Colonial Policing and the Transnational Legacy

This compilation represents the first study to examine the historical evolution and shifting global dynamics of policing across the Lusophone community. With contributions from a multi-disciplinary range of experts, it traces the role of policing within and across settings that are connected by the shared legacy of Portuguese colonialism. Previously neglected within studies of the globalisation of policing, the Lusophone experience brings novel insights to established analyses of colonial, post-colonial and transnational policing. This compilation draws research attention to the policing peculiarities of the Lusophone community. It proposes new cultural settings within which to test dominant theories of policing research. It uncovers an important piece of the jigsaw that is policing across the globe. Key research questions that it addresses include:

- What were the patterns of policing, and policing transfers, across Portuguese colonial settings?
- How did Portugal's dual status as both fascist regime and imperial power shape its late colonial policing?
- What have been the different experiences of post-colonial and transitional policing across the former Portuguese colonies?
- In what ways are Lusophone nations contributing to, and indeed shaping, patterns of transnational policing?
- What comparative lessons can be drawn from the Lusophone policing experience?

Conor O'Reilly is Associate Professor in Transnational Crime and Security at the School of Law, University of Leeds. His research interests focus upon the transnational dynamics of crime, policing and security. He has published widely on these and related research themes in leading journals, including: *British Journal of Criminology; Crime, Law and Social Change; International Political Sociology; Police Quarterly;* and *Theoretical Criminology.* He is also author of the forthcoming monograph, *Policing Global Risks: The Transnational Security Consultancy Industry.* He has worked on a range of international research projects, including the COPP-LAB project on Lusophone policing, and is currently leading a three-year project on kidnapping in Mexico.

'Until now, the field of Police Studies has not had a definitive account of the Portuguese colonial empire and its effects on the global dynamics of policing. This book is an excellent example of critical interdisciplinary scholarship that casts new and welcome light on to European colonialism and colonial policing.'

James Sheptycki, *McLaughlin College,*
York University, Toronto, Canada

Colonial Policing and the Transnational Legacy

The Global Dynamics of Policing Across the Lusophone Community

Edited by
Conor O'Reilly

LONDON AND NEW YORK

First published 2018
by Routledge
2 Park Square, Milton Park, Abingdon, Oxon, OX14 4RN

and by Routledge
711 Third Avenue, New York, NY 10017

*Routledge is an imprint of the Taylor & Francis Group,
an informa business*

© 2018 selection and editorial matter, Conor O'Reilly; individual
chapters, the contributors

The right of Conor O'Reilly to be identified as the author of the
editorial material, and of the authors for their individual chapters,
has been asserted in accordance with sections 77 and 78 of the
Copyright, Designs and Patents Act 1988.

All rights reserved. No part of this book may be reprinted or
reproduced or utilised in any form or by any electronic, mechanical,
or other means, now known or hereafter invented, including
photocopying and recording, or in any information storage or
retrieval system, without permission in writing from the publishers.

Trademark notice: Product or corporate names may be trademarks
or registered trademarks, and are used only for identification and
explanation without intent to infringe.

British Library Cataloguing-in-Publication Data
A catalogue record for this book is available from the British Library

Library of Congress Cataloging-in-Publication Data
Names: O'Reilly, Conor (Conor Francis), editor.
Title: Colonial policing and the transnational legacy : the global
    dynamics of policing across the Lusophone community / [edited by]
    Conor O'Reilly.
Description: Abingdon, Oxon ; New York, NY : Routledge, 2017. |
    Includes bibliographical references and index.
Identifiers: LCCN 2017007941 | ISBN 9781409465300 (hardback) |
    ISBN 9781317164142 (adobe reader) | ISBN 9781317164135
    (epub) | ISBN 9781317164128 (mobipocket)
Subjects: LCSH: Police—Portugal—Colonies—History.
Classification: LCC HV8239.A2 C65 2017 | DDC 363.209171/
    2469—dc23
LC record available at https://lccn.loc.gov/2017007941

ISBN: 978-1-409-46530-0 (hbk)
ISBN: 978-1-315-57273-4 (ebk)

Typeset in Galliard
by Apex CoVantage, LLC

For Pílar and Tomás

Contents

List of tables	xiv
Notes on contributors	xv
Acknowledgements	xix

Introduction: policing and the Lusophone community across time and space CONOR O'REILLY	1

PART ONE
The colonial policing mission   15

1 **Colonial policing and the Portuguese Empire (c.1870–1961)** GONÇALO ROCHA GONÇALVES AND RITA ÁVILA CACHADO	17
2 **The military and the (colonial) policing of mainland Portugal (1850–1910)** DIEGO PALACIOS CEREZALES	35
3 **Militarism in the São Paulo police force (1868–1924)** ANDRÉ ROSEMBERG	55
Comment: the Portuguese colonial policing mission in comparative perspective RICHARD S. HILL	67

PART TWO
Policing at the end of Empire   89

4 **PIDE's racial strategy in Angola (1957–1961)** FERNANDO TAVARES PIMENTA	91

viii *Contents*

5 Knowing 'Mozambican Islam': the *Confidential Questionnaire on Islam* and colonial governance during the liberation war 105
SANDRA ARAÚJO

6 Intelligence-centric counterinsurgency as late colonial policing: comparing Portugal with Britain and France 129
BRUNO CARDOSO REIS

Comment: reflections on Portuguese late colonial policing 152
MARTIN THOMAS

PART THREE
Post-colonial, transitional and transnational policing dynamics 161

7 Post-war police reform in Mozambique: the case of community policing 163
HELENE MARIA KYED

8 Transformation of Macau policing: from a Portuguese colony to China's SAR 183
LAWRENCE K.K. HO AND AGNES I.F. LAM

9 Faint echoes of Portugal but strong accents of Indonesia: hidden influences on police development in Timor-Leste 208
GORDON PEAKE

10 Branding Rio de Janeiro's pacification model: a silver bullet for the 'planet of slums'? 227
CONOR O'REILLY

Comment: 'never mind the similarities, focus on the differences': imposition, imitation and intransigence in post-colonial global policing reform 253
ANDREW GOLDSMITH

Index 265

Detailed contents

List of tables   xiv
Notes on contributors   xv
Acknowledgements   xix

Introduction: policing and the Lusophone community across time and space   1
CONOR O'REILLY

Policing and the Lusophone community across time and space 3
    Policiamentos-Lusos e o Futuro? 5
The chapters 7

PART ONE
The colonial policing mission   15

1 **Colonial policing and the Portuguese Empire (c.1870–1961)**   17
GONÇALO ROCHA GONÇALVES AND RITA ÁVILA CACHADO

Introduction 17
Territorial occupation and the emergence of 'colonial policing' 19
*Eduardo Costa and the appearance of colonial police in the
    Portuguese colonial thinking 21*
The institutional landscape and the circulation of personnel 25
    Salgueiro Rêgo and colonial policing during the New State 26
Conclusion 31

2 **The military and the (colonial) policing of mainland Portugal (1850–1910)**   35
DIEGO PALACIOS CEREZALES

Introduction: the military and policing 35
A country without a gendarmerie 36

x *Detailed contents*

Policing alternatives in the early years of liberalism 37
Self-policing: the parish constables 38
The army as police 39
Internal colonialism 43
Learning to police 46
Africanism and militarism 48
Conclusion 50

3 Militarism in the São Paulo police force (1868–1924) 55
ANDRÉ ROSEMBERG

Introduction 55
Policing Brazil in the 19th century 57
The police under the republic 60
Conclusion 64

Comment: the Portuguese colonial policing mission in comparative perspective 67
RICHARD S. HILL

Introduction 67
Policing 68
Knowledge circulation 71
Military 72
Multilayered control 75
Civilising mission 79
Professionalisation 83
Conclusion 84

PART TWO
Policing at the end of Empire 89

4 PIDE's racial strategy in Angola (1957–1961) 91
FERNANDO TAVARES PIMENTA

Introduction 91
Racial segmentation in colonial Angola 91
PIDE 94
PIDE in Angola 95
Racialised incarceration and divide to rule 97
The shantytown massacres 98
Combating the Angolan United Front (FUA) 99
Conclusion 101

Detailed contents xi

5 Knowing 'Mozambican Islam': the *Confidential Questionnaire on Islam* and colonial governance during the liberation war 105

SANDRA ARAÚJO

Introduction 105
Colonial governance of Islam in Mozambique 107
The Mozambique information, centralisation and coordination services (1961–1974) 110
Knowing 'Mozambican Islam': the Confidential Questionnaire *114*
The questionnaire implementation 117
Remarks on the questionnaire outcomes 121
Conclusion 124

6 Intelligence-centric counterinsurgency as late colonial policing: comparing Portugal with Britain and France 129

BRUNO CARDOSO REIS

Introduction 129
Locating Portuguese colonial policing 130
Framing late colonial counterinsurgency as policing 133
Diffusion of counterinsurgency as high policing – the intelligence-centric dimension 138
Late colonial counterinsurgency as policing – some wider implications 144
Conclusion 147

Comment: reflections on Portuguese late colonial policing 152

MARTIN THOMAS

PART THREE
Post-colonial, transitional and transnational policing dynamics 161

7 Post-war police reform in Mozambique: the case of community policing 163

HELENE MARIA KYED

Introduction 163
The contested police reform process 165

xii *Detailed contents*

International involvement – the UNDP-led process 167
The Mozambican community policing model 169
    National expansion and pilot projects outside official
       reform 170
Rural case-study: new civilian agents of the state police 172
    Everyday policing: state outsourcing and autonomous
       actions 173
Urban case-study: a new neighbourhood court 175
    Everyday policing: legal defiance and political
       instrumentalisation 176
Conclusion 179

8 Transformation of Macau policing: from a Portuguese colony to China's SAR 183

LAWRENCE K.K. HO AND AGNES I.F. LAM

Introduction 183
Three key organisational features of colonial Macau policing 186
Dual police forces 187
    The Public Security Police (PSP) or Corpo de Polícia de
       Segurança Pública (CPSP) 188
    The Judiciary Police (JP) or polícia judiciária de Macau 189
    Operational conflicts between PSP and JP 190
Non-local police forces distant from the community 192
Limited capacity and professional ability 193
Transformation of policing in the MSAR 195
Triggers for police reform after 1999 195
    De-monopolisation of the gaming industry 195
    Emergence of new civil groups 197
    Emergence of outspoken media and the 2007 Labour
       Day Rally 198
Attempts to reform Macau police agencies and policies 199
    Establishment of the Unitary Police Services (Servicos de
       Polícia Unitarios) in 2001 199
    Adjustment of salary scale and amount 200
    Upgrading police professionalism 200
    Public relations 202
    Assessing reform 202
Conclusion: further change ahead 203

9 Faint echoes of Portugal but strong accents of Indonesia: hidden influences on police development in timor-leste 208

GORDON PEAKE

Introduction 208

Timor-Leste as the epitome of the conflict paradigm *210*
Colonial genealogies and historical continuities *212*
*Lots of investment but little dividend: attempts to mould the
Timorese police into an international image of best practice 214*
Post-colonial and post-authoritarian echoes 219
Conclusion 223

**10 Branding Rio de Janeiro's pacification model: a silver
bullet for the 'planet of slums'?**   **227**
CONOR O'REILLY

Introduction 227
*Global promotionalism and the creation of a geo-policial
brand 230*
Of complex dualities and the segmented brand 235
*Elite transnational security networks: a scene that celebrates
itself? 237*
*International peacekeeping and the Rio-MINUSTAH
feedback loop 241*
Conclusion 244

**Comment: 'never mind the similarities, focus on the
differences': imposition, imitation and intransigence
in post-colonial global policing reform**   **253**
ANDREW GOLDSMITH

Introduction 253
Imperial impositions 254
Intransigence and resistance 257
'Cherry pie or knuckle sandwich?' 259
Glocality, co-optation and hybridity 260
From missionaries to marketeers 261
Conclusion 262

Index   265

Tables

5.1	SCCIM Surveys	113
8.1	Informant Profiles	205

Contributors

Sandra Araújo is currently concluding a PhD in Anthropology at CRIA-FCSH/ NOVA (Centro em Rede de Investigação em Antropologia/Faculdade de Ciências Sociais e Humanas – Universidade Nova de Lisboa). She is studying the role of intelligence in the governance of Mozambican Muslims during the liberation war. Her research interests include the cultural dimensions related to surveillance, intelligence and security services in colonial contexts. Recently she published the following chapter 'Shaping an Empire of Predictions: The Mozambique Information Centralization and Coordination Services (1961– 1974)' in *Policing in Colonial Situations. Cases, Connections, Boundaries (ca. 1850–1970)* edited by E. Blanchard, M. Bloembergen and A. Lauro. Frankfurt am Main, Berlin, Bern, Bruxelles, New York, Oxford, Wien: PIE-Peter Lang. 2017

Rita Ávila Cachado, b. 1975, graduated in Anthropology in 1999 in Lisbon (FCSH-Nova). PhD in Urban Anthropology, Lisbon University Institute (ISCTE-IUL), 2008, and Masters in Anthropology. Colonialism and Post-Colonialism (2004, ISCTE-IUL). Invited Teacher, ESAD-IPL Leiria 2010– 2013; ISCTE-IUL 2012-. Post-doc current project about Urban Ethnography in CIES-IUL (Fellowship from Science and Technology Foundation – FCT, Portugal). Academic writings in Social Housing in Portugal; Hindu-Gujaratis in Lisbon; Transnationality; Portuguese Colonialism in India (Master Thesis). Fieldwork in Portugal, India, United Kingdom and in Mozambique. Current academic interests include ethnographic archives, revisitation, and history of science.

Andrew Goldsmith is Strategic Professor of Criminology at Flinders University, Adelaide, South Australia, where he is also director of the Centre for Crime Policy & Research. His research interests include transnational policing, organised crime, corruption and Internet criminality. Between 2005 and 2012 he led a major empirical study of transnational policing in Timor-Leste and the Solomon Islands, the results of which have appeared in various journal articles and book chapters. He also co-edited with James Sheptycki, *Crafting Transnational Policing: Police Capacity-Building and Global Policing Reform* (Hart 2007).

xvi *Contributors*

Gonçalo Rocha Gonçalves is a Post-Doctoral Researcher and Invited Assistant Professor at ISCTE – University Institute of Lisbon. Visiting Fulbright Scholar at Macmillan Center, Yale University in 2016. He holds a PhD in History from The Open University, UK, with the thesis 'Civilizing the policeman: police reform, culture and practice in Lisbon, c.1860–1910' (2012). Among his latest publications is '*O aparelho policial e a construção do Estado em Portugal*', *Análise Social*, Vol. L (3.º), 2015 (n.º 216), pp. 470–493, 'Police reform and the transnational circulation of police models: The Portuguese case in the 1860s', *Crime, Histoire & Sociétés/Crime, History & Societies* 2014, vol.18, no.1, pp. 5–29 (awarded with The Herman Diederiks Prize Essay for 2013 Lauréat du prix Herman Diederiks 2013).

Richard S. Hill is an historian at the Stout Research Centre for New Zealand Studies at Victoria University of Wellington, New Zealand, where he is also Director of the Treaty of Waitangi Research Unit. Professor Hill has specialised in both policing history and the relationship between states and indigenous peoples, and has written six books on these subjects. He is presently researching the history of covert state surveillance in New Zealand. His interests extend to global history (he was recently based at Oxford University's Centre for Global History), and he is now preparing a comparative history of policing in colonies.

Lawrence K.K. Ho is Assistant Professor at the Department of Social Sciences, Education University of Hong Kong.

Helene Maria Kyed is senior researcher at the Danish Institute for International Studies (DIIS), and has a background in anthropology and international development studies. Her area of research is policing and justice enforcement, with a particular focus on non-state, informal and customary actors and practices, although she has also researched the state police. Theoretically she works with questions of public authority, violence and sovereignty. Research is based on ethnographic fieldwork in Mozambique and more recently in Myanmar. Her most recent book is *Policing and the Politics of Order-Making* (London: Routledge, 2015).

Agnes I.F. Lam is Assistant Professor at the Department of Communication, Faculty of Social Science, University of Macau.

Conor O'Reilly is Associate Professor in Transnational Crime and Security at the School of Law, University of Leeds. His research interests focus upon the transnational dynamics of crime, policing and security. He has published widely on these and related research themes in leading journals, including: *British Journal of Criminology*; *Crime, Law and Social Change*; *International Political Sociology*; *Police Quarterly*; and *Theoretical Criminology*. He is also author of the forthcoming monograph, *Policing Global Risks: The Transnational Security Consultancy Industry* (Hart Publishing). He has worked on a range of international research projects, including the COPP-LAB project on Lusophone

Contributors xvii

policing, and is currently leading a three-year project on kidnapping in Mexico.

Diego Palacios Cerezales is a Lecturer in European History at the University of Stirling. Diego has published widely on protest, policing, popular politics and social movements in Spain and Portugal in the modern era. His books include *O poder caiu na rua. Crise de Estado e acções colectivas na revolução portuguesa, 1974–1975* (Lisbon: Imprensa de Ciencias Sociais, 2003); *A culatazos. Protesta popular y orden público en el Portugal contemporáneo* (Palma de Mallorca: Genueve Ediciones, 2011); *Estranhos corpos políticos. Protesto e mobilização no Portugal do século XIX* (Lisbon: Unipop, 2014). He is currently writing a transnational history of petitioning.

Gordon Peake is a consultant and Visiting Fellow at the Development Policy Centre, Australian National University, Canberra. His book, *Beloved Land: Stories, Struggles and Secrets from Timor-Leste* was the winner of two Australian book awards.

Fernando Tavares Pimenta graduated in History at Coimbra University and completed a PhD degree in History and Civilisation at the European University Institute of Florence in 2007. He is currently a researcher at the School of Social and Human Sciences, New University of Lisbon (FCSH-UNL). He has published several books on Portuguese Colonial History and also on Portuguese Contemporary History, namely: *Angola. Os Brancos e a Independência* (Porto, Afrontamento, 2008); *Portugal e o Século XX. Estado-Império e Descolonização, 1890–1975* (Porto: Afrontamento, 2010); *Storia Politica del Portogallo Contemporaneo, 1800–2000* (Florence, Le Monnier, 2011) *and Descolonização de Angola e de Moçambique. O Comportamento das Minorias Brancas* (Goiânia, Editora Universidade Federal de Goiânia, 2015).

Bruno C Reis is since 2017, a Professor at the Center of International Studies (CEI) of ISCTE-IUL. He holds a M. Phil. in Historical Studies from Cambridge University and a Ph.D. in War Studies from King's College. He was a research fellow at ICS-University of Lisbon from 2011-2017. Since 2011 he has been an adviser to National Defence Institute of Portugal (IDN) namely on the new strategic concept of Portugal. He is a member of the Sir Michael Howard Center for the History of War at King's College London. He has been a guest reader at a number of Portuguese universities where he has taught courses in the History of International Relations, History of Colonialism and Decolonization, Security Studies, Leadership and Grand Strategy. He has conducted research and published on these topics, namely with Andrew Mumford, *The Theory and Practice of Irregular Warfare* (London: Routledge, 2013).

André Rosemberg obtained his PhD in History from Universidade de São Paulo. He is an invited researcher in *Observatório da Segurança Pública* (UNESP/ Marília) and post-doctorate and PUC/SP. Amongst other articles, books and

xviii   *Contributors*

chapters, he is the author of *De chumbo e festim – uma história da polícia Paulista no final do Império* (EDUSP, 2010).

Martin Thomas is Professor of Imperial History and Director of the Centre for War, State and Society at the University of Exeter. He has written extensively on colonialism and decolonisation. His most recent book is *Fight or Flight: Britain, France, and their Roads from Empire*, published by Oxford University Press in 2014.

Acknowledgements

The inception of this compilation traces back to a workshop entitled, 'Reflections on Colonial and Post-colonial Policing in the (Former) Portuguese Empire' convened at the University of Porto in 2011. As a novice of Lusophone policing scholarship at the time, I can recall accepting the task of organising this event with some trepidation when approached by Cândido da Agra – then Director of the School of Criminology at the University of Porto. However, I am now extremely grateful that he came to me with this proposal. The research endeavour his request catalysed has not only afforded me a more developed knowledge of policing patterns across the Lusophone world, but has also culminated in this edited volume which I hope will encourage further academic exploration of this under-researched terrain.

Some years have passed since the Porto meeting and many people have contributed to the journey from that event to this output; all deserve thanks. The initial workshop was part of a series of events organised by the GERN Working Group on Colonial Policing and I am grateful for the long-term support of its members, Emmanuel Blanchard, Georgina Sinclair, Chris Williams, Margo de Koster, Marieke Bloembergen, Amandine Lauro and Cyrille Fijnaut. The workshop also received financial and institutional support from the French *Groupe Européen de Recherche sur les Normativités* (GERN), the Portuguese *Fundação para Ciencia e Tecnologia*, and from the Faculty of Law of the University of Porto, to each of which I express gratitude. The event itself also received significant logistical support from the *Escola de Criminologia* of the University of Porto, not least through the efforts of Ana Faria. Insofar as the academic content of this event was concerned, Cândido da Agra and António Costa Pinto both provided valuable counsel in my initial search to identify scholars, both from within Portugal and beyond, working on Portuguese colonial policing and related themes.

For their individual contributions and their commitment to this project, I am grateful to the authors of the chapters and the expert comments that follow. Most contributors have been involved since the initial workshop, whilst some others joined the project at later stages. All deserve thanks for their availability, their efforts, their patience, and their openness to constructive critique. In this context, I also wish to thank over thirty peer-reviewers who, whilst remaining anonymous, played a crucial role in enhancing the quality of each chapter. Their insights have

xx *Acknowledgements*

helped us better map and better understand Lusophone policing patterns, as well as to situate them in some comparative perspective. Chapter Nine is a reprint of an article by Lawrence Ho and Agnes Lam, entitled 'Transformation of Macau Policing: from a Portuguese Colony to China's SAR', that was originally published in *Crime, Law and Social Change*, 61(4) in 2014. I am grateful to Springer publications for granting permission to reprint this material.

Sole-editing a compilation is not a task I plan to undertake again either lightly or soon. However, the challenges that it presented were made much more bearable by constant support from Alison Kirk, Senior Editor at Routledge, as well as by Amrisha Pandey, a PhD candidate at the University of Leeds who greatly assisted preparation of the final manuscript. In the Faculty of Law of the University of Porto and the School of Law at the University of Leeds, I have been fortunate to work at institutions willing to provide logistical and financial support during key stages of this work. I am also grateful for the kindness and support of new Lusophone colleagues and friendships that I have gained through this process, not least those of Rita Faria, Susana Durão and Marcio Darck.

Finally, I wish to thank my wife, Rita de la Feria. I hesitate to use the term 'my Portuguese wife' (I have no other wives of other nationalities!), but she is Portuguese and brought me to her home country, triggering the life-changes that eventually led to this compilation. She has always supported, and remains a necessary motivator for, my work. Indeed, I usually persuade her to read every academic piece that I write. I am confident that this will include these acknowledgements.

Introduction

Policing and the Lusophone community across time and space

Conor O'Reilly

Scholarship concerning the globalisation of policing has witnessed cross-disciplinary convergence in recent years – a process from which this volume has itself emerged. Criminologists and policing scholars concerned with transnational policing have recognised the formative influence that colonial policing has exerted upon this field (see, for example: Bowling 2010: 69–74, Bowling and Sheptycki 2012: 20–22, Ellison and O'Reilly 2008). Renewed historical interest in colonial policing has also witnessed research attention directed towards transfers between European Metropoles and their colonies, intercolonial exchanges, and transnational connections (see, for example: Blanchard and Glasman 2012, Sinclair and Williams 2007, Sinclair 2011, 2016). Post-colonial studies also play an important role, pushing scholars of diverse research ilks to venture out of disciplinary silos and engage with complex interactions between the colonial, the post-colonial and the transnational (Agozino 2007, Brogden and Ellison 2012, Comaroff and Comaroff 2006, 2014, Hönke and Müller 2012, 2016).

In their aptly titled collection, *The Global Making of Policing: Postcolonial Perspectives*, Hönke and Müller (2016) have recently noted that 'practices of policing are dynamically co-produced: they are an outcome of entangled histories' (p. 2). Their words are highly appropriate for this volume and offer analytical extension to earlier observations of policing as a by-product of complex transterritorial interaction. Some 30 years ago Mike Brogden drew attention to patterns of 'internal colonialism' within British policing (1987a, 1987b), whilst Michel Foucault had previously forewarned of colonialism's 'boomerang effects' (2003: 103). Certainly, their prescient statements resonate across this collection, albeit that the complex patterns to which Hönke and Müller (2016) refer have only recently been recognised. By grappling with *Colonial Policing and the Transnational Legacy*, the contributors to this volume make valuable connections with, and additions to, these preceding research insights. However, this collection's efforts to disentangle the global policing web differ, in that it gathers together research regarding colonial, late-colonial, post-colonial, transitional and transnational policing that has emerged from within the genealogical framework of the Lusophone community. For the unfamiliar, Lusophone speaks to much more than some linguistic commonality – many Lusophone contexts include languages other than Portuguese – but rather refers to that transnational assemblage of nations and

2   Conor O'Reilly

peoples linked by a shared legacy of Portuguese colonialism.[1] Drawing on research expertise from anthropology, colonial and modern history, criminology, international relations, security studies and sociology, this collection not only houses diverse disciplinary perspectives, but also spotlights a highly significant, yet hitherto neglected, research field: *the global dynamics of policing across the Lusophone community.*

From colonial origins in the most enduring modern European Empire to more contemporary trends across a burgeoning global community approaching 270 million, this compilation addresses a major *lacuna* of policing scholarship. This is not to say that policing in Portugal and its former colonies have escaped academic scrutiny – see, for example the work of Durão (2008) on Portugal, Bretas (1997) on Brazil, or Mateus (2004) on the Portuguese political police during the colonial wars – but rather to recognise that in terms of its scale and diversity, Lusophone policing is dramatically under-researched.[2] This knowledge gap becomes even more evident when the geographic expanse of the Lusophone community is set against the various significant historical transformations through which it has passed.

Not only does this collection furnish insights into policing across Luso-Brazilian, Luso-African and Luso-Asian settings but it also offers unique research issues that span from the colonial to the contemporary. In a policing field where Anglophone and Western perspectives are recognised as problematically dominant, examination of policing across the Lusophone community presents an opportunity to challenge orthodox conceptions, as well as to uncover an important piece of the jigsaw that is policing across the globe.[3]

It is useful to highlight some singularities of the Lusophone case. It includes an instance of metropolitan reversal whereby a European Empire was temporarily ruled from within one of its own colonies – in this case from Rio de Janeiro at the start of the 19th century (see, Bretas and Rosemberg 2013). Later, Portugal would hold the dubious dual status of being both imperial power and fascist regime under Salazar during the 20th century. Such distinctiveness continues at the end of

---

1   Whilst the Lusophone community extends to various diasporas, it is principally recognised as including the independent nations of Portugal, Angola, Brazil, Cape Verde, Guinea-Bissau, Macau, Mozambique, São Tomé and Príncipe, and Timor-Leste, as well as the former colonial territories of Goa and, Daman and Diu in India. For a useful definition of the term Lusophone, see the work of Arenas (2011: 205).

2   It is noteworthy that there is a sizeable body of academic research focused upon systems of Portuguese colonial control and mechanisms of economic exploitation in its colonies (see, for example: Jerónimo 2015, Jerónimo and Monteiro 2013) but this has not been brought within the colonial policing research framework and is gathered under general reflections on Portuguese colonialism.

3   In challenging the dominant Anglophone and Western narratives of policing research, this collection also benefits from the fact that the majority of contributing scholars are themselves drawn from within the Lusophone community – albeit predominantly from Portugal and Brazil. These academics are developing a distinctly Lusophone voice within the policing research field.

Empire, when late-colonial policing took place against the impending, and interconnected, political transformations of democratisation at home and decolonisation overseas. The violent decolonialisations of Luso-Africa also rest in sharp contrast to the more *laissez-faire* colonial departures from Luso-Asia; differing transitional processes shaping divergent trajectories for policing change. The opportunity for new insights continues into contemporary contexts of transnational policing and post-colonial settings. The idea that those on the receiving end of policing transfers are evolving beyond passive and grateful recipients is appropriate to several Lusophone cases. Police organisations in sites such as Mozambique and Timor-Leste are progressing towards more active agency and more knowing consumption of those foreign exports proffered through transnational policing exchange. Indeed, the emergent superpower of Brazil has gone further still, assuming donor-traits by promoting its policing and security wares in the transnational marketplace.

Policing and the Lusophone community across time and space

Reflecting upon recurrent themes that emerge from Lusophone policing contexts, this section identifies some points of interest that bridge colonial, post-colonial and transnational considerations. As Cunneen (2011) has previously observed on the merits of post-colonial perspectives, our research aspirations should reach beyond specific time-periods, as after all 'colonization and the postcolonial are not historical events' (p. 249), they are complex continuing processes that are re-invented. A case in point is that regular creature of colonial discourse, the Other (Said 1978). The Other's place in colonial policing research is well established with scholars such as Brogden (1987a, 1987b) noting how the mission to civilise savage indigenes reflected back to the Metropole through processes of internal colonialism; policing practice at home being re-shaped towards governing the unruly, uneducated and criminal classes (see also: Sinclair and Williams 2007). As Palacios Cerezales makes clear in his contribution, such patterns are also evident in the Lusophone experience. The Portuguese military were delegated civilising missions in both the colonial hinterland and the Metropole's rural interior. Policing the Other has more recently come to the fore in governing urban poor within the Global South. Rio de Janeiro's pacification programme has been described as linking 'domestic postcolonial legacies of Brazilian policing and its deeply embedded practice of suppressing the racialized urban 'other' (Hönke and Müller 2016: 13, see also Müller 2016 and O'Reilly in this collection). The Other as a target for police action – whether in the form of civilising missions or re-branded pacifications – has become more globally diffuse. Brogden and Ellison (2012) even link 'international policing of the Other' (p. 99) to commodifying tendencies in the export of policing and security expertise. Rio's *favelas* may furnish a 'spectacular' (Robb Larkins 2015) coalescence – if not a collision – of patterns of colonisation and post-colonialism, commodification and transnational forces, but there is much more to be said about the Lusophone Other. From multiple mechanisms of

4   *Conor O'Reilly*

colonial control, to more contemporary strategies to govern urban (in)security – for example, moral panics and policing urban youth in Cape Verdean shantytowns (Zoettl 2014, 2015) – there are multiple sites within which to explore the recru descence of civilising, pacifying and policing the Other.

Policing transfers have evidently become more complex than reverberation between the colonies and the Metropole. The circulation of policing knowledge and techniques has progressed through cross-colonial mobilities and early international emulations of 'best practice' towards late-colonial intelligence exchange amongst imperial powers as colonial grasps began to slip. Ensuing colonial wars accelerated such intelligence-sharing, as well as catalysing lesson-drawing in counterinsurgency. In the wake of these various transfers born of colonialism, we now witness more complex transnational patterns; undoubtedly influenced by what has gone before but also pursuing new, less predictable, directions. However, none of these police transfers travel of their own free will; they are catalysed by both push and pull factors. Cultural connections, political imperatives, organisational needs, and individual motivations may all trigger policing mobilities. Indeed, the role of human agency (Stone 2004) in such processes is apparent across several contributions to this volume. They demonstrate how human vessels for policing innovations and transfers have progressed from 'roaming police advisors' (Sinclair 2006) and colonial 'police intellectuals' (McMullen 1998) like Captain Salgueiro Rego (see Gonçalves and Cachado) or General Pedro Cardoso (see Reis), to more contemporary 'policy entrepreneurs' (Newburn and Jones 2007) such as Sergio Cabral and José Mariano Beltrame in the case of Rio de Janeiro (see O'Reilly), or policing policy converts like General Macamo in Mozambique (see Kyed). Tracing these figures' transnational interactions and influence provides a window on to how human agency has shaped the global dynamics of policing across the Lusophone community and beyond. Perhaps when compared with Anglophone policing, the Lusophone case might not present the same intensity of circulations. However, whether to enforce colonial control, to professionalise policing, to suppress anti-colonial movements, or to market new brands of policing and security intervention, key Lusophone figures have been active participants in forging transnational policing networks.

Another brief observation is merited regarding the degree of police-military blur in Lusophone policing. Whilst police and military domains are often treated as distinct in their respective academic traditions, the Lusophone cases here presented are marked by high incidence of overlap and blurring. Early forms of colonial policing were heavily reliant on the Portuguese military (see Palacios Cerezales), late 19th Century policing in São Paulo took a highly militarised trajectory (see Rosemberg), PIDE, Portugal's political police, ran its own paramilitary forces during the colonial wars (see Reis). More recently police in post-colonial African contexts such as Mozambique are being coaxed away from militarised policing (see Kyed), whilst the military police in Rio de Janeiro engage in militarised humanitarianism in the *favelas* (see O'Reilly). Each Lusophone context has its own story to tell, and some – such as Portugal – have indeed progressed far from the militarised policing of the past. However, as Richard Hill later considers in more depth,

Introduction 5

we cannot consider policing across the Lusophone community without attention to this enduring military flavour.

Policiamentos-Lusos e o Futuro?[4]

In advance of introducing this volume's structure and contributions, it is worth reiterating that this book seeks to better understand the complex dynamics of Lusophone policing(s), as well as to provide a platform for further exploration. Whilst there is certainly much *terra incognita* within the Lusophone case, it is instructive to acknowledge existing academic efforts that make important inroads into this research field. By providing a window onto some recent projects and publications, as well as suggesting some pathways for future research, I hope to provide orientation, and some motivation, for further scholarly interest in policing across the Lusophone community.

To recognise two significant research projects that locate Lusophone policing within a more transnational setting is a useful starting point. In terms of political policing during the late-colonial period, the project, 'Defying the winds of change: Portugal, Rhodesia and South Africa 1961–1980' led by historian Filipe de Meneses, together with Robert McNamara, has shed light on how these three regimes collaborated to suppress independence movements across Southern Africa. Working with declassified documents, De Meneses and McNamara uncover the covert alliance of Project Alcora that blended mutual support in areas of military intelligence, counterinsurgency and political policing. These arrangements even extended to secret annual conferences that brought together collaborating intelligence agencies. Whilst Project Alcora was ultimately a failed endeavour in its attempts to forestall both decolonisation and progression towards racial equality, this project's revelations remind us that there are darker transnational policing and security networks; dubious connections where intertwined national security interests are deliberately obfuscated (for more on this research, see: De Meneses and McNamara 2012, 2013, 2014a, 2014b). Struggling through the 'endarkened governance' (De Lint 2004, Taylor 2014) of such shadow networks is a challenge encountered by criminologists as well as historians, and there is scope for productive collaboration and exchange between scholars of Lusophone policing from these two research communities.

Another recent project that makes an important contribution to understanding policing mobilities across the Lusophone Community is *Project COPP-LAB: Circulações de Oficiais de Polícia em Portugal, África Lusófona e Brasil* ('Circulation of Police Officers in Portugal, Lusophone Africa and Brasil'). Under the research direction of Susana Durão, this project has charted patterns of knowledge and personnel transfer, concentrating upon the experiences of police cadets from former Luso-African colonies attending the officer-training programme at the Higher Institute for Police Science and Internal Security in Lisbon. This re-animation of

---

4 This can be translated as 'The Future for Lusophone Policings?'

6   Conor O'Reilly

policing connections with the former Metropole is all the more symbolic given that this training institute was itself initiated to shift Portuguese policing away from the anti-democratic traits associated with *O Estado Novo*. Consequently, this project has engaged with attempts to foster democratic policing in post-colonial settings by inculcating future police leaders with the policing knowledge and ethos developed for Portuguese democratic society. With graduates from this officer training now spread throughout the Lusophone community, there is a loose transnational network and epistemic community bound by shared training experience and the knowledge that it imparted, what Durão and Lopes (2015) have termed '*comunidades de saberes*' ('communities of knowledge'). This project's field missions to the former Portuguese colonies also furnished insights into the shifting patterns of policing transfers to which Luso-African police forces have been exposed throughout their history (for more on this research, see: O'Reilly 2015, Udelsman Rodrigues 2015, 2016).

Contributors to this volume are also independently engaged in further expanding knowledge regarding Lusophone policing dynamics (see Gonçalves 2014 on transnational police exchanges during the 19th century). Other important work is also emerging out of research that analyses Lusophone countries' policing role in both suffering the effects of global insecurities, as well as combatting them (for example, see Shaw 2015 on narco-trafficking's destructive impact on Guinea-Bissau).

This brief panorama of recent and ongoing research, when combined with the contributions that follow, paints a picture of high times for research into Lusophone policing and a field where research interest is gathering pace. However, these are initial forays and the transnational pathways that have shaped policing across the Lusophone community are only starting to be discovered. With this in mind, this section is brought to a close with a few research questions triggered by this collection. From its earliest manifestations colonial policing involved mobilities – predominantly from the Metropole to the colonies – but to what extent did Portuguese colonial policing manifest the mobility of personnel through 'strangers policing strangers'? Certainly, this distanciating practice existed at home via internal colonialism (see Palacios Cerezales in this volume) but to what extent did Portuguese colonial structures manipulate racial/tribal difference and deploy colonial intermediaries in this manner? What was the traffic in colonial subjects from one colonial territory to police those who resided in others? Whilst analysis of the global dynamics of policing across the Lusophone community uncovers both connections between patterns of colonial policing exchange and new transnational dimensions, have existing research orientations neglected those regional policing links born of shared colonial legacies? For example, what patterns of police transfers exist between Luso-African nations? What is Brazil's regional impact upon policing in Latin America or indeed its transatlantics reach into Luso-Africa? Anecdotal evidence from the aforementioned COPP-LAB project suggests that regional transfers and those between countries with a shared colonial heritage are increasing (for example, between Angola and Cape Verde), whilst Brazil's regional leadership role countering transnational organised crime

Introduction 7

has also been spotlighted (Muggah and Diniz 2013). However, the details of such transnational policing arrangements certainly require greater empirical investigation. It is hoped that the transnational and interdisciplinary research connections forged in the process of this compilation may play some part in exploring these issues further.

The chapters

Part One focuses upon policing in Lusophone contexts during the late 19th and early 20th centuries. It picks up the emerging story of Portuguese colonial policing during the third phase of this global Empire, after it had lost its Brazilian colony in the Americas. Across the three chapters and expert comment, a range of policing traffic is spotlighted: between colonies and the Metropole; between urban and rural settings; between domestic/colonial police forces and foreign policing exemplars; and, between the military and the police. Indeed, the place of the military in the story of Portuguese colonial policing emerges as highly significant. Even if the late 19th century witnessed a shift away from reliance on the army to assert and maintain colonial control, the army would continue to sporadically perform policing roles at home whilst colonial policing also retained a certain military infusion.

Gonçalo Gonçalves and Rita Ávila Cachado's chapter provides a panoramic opening historical analysis of the emergence and evolution of Portuguese colonial policing, linking it with a shift towards more developed colonial governance through civil administration. They depict early colonial policing as a fragmented endeavour with limited coherence in organisational structures across the diverse Lusophone settings. The colonial policing arrangements that took shape were influenced by a variety of factors, including: domestic political debates around policing; international transfers of early best practice; emulation of policing structures from both the Metropole, as well as from other European Empires; and, renewed political attention to the *Ultramar* (overseas territories) triggered by the imperial ambitions of Salazar's dictatorship. Diego Palacios Cerezales next explores patterns of internal colonialism in the Portuguese context, with specific attention to the role of the army in police action directed towards the Metropolitan rural poor. He reiterates how patterns of colonisation and its tutelary relationships were not unique to foreign lands: military policing of the *povo* (the uneducated and the unruly) mirrored colonial policing of the indigene; colonial racial hierarchies echoed class hierarchies of the Metropole. Police-military blurring again comes to the fore in André Rosemberg's examination of how the São Paulo police force emerged as a militarised police institution in the post-colonial context of 19th century Brazil. His contribution explores the factors that contributed to these traits and reiterates that the militarised DNA of much Brazilian policing is both historically engrained and incompatible with democratic objectives – albeit here under the specific contingencies of São Paulo. This attention towards hybridisation of police and military is accompanied by consideration of the deployment of these militarised police as a civilising force; this 'little army of São

8   *Conor O'Reilly*

Paulo' also being connected to local political elites. In his expert comment, Richard Hill digs deeper into common themes emerging from these chapters. Indeed, his contribution goes beyond mere commentary to locate Portuguese colonial policing within wider consideration of violence and social control in colonial settings. He also compares Portuguese colonial policing with parallel structures in other European Empires and identifies productive avenues for further research.

Part Two progresses towards Portuguese late colonial policing, exploring its responses to militant decolonisation movements. In confronting nationalist sentiment in its African colonies, Salazar cast the Portuguese political police, PIDE, as the protagonist of colonial policing. Its dubious work progressing from initial attempts to undermine organised nationalism in the colonies during the late 1950s and early 1960s, to eventually engage with ensuing colonial wars: in Angola from 1961; in Guinea-Bissau from 1963; and, in Mozambique from 1964. Colonial policing during this period thus enmeshed high policing with counterinsurgency. The depth of Portuguese resistance to decolonisation – not least simultaneously fighting colonial wars on three fronts – linked with the intransigent nature of Salazar's dictatorship. As Costa Pinto (2003) has observed, 'The future of the regime . . . was inextricably linked to the outcome of the wars' (p. 17) and ultimately both at home and abroad, attempts to maintain the *status quo* were unsuccessful. The democratisation delivered through the Carnation Revolution of 1974 in Portugal, served to accelerate decolonisation. Indeed, despite Portugal's longevity as a colonial power, its efforts to stem the tide of decolonisation arrived too late and its recourse to force further exposed the failures of its colonial governance.

In his chapter, Fernando Tavares Pimenta charts early PIDE attempts to suppress nascent Angolan nationalism in the period before colonial war. Focusing upon what he terms PIDE's 'racial strategy', he explores how racial difference was manipulated to sow division and distrust within multi-racial nationalist movements. In so doing, he reminds us that strategies of colonial control were not limited to African natives, but extended to settled white communities who also harboured nationalist ambitions. Albeit that, as Pimenta explains, the racialisation of punishment witnessed the latter receive less harsh treatment than African natives. In focussing upon a lesser-known Portuguese intelligence actor, SCCIM (Mozambique Information Coordination and Centralisation Services), Sandra Araújo's chapter examines an agency whose work was located at the nexus of administrative intelligence, colonial governance and academic research. She explores SCCIM's work through its confidential questionaire on Islam; an attempt to accumulate knowledge that might facilitate Portuguese approximation to Mozambican Muslim communities and subsequently co-opt them into the struggle against anti-colonial forces. Reiterating the centrality of intelligence-work within colonial governance (Thomas 2007), Araújo highlights significant failings of this scientification of intelligence, whilst also depicting the complex web of colonial intelligence actors operating during this period. Analysing the relationship between police action and military action, Bruno Cardoso Reis reiterates overlap between these spheres. Through comparative analysis, he also questions whether the brutality of Portuguese colonial control differed from that of other European Empires by virtue of the fact that, unlike them, it was authoritarian at home, as well as in the colonies. Part Two concludes with an expert comment from Martin Thomas that flags the significance of civil-military frictions as well as overlaps. He also emphasises how macro-political factors – both in Portugal and in Lusophone Africa – shaped late-colonial policing and counterinsurgency, and draws attention to transnational counter-colonial connections during this period.

Part Three progresses this compilation towards analysis of more contemporary policing patterns and forms across the Lusophone world. These include: post-colonial legacies of conflict, including political instability, militarisation and politicisation of policing; transitional processes that have involved efforts to reform and democratise police; and, transnational forces, predominantly transfers into Lusophone settings but increasingly also encompassing more complex and multidirectional policing traffic. The four contributions in Part Three explore how policing in Luso-Africa, Luso-Asia and Luso-Brazil emerges from what Hönke and Müller (2012) call 'the entangled histories of (in)security governance in the (post)colonial world' (p. 383). As these chapters make clear, policing in these Lusophone contexts has been forged by both the legacy of colonialism and transnational exchange; the latter increasingly being forged out of 'co-constitutive' (Bilgin 2016) policing relationships whereby the agency of Northern donors and Southern recipients (sometimes aspirant donors) intersects.

In the first chapter of Part Three, Helene Maria Kyed examines the complexity of police reforms in post-conflict Mozambique, contrasting the importation of two of the most prominent models: the professional reform model; and, community policing. Taking place under different auspices, these reform efforts occur against the backdrop of a country that was experiencing multiple transitions: from war to peace; from authoritarianism to multi-party democracy; and, from a centralised towards a market-oriented economy. In her critical examination of police reform implementation, Kyed highlights how the practical translation of international police reform models is impacted by local contingencies. In the Mozambican case, the variant effects of these policing imports were influenced by the shifting topography of political power across urban/rural settings, as well as the plural and contested nature of security governance; a feature common to many post-colonial settings. In the re-published piece from Lawrence Ho and Agnes Lam, the authors trace the comparatively calmer policing evolution in Macau and its progression from Portuguese colony to Chinese SAR (Special Administrative Region). Indeed, whereas the colonial legacy of policing in key Luso-African contexts was largely born out of oppression and conflict, the case of Macau offers a narrative of imperial neglect. The authors outline systematic organisational failings and capacity shortcomings within policing in this distant colonial enclave, noting that China and the Anglophone world also exerted influence on its policing patterns. Historical analysis is complemented by more contemporary empirical work that spotlights the impact of recent attempts to reform the police, as well as the challenges that confront policing in Macau; for example, the presence of organised crime and corruption due to its gambling industry. The

10   *Conor O'Reilly*

reinvention and modernisation of policing in Macau thus takes place against the transitional backdrop of sovereignty retrocession to China.

Gordon Peake's chapter offers a novel perspective on policing in Timor-Leste, the Lusophone policing setting that has probably received the most academic attention, certainly as regards transnational interactions. Whilst police development and reform in this young nation have certainly been the focus of much international endeavour, Peake argues that (the many) scholarly works conducted on policing in Timor-Leste have neglected one of its most significant influences; the legacy of authoritarianism from its former occupier and closest neighbour, Indonesia. Proposing deeper reflection upon these hidden imprints upon Timorese policing, Peake works to unravel the schizophrenic entanglements of its post-colonial, post-conflict and post-authoritarian status. Whilst the colonial influence of Portugal is evident in the titles and trappings of policing in Timor-Leste (Portuguese superceding *Tetum* in formal settings), Indonesian influence is more significant in terms of its residual effects upon police practice and culture. This chapter reminds us that Timor-Leste has the dubious privilege of not one, but two former Metropoles and reiterates that policing often emerges from a mesh of multiple influences.

My own contribution to this volume focuses upon recent efforts to pacify the *favelas* in Rio de Janeiro, drawing attention to both the forces that catalysed this model for urban security intervention, as well as how it has been strategically promoted in the transnational policing marketplace. Whilst Rio de Janeiro's Pacification Model was forged in the *favelas*, it is also born of legacies of colonialism, dictatorship and subjugation of the other, as well as complex transnational interactions and feedback loops. Rio de Janeiro, like other Latin American contexts, has longstanding status as a laboratory for policing and security experimentation. What this chapter highlights is the by-product of this experience: a model for urban security intervention that not only builds on the platform of previous transnational exchanges, but which also appears to be replicating them through pursuit of its own global profile. This chapter conceptualises Rio de Janeiro's Pacification Model as a *geo-policial brand*; a policing model that seeks to harness and transform the notoriety associated with policing in the *favela* to market a new security narrative for the *Cidade Maravilhosa*; one that sits comfortably with Brazilian attempts to secure its status as an emerging superpower. Reverberating across history, across contexts of deployment, across the police and military spheres, and also across militarisation and humanitarianism, the Rio de Janeiro Pacification Model represents a new brand for police action, one that has emerged from within – rather than being an export to – the Global South.

The compilation concludes with a final reflection from Andrew Goldsmith that calls for more nuanced consideration of the patterns of global policing; more accurately, its *glocal* dynamics. He spotlights how academic commentary must move away from grand narratives of (predominantly Western) policing exports towards a deeper understanding of local forces of resistance and how these mediate foreign transfers. He further points to evolving directions of policing exchange and how the transnational policing field is behaving more like a busy transnational

Introduction 11

policing marketplace. One where the wares on offer now include a growing array of exotic post-colonial policing brands that are seeking to carve-out their own market space alongside more recognisable Western policing staples.

References

Agozino, B. 2007. *Counter-Colonial Criminology: A Critique of Imperialist Reason.* Bristol: Pluto Press.

Arenas, F. 2011. *Lusophone Africa: Beyond Independence.* Minnesotta, MN: University of Minnesotta Press.

Bilgin, P. 2016. Unpacking the 'global', in *The Global Making of Policing: Postcolonial Perspectives,* edited by J. Hönke and M.M. Müller. Abingdon, Oxford: Routledge, 167–177.

Blanchard, E. and Glasman, J. 2012. Le maintien de l'ordre dans l'empire français: une historiagraphie émergente, in *Maintien L'Ordre Colonial,* edited by J.-P. Bat and N. Courtin. Rennes: Presses Universitaires de Rennes, 11–41.

Bowling, B. 2010. *Policing the Caribbean: Transnational Security Cooperation in Practice.* Oxford: Oxford University Press.

Bowling, B. and Sheptycki, J.W.E. 2012. *Global Policing.* Sage: London.

Bretas, M. 1997. *Ordem na Cidade: O Cotidiano da Autoridade Policial no Rio de Janeiro, 1907–1930.* Rio de Janeiro: Rocco.

Bretas, M. and Rosemberg, A. 2013. A história da polícia no Brasil: balanço e perspectivas. *Topoi (Rio de Janeiro),* 14(26): 162–173.

Brogden, M. 1987a. An act to colonise the internal lands of the island: Empire and the origins of the professional police. *International Journal of the Sociology of Law,* 15: 179–208.

Brogden, M. 1987b. The emergence of the police: The colonial dimension. *British Journal of Criminology,* 27: 4–14.

Brogden, M. and Ellison, G. 2012. *Policing in an Age of Austerity: A Postcolonial Perspective.* Abingdon, Oxford: Routledge.

Comaroff, J. and Comaroff, J.L. 2006. *Law and Disorder in the Postcolony.* Chicago: University of Chicago Press.

Comaroff, J. and Comaroff, J.L. 2014. *Theory From the South: Or, How Euro-America is Evolving Toward Africa.* Boulder, CO: Paradigm.

Costa Pinto, A. 2003. The transition to democracy and Portugal's decolonization, in *The Last Empire: 30 Years of Portuguese Decolonization,* edited by S. Lloyd-Jones and A. Costa Pinto. Bristol: Intellect, 17–35.

Cunneen, C. 2011. Postcolonial perspectives for criminology, in *What Is Criminology?,* edited by M. Bosworth and C. Hoyle. Oxford: Oxford University Press, 249–266.

Durão, S.S.B. 2008. *Patrulha e Proximidade: Uma Etnografia da Polícia em Lisboa.* Lisbon: Almedina.

Durão, S.S.B. and Lopes, D. 2015. Formação internacional, comunidades de saberes e mudança institucional: os oficiais de polícia africanos formados em Lisboa. *Fórum Brasileiro de Segurança Pública,* 9(1): 122–139.

Ellison, G. and O'Reilly, C. 2008. From empire to Iraq and the War on Terror: The transplantation and commodification of the (Northern) Irish policing experience. *Police Quarterly,* 11(4): 395–426.

12 Conor O'Reilly

Foucault, M. 2003. *Society Must Be Defended: Lectures at the Collège de France, 1975–76*. London/New York: Penguin.

Gonçalves, G.R. 2014. Police reform and the transnational circulation of police models: The Portuguese case in the 1860s. *Crime, Histoire & Sociétés/Crime, History & Societies*, 18(1): 5–29.

Hönke, J. and Müller, M.-M. 2012. Governing (in)security in a postcolonial world: Transnational entanglements and the worldliness of 'local' practice. *Security Dialogue*, 43(5): 383–401.

Hönke, J. and Müller, M.-M. 2016. *The Global Making of Policing: Postcolonial Perspectives*. Abingdon, Oxford: Routledge.

Jerónimo, M.B. 2015. *The 'Civilizing Mission' of Portuguese Colonialism (c.1870–1930)*. London: Palgrave Macmillan.

Jerónimo, M.B. and Monteiro, J.-P. 2013. Internationalism and the labours of the Portuguese colonial empire (1945–1974). *Portuguese Studies*, 29(2): 142–163.

Lint, W. de 2004. Neoconservatism and American counter-terrorism: Endarkened policy?, in *Terrorism and Counter-Terrorism: Criminological Perspectives*, edited by M. Deflem. Amsterdam: Elsevier/JAI Press, 131–153.

McMullen, J. 1998. Policing reform and moral discourse: The genesis of a modern institution. *Policing: An International Journal of Police Strategies & Management*, 21(1): 137–158.

Mateus, D.C. 2004. *A PIDE/DGS na Guerra Colonial 1961–1974*. Lisbon: Terramar.

Meneses, F. de and McNamara, R. 2012. The last throw of the dice: Portugal, Rhodesia and South Africa, 1970–74. *Portuguese Studies*, 28: 201–215.

Meneses, F. de and McNamara, R. 2013. The origins of exercise ALCORA, 1960–71. *International History Review*, 35: 1113–1134.

Meneses, F. de and McNamara, R. 2014a. Parallel diplomacy, parallel war: The PIDE/DGS's dealings with Rhodesia and South Africa, 1961–74. *Journal of Contemporary History*, 49: 366–389.

Meneses, F. de and McNamara, R. 2014b. Exercise ALCORA: Expansion and demise, 1971–74. *International History Review*, 36: 89–111.

Muggah, R. and Diniz, G. October 2013. *Securing the Border: Brazil's 'South America First' Approach to Transnational Organised Crime*. Strategic Paper 5. Igarapé Institute: Rio de Janeiro.

Müller, M.-M. 2016. Entangled pacifications: Peacekeeping, counterinsurgency and policing in Port-au-Prince and Rio de Janeiro, in *The Global Making of Policing: Postcolonial Perspectives*, edited by J. Hönke and M.-M. Müller. Abingdon, Oxford: Routledge, 77–95.

Newburn, T. and Jones, T. 2007. Symbolizing crime control: Reflections on zero tolerance. *Theoretical Criminology*, 11(2): 221–243.

O'Reilly, C. October 2015. *Morabeza for Transnational Policing? The Cape Verdean Experience of Foreign Police Assistance*. COPP-LAB Workshop, Leeds, UK.

Robb Larkins, E. 2015. *The Spectacular Favela: Violence in Modern Brazil*. Berkeley: University of California Press.

Said, E. 1978. *Orientalism*. New York: Vintage.

Shaw, M. 2015. Drug trafficking in Guinea-Bissau 1998–2014: The evolution of an elite protection network. *Journal for Modern African Studies*, 53(3): 339–364.

Sinclair, G. 2011. Globalising British policing, Vol. IV, in *The History of Policing*, edited by Clive Emsley (Series Editor). Aldershot: Ashgate.

Sinclair, G. 2016. 'British cop or international cop?' Global makings of international police assistance, 2000–2014, in *The Global Making of Policing: Postcolonial Perspectives*, edited by J. Hönke and M.-M. Müller. Abingdon, Oxford: Routledge, 132–148.

Sinclair, G. 2006. Get into a crack force and earn £20 a month and all found: The influence of the Palestine police on colonial policing. *European Review of History*, 13(1): 49–65.

Sinclair, G. and Williams, C.A. 2007. 'Home and away': The cross-fertilisation between 'Colonial' and 'British' policing, 1921–85. *Journal of Imperial and Commonwealth History*, 35(2): 221–238.

Stone, D. 2004. Transfer agents and global networks in the 'transnationalization' of policy. *Journal of European Public Policy*, 11(3): 545–566.

Taylor, P. 2014. *Endarkened Governance: A Genealogical Analysis of the Pentagon Papers and the Global Intelligence Files*. Electronic Theses and Dissertations, paper 5083, University of Windsor.

Thomas, M. 2007. *Empires of Intelligence. Security Services and Colonial Disorder After 1914*. Berkeley: University of California Press.

Udelsman Rodrigues, C. 2015. Cooperação internacional e construção de um modelo original de polícia em Angola. *Fórum Brasileiro de Segurança Pública*, 9(1): 102–121.

Udelsman Rodrigues, C. 2016. The *Portuguesinhos*: Experiences of return and reintegration of Angolan police commissioned officers who studied in Portugal. *Journal of Global Initiatives: Policy, Pedagogy, Perspective*, 11(1): 77–98.

Zoettl, P.A. 2014. *Morabeza*, cash or body: Prison, violence and the state in Praia, Cape Verde. *International Journal of Cultural Studies*, 19(4): 1–16.

Zoettl, P.A. 2015. My body imprisoned, my soul relieved: Youth, gangs and prison in Cape Verde. *European Journal of Cultural Studies*, 1–17.

Part One

The colonial policing mission

1 Colonial policing and the Portuguese Empire (c.1870–1961)

Gonçalo Rocha Gonçalves and Rita Ávila Cachado[1]

Introduction

The colonial state and its crime, public order and public safety law enforcement agencies remains a poorly researched subject in the historiography of the Portuguese Empire in the 19th and 20th centuries. Despite some occasional references, the police and policing practices have not proved a subject able to attract the interest of Portuguese scholars of colonialism. This constitutes little surprise as the historical works on Portugal's mainland continental police force from the mid-19th century onwards – which marks the beginning of police *modernisation* – are only a recent theme within Portuguese historiography.

Examining the most recent works on the Portuguese colonial Empire it is possible to conclude that the studies specifically devoted to the subject are rare and more directly focused on political policing (Nascimento 2001: 226–228, 236–237, Mateus 2004, Curto and Cruz 2013: 113–165). Other works indirectly touch upon the issue of policing, though the issue remains partly hidden in the main subjects and arguments of these works. This is the case with Ricardo Roque's study on colonial resistance in India (Roque 2001), Maria Conceição Neto's social history of Huambo (Angola) (Neto 2012: 265–278), or Valdemir Donizette Zamparoni work on urban development and labour relations in Lourenço Marques, Moçambique (Zamparoni 1998).

During the last decades of the 19th century, the renewed interest and stabilisation of colonial powers in their 'scramble for Africa' translated into the reform of colonial police institutions and the development of specialised, professional policing structures (Thomas 2012: 17–42). Although the Portuguese colonial police never reached the degree of complexity of the British Empire, which contained more than 200 different police forces in the early 20th century (Emsley 2012), its dispersion and diversity over time and space still produces nebulous contours in the associated subjects. Beyond Portuguese historiography, the attention of

---

1 The authors would like to thank Conor O'Reilly for his comments and help editing this chapter and the valuable comments of the anonymous referees.

18 Gonçalo Rocha Gonçalves and Rita Ávila Cachado

historians to colonial policing has been growing since sociologist Mike Brogden (1987) adopted a metropolitan point-of-view to draw attention to the importance of the 'colonial dimension' in the emergence of the *new police* in the 19th century. Since then the study of the various forms of colonial policing institutions, of police personnel and their circulation within colonial and metropolitan territories, as well as the characteristics of police functions and practices have witnessed numerous developments.[2] Irradiating from the main urban settlements, the places where the presence of Europeans attained greatest significance became the locations that experienced the most pressing demands for organisation of a policing system. This is not surprising given that 'the increasingly careful organisation of urban living' was among the reasons that enabled the growth of the European presence and influence in colonial settlements (Porter 1994: 75). However, the development of a 'colonial policing' sphere of administration may unveil many other features of European colonialism.

This chapter aims to identify the emergence and contours of colonial policing as a government issue in Portugal, the debates and main measures undertaken at the end of the 19th century and throughout the first-half of the 20th century. The notion of 'colonial policing' emerges as problematic as it was often deployed as a misleading analytical category. Because this conveys an idea of institutional centralisation (if not of everyday operational control at least of inception rationalisation) and the existence of a standardised set of practices, 'colonial policing' sometimes gets assumed to be a coherent system. This was something that never proved the case in the Portuguese colonial territories. This also holds true for other Portuguese colonial institutions and programs (Domingos and Peralta 2013) Nevertheless, this chapter adopts this concept in the sense of a category that was a political construction by politicians as well as by the civil and military authorities and which was deployed in public debates on the nature and place of colonialism in Portugal. Portraying the emergence of this category within discussions about the colonial state and some of the institutional reforms enacted over time in this area as well as the distinct types of state agents operating in the field constitute the core objectives of this chapter.

For this, the text draws on multiple primary and secondary sources. The legislation enacted throughout the years – creating or reforming police forces and policing services – is the main anchor source used. Moreover, the writings of administrators and police officers that reflected on this subject are also drawn into the analysis. Many other sources could possibly give a more comprehensive view on this subject – parliamentary debates, Navy Ministry documentation, for example – but given the lack of works providing a general overview of the development of

---

2 The British case is the most thoroughly studied in its colonial settlements following the precursor work by McCracken (1986) and book edited by Anderson and Killingray (1991), the subject continues to register a significant body of works (for a recent work see Sinclair 2011). Elsewhere the subject has also deserved the attention of historians: for an overview of this new field of research about French colonialism, see Blanchard (2014); for the German African possessions, see Zollmann (2011).

colonial policing in Portuguese territories, the analysis of the legislation produced anchored in other contemporary writings provide an introduction to the subject that is capable of both inciting and assisting further, deeper, works. Also, we should clarify at this stage just what this text will and will not deal with. Thus, the focus is very much placed on those public institutions that have been directly characterised as 'police'. This excludes one important sphere of colonial policing that was particularly important in the case of the Portuguese colonies due to the incipient nature of the colonial state well into the 20th century: the privatisation of policing practices and other social disciplinary strategies. As Jerónimo has pointed out, plantations, concessions, native lands were places and domains where formal rules and means of enforcement held little if any real impact (Jerónimo & Monteiro 2013: 168). Although outside the objectives of this work, we should indeed point out the importance of private policing within Portuguese colonial territories. In part, it was the persistent fragility of public policing institutions – that consist the core objective of this text – one factor that explains the continuous importance of private forms to keep the order.[3]

The first section of this chapter focuses on the emergence of the police as an issue in the debate on the nature of the colonial state at the end of the 19th century. In fact, in this period there were only a few, but nonetheless, significant references to the subject. Furthermore, these references interlinked with police reforms that were being undertaken in metropolitan Portugal. Despite the insertion of police and policing into thinking about the colonial state, institutional reforms would continue in a piecemeal fashion without any overall policy implemented in a universal fashion across all colonial territories. The second half of the chapter focuses on the period from the 1930s through to the outbreak of colonial warfare in 1961; a period marked by the emergence and consolidation of an authoritarian dictatorship headed by António Oliveira Salazar. Within the Estado Novo's political project, the empire took on a new and central role in defining the nature and historical mission of the Portuguese nation. Therefore, centralised control over colonial territories and populations emerged as a prominent political issue and the colonial policing system and institutions fell within this context. On this point, a comparison between police reform in metropolitan Portugal and colonial policing proves helpful. Despite police force centralisation in continental Portugal, the piecemeal organisation and the diversity present in the police institutions and policing strategies of the colonies still persisted.

Territorial occupation and the emergence of 'colonial policing'

In the 1880s, the new imperial order emerging in the wake of the Berlin Conference instituted the effective occupation, administration and colonisation of territories under the sovereignty of European imperial powers. For Portugal, these

---

3 On the development of police institutions in the context of territorial concessions to private companies, see Direito (2013: 97, 108, 111).

changes in imperial policy meant that the country had to introduce significant changes to its colonial relationships. The existing relationships existing between metropolitan Portugal and its overseas territories were adamantly based on a type of colonial exploitation within the framework of which a small number of settlements, the sites of trading and commercial activities, constituted the only presence that the country actually held in its colonies. The new imperial order meant that new arrangements had to be crafted almost from scratch out of the existing, highly blurred, definition of the colonial state. The Portuguese elites were entirely aware of the need for new institutions, personnel and administrative procedures that were capable of enforcing colonial order and installing more effective control over the territories and the populations. They were well aware that these measures represented crucial factors for the success of the new colonial project that they correspondingly advocated (Costa 1903). The nature and characteristics of these institutions, agents and practices were subject to a growing number of debates and 'trial and error' strategies of reform that had been put into practice by different governments. These debates and political processes in the defining of Portuguese colonial policing constitute the core material of this chapter.

How was policing traditionally carried out in the period preceding the renewed attentions to Africa in the late 19th century? Portuguese colonial administration was characterised by its weakness and its fragmented nature. From the mid-19th century onwards, there had been no major significant European settlements in the existing colonial territories (with Brazil having for centuries been the main colonial destination of Portuguese population migrations) and the existing settlements (for example, Luanda) were perceived as destinations to which convicts were transported alongside the perception that there was no need for any major policing arrangements. In the traces existing of what might be termed a state, there remained a permanent confusion between the public and private spheres, with the intertwining of the exercise of state powers with commercial activities; the accumulation of posts holding different functional natures and the limited number of individuals despatched from metropolitan Portugal (Alexandre 1999). The exercise of police powers certainly followed this pattern. In the small Asian territory of Macau, for example, police officers were traditionally paid for by local merchants and the rank and file was composed of men from Portugal's Indian colony of Goa (Teixeira 1970: 22–23, 26–29).[4]

Very differently to the conclusions reached about the British case, where one can claim 'the centrality of colonial conquest and imperial legitimation of institutional development in Victorian England' (Brogden 1987: 5), in the Portuguese case, the link between modernisation and the development of metropolitan policing and imperial legitimation proved non-existent. Thus, in 1860s metropolitan Portugal, police reform was a central issue on the government agenda with politicians looking to European police systems and not to any colonial experience as happened in the

---

4 For an analysis of the policing system in Macau and its recent transition to China's SAR see Ho and Lam (2014) and the chapter published by these authors in this volume.

case of the Anglo-Irish experience. In this period, while policing in continental Portugal became the subject of multiple discussions, there was no parallel debate about policing in the colonial territories (Gonçalves 2014). Not only was there no interexchange of either personnel or of experiences between metropolitan and colonial police forces but also the theme of the colonial police was almost totally absent in the early second half of the 19th century at least in terms of more general discussion rather than gaining just the occasional reference.[5]

In fact, policing was largely perceived as an army function (see the contribution of Palacios Cerezales in this collection). The second half of the 1870s, however, brought about a new impetus to the Portuguese colonial project due to the international pressure that was being experienced in the African territories. This prompted the first debates on this issue beyond the strictly military sphere. Issues such as the abolition of the slave trade and the existence of forced labour attracted criticism of the Portuguese administration and its lack of police structures capable to efficiently control such practices.[6] One central issue emerges frequently: the discrepancy between written legislation and the actual practices on the ground. Portuguese colonialism in general seemed more concerned with establishing administrative rules and maintaining good relations within the administrative apparatus than with enforcing those same rules. However, the internationalisation of colonial questions towards the end of the 19th century required the Portuguese authorities to put forward if not actual effective responses to safety and public order problems, at least the framework for discussing these issues in more detailed terms.

Eduardo Costa and the appearance of colonial police in the Portuguese colonial thinking

One case that clearly illustrates the progressive advance of the colonial policing question and its diversity beyond simple military territorial occupation stems from Mozambique. The reasons for the policing issue to surge more strongly in Mozambique than in other territories (Angola for example, which does not have the same body of legislation) remain somewhat ambiguous but might derive from the prevalence of a more heterogeneous and complex society in this territory; in some ways it was more 'modern' due to commerce and migration from Asia. In an extensive work about the Portuguese colonial administration, Eduardo Costa, an army officer, former governor of Mozambique and a proponent of the new 'science of colonial administration', theorised extensively on just what the government's territorial occupation policy should be (Alexandre 2000: 182). In his works, the author dedicated a few pages to the organisation of the colonial police

---

5 As for colonial policing, although there are but a few specific studies, there are many works that pay attention to the control over the population, especially when there were threats to colonial rule. The fear of loss, regarding colonial possessions, led the colonial Portuguese state to take control actions. One of the first big menaces was with the Indian Portuguese State in the late 1950s (see Rodrigues 2002, Cachado 2004).

6 For the existence of forced labour in the late colonial Portuguese rule, see Garcia 2012.

22   Gonçalo Rocha Gonçalves and Rita Ávila Cachado

system in what was one of the earliest positions articulated on the specificities of colonial policing within the Portuguese colonial administrative elite (Costa 1903: 180–188). Drawing on foreign examples (mainly British and German) and Portuguese metropolitan police institutions (the *Polícia Civil* and the *Guarda Municipal*) as sources of inspiration, this work's significance derives from how it provides an insight into the existence of a broader discussion undertaken by a growing colonial administrative elite on the subject of territorial occupation. Within this framework, the military and the policing structures were placed at the core of this discussion, with 'colonial policing' correspondingly beginning to emerge as an autonomous subject of debate within the colonial administration.

Eduardo Costa distinguishes between three different types of police. The first was the 'high police' whose primary function was to preserve Portuguese rule of its colonial territories and to combat indigenous rebellions and all kinds of banditry. The army therefore was to be encharged with this function. Second, the police took charge of maintaining public safety and public order in urban settlements. Finally, there came the 'private' indigenous police force which was attributed the function of maintaining order and enforcing the law in areas inhabited exclusively by the indigenous population. Under colonial government supervision, Costa held that this latter type of policing should be carried out by local people under military command. However, the second kind of policing, the police in charge of overseeing order and tranquility in urban settlements, received a more extensive discussion from the author. The most immediate issues arising involved choosing firstly between military or civilian police forces and secondly between forces composed of white European personnel or indigenous police officers. Costa posed the question and sought to open a debate: 'what would be most convenient?' (Costa 1903: 180). However, instead of putting forward answers, he opted to analyse the existing reality according to the example he knew best: Mozambique.

The existing policing structures were, according to Costa, utterly chaotic in nature. In the Portuguese colonies, 'we have of everything . . . [but] without any defined criteria' (Costa 1903: 180). Mozambique was an especially complex example as part of the territory was outsourced to administration by a private company (*Companhia de Moçambique*). Thus, any reforms introduced by the government into the rest of the territory coexisted with whatever developments were introduced in the meanwhile by the *Companhia de Moçambique*. Despite the fact that Mozambique was, considering all the Portuguese colonies, the territory that witnessed the most policing related measures, the force then available was still considered blatantly insufficient for the task. To demonstrate this state of affairs, Costa provides the example of the then recent appointment of British detectives in Beira to resolve the case of a gang that had been causing trouble. Whilst the appointment had 'hurt the national self-esteem', the hiring of foreign policemen nevertheless yielded positive results (Costa 1903: 183). Furthermore, in addition to its clear shortcomings, urban policing, the second type defined by Costa, was characterised by its diversity throughout Mozambique. Considering only those parts of Mozambican territory that were directly administered by the

Portuguese Government, there was Lourenço Marques, with a military police force composed of European personnel alongside some indigenous assistants; in Beira, in the central region, there was a civil police composed almost exclusively of policemen of European origins; and, finally, the cases of Quelimane, a seaport further to the north and Mozambique island with their civilian police forces that were exclusively composed of men of African origin who were commanded by a small number of European military officers. In whatever the respective arrangements, the government in Lisbon seemed to have played very little role in the eventual outcome.

Reproducing almost verbatim the discourses about police reform made in continental Portugal in the 1860s (Gonçalves 2014), Costa endorsed the option for civil police forces in urban colonial settlements. In the cities, he acknowledged, 'the police service [. . .] requires from its officers prudence and restraint that only the long practice of the same service and experience of life can give'. In urban settlements, the application of force required more selective deployment and thus only experienced and carefully recruited men would be able to perform the job. Taking the example of Lisbon's 1893 police reform and the British model in Lagos, Sierra Leone, Eduardo Costa advocated a semi-military organisation, with the personnel in these police forces containing varying proportions of European and indigenous members depending on the prevailing circumstances in each region. Nevertheless, Costa also noted an important difference between Lisbon's policing structures and those supposedly existing in its colonial cities. Whereas in Lisbon, the *Polícia Civil* was undergoing a process of specialisation with the restructuring of individual police services (municipal, public safety and criminal investigation), due to the existing social conditions but especially due to the limited financial resources available, the introduction of this organisational complex into colonial policing in its African colonies was not yet feasible.

The issues addressed by Eduardo Costa in his writings on civil administration in the Portuguese colonial territories arose out of a context in which the number of legislative reforms directly addressing the nature and composition of colonial police forces grew significantly after the 1860s. In 1861, the Government of Macau centralised what had hitherto been a police force paid for by local merchants and set up the *Corpo de Polícia de Macau* (Police Corps of Macau) proceeding, in 1869, with its militarisation (Teixeira 1970: 48–49, 54–61). At the end of 1872, the Cape Verdean government launched the Praia police force.[7] In June 1875, another local government ordinance led to the *Companhia de Polícia* (Police Company) in the City of Mozambique. This was a military police force funded by the local municipality with the stated reasons behind its creation being 'the need to provide for individual security and property in a city, where the influx of national citizens and foreign people is increasing'.[8] Two years later, the

---

7 *Portaria* (Ordinance) 24, 24–12–1872, sanctioned by government decree on 13–08–1873 in *Diário do Governo* Nº 144, 29–08–1873.

8 *Portaria* (Ordinance) of the General Government of Mozambique 16–06–1875.

24   Gonçalo Rocha Gonçalves and Rita Ávila Cachado

government of Angola acted to endow the city of Luanda with the *Corpo de Polícia da Cidade de Luanda* (Police Corps of Luanda City).[9] In 1879, the authorities set up the *Polícia Civil da Cidade de Nova Goa* (Civil Police of Nova Goa City) in India.[10] These represent just some initial examples with others following in the 1880s and 1890s with reforms introduced to the policing arrangements in the most urbanised (normally port towns) settlements in the Portuguese colonial territories. These reforms were very much piecemeal and were introduced by local government with very little, if any, intervention from the metropolitan government in Lisbon. These police forces almost always took inspiration from the models of the Municipal Guard and the Civil Police of Lisbon and Porto. In common, the locations for these reforms were all places where urbanisation and the presence of a more diverse social and ethnic landscape represented significant factors. The continuous passing, altering and revoking of measures in relation to local police forces provides a broader picture of just what Eduardo Costa had described regarding Mozambique.[11]

Evidence that the policing arrangements evolving in Mozambique attained a significantly greater degree of complexity than in other Portuguese colonies stems from the personnel serving in the main urban settlements of this territory. Only rarely did the Ministry of Interior handle issues related to colonial policing and public safety, the state referred issues related to colonial territories to the Department of the Navy. However, some documentation in the archives of the Portuguese Ministry of the Interior suggests that, in the end of the 19th century, the number of police officers from the *Guarda Municipal de Lisboa* (Lisbon Municipal Guard) joining forces in Mozambique became a regular process. Whether through officers voluntarily joining these forces, or because military hierarchy transferred them to the colonies, the number of men, formally under the direction of civil authorities that circulated from Lisbon to the colonies unquestionably grew significantly in this period.[12] Thus far, only fragmentary evidence is available irrespective of the fact that the circulation of civil administration personnel from continental Portugal to the colonies had begun in this period and has already been identified by some authors (Castelo 2007: 46–47, 61–65). The assumption that this movement also began to occur in the police forces, entities distinct from the regular military structures, can, from the evidence of the Ministry of Interior cited above, also be pointed to. As with all colonial administrations, the transition from a colonial state dominated by the military to a civilian authority should also have taken place in the case of the police (Alexandre 1999). As the 19th century ended,

---

9 *Boletim Oficial do Governo-geral da Província de Angola*, Nº9 and 10, 3 and 10–03–1877.

10 Portaria Nº667, 07–10–1879.

11 Furthermore, for the case of Lourenço Marques, the description of a state of constant reform in the police organisation ongoing throughout the last decade of the 19th century proves illustrative (Pereira 1940: 4–20).

12 For some examples of transferences of men from Lisbon to Lourenço Marques, see IANTT-MR, Mç.2854, L°39, Nº929 (1889); Mç.2860, L°40, Nº475 (1890); Mç.2866, L°41, Nº310 (1891); Mç.2345, L°47, Nº272 (1897).

the circulation of policemen from Lisbon to the colonies seemed to be restricted to the urbanised settlements in Mozambique. From evidence gathered from documentation from the Ministry of Interior, no other colony experienced any similar processes of personnel transfer in the late 19th century. The completion of railways in 1895 in Lourenço Marques and Beira in 1898 marked the late 19th century in Mozambique and fostered an environment that was conducive to the already traditional correlation between increased mobility and growing feelings of insecurity (Knepper 2010: 14–18). The need for a bylaws code – a code designed to regulate multifarious aspects of everyday life – in Lourenço Marques followed the same pattern that had occurred decades earlier in Lisbon when the establishment of an urban civil police force was accompanied by the enactment of the first modern bylaws code. In a similar pattern to the metropolitan context, the development of more complex urban societies, as was then the case in Mozambican cities, also triggered debates about policing the colonies.

However, outside the main towns, and well into the 20th century, the military continued to perform policing duties on a routine basis (see Palacios Cerezales' contribution in this collection). The *colunas móveis de polícia* (mobile police columns) (Angola 1913) were deployed to bring the state, even if only on a temporary basis, to regions and populations where the European administrative state remained little more than a mirage. The army officer thus frequently served as an administrative handyman (Roque 2001: 303).

The institutional landscape and the circulation of personnel

The final years of the Republic (1918–1926) and the period of military dictatorship (1926–1933) normally get described as the period that marked the end of the 'pacification campaigns' with the corresponding 'introduction of the civil service' in place of the military for running the colonial territories (Castelo 2007: 16, Pélissier 1986, Newitt 1997). The non-military components of the state thus registered a period of exponential growth (Domingos and Peralta 2013), capable of ascertaining Portuguese sovereignty over the entirety of the colonial territories and claiming a civilising mission (Rosaldo 1989), particularly in the cases of Angola and Mozambique. However, whether or not this objective was actually achieved, the circumstances prevailing on the ground were not normally well-defined, meaning that in the Portuguese colonial landscape policing was always based on a patchwork system. The police and the entire administrative structure were at the very centre of this process and encapsulated the persistent weakness of the Portuguese state. Similar to the situation in metropolitan police institutions where, apart from the creation of the *Guarda Nacional Republicana* (Portuguese National Gendarmerie), no more significant changes were introduced. Furthermore, the Republic that took power in 1910 did not make any apparent structural changes to Portuguese colonial policing.

Nevertheless, this did not prevent important local developments in some territories. In this respect, Mozambique and particularly its capital, Lourenço Marques,

26 Gonçalo Rocha Gonçalves and Rita Ávila Cachado

pioneered changes and undertook important measures to develop its police services. In fact, following a pattern seen elsewhere in Europe and showing how Portuguese took part in police modernisation, towards the end of the 1910s and at the beginning of the 1920s, criminal investigation as a specific field of policing techniques – with its several different techniques for identifying large parts of the population within the framework of investigating specific crimes – which was undertaken by a specialist branch within the territorial police or by an independent institution, achieved significant advances in Mozambique. More than any other place in the Empire, the *scientific police* that had been witnessing significant progress in metropolitan Portugal in the two preceding decades, now reached one of its colonial territories. In 1916, a branch of the judicial police was set up in the *Polícia Civil de Lourenço Marques*, composed of 27 members (including 12 of the indigenous population, probably *assimilados*).[13] Five years later, on the grounds of the great increase in the population of Lourenço Marques, which was by then generating a heavy work burden for the police commissioner alongside the need to integrate someone specialised in legal knowledge (a judge) into this police service, an independent branch of the judicial police was established there.[14] Between 1917 and 1920, this service was set up with the help of a well-known republican, medical anthropologist and the director of the *Intituto de Criminologia de Lisboa*, Rodolfo Xavier da Silva (Silva 1932). To what extent did these technical developments also take place in other territories remains unclear? However, we do know that, when the new commandant, Salgueiro Rego, arrived at the police force in the small colony of Sao Tomé e Principe in the early 1950s, he registered dismay at the lack of any police identification services (Rego 1955: 138).

Salgueiro Rêgo and colonial policing during the New State

The colonial nature of the Portuguese nation was a cornerstone ideology of the Estado Novo and translated into a whole new set of political, economic, social and administrative agendas. The police – its institutional system, the nature and quality of its personnel and operational strategies – naturally reappeared as an issue in the widespread colonial debates. In the founding year of the New State, 1933, the *Reforma Administrativa Ultramarina* (Overseas Administration Reform) restructured – at least in the *letter of the law* – the state machinery in the colonial territories.[15] The administrative officers assigned to new administrative institutions (*circunscrições, concelhos* and *postos administrativos*) were expected to perform

---

13 Ordinance of 10–02–1916 in Boletim Oficial de Moçambique N°7, 12–02–1916. *Assimilados* was a term that designated both a juridical and cultural category. *Assimilados* were those indigenous people who proved that they had adopted European cultural rules and were therefore envisioned as citizens, in opposition to *indígena*, not citizens. *Assimilados* remained only a minority group, which proves that Portuguese colonialism was not as assimilationist as advocated, see Silva (2012).

14 Law-Decree n° 7348 of 19–02–1921 in *Boletim Oficial de Moçambique* N°14, 02–04–1921.

15 Decree-law number 23229, 15–11–1933.

Colonial policing and the Portuguese Empire   27

many police functions. However, as the renewed and growing levels of attention to colonial policing was reflected in the number of works published about the subject in Portugal, it is possible to observe how on the ground policing was still based on complex arrangements. Through monographic volumes about individual police forces or works addressing a more general discussion of colonial policing and offering different solutions for a colonial police system, we may trace the growing attention paid to this issue. Amongst those authors paying renewed attention to colonial policing, the works (and the career) of Captain Salgueiro Rego constitute a significant source, detailing some of the trends of change within the colonial policing field during the early decades of the Estado Novo.

Right from his birth, Salgueiro Rego's life was interlinked with the police: his father was a cavalry officer in Lisbon's *Guarda Municipal*. At the age of eight, however, tragedy beset his life with the death of his father in *Quartel do Carmo*. Aided by the money his father had discounted with the corporation's mutuality and, following a subsidy from the queen, he was educated at the Military College. At a young age, he joined Lisbon's municipal services as an accountancy officer. During the First World War, he re-joined the army and saw active service in Belgium. From its very outset in 1926, he was a supporter of the military coup that established the dictatorship. At the end of the 1920s and throughout most of the 1930s, he worked as a high-ranking officer in the Agriculture Ministry and as an *aide-de-camp* to some military generals. In the late 1930s, he joined the *Polícia de Segurança Pública* (Public Security Police), directing provincial commands (Viseu and Leiria) and one of the three Lisbon police divisions (between 1939 and 1942). It was in this latter period that Rego became part of a small intellectual elite of PSP officers (another member of this group subsequently served as the director of PIDE, Fernando Silva Pais) that through extensive study began examining the nature, functions and social status of the police and policemen. There were numerous publications with the group launching an official journal, *Polícia Portuguesa*, in 1937 as well as playing a central role and constituting a body of police thinking in which the 'police of the colonies' emerged as a topic of clear interest.[16] After being outside of the police force for a period in the 1940s (working at the censorship services), in 1951, after having been considered for the command of the PSP of Portuguese India, he was nominated chief of police in the small colony of Sao Tome and Principe, where he would stay until 1953 (Rego 1955).[17]

---

16 See for example, 'Polícias do Império Português. A PSP de Luanda', *Polícia Portuguesa*, nº14, Jul–Ago, 1939; Fernando Silva Pais, 'O Corpo de Polícia Civil de Lourenço Marques', *Polícia Portuguesa*, nº20, Jul–Ago, 1940; Antero das Mercês Afonso, 'Subsídios para a história da polícia de segurança pública de Angola', *Polícia Portuguesa*, nº40, Nov–Dez, 1943.

17 Rego's assignment to the Sao Tome police ended controversially in 1953. At the beginning of that year, he refused to comply with the Governor's orders forcing indigenous people to work on the plantations and on the public works. For this he was dismissed and held for eight days before being shipped back to Lisbon. In the following days, with the governor

28 *Gonçalo Rocha Gonçalves and Rita Ávila Cachado*

From the end of the 1930s until his death in the 1960s, Rego was a regular contributor to the daily press and amongst the various topics he discussed, policing issues was one of the main subjects. Among the many aspects of police organisation and policing functions that drew his attention, Salgueiro Rego thoroughly discussed the need to establish a new police system in the Portuguese colonial territories in Africa (Rego 1946). By a new system, he meant going beyond a mere institutional framework and into the system of recruitment, training and discipline. Overall, the colonial policing system needed to be 'properly studied and organized'. His works are particularly relevant because of the wide range of sources he deploys when arguing for new solutions. First of all, he relies on his own experience, whether as a police officer in continental Portugal or in Sao Tome and Principe. Additionally, while he does not make any exhaustive comparative exercise with other national police systems, he actually reveals a fairly rich international bibliography. For example, in a paper delivered to a colonial congress, he extensively discusses John Moylan's works about the British police, whose books he was given by the British Embassy in Lisbon (Rego 1967: 58), and the desirability of applying some of its features into Portuguese colonial policing. Amongst other aspects, Salgueiro Rego emphatically stressed the need to set up schools in metropolitan Portugal to train police officers for deployment in colonial police forces.[18] It was, he argued, crucially important to have policemen who knew how to deal with the indigenous populations as they adapted their uses, customs and civilisation to the colonial order (Silva 2012). This was not a particularly new type of discourse even in the Portuguese context, but if, for instance, at the beginning of the 20th century this was a discourse applied to discuss the colonial administration as a whole, it was deemed specifically relevant to the context of police action in the 1940s. Only the structural growth ongoing since the beginning of the century enabled the existence of these more specialised discussions.

On the ground, according to Salgueiro Rego, the situation still remained grim with each colony running only the police force that each colony's governor adjudged to be appropriate, with the government in Lisbon having little say in the matter. In fact, the continued lack of central government intervention remained a motive for criticism. In contrast with the rationalised national model consolidated in continental Portugal during the 1930s, a national urban police

---

commanding the police force, a series of now tragically renowned massacres took place. When, in 1955, Salgueiro Rego published his memoirs (with one chapter dedicated to these events), the book was an editorial sensation and, despite being authorised by the Lisbon censorship, was banned in Sao Tome by its new governor. On the events of 1953, see Seibert (2002).

18 This practice took shape, post-decolonisation and post-democratisation, with police officers from the former African Portuguese colonies receiving training at the *Instituto Superior de Ciências Policiais e Segurança Interna*, in Lisbon (Higher Institute of Police Sciences and Internal Security). The study of the circulation and training of these officers is currently being undertaken in the collective research project 'COPP-LAB: Circulações de Polícias em Portugal, África Lusófona e Brasil' coordinated by Susana Durão at the Social Sciences Institute – University of Lisbon.

force, the *Polícia de Segurança Pública*, and a national rural military police force, the *Guarda Nacional Republicana*, colonial policing was thus still characterised by institutional and organisational diversity across the different territories under Portuguese rule. This diversity affected many issues inherent to police functioning with one that was deeply regretted by Salgueiro Rego, being the question of the disparity in wages from colony to colony that effectively prevented the cultivation of a homogeneous group of colonial police officers. Given the different currencies circulating in the different colonial territories and variations in the cost of living, uniformity of wages would have always been practically impossible to achieve but the sheer fact of the subject being raised already indicates the desire of some within the institution, to attain trans-territorial unity in the policing system. Whilst some colonies still maintained their police force integrated within the army, others had independent police services while differing in the composition of their personnel structures. Nevertheless, the career of Salgueiro Rego represents an example of the intensification in the circulation of police personnel from continental Portugal to the colonies. This movement of policemen was favoured by the institutional reforms introduced by the Estado Novo. By fashioning the *Polícia de Segurança Pública* of Angola, Mozambique, for example, as intended copies of the metropolitan PSP, and despite the fact that they retained independent commands, the state acted to nurture an organisational continuity between metropolitan Portugal and the colonies in keeping with an ever increasing circulation of personnel.

In fact, in an attempt to overcome the colonial police system's institutional patchwork, the early 1940s witnessed a major reform movement, which spanned not only the engendering of new solutions for colonial policing but also much more active central government intervention. This was indeed a movement within the scope of a broader rationalisation of the colonial administrative institutions undertaken by the Estado Novo. This reform movement resulted in the setting up or restructuring of police forces in all of the most important colonial territories in Africa. The *Polícia de Segurança Pública de Angola* evolved through a succession of legislative reforms ranging from the end of the 1920s through to the 1960s and institutionally extending from the local police in Luanda to the main police force for the colony's entire territory alongside the corresponding growth in the institution's manpower.[19] Although the institution was already formally referred to as the *police of Angola*, the organisational scope outside Luanda remained restricted. While the police force had in its ranks only the small number of 293 formal employees in 1942, the number had grown to the

---

19 Diploma Legislativo Colonial nº126, 27–07–1929 established 'Polícia de Segurança Pública da Colónia de Angola'; Diploma Legislativo Colonial nº1030 of 08–10–1938 (Polícia Segurança Pública Angola 1938); Decreto-Lei nº 31995 in Diário da República Nº 99, Série I, 30–04–1942. In the 1960s and already in the context of the colonial war, PSP Angola was again reformed by Decreto-Lei, in Diário da República nº 279, Série I, 27–11–1964 and Decreto-Lei nº 47360, in Diário da Républica, nº 279, Série I, 02–12–1966.

30 Gonçalo Rocha Gonçalves and Rita Ávila Cachado

astonishing sum of 13,157 policemen in 1964.[20] In Mozambique, the police force underwent reorganisation in 1943 as the *Polícia de Segurança Pública*, although a number of features (for example, the uniforms) had already indicated an earlier approximation to the PSP model.[21] In the smaller territories, a similar set of reforms was also put into practice. 1944, for example, saw the founding of the *Polícia de Segurança Pública of Guiné*.[22] In the Cape Verde archipelago, a series of reforms in 1936, 1952 and 1956 shaped the local *Polícia de Segurança Pública*.[23] Even in the territories where the police did not formally assume the name of *Polícia de Segurança Pública*, such as in Sao Tomé e Principe, where Salgueiro Rego had served as police commandant between 1951 and 1953, its organisation was copied on the metropolitan institution and the circulation of personnel set in motion (Rego 1955).

At least through to the end of the Second World War, the results of the reforms appear only limited in scope. According to Salgueiro Rego, writing in the mid-1950s, a confusion of ranks and hierarchical structures remained and only served to spread confusion and to prevent the consolidation of a uniform system. Despite the reform movement and the reorganisation and standardisation of colonial police institutions, organisational diversity persisted and consequently enabled the existence of different policing patterns. Only with the colonial wars was the rationalisation that imposed uniformity based on a metropolitan institution completed even while this represented the fruits of a movement that had timidly taken its first steps decades earlier.

In comparison with earlier periods, the reforms of the police system implemented during the Estado Novo revealed the transfer of political decision-making from the local colonial authorities to the central government in Lisbon. More importantly, and more specifically related to the definition of 'colonial police', the changeover reflects an important political decision regarding the reform of the colonial policing system that, whilst beyond the scope of this chapter, merits thorough research attention. Between the rise to power of the Estado Novo and the end of the Second World War, there was a continuous replication throughout the colonial territories of the metropolitan *Polícia de Segurança Pública* institution. First, this meant that, contrary to what had happened in France, for example, with a strong presence of its *Gendarmerie* in the French colonies (Lorcy 2011), the Portuguese *Guarda Nacional Republicana* was not transposed to Africa. Second, this necessarily meant the rejection of designing specific police institutions for the colonies from scratch. Instead, the government elected the PSP as the model for Portuguese colonial police forces.

---

20 See the Laws cited above.

21 Fernando Silva Pais, 'O Corpo de Polícia Civil de Lourenço Marques', *Polícia Portuguesa*, nº 20, Jul–Ago, 1940.

22 Decreto-Lei nº 33826, Diário da República, nº 167, Série I, 01–08–1944.

23 See Polícia de Segurança Pública de Cabo Verde, *Regulamento Geral do Corpo de Polícia de Segurança Pública de Cabo Verde: Aprovado pela portaria nº 4993 de 12 de Maio de 1956*, Cidade da Praia: Imprensa Nacional, 1956.

Even if, with the outbreak of the colonial wars, colonial policing primacy shifted from PSP to PIDE (Mateus 2004), the decision do adopt PSP in the colonies had numerous consequences in the colonies, obviously, but also, during the decolonisation process, in metropolitan Portugal. In Africa, with the outbreak of the colonial war the considerable growth of the PSP organisational structure had significant operational, technical and even cultural consequences on the different colonial PSP forces. In metropolitan Portugal, colonial wars and the decolonisation process must have also impacted considerably on the organisational structure of the PSP. The substantial growth of colonial PSP happened, in part, through the circulation of personnel from Europe to Africa. After, the 25th of April the return of these men and their re-integration in the metropolitan police force produced within the PSP its own *retornados* process. Both issues, the decision to replicate the PSP in the colonial territories to the detriment of possible other options, and the long term consequences of this political decision for the metropolitan institution and its organisation, constitute important topics for future researches.

Conclusion

The history of Portuguese colonial policing has not yet even attained its infancy and in fact remains a subject that still needs greater definition across multiple aspects. What type of institutions held effective policing powers in the Portuguese colonies? The military or civilian nature of police forces proves a recurrent topic in police historiography, the question posed here is just how did these two categories take on specific 'colonial' characteristics? Who were the men that joined the ranks of these police forces and what professional careers did they accomplish? Topics like the social profile of recruits, the process of recruitment, the longevity of careers and the circulation between forces (between metropolitan Portugal and the colonies and also from colony to colony) constitute important fields of research within this framework. How did the practices that they carried out evolve and what were their respective results? These are all questions that still require asking and answering in further research projects. In this chapter, we have attempted to map out this subject, to provide both a set of clues for future research and some hypotheses towards potential answers.

Our core focus has been on the movements shaping and reshaping the colonial police institutional system. From a patchwork system, constructed case by case almost at the complete free will of each colonial governor to a movement towards institutional rationalisation enacted by the Estado Novo, we portray how the police emerged as a subject within the framework of colonial government practices. Actors such as Eduardo da Costa, for whom the colonial police represented but one among many subjects in the overall exercise of conceptualising the colonial state, and Salgueiro Rego, who engaged in a similar exercise but acting within the colonial police force, represent examples of the emergence of this subject in the political economy of the Empire. Thus, we suggest that the police in the colonies became somehow institutionalised within the Estado Novo context and,

32   Gonçalo Rocha Gonçalves and Rita Ávila Cachado

more importantly, the attention paid to the police in the colonies derives from the attention in general attributed by the Estado Novo to the colonies. As shown above, the complexity of Mozambique and Angola concerning the police proves greater than in the smaller Portuguese colonies, where the socio-economic colonial concern was lower.

While this chapter puts forward some clues as to the analysis of the human composition of these police forces, it disregards the relationships established between the police forces and their colonial populations (whether settlers, indigenous, *assimilados* or foreign nationals). Furthermore, if these already constitute complex subjects in the case of metropolitan police forces and policing practices, in urban colonial contexts, where the existence of multi-ethnic police forces and societies certainly resulted in a very rich palette of hierarchical and power relations, there is still much to discover for historians of Portuguese colonialism. The famous phrasing *know to dominate* when addressing colonialism (see Saïd 1978 and Cohn 1997) was changed by Roque to 'know to pacify' (Roque 2001: 86), which, in our perspective, provides a useful means of addressing the role of colonial policing in the Portuguese context.

In conclusion, any history of the police and policing Portuguese colonial territories in the periods before the 1940s shall always have to confront the diversity of the multiple solutions, strategies and institutional and material configurations that took shape over years. In fact, analysis of this diversity may indeed open up a fruitful path for understanding the unsteady ground of colonial public policies and the central importance of the local dynamics of social life in the definition of the police system and policing styles. The history of colonial police in the context of the Estado Novo should acknowledge, on the one hand, the history of the broader strategies of control and security in the Portuguese colonies, and on the other hand, the complexity of the international environmental history that accompanied the Estado Novo and the colonial state, which lived under a constant threat from the end of World War II, and that seems to have reacted only in very sparse and irresolute ways.

References

Alexandre, V. 1999. Administração Colonial, in *Dicionário de História de Portugal,* Vol. 7, edited by M.F. Mónica and A. Barreto. Porto: Figueirinhas, 45–49.

Alexandre, V. 2000. *Velho Brasil, Novas Áfricas: Portugal e o Império (1808–1975).* Porto: Edições Afrontamento.

Anderson, D.M. and Killingray, D. 1991. *Policing the Empire: Government, Authority and Control, 1830–1940.* Manchester: Manchester University Press.

Angola. 1913. *Instruções provisórias para os serviços das colunas volantes de polícia no distrito de Luanda.* Luanda: Imprensa Nacional.

Blanchard, E. 2014. The French colonial police, in *Encyclopedia of Criminology and Criminal Justice,* Vol. 8, edited by G. Bruinsma and D. Weisburd. New York: Springer, 1836–1846.

Brogden, M. 1987. The emergence of the police – The colonial dimension. *British Journal of Criminology,* 27(1): 4–14.

Colonial policing and the Portuguese Empire   33

Cachado, Rita Ávila. 2004. On the annexation of Diu by the Indian Union: The political environment and personal memories. *Oriente*, 10: 94–106.

Castelo, C. 2007. *Passagens para África: O povoamento de Angola e Moçambique com naturais da metrópole (1920–1974)*. Porto: Edições Afrontamento.

Cohn, B. 1997. *Colonialism and Its Forms of Knowledge: The British in India*. Delhi: Oxford University Press.

Costa, E. da. 1903. *Estudo sobre a Administração Civil das Nossas Possessões Africanas*. Lisbon: Imprensa Nacional.

Curto, Diogo Ramada and Bernardo Pinto da Cruz. 2013. Cidades coloniais: fomento ou controlo?, in *Cidade e Império. Dinâmicas coloniais e reconfigurações pós-coloniais*, edited by N. Domingos and E. Peralta. Lisbon: Edições 70, 113–165.

Direito, B.P.T. 2013. *Políticas coloniais de terras em moçambique: o caso de Manique e Sofala sob a Companhia de Moçambique, 1892–1942*. Unpublished PhD Thesis, University of Lisbon, Lisbon.

Domingos, N. and Peralta, E. 2013. A Cidade e o Colonial, in *Cidade e Império. Dinâmicas coloniais e reconfigurações pós-coloniais*, edited by N. Domingos and E. Peralta. Lisbon: Edições 70, ix–l.

Emsley, C. 2012. Marketing the brand: Exporting British Police Models 1829–1950. *Policing: A Journal of Policy and Practice*, 6(1): 43–54.

Garcia, J.L. 2012. 'Um mulato contra o império português. Descobrir Mário Domingues no século XXI', in Carlos Gaspar, *Fátima Patriarca e Luís Salgado de Matos (org), Estado, Regimes e Revoluções. Estudos em homenagem a Manuel de Lucena, Lisboa, Imprensa de Ciências Sociais*, 457–483.

Gonçalves, G.R. 2014. Police reform and the transnational circulation of police models: The Portuguese case in the 1860s. *Crime, Histoire & Sociétés/Crime, History & Societies*, 18(1): 5–29.

Ho, L.K.K. and Lam, A.I.F. 2014. Transformation of Macau policing: From Portuguese colony to China's SAR. *Crime, Law and Social Change*, 61: 417–437.

Knepper, P. 2010. *The Invention of International Crime: A Global Issue in the Making, 1881–1914*. Basingstoke: Palgrave Macmillan.

Lorcy, D. 2011. *Sous le régime du sabre: Le gendarmerie en Algérie, 1830–1870*. Rennes: Presses Universitaires de Rennes.

McCracken, J. 1986. Coercion and control in Nyasaland: Aspects of the history of a colonial police force. *Journal of African History*, 27: 127–148.

Mateus, D.C. 2004. *A PIDE/DGS na Guerra Colonial 1961–1974*. Lisbon: Terramar.

Nascimento, A. 2001. S. Tomé e Príncipe, in *Nova História da Expansão Portuguesa: Vol. XI: O Império Africano, 1890–1930*, edited by A.H. de Oliveira Marques. Lisbon: Editorial Estampa.

Neto, M.C. 2012. *In Town and Out of Town: A Social History of Huambo (Angola), 1902–1961*. PhD Thesis, SOAS, University of London, London.

Newitt, M. 1997. *História de Moçambique*. Mem Martins: Europa-América.

Pélissier, R. 1986. *História das campanhas de Angola: Resistência e Revoltas (1845–1941)*. Lisbon: Estampa.

Pereira, A.S. 1940. *Monografia do Corpo de Polícia Civil de Lourenço Marques*. Lourenço Marques: Imprensa Nacional.

Polícia de Segurança Pública de Angola. 1938. *Organização do Corpo de Polícia de Segurança Pública*. Luanda: Imprensa Nacional.

Porter, A. 1994. *European Imperialism, 1860–1914*. London: Palgrave Macmillan.

34   Gonçalo Rocha Gonçalves and Rita Ávila Cachado

Rego, S. 1946. *Organização Policial e Assistencial no Império Colonial Português: Tese apresentada ao 'Congresso da Guiné' de 1946*. Lisbon: Bertrand.

Rego, S. 1955. *Memórias de Um Ajudante de Campo e Comandante da Polícia*. Lisbon: Tipografia Severo de Freitas.

Rego, S. 1967. *Memórias de um ajudante de campo e comandante da polícia: II Volume*. Lisbon: Tipografia Severo de Freitas.

Rodrigues, L.N., 2002. Os Estados Unidos e a Questão de Goa em 1961. *Ler História* 42, 41–90

Roque, R. 2001. *Antropologia e Império: Fonseca Cardoso e a expedição à Índia em 1895*. Lisbon: Imprensa de Ciências Sociais.

Rosaldo, R. 1989. Imperialista nostalgia. *Representations*, 26: 107–122.

Saïd, E. 1978. *Orientalism: Westerns Conceptions of the Orient*. New York: Pantheon.

Seibert, G. 2002. The February 1953 Massacre in São Tomé: Crack in the salazarist image of multiracial harmony and impetus for nationalist demands for independence. *Portuguese Studies Review*, 10(2): 53–80.

Silva, C.N. da. 2012. Natives who were Citizens and natives who were Indigenas in Portuguese Empire (1900–1926), in *Endless Empire: Spain's Retreat, Europe's Eclipse, America's Decline*, edited by A.W. McCoy, J.M. Fradera and S. Jacobson. Madison, WI: University of Wisconsin Press, 295–306.

Silva, R.X. da. 1932. *A dactiloscopia em Moçambique*. Lisbon: Tipografia da Cadeia Penitenciária.

Sinclair, G. 2011. *Globalising British Policing*. Farnham: Ashgate.

Teixeira, M. 1970. *A Polícia de Macau*. Macau: Imprensa Nacional.

Thomas, M. 2012. *Violence and Colonial Order: Police, Workers and Protest in the European Colonial Empires, 1918–1940*. Cambridge: Cambridge University Press.

Zamparoni, V.D. 1998. *Entre Narros & Mulungos: Colonialismo e paisagem social em Lourenço Marques, c. 1890- c.1940*. Tese de Doutorado. São Paulo: Faculdade de Filosofia, Letras e Ciências Humanas da Universidade de São Paulo.

Zollmann, J. 2011. Communicating colonial order: The police of German South-West-Africa (c. 1894–1915). *Crime, Histoire & Sociétés/Crime, History & Societies*, 15(1): 33–57.

2 The military and the (colonial) policing of mainland Portugal (1850–1910)

Diego Palacios Cerezales

> Living among the rank and file while policing the remote countryside, marching with the recruits and making them police popular fairs, religious pilgrimages and election days, was the way my generation learnt the soldier's psychology
> (Marshall Gomes da Costa 1930b: 34).[1]

Introduction: the military and policing

Policing the countryside was the main task of the Portuguese army during the second half of the 19th century. The military also had a crucial role in the policing of the Portuguese colonies, especially after the occupation campaigns of the 1890s. In order to understand how they approached that task in the colonies, it is essential to have a clear picture of the centrality of the army as police in metropolitan Portugal. This chapter assesses the nature and extent of these policing duties from the 1850s (when the constitutional monarchy became a stable regime) to the 1920s (when the republican reforms changed the picture), underlining the links between the military policing of both European and colonial Portugal. In addition, as both the civilian and the military elite depicted the rural and illiterate populations that they policed as a savage *other*, this chapter also sketches the quasi-colonial appreciation of the metropolitan rural poor that guided the military's policing actions. Michel Foucault's insights on the continuities between colonial and internal governance led to a new approach to the history of policing during the 1980s and Mike Brogden (1987) made the case for the colonial undertones of the British new police in the 19th century. This chapter situates Portugal within these debates, also stressing that the military fully belong to the history of policing, both in the colonial and in the metropolitan contexts.

---

1 Marshall Gomes de Costa (1863–1929) was one of the most respected officers of the Portuguese Army. He had a long military career in Africa, took part in colonial administration and commanded the Portuguese Forces in France during the World War I. In 1926 he headed the coup that overthrew the democratic republic, but he soon ceded leadership to General Oscar Carmona.

36 Diego Palacios Cerezales

The following pages first propose a comparative assessment of the role of the army in the policing of metropolitan Portugal during the second half of the 19th century. The discussion then moves on to explain the underdevelopment of the Portuguese professional police forces and to assess the workings of the policing arrangements that constitutional governments put in place. Subsequently, the chapter discusses the validity of the idea of internal colonialism to make sense of the policing of the Portuguese countryside. The final section explores the values attached to the experience of policing by the military and the looping circulations between the military policing of colonial and metropolitan Portugal.

A country without a gendarmerie

Historians like to pinpoint novelty, foundation dates and first usages. On the other hand, as the revisionist accounts of the history of technology remark, in order to make sense of what was going on in a particular time and place, we should not focus on innovation, but on technological volume, that is, in 'the sheer amount of technologies in use at a specific time' (Cordeiro 2013: 106). This change of emphasis is also an interesting reminder for the history of police and policing. Traditional histories of the Portuguese police were focused on the first modern and professional Portuguese policemen, bringing attention to the foundation dates of the Royal Police Guard (1802), the Municipal Guard (1834) or the Civil Police (1867) (Noronha 1950, Lapa 1953, 1955, Barreto 1979). However, all these dates have a blind spot: while the three cited forces were urban police, 19th century Portugal was a predominantly rural country. Lisbon was a big city by European standards and the policing of the capital was an important issue (Gonçalves 2012), but at the beginning of the 20th century, three-quarters of the population still lived in villages of less than 2,000 inhabitants. Portugal became an urbanised country much later, specifically in the 1960s (Valério 2001). The same point is valid when applied to the Portuguese African colonies – although not so much to Goa or Macau – where a clear distinction has to be drawn between urban and rural policing, as Gonçalves and Cachado highlight in their contribution to this volume.

To understand how most of the Portuguese land and its people were policed during the 19th century, we have to turn to the organisation of policing duties in the countryside. At the same time, if we want to understand transfers and continuities between metropolitan and colonial policing in the Portuguese Empire, we may well begin by stressing that policing in metropolitan Portugal was not something that was only performed by salaried state appointed policemen.

The Portuguese military had a central role in policing. This would not come as a surprise, as it is well known that, during the 19th century, the army was used for crowd control all over Europe (Johansen 2005). Nonetheless, there was a crucial difference between Portugal and the other colonial powers. Although from the 1830s onwards, liberal Portugal broke with the *Ancien Régime* and followed the well-known Napoleonic blueprint of centralisation, the Portuguese government did not establish its usual policing companion, a national gendarmerie, at that particular time. This left a void in the grid of policing that the army was called to fill.

Gendarmeries were a common feature of most European 19th century landscapes. The original French model was first exported during the Napoleonic Wars: Bavaria and Prussia adopted their own forces in 1812, followed in 1814 by the Low Countries, Piedmont, Tyrol and the Austrian Lombardy. The Spanish Civil Guard, in turn, was created in 1844. After the suppression of the 1848 revolutions, Vienna's government deployed its gendarmerie across the Austro-Hungarian Empire. In addition, in the newly unified Italy of the 1870s, the *Carabinieri*, already in place in Piedmont, became one of the tools for the administrative integration of the country (Emsley 1999).

'Since the deployment of the Civil Guard in Spain', read the Portuguese *Revista Militar* in 1861 'the Army there does not patrol the streets anymore, or police theatres and bullfights' (RM, XIII, 1861: 12). In most of Europe the deployment of constabularies allowed the Army to reduce its policing role to crowd control during big collective threats, such as waves of rioting and large labour strikes (González Calleja 1998, Johansen 2005, Emsley 2005). At first, Portugal seemed to be following the same pattern, but the embryonic gendarmerie that was created in 1838 was disbanded in 1842. The renunciation of professional police for the countryside meant that the military remained a cornerstone of policing during the second half of the 19th century. This military pre-eminence endured until the deployment of a true national gendarmerie, the GNR (*Guarda Nacional Republicana* – National Republican Guard) in the aftermath of the 1910 republican revolution (Lloyd-Jones and Palacios Cerezales 2007).

Policing alternatives in the early years of liberalism

Some kind of gendarmerie for Portugal had been projected since the short-lived times of the 1822 constitution. The idea resurfaced after 1834, when absolutism was defeated for good, and liberals had the opportunity to devise a new administrative structure for the country. Liberals divided metropolitan Portugal into 'districts', inspired by the French *departements*, and a government-named 'civil governor' was put at the top of each of them (Silveira 1997, Manique 1989). Then the government created a civil police for Lisbon and Porto, called the Municipal Guard (1834), a citizen's militia called the National Guard (1835) and, finally, the so-called Public Security Corps (*Corpos de Segurança Pública*), which were small military detachments who served under the supervision of the provincial civil governors and could have become the embryo of a national gendarmerie-type force.

The consolidation of these forces became problematic. The following two decades were full of political turmoil, division among conservative and radical liberals, popular resistance against the new liberal State and renewed civil war (Ferreira 2002, Bonifácio 1992). During those struggles, it became apparent that some of the citizen militias and security corps were just a formalisation of the power that local bosses had hoarded during the civil war. Meanwhile, popular resistance hindered the normal workings of justice and taxation.

As open confrontation seemed endemic, pacification grew into a key concern for leading politicians in Lisbon, who sought to gain control of every armed body

38 *Diego Palacios Cerezales*

in the country as well as the general disarmament of the population. In 1838, most of Lisbon's National Guard was disbanded after some bloody clashes with the Army, and the same was done all over the country when guardsmen appeared to act with independence vis-à-vis the wishes of the government. In fact, during the 1840s the citizen militia almost disappeared thanks to governmental abandonment (Pata 2004). In 1842, it was the turn of the provincial Public Security Corps. Some units had sided with the liberal left during political disturbances, while others had mutinied due to the late payment of their salaries. Despite some civil governors' claims that more regular salary payment and some organisational improvements were a better option, the government also disbanded this nascent gendarmerie. Lisbon's and Porto's Municipal guards, in turn, were fully militarised. The militarisation had begun as early as 1836, but in 1851 these constabularies were integrated into the army as special units for the garrisoning of the two main cities. Finally, the army also campaigned for the confiscation of those military weapons in the hands of the Portuguese civilian population.

General disarmament and the monopolisation of organised armed force by the military allowed the country to enter into a more pacific phase during the 1850s. This came in tandem with political reconciliation within both the civilian elites and the military, which were awarded with a so-called 'monster promotion' of all officers, regardless of their past political allegiances. On the other hand, as the National Guard and the Security Corps had been disbanded, in most of the country the army was the only institution left with the potential to mobilise organised coercive force to enforce the law. Pacification came at the price of institutional underdevelopment. Future projects for the creation of provincial police recommended prudence and highlighted how past experiences with militias and security corps ran the risk of them becoming uncontrolled guerrilla bands (*DCD*, 20 June 1854: 286; *REAP Beja*, 15 September 1859).

Self-policing: the parish constables

Another alternative to the creation of police forces was the mobilisation of local communities for self-policing. Different forms of self-policing had existed during the *Ancien Regime* and the National Guard had somehow revived that tradition, but the centralising drive that marked Portuguese liberalism in the 1840s meant that most of the policing duties were entrusted to a top-down hierarchy of delegates under the supervision of the civil governor: an 'administrator' in every municipality – usually recruited among the locally rooted gentry; and, one sheriff (*regedor*) under him in every parish. This parish sheriff was to be assisted by a number of parish constables (*cabos de polícia*), one for every eight houses.

Teixeira de Macedo, following the administrative code, calculated that there were 4,000 parish sheriffs and 30,000 constables all over the country (Macedo 1984 [1880]). On paper, the system could appear as a vast and powerful machine of civil governors, administrators, sheriffs and constables running from the heights of the *Ministério do Reino* (Ministry of the Realm) in Lisbon to the most remote mountain parish (Catroga 2006, Santos 2001). In fact, 'the rays of central power become weak and colourless as they reach the extremities', wrote Aveiro's civil governor in 1858 (*REAP*, Aveiro 1858). The vast numbers of parish sheriffs and constables were a theoretical proposition that was never achieved in practice. In addition, these men were part-time non-professional police; they were neither trained, nor armed, nor paid, nor uniformed. They were not even integrated into a defined command structure. Constables had no working schedule and were not paid for their services. Instead, they were at the orders of the administrator whenever he needed them, and even then, only for services within the parish where they lived.

The collection of the civil governor's yearly reports about the administrative improvements of their districts offers a useful bottom-up evaluation of the rural police (*REAP*, 1856–62). The spirit of the law supposed that these were voluntary offices to be held by the socially prominent, but the gentry very often refused to collaborate. As there were not many volunteers, the administrator could force any citizen to serve as parish constable for a year. Occasionally, 'appointing someone constable meant making a new political foe' (*REAP*, Portalegre, 1865: 5). Nomination for policing service was a kind of punishment, and during election time the political opponents' supporters could be appointed constables 'and receive the order to guard their own houses in order to prevent them from campaigning'. In the 1880 election, 'in Vila Nova de Gaia 580 parish constables were named; in Vila do Conde, 605; in Sintra, 638, and most of them because they were against the government' (*DCD*, 16 January 1880: 461). Due to the refusal to serve by the socially prominent, added to the coercive nature of the nomination and the elasticity of the constable's obligations, the administrators used their power to nominate constables in order to reinforce their own patronage networks (Macedo 1984, Um liberal 1858). As a result, the parish constables were conscripted among the less powerful, usually workingmen who lost their subsistence wages every time they made a policing service. The quality and reliability of this police were low. As a former civil governor said 'sometimes the constables accomplish a valuable policing service [. . .] if they are not knifing someone in a tavern' (*DCP*, 2 July 1878: 35). The civil governors yearly reports repeat the same idea: the system was 'a simulacrum of police' (*REAP, Leiria* 1858: 12); the constables had neither social authority nor motivation and were not reliable enough to grant them arms permits (Bulhões 1867, Mendonça 1866). The fiscal authorities also complained that, during open conflicts, sheriffs and constables were prone to side with the people they belonged to (Roma 1857, AMR – ANTT, L 38 n°904, 23 July 1888).

The army as police

The parish constables' shortcomings as police meant that civil governors and municipal administrators requested military support whenever they needed to capture a criminal, police a rural fair or a seasonal market, maintain order during court hearings, or control civil unrest. Harvest policing, riot suppression, customs enforcement, tax collection, criminal detention, elections, prison guarding, and

40 Diego Palacios Cerezales

even collecting tolls in roads and bridges were duties the Portuguese army performed during the 19th century.

The 1842 decree that dissolved the regional Public Security Corps outlined how the Army's policing role would function:

> The Army's duty, during peacetime, is to maintain the State's internal security and to enforce the Law, supplying all the support that the due magistrates may ask for. [. . .] The policing service will be performed by the regular army regiments. The civil governors have to accord the service with the commander of each regional military division, who should give orders to provide the necessary force for the said service, following the guidelines agreed by both authorities.
>
> (Diário do Governo n° 239, 10 October 1842)

This arrangement stayed in full force for more than 60 years, and only began to lose its validity in the 1910s, when the GNR was deployed. That said, it is important to notice that the army did not perform policing duties as an inborn mission. Despite some projects favouring such development, it did not become a *de facto* gendarmerie. Its policing role, albeit constant, was that of a military aid to the civil power – in short, a muscle provided to unarmed civil authorities.

The contrast between the Portuguese and the Spanish case also is worth stressing, as the army's policing role did not lead to a militarisation of the administration similar to that of the neighbouring country. Spain, in addition to deploying the Civil Guard since the late 1840s, widely used the army to quell civil disorder. In contrast to Portugal, however, the Spanish army did not agree to act as an aid to the civil power and, in order to intervene, stepped into the civilian prerogative, imposed martial law, and acting as a military government (Ballbé 1984, Risques I Corbella 1995, González Calleja 1998). The Spanish army did not wait for the government or parliament to decree martial law. The regional army commander (*Capitan General*) would make a consultation with the local civil governor and would then take the decision himself. Rioters or strikers detained by the army in Spain were court-martialled; in Portugal, the army delivered them to the civil justice.

This greater respect for civilian power in Portugal was a legacy from William Carr Beresford's reconstruction of the Portuguese Army, which he had headed from 1809–1820, when he was ousted by a revolution. His 1816 army regulations departed from the previously practiced extension of military jurisdiction over rioters.[2] Beresford's role as Lord Protector in Portugal during the 1810s, while the Portuguese Royal family resided in Brazil, in tandem with the prominence of British officers within the Portuguese Army, were often depicted as a kind of

---

2 *Regulamento para a organização do exército em Portugal.* Lisboa, Imprensa Régia. Esp. Art. XXX n 2 and Art.XXXII n 7. These army regulations overwrote the *alvarás* of 20 December 1784 and 10 August 1790, which had subjected rioters to military authority.

The military and the (colonial) policing 41

British colonialism (Carvalho 1830: 212). In this vein, this civilian legacy may also be understood as a kind of colonial transfer of policing practices that lasted until the further militarisation of public order during the 1910–1926 republic.

During the second half of the 19th century, neither the military nor the civil governors liked the army to be used as police. The army only policed at the request of the civil authorities, but the latter complained that, once the military received their orders, they didn't have any say on how policing operations were to be conducted. For the civil governors, the military as policemen were insufficiently flexible and, as their network of barracks was not designed for policing purposes, they often arrived too late. For the army, as will late be discussed, the scattering of the regiments on small police detachments meant that they could not focus on their main purpose: preparation for war.

The Portuguese army has not retained any institutional memory of this policing role. Even the recent publications, such as the *New Military History of Portugal* (Barata 2003), do not address policing in the volume dealing with the 19th century. In addition, the Portuguese Army's archives are organised in such a way that scholars can only do research into military campaigns, or on some major mobilisations for crowd control. All the paperwork on everyday policing activities such as the maps of the territorial distribution and the movement of military patrols, that regional military headquarters had to produce on a monthly basis, have hitherto escaped from historians. Only one such map, published in *Revista Militar* in 1849 (Vol. I, 1849: 21–22), makes a first approach to the volume of the Army's policing activity possible. In that year, 60 infantry detachments ranging in size from 3 to 295 men slept all over the country, away from their regimental barracks, on a daily basis, guarding posts and dealing with policing activities. These numbers did not comprise the cavalry squadrons that usually patrolled highways, nor the short-term detachments that the civil authorities asked for when they needed to perform special tax collection operations, capture criminals, organise quarantine lines, enforce the monopolistic cultivation of the tobacco plant or police seasonal courts and fairs.

Policing was such a central activity for the army that, in 1850, when the government tried to cut the military budget, it asked the provincial civil governors if the number of soldiers could be reduced 'without making public service suffer.'[3] Contrary to the desired response, they answered that they needed more troops on an everyday basis, and that they also feared renewed waves of food and tax rioting such as that of 1846 (AHM, 3ª Div, Secç. 50 Cx. 6 Doc. 3). Their worries were not groundless, and major waves of rural rioting took place again in 1861–1862, 1867–1870, 1882, 1888 and 1893–1894.

Despite the 'aid to the civil power' role that was assumed by the army, its network of barracks was not designed for policing the countryside, nor was it designed for defence against Spain. The border fortresses were almost abandoned,

---

3 Circular do Ministerio da Guerra para os governadores civis, 26 February 1849 AHM, 3ª Divisão, Secção 50 (Diversos) *Cx.* 6 Doc. nº3.

42   Diego Palacios Cerezales

while the barracks were distributed following a non-systematic pattern derived from the contingencies of the civil war and the availability of suitable buildings such as confiscated monasteries (Maya 1887, Oliveira 1993). The lack of a planned deployment meant that policing services sometimes necessitated that the troops march for three or four days in order to get to the designated place. Coastal naval transport was often used for the deployment of troops during periods of major unrest and from the 1860s onwards, the telegraph and the first railroads improved the logistics of the army in fulfilling its internal mission. Nevertheless, the infrastructural capabilities of the Portuguese State remained low. In 1893, when riots were expected in Fafe due to rising grain prices, an infantry detachment was sent from Viana do Castelo. It took four days marching for them to cover the 85 km (Castro 1947).

Many of the reformers who dreamed of a proficient and war-ready army saw the policing service as the main obstacle to the army improving its military performance. For the military, acting as 'vile policemen' was not their true mission (Salgado 1862). They resented the regiments being subdivided into policing detachments, which meant that they could hardly be trained for external and colonial war: 'the *esprit-de-corps* vanished' and 'discipline suffered' (Pimentel 1868: 6). According to Fontes Pereira de Melo, the most prominent Portuguese statesman of the second half of the 19th century, the arrangement meant that Portugal had 'neither a true police nor a true army' (Coelho 1877: 238). In addition, the strategic defence of the realm against Spain was in hands of the British alliance, which hurt the patriotic pride of some officers. The status quo satisfied nobody, but as the Minister of War declared in the 1860s, 'as no war is probable for the next 30 years and the treasury is paying for an army, it is reasonable to make something useful of it as police' (Sá da Bandeira: *DCD* n° 92, 14 June 1862: 1644).

In fact, the half a dozen aborted projects for the deployment of a new national gendarmerie discussed in Parliament between 1850 and 1910 always stressed that both the army and the civil policing service would benefit from it. Nevertheless, the political power of the big landowners was strong enough to abort the gendarmerie projects. Big property was neither pressed by criminality nor by social struggle, so landowners did not want to pay for a gendarmerie. At the same time, they dodged taxation thanks to the State's low infrastructural power. In fact, big landowners were the main beneficiaries of the anti-tax riots of the 1860s and 1880s, which succeeded in maintaining rural wealth outside the State's fiscal knowledge (Palacios Cerezales 2013).

In 1888, Vizconde de S. Januário, a general seasoned in colonial government, became the Minister of War. He was determined to improve the army's training for war, so he wanted to force parliament to approve the creation of a national gendarmerie. That year had been riotous during winter and spring, but he established higher requirements for the civil authorities to obtain military aid (*DCD*, 14 June 1888, p. 1976). Then, in August, he announced that during September and October the Army would perform large military exercises, and would not, therefore, be available for policing duties. He subsequently ordered

The military and the (colonial) policing 43

every military detachment to join its original regiment: sentries disappeared from public vaults, judicial buildings and prisons, while cavalry squadrons ceased to patrol the major highways. In order to fill the gaps, civil governors overloaded their small civil police forces and ordered the unpaid parish constables to abandon their private occupations in favour of public service, resulting in an explosion of complaints. Civil governors were alarmed, especially when their requests for military aid for major fairs and markets were declined. The *Ministério do Reino* (Ministry of the Realm – in charge of home affairs) was flooded with letters: the menace of riots was widespread and civil authorities feared that the 'bad tempered' rural populations would take advantage of the lack of armed support to renew the customary attacks on tax and recruitment offices. They also feared robberies by wandering gypsies and all kinds of moral and social disorder caused by railway construction workers. Appealing to the military's self-interest, the civil authorities underlined that, without armed support, the recruitment of new conscripts had to be halted.[4]

The general clamour increased tension between the *Ministério do Reino* and the *Ministério da Guerra* ('Ministry of War'). Finally, short-term security concerns prevailed, and the Ministry of War had to concede. By the middle of September the army was again policing fairs and festivals; sentries returned and, once again, the desired gendarmerie was postponed. The Army's challenge had failed.

The centralisation of the Army's policing operations payments in the *Ministério do Reino* offers the opportunity to obtain some systematic information about the Army's involvement in policing during the 1880s. Over 60% of the policing services for pilgrimages and fairs were provided during the summer when most of these gatherings took place. Archival sources also confirm something already pointed out in several military memoirs: there was no policing specialisation among the different regiments and only the aristocratic units around the Royal Palace in Lisbon were free from policing duties (Costa 1930b). Each season, it was the factors of recruitment and training that determined which units would be more involved in policing. During summer, one third of the regiments were scattered into policing detachments, while the rest only performed a couple of policing missions and concentrated on drilling and manoeuvres.

Internal colonialism

The image of the domestic missionary Robert Storch applied to the English policeman in 'a battle with local custom and popular culture' cannot be directly projected on to the policing service of the Portuguese military (Storch 1976: 481). Their more restricted role as an aid to the civil power limited their interaction with the civil population. On the other hand, numerous military reformers proposed the army itself as a school for the nation. A true national army would

---

4 Cf. Copiador de correspondencia expedida, AMR-ANTT L 38 n°209, 239, 864, 1091, 1103, 1051, 1156, September–October 1888.

44 Diego Palacios Cerezales

make all classes of society serve in equal terms, and teach the illiterate rank and file how to read and write, uprooting superstition and favouring patriotism. In fact, conscription was far from universal, and it was suffered only by the powerless. In addition, regimental schools hardly functioned, so the army seldom played this educational and nationalising role.

In connection with the civilising role towards the whole population, numerous military writers affirmed that the Army, by deterrence, guaranteed that Portuguese society did not disintegrate into chaos. However, they agreed that a true civilising result could only be achieved if a gendarmerie was deployed (Breyner 1862, Maya 1887). To exemplify the civilising role of a gendarmerie, they usually made comparisons with Spain. According to them, in Portugal, twenty soldiers were needed to patrol a fair and prevent brawls, while in the other side of the border, despite the hypothetical hot blood of the Spaniards, a couple of Civil Guards were usually enough (Machado 1888)

Not being a civilising force, the Army was nonetheless an active part of the apparatus to impose national law over local custom and popular resistance. The military officers belonged to the social and political elite and shared the same distant view of the ordinary people – '*o povo*'. By '*povo*' they meant the illiterate peasants they had to deal with during seasonal fairs and food and tax riots, the masses that, at the same time, were the pool of recruitment for their rank and file. As Rui Ramos (2004) has argued, the liberal elite recognised themselves as those who had recently risen above the general mass of the people and the only ones to have a vested interest in the independence of the nation. They assumed that the populace were indifferent to their patriotic and progressive sentiment. Persistently high illiteracy levels came to illustrate the reluctance or incapacity of the rural masses – that is, most of the Portuguese – to join the liberal community. Thus they saw the state as an instrument through which to create a community of civic-minded individuals out of a hostile mass of superstitious and unpatriotic peasants. In general, liberals treated the *povo* as children under tutelage. This was the same as they treated indigenous peoples in the colonies; and a suspicion of the masses led liberals, who did not share the traditional reverence for religious traditions, to use the Catholic clergy as an instrument of popular control (Neto 1998). When in 1911 the Republican government divided the inhabitants of the colonies into *citizens* and *natives*: 'those born of native parents and who by education and habits were not distinct from the common of their race' (Silva 2010: 53), the Portuguese authorities were resorting to a distinction between nationality and citizenship that had been commonplace since the 1830s to deal with the rural poor. The natives were nationals, and had rights guaranteed by the Portuguese state. But they were not citizens. Thus, the 'colonial utilization of the citizen/national dichotomy reveals the relation between the enlightened urban elite and the illiterate rural masses in Portugal itself as a case of internal colonialism [. . .] As in Africa, the citizens awarded themselves the right to rule and direct their backward compatriots in the name of a natural superiority' (Ramos 2004: 102).

The political elite saw popular protest as a kind of natural phenomenon. The passivity of the *povo* or their mobilisation in the face of any public policy, such as taxation, was something that defined the field of possibilities in the political system, but the political elites never thought of the lower classes as potential allies. They were just *povo*, not citizens, not identifiable groups with partial interests that could be incorporated into the political game. The category of *'povo'* worked as a tag of exclusion; it was the name for all the social groups excluded from political decision-making (Valente 1981).

The military elite often depicted the rural and illiterate populations that they policed as a savage *other* who, like the soldiers, only understood force (Mendonça 1866, Gonçalves 1921). 'Iroquois' (a derogatory comparison alluding to Native American tribes), 'imbecile' and 'savage' could easily combine in a paragraph about Portuguese rural rioters (Guimarães 1863)

In the absence of day-to-day policing, and not believing that 'in the actual state of civilisation' the rural populations could voluntarily comply with the law, the military devised a routine of intervention in rural disturbances based on what they called 'the re-establishment of the authority principle' (Palacios Cerezales 2007). This meant that any punctual victory of the rioters over the authorities had to be erased from the public imagination by an energetic display of force, and by making the rebel communities pay, often through the billeting of troops. In 1862 and 1868, when tax riots became widespread, the military established special 'flying police columns' (*colunas volantes de policia*). Located in key communications points, these mobile units were always ready to be dispatched wherever necessary. Mike Brogden, dealing with the British case, identified task forces for outside excursions as a mode of intervention at odds with consent-based policing that linked colonial and metropolitan practices in Britain (Brogden 1987). In Portugal, this mode of deployment of military force was to be replicated in the African colonies after the 1901 military reorganisation (Castro 1908).

All the same, while minor technological and logistical advantages over the native chiefdoms, such as patrolling gunboats, made it possible for small Portugal to acquire and control big chunks of Africa (Telo 1994), the military saw their cohesion, communications and superior weaponry as the basis of their ultimate success during the campaigns against rural rioting in metropolitan Portugal. As one military commander explained during the 1862 riots, the long range of the new Enfield rifle made it possible for 40 soldiers to stop a crowd of 'four or five thousand peasants' (AMR – ANTT, *Mç*. 3004, L 13 Oficio 1092, 5th of May 1862 Telgr. nº2).

Rural policing would only be revamped after the 1910 republican revolution, but the new policing trends, amidst anxieties with the new workers militancy and fear of counter-revolutionary revolts, would also have a quasi-colonial flavour. Republicans were an urban minority that, considering the backwardness of the *povo*, feared that 'only the reactionary priests and landowners who dominated the rural masses would benefit from universal suffrage and the devolution of power to the provinces' (Ramos 2004: 101). They had a democratic program, but 'democracy' for them was a future stage in the development of the country, something that could only come about once they had eradicated illiteracy and superstition. Therefore, they stripped 375.000 illiterate heads of household of the voting rights they previously had enjoyed (Almeida 2006).

46 Diego Palacios Cerezales

The military were also employed to conquer the hearts and minds of the rural populations. During 1911 and 1912 the republican military embarked on a series of propaganda missions in the rural north 'to publicize the benign accomplishments of the provisional government' (AHM, I Div, sec. 34 cx. 6 doc. 14). This was a kind of propaganda action that the military would again do in Africa in the 1960s, trying to undermine the appeal of the independence movements (Cann 1997). Then, the deployment of the new national gendarmerie, the GNR, was not conceived just as a provision of policing, but also as the arrival of the republic to the countryside. With the GNR, the Portuguese government, the new national colours and the Republic itself were made present in every small village at least once a week. The guards had to collaborate with local authorities, but they only obeyed their own chain of command; they belonged to a centralised national organisation that represented the Republic and, as dutiful bearers of the Republican promise of national resurgence, they didn't easily compromise with local power equilibria (Lloyd-Jones and Palacios Cerezales 2007).

Learning to police

Despite its everyday involvement as an aid to the civil power, the army did not develop a training program for policing duties. In fact, as we have seen, military writers usually despised policing operations and blamed the continual scattering of the regiments for their poor level of battle readiness. On the other hand, a few officers welcomed the policing operations as an opportunity to see some real action. In addition, policing services were paid by the *Ministério do Reino*, and the extra money that younger officers and NCOs received from civil authorities was an interesting reward. 'I have never been so rich', remembered Gomes da Costa, 'as a lieutenant in 1885, when I was paid for 15 months of duty in a sanitary cordon in the Spanish frontier. I had saved 20,000 reis; I was a prince!' (Costa 1930b: 39)

Army officers learned how to deal with policing duties by on-the-job training. After the 1842 general instructions for the military to aid the civil power cited above, several army general orders (*ordens de serviço*) tried to clarify how different policing missions had to be performed. Since the 1870s, compilations of orders were regularly reprinted in policing handbooks for army officers (Silva 1876, Costa 1889, Vidigal 1905). These unofficial manuals also gave advice based on 'experience and common sense', because a lot of services 'were not clearly fixed by law and only experience and practice may teach the better methods' (Silva 1876: 66).

In 1889 a new army code thoughtfully explained the principles of military aid to the civil authorities. First, in every barracks a picket should always be ready to answer the call of duty. When a detachment was mobilised to help the civil power, its mission had to be clearly stated and the civil authorities could not employ the men for any other purpose without previous authorisation from the provincial military government. Only in cases of urgent need could the civil authorities ask the commanding officer to perform a different policing duty, but even then the request had to be made in writing or in the presence of some witnesses. This was crucial to maintain the functional distinction between the military and civilian authorities. The former should not invade the civilians' jurisdiction, while the later should not resign their responsibility. The commanding officer or NCO had sole responsibility for the operational performance of the mission and a soldier, not even rank and file, should never take direct orders from a civilian, regardless of their administrative status (Secr. de Estado dos Negócios da Guerra 1889).

How did the army perform the more common policing operations? The most reprinted handbook recommended that for the policing of a rural market, a fair or any other collective gathering, the military force had to be stationed in a cleared position 200 metres apart from the gathering. The commanding officer had to resist any demand from the civil authorities to scatter the force in patrols or sentries and had to maintain it ready for collective intervention. Diverse evidence, however, shows that sometimes administrators and excise collectors managed to get personal escorts from the Army during periods of riots but, since the 1880s, civil policemen detached from the provincial capitals began to perform those roles, the Army acting only as a reserve force (Palacios Cerezales 2008).

During policing services, it was usual for the Army officers to train their men to swing the rifle as a blunt weapon, contrary to service orders, because the bayonet was potentially lethal. In the 1890s the more common non-lethal usages of military weaponry, such as hitting with the stock of the rifle, firing blank ammo, or firing overhead during crowd control operations were forbidden by army regulations, but infantry officers widely used them during policing operations 'in order to avoid injuries' (Castro 1947: 10). In practice, the military aimed at a proportionate usage of force, but they did not want to be constrained to it by law (Palacios Cerezales 2011). During the parliamentary discussions that followed some fatal casualties in crowd control operations, some important differences between the ethos of a police force and that of the military surfaced. As one parliamentarian with a military background explained: the army sometimes had to kill in order to 'maintain its dignity' in the face of the crowd, while the police did not (Dantas Baracho, *DCP*, 23 April 1900: 10).

Policing elections was another important task for the military. Sometimes electoral competition made strong networks of patronage clash and the army was needed in order to maintain the peace. During the 1878 national elections 4,258 soldiers were mobilised, which meant that in some districts 80% of available soldiers were on electoral duty (*DCD*, 16 February 1880: 478–479). At times the presence of troops on election-day was seen as government interference against the opposition. Even so, troops could only approach the ballot box in situations where the civil authority asked them to come 'to prevent brawls and aggressions', and from then on the ballot was suspended until peace was re-established and the troops departed (*Ordem do Exército* nº 48 1870).

To capture a criminal, a civil magistrate had to organise the operation. One manual recommended the military to surround the habitation of the criminal at night and to wait until dawn in order to break the door, as the constitution forbade the officials from entering a citizen's home at night (Silva 1876: 64).

48   Diego Palacios Cerezales

The creation and growth of the civil police in the provincial capitals since the late 1860s (Gonçalves 2012), the deployment of a new and militarised customs guard (the *Guarda Fiscal*) in the 1880s and the modernisation of the civil police in the 1890s diminished some of the army's policing duties. Nevertheless, as late as 1903 the civil governor of Porto – a district with a high density of police, comprising the Municipal Guard, the Civil Police and the Custom's Guard – asked the army for 65 ordinary policing services: 31 for rural fairs; seven for low level public order threats; five for court or prison guarding; two for tax collection enforcement; and, one for escorting a magistrate during criminal investigations (*Arquivo do Governo Civil do Porto* L 737). All of these services were performed in the rural municipalities near Porto. Furthermore, that same year there was a major strike in Porto and the city's police was reinforced with several cavalry squadrons for almost two months.

Additionally, the military did not only perform policing duties in the Army. The Municipal Guards of Lisbon and Porto had been militarised in the 1850s, and the customs guard was also a military body. Moreover, in the rest of the country municipal administrators were sometimes recruited among reserve officers, who also looked for retired NCOs to serve as parish sheriffs.

Africanism and militarism

At the end of the century, some colonial military successes and the new European-wide militaristic ethos allowed for the enhancement of the status of the military within the Portuguese elite. During the 1860s and 1870s, the project of a civilian police had been advanced as the most in tune with the liberal ethos of constitutional Portugal. The heavy militarisation of the Municipal Guards had not been presented as an intrinsic virtue, but as a transitory necessity derived from the *povo*'s low level of civilisation. As the Minister of the Realm, Rodrigo da Fonseca, explained in 1855 'here [in Portugal] only a fully armed soldier is able to command respect from the masses' (*DCD*, 22 May 1855: 239). In contrast, after the 1890 British *ultimatum*, that thwarted the Portuguese great colonial plans and humiliated its governing elite, the new generation of bold politicians that took the reins of government presented the military as a source of patriotic renewal (Cabral 1989, Sardica 2001, Cabral 1993). They promised 'new life' for a system that, according to Oliveira Martins, Eça de Queiros and other leading intellectuals of the time, had become exhausted by partisan, clientelistic and corrupt politicking (Ramos 1998).

In the wake of the *ultimatum*, nationalist and republican mobilisation in the streets of the main Portuguese cities foreshadowed a revolution, making the Constitutional Monarchy seek a stronger defence. First, military men with colonial experience were put in charge of Lisbon's and Porto's civil government, such as the Visconde de Paço d'Arcos, who served in Lisbon after having been governor of India and Moçambique. Then, the Municipal Guard was reinforced and the urban 'civil' police underwent a process of militarisation. The *28 August 1893 decree* reorganised the patrolling section of the civil police as a 'special body

The military and the (colonial) policing 49

organized, instructed and disciplined under the direction of army officers, far from any suspected influence of favouritism'. Militarism was on the rise and the government thought that army officers were the only individuals capable of 'directing, educating, disciplining and commanding groups of men armed by the state'. Finally, the new legislation imposed that all the new recruits for the police had to be discharged soldiers (*Decree of 28 August 1893*).

Despite its influence on government and public opinion, the militaristic ethos did not become hegemonic (Sardica 2001). In fact, it was not able reach the goal of creating a gendarmerie that would permit the army to concentrate upon military training and readiness for war. In fact, the military reform of 1900 aimed at a cost-free improvement of the military aid to the civil power. Eight regiments of four squadrons were each transformed into 10 regiments of three squadrons each, aiming at favouring two additional towns with a full regiment (Ramos 1998).

At the beginning of the 20th century, policing was still the main occupation of the Metropolitan army (Sousa 1938). 'For the military in the provinces', as one army officer recalled, 'service meant commanding policing forces during fairs, pilgrimages and election days' (Castro 1947: 7). In 1907, a young officer with militaristic projects offered an acid view:

> ... service is mounting guard, escorting a religious procession, going to those villages where there is disorder, or where the local politicians ask for some troops for the adornment of the place; service is being on parade, exposed to the curiosity and the gossiping of the public, writing down corpus delicto, selling some stuff in public auction, [. . .] in such a way that some get the idea that the army's purpose is to perform policing activities and that it has nothing to do with war.
>
> (Esteves 1907: 8).

For the most dynamic among the military, policing mainland Portugal was not a fulfilling experience. As Marshall Gomes da Costa recalled years later. '[By means of policing duties] we officers learnt how to command, and we naturally acquired our military spirit, the science of making men obey and our authority and prestige [. . .] [yet], in order to become true soldiers, we had to ask for a commission in Africa' (Costa 1930b: 34). His contemporary Gonçalo Pimenta de Castro agreed: 'my dream would come true in Africa; I would become a true soldier, not just a policeman for fairs, pilgrimages and elections' (Castro 1947: 14). In the Portuguese African territories, both the Army and the Navy were involved in authentic military operations aimed at asserting sovereignty, especially from 1895 to the end of the Great War. The colonies thus held the promise of real military action, even if most of the time the use of troops for preventive policing was the rule, not combat against insurgents. That last possibility, nonetheless, was often also portrayed as an imperial policing endeavour, reflecting the blurred line between the military and the police so common in colonial contexts (see Reis in this collection). Finally, the colonial successes of the military served to enhance their status, also favouring, as we already mentioned, the militarisation of the metropolitan police.

50 *Diego Palacios Cerezales*

In 1891, the Portuguese military comprised around 17,000 men in metropolitan Portugal, including the navy, the Municipal Guard and the Customs Guard. The three African possessions, in turn, were supposed to have 8,000 soldiers, of which only one battalion of 374 were Europeans, most of them serving in Africa due to disciplinary reasons. The colonial army was not an integral part of the Portuguese army, but a series of scattered forces under the supervision of the colonial governors. The officers were Europeans, while most of the troops were recruited among the colonised. The colonial troops were chiefly used for policing duties, not for combat. As the officers did not trust their loyalty, when strong action was needed they would rely on the extraordinary, and expensive, deployment of metropolitan forces in Africa (Carrilho 1985).

In 1901 a new reorganisation of the colonial forces sought to further integrate the metropolitan and the colonial armies. At the same time, for the purpose of occupying and 'pacifying' the large African territories under the nominal Portuguese sovereignty, the state began to deploy the so-called 'mobile police columns'. Those were military detachments that, albeit in a temporary basis, brought the State to regions where the European administrative state seldom arrived (Castro 1908). These mobile forces re-enacted the 'flying columns' that the metropolitan army had used during waves of rioting up until the improvement of railway communications in the 1870s.

The proclamation of the republic in 1910 and the foundation of the GNR in 1911 did not mean an abrupt disconnection of the army from policing duties. On the contrary, the republic strengthened and multiplied the links between the military policing of the metropolis and that of the colonies. The GNR itself was a fully militarised institution. The guards were soldiers and the officers fully belonged to the army. Despite some specialisation in rural patrol, most of the GNR's policing practices were a development of the traditional military involvement in policing operations. A new edition of the traditional policing handbooks for military officers was published as late as 1937, this time aptly addressed to 'officers of the army, GNR, customs guard and police' (Delgado and Oliveira 1937: I). Finally, the exacerbation of social and political conflict during the republic – aggravated between 1916 and 1918 by the state of war – led to a further militarisation of public order policing. The temporal suspension of constitutional guarantees, very sparsely used during the second half of the 19th century, became a common feature from the January 1912 general strike onwards. The state of siege, massive deportations and military courts were used to subdue monarchist unrest, strikes and bread riots, multiplying the involvement of the military in policing (Palacios Cerezales 2011). The suspensions of guarantees undermined the civil rights protection in the metropolis, creating a de facto juridical situation close to that of the colonies.

Conclusion

In bringing this chapter to a close, it is important to highlight some important connections with other works included in this collection. As Bruno Cardoso Reis underlines, military operations in Africa would be understood as imperial policing, rather than colonial war, well into the 20th century. The long involvement of the military in metropolitan policing, addressed in this chapter, may explain his comparative finding of a more blurred line between the police and the military in the Portuguese colonies. In addition, as the chapter by Gonçalves and Cachado describes, during the decades surrounding the turn of the 20th century, new police forces were put on foot for the capital of each colony: Praia, Sao Tomé, Luanda, Lourenço Marques, Nova Goa and Macau. These were a new kind of colonial police, but circumscribed to urban spaces and hardly reaching the vast countryside, which was largely left to the army to patrol. At the same time, these forces were strongly militarised and commanded by European officers.

The threads that linked the military to colonial policing were inextricable. When metropolitan officers first disembarked in Africa, heading for a policing post, they came from an organisation that was already accustomed to a vast array of policing duties. During their career they could have served as police in the regular army, but also in the civil police and in the two specialised paramilitary constabularies: the Municipal Guards of Lisbon and Porto and the Customs Guard. Unfortunately, we do not have numbers to assess the proportion of colonial officers that had previously served in either of the metropolitan police forces, but a survey of the published memoirs shows that temporary commissions with the police forces were quite common. At the same time, the colonial attitude in Africa shared important elements with the internal colonialism elements of the military policing of the metropolitan countryside. Both trends were be reinforced after 1911 with the establishment of the National Republican Guard, as serving for some years in its ranks became common for an army officer's career. When the colonial army was used as police and when military officers were put in charge of the colonial police forces, they already knew the business.

References

REAP: Relatórios sobre o Estado da Administração Pública, Imprensa Nacional, 1856–1866.
AHM: Arquivo Histórico Militar
AMR – ANTT: Arquivo do Ministério do Reino – Arquivos Nacionais da Torre do Tombo, Lisbon.
DCD: Diário da Câmara dos Deputados (1834–1910)
DCP: Diário da Câmara dos Pares do Reino 1834–1910)
RM: Revista Militar, 1849–1910

Bibliography

Almeida, P.T. 2006. 'Materials for the History of Elections and Parliament in Portugal.' Online Resource, Biblioteca Nacional de Portugal from: http://purl.pt/5854/2/index.html [accessed 24 April 2017]
Ballbé, M. 1984. *Orden Público y Militarismo en la España Constitucional, 1812–1978.* Madrid: Alianza.
Barata, M.T. 2003. *Nova História Militar de Portugal – O Século XIX.* Lisbon: Círculo de Leitores.

52 Diego Palacios Cerezales

Barreto, M. 1979. *História da Polícia em Portugal*. Braga: Braga Editora.

Bonifácio, F. 1992. A guerra de todos contra todos (ensaio sobre a instabilidade política antes da Regeneração). *Análise Social*, 27: 91–134.

Breyner, A. 1862. O Exército e a Polícia. *Revista Militar*, 14: 11–16.

Brogden, M. 1987. An act to colonise the internal lands of the island: Empire and the origins of the professional police. *International Journal of the Sociology of Law*, 15: 179–208.

Bulhões, M.L.d. 1867. *La Réforme de la Administration Civile au Portugal*. Lisbon: Imprensa Nacional.

Cabral, M.V. 1989. *Portugal Na Alvorada do Século XX: Forças Sociais, Poder Político e Crescimento Económico de 1890–1914*. Lisbon: Presença.

Cabral, M.V. 1993. *The Demise of Liberalism and the Rise of Authoritarism in Portugal, 1880–1930*. London: Kings College.

Cann, J.P. 1997. *Counterinsurgency in Africa: The Portuguese Way of War, 1961–1974*. London: Greenwood.

Carrilho, M. 1985. *Forças Armadas e Mudança Política em Portugal no Século XX*. Lisbon: INCM.

Carvalho, J.L.F.d. 1830. *Ensaio Historico – Politico Sobre a Constituição e Governo do Reino de Portugal*. Paris: H. Bossange.

Castro, G.P.P.d. 1947. *As Minhas Memórias. Na Metropole e Nas Colónias*. Oporto: Livraria Progriedor.

Castro, Veloso de. 1908. *A Campanha do Cuamato em 1907. Breve Narrativa Acompanhada de Photographias*. Luanda: Imprensa Nacional.

Catroga, F. 2006. O poder paroquial como Polícia no século XIX português, in *Lei e Ordem. Justiça Penal, Criminalidade e Polícia. Séculos XIX e XX*, edited by P.T.d. Almeida and T.P. Marques. Lisbon: Horizonte.

Coelho, F.J.P. 1877. *Contemporâneos Ilustres*. Lisbon: Tyographia da rua dos Calafates.

Cordeiro, B. 2013. A technology of government in Portugal: Public lighting and the use of studying disuse, 1848–1965, in *The Making of Modern Portugal: Power, State, Society*, edited by L. Trindade. Newcastle: Cambridge Scholars.

Costa, J.J. 1889. *Instrucções Auxiliares Para os Comandantes dos Destacamentos, Diligências e Escoltas das Tropas de Infanteria*. Lisbon: Typographia Instantanea.

Costa, M.G.d. 1930a. *A vida Agitada do Marechal Gomes da Costa*. Lisbon: Livraria Franco.

Costa, M.G.d. 1930b. *Memórias*. Oporto: Classica Editora.

Delgado, H. and F. Oliveira. 1937. *Auxiliar do Graduado do Exército, GNR, Guarda Fiscal e Polícias*. Tomar: Tipografia A Grafica.

Emsley, C. 1999. *Gendarmes and the State in Nineteenth Century Europe*. Oxford: Oxford University Press.

Emsley, C. 2005. El Ejército, la policía y el mantenimiento del orden público en Inglaterra (1750–1950). *Política y Sociedad*, 42(3): 15–29.

Esteves, R. 1907. *A função do Exército*. Lisbon: Papelaria Fernandes.

Ferreira, F.d.S.e.M. 2002. *Rebeldes e Insubmissos. Resistências Populares ao Liberalismo*. Oporto: Afrontamento.

Gonçalves, G.R. 2012. *Urban Police and the Modernization of Contemporary State, Lisbon 1867–1935*. PhD Thesis, Open University, Milton Keynes.

Gonçalves, H.d.A. 1921. *Necessidade da Força Armada*. Oporto: Tipografia Sociedade Astória.

The military and the (colonial) policing   53

González Calleja, E. 1998. *La Razón de la Fuerza. Orden Público, Subversión y Violencia Política en la Restauración 1875–1917)*. Madrid: CSIC.

Guimarães, R. 1863. *Narrativas e Episódios da Vida Política e Parlamentar de 1862 e 1863.* Lisboa: Typographia Universal.

Johansen, A. 2005. *Soldiers as Police: The French and Prussian Armies and the Policing of Popular Protest, 1889–1914.* London: Ashgate.

Lapa, A. 1953. *Subsídios Para a História de PSP de Lisboa – Vinte e cinco anos ao serviço da Nação.* Lisbon: PSP.

Lapa, A. 1955. *Subsídios Para a História da Polícia de Segurança Pública do Porto.* Oporto.

Lloyd-Jones, S. and Palacios Cerezales, D. 2007. Guardians of the republic? Portugal's GNR and the politicians during the 'new old republic', 1919–1922, in *Policing Interwar Europe*, edited by G. Blaney. Basingstoke, UK: Palgrave.

Macedo, A.T.d. 1984 (first imprint 1880). *Traços de História Contemporânea.* Lisbon: Rolim.

Machado, J.E.X. 1888. *Ensaio Sobre a Organisação da Guarda Civil em Portugal.* Lisbon: Typographia das Novidades.

Manique, A.P. 1989. *Mouzinho da Silveira. Liberalismo e Administração Pública.* Lisbon: Livros Horizonte.

Maya, T.F. 1887. *Notas Sobre a Cavalaria Na Actualidade.* Porto: Livraria Portuense.

Mendonça, M.F.d. 1866. *O Progresso do Exército, Ou Alguns Pensamentos Sobre O Sistema Militar Dum Povo Livre.* Coimbra: Imprensa da Universidade.

Neto, V. 1998. *O Estado, a Igreja e a Sociedade em Portugal.* Lisbon: INCM.

Noronha, E. 1950. *Origens da Guarda Nacional Republicana. A Guarda Municipal.* Lisboa: Comando Geral da GNR.

Oliveira, G.A.N.R.d. 1993. *História do Exército português,1910–1945.* Lisbon: EME.

Palacios Cerezales, D. 2007. O princípio de autoridade e os motins antifiscais de 1862. *Análise Social*, 42: 35–53.

Palacios Cerezales, D. 2008. *Estado, Régimen Y Orden Público En El Portugal Contemporáneo 1834–2000).* PhD Thesis, Complutense, Madrid.

Palacios Cerezales, D. 2011. *Portugal à Coronhada. Protesto Popular e Orden Pública Nos Séculos XIX e XX.* Lisbon: Tinta da China.

Palacios Cerezales, D. 2013. Weak state and civic culture in liberal Portugal (1851–1926), in *The Making of Modern Portugal: Power, State, Society*, edited by L. Trindade. Newcastle: Cambridge Scholars Publishing, 44–64.

Pata, A.d.S.M. 2004. *Revolução e Cidadania. Organização Funcionamento e Ideologia da Guarda Nacional (1820–39).* Lisbon: Colibrí.

Pimentel, L.A. 1868. O Regimento de Infantaria 12. *Jornal do Exército*, II(1): 1–2.

Ramos, R. 1998. *A Segunda Fundação.* Lisbon: Estampa.

Ramos, R. 2004. Portuguese, but not citizens: Restricted citizenship in Portugal, in *Lineages of European Citizenship: Rights, Belonging, and Participation in Eleven Nation – States*, edited by R. Bellamy, D. Castiglone and E. Santoro. Houndmills, Hampshire/New York: Palgrave.

Risques I Corbella, M. 1995. *El Govern Civil de Barcelona al Segle XIX.* Barcelona: Publicacions de l'Abadia de Montserrat.

Roma, C.M. 1857. *Considerações Sobre as Questões Urgentes da Governação Publica e Em Especial Sobre a Dos Caminhos de Ferro.* Lisbon: Typ. da Revista Universal.

Salgado 1862. O Exército. *Revista Militar*, XIII: 101–108.

54 Diego Palacios Cerezales

Santos, M.J.M.d. 2001. *Bonfim-Século XIX. A Regedoria na Segurança Urbana*. Porto: Junta de Freguesia de Bonfim.

Sardica, J.M. 2001. Os militares e a politica entre o Ultimato e a Republica, in *Diplomacia e guerra*, edited by F. Martins. Evora: CIDEHUS/Colibrí: 9–44.

Secr. de Estado dos Negócios da Guerra. 1889. *Regulamento Para o Serviço Interno do Exército*. Lisbon: Imprensa Nacional.

Silva, C. Nogueira da. 2010. Povo e Cidadania no Século XIX, in *Como se faz um Povo*, edited by J. Neves. Lisboa: Tinta da China, 41–53.

Silva, F.P.S.e. 1876. *Guia dos Oficiais, Oficiais Inferiores e Mais Praças Comandantes de Destacamentos, Diligências e Escoltas*. Lisbon: Livraria Verol Senior.

Silveira, L.N. Espinha da (ed.). 1997. *Poder Central, Poder Regional, Poder Local. Uma Perspectiva Histórica*. Lisbon: Cosmos.

Sousa, G.G.d. 1938. *Meio Século de Vida Militar*. Coimbra: Coimbra editora.

Storch, R.D. 1976. The policeman as domestic missionary: Urban discipline and popular culture in Northern England, 1850–1880. *Journal of Social History*, 9: 481–509.

Telo, A.J. 1994. *Economia e Império no Portugal Contemporâneo*. Lisbon: Cosmos.

Um liberal 1858. *Coisas Que Fazem Rir, e Golpe de Vista Sobre as Questões Lazzarista e Charles et George*. Porto: I.A.d'Almeida Junior & Irmão.

Valente, V.P. 1981. A 'Revolta do Grelo', Ensaio de Análise Política in *Tentar Perceber*. Lisbon: INCM.

Valério, N. (ed.). 2001. *Estatísticas Históricas Portuguesas*. Lisbon: INE.

Vidigal, A.E.A.d.Z.e.S. 1905. *Guia Auxiliar Para os Officiaes, Officiaes Inferiores e Demais Praças no Commando de Destacamentos, Diligencias e Escoltas*. Nova Goa: Imprensa Nacional.

3 Militarism in the São Paulo police force (1868–1924)

André Rosemberg

Introduction

This chapter examines the militarisation of the São Paulo police force between 1868 and 1924. In a period marked by political regime change and subsequent realignments of power groups and ideological discourse, the São Paulo police force was transformed from a makeshift, debauched institution into 'the little army of São Paulo' – to use the laudatory rhetoric of its administrators. In fact, after the 1870s, the state police force not only played an essential role in São Paulo's social and crime control, but also acted as a potentially civilising instrument – one that could organise public administrative processes while still enjoying significant institutional autonomy. During the Republican era, the approximation of this police force to the dominant political party machinery (*Partido Republicano Paulista*) further strengthened its military connections. Moreover, the early years of the 20th century were decisive in consolidating the militaristic, bellicose nature of the São Paulo police force, causing an 'identity crisis' that persists until today. Features inherent to policing, delineated and constituted as functions of police bureaucracies in the United States and Europe, were passed over in São Paulo in favour of an emphasis on its martial nature. This was made explicit in the regulations of the police force, in its institutional relations and also in its dealings with the population. This chapter analyses these intersecting dynamics and the means by which the new bases of militaristic rhetoric were assimilated across several institutional spheres.

The recent incursions by the Rio de Janeiro police into the slums of Rio de Janeiro as part of the implementation of the UPPs (Police Pacification Units) program have gained wide publicity in the national and international media and have been described and broadcast in spectacular colour. In the dramatics of these actions (Larkins 2013), the metaphors employed in interviews and debates, as well as the symbols displayed (reporters using bullet-proof vests during broadcasts) recall battlefield images: of the war against crime and of a government retaking 'lawless territories'. A conflict has developed wherein it has been imperative to subjugate the enemy by governmental forces that have been legitimised, so they would have us believe, by the will of civil society. Martial tropes were on the table: a war; two 'equivalent' armies; an opponent to be

56   *André Rosemberg*

expunged, and a morally legitimate mission. On one side, the police; on the other, the criminals.[1]

If Brazilian public opinion does not find it strange that a warlike force in the guise of the police is participating in an urban operation, this is largely due to the fact that Brazilian police groups have historically incorporated many traits usually associated with the military. Some 25 years after the democratisation of 1988, this debate is gaining force, since the permanence of the military 'scent' has come to define not just the police organisations but their very culture, with the uniformed police subject to acerbic criticism by some commentators (Costa and Medeiros 2003, Muniz 2001, Pinheiro 1991). According to this interpretation, neither military characteristics nor the military ethos fit easily with an institution that is set in a democratic context where respect for the law and basic rights is the main priority to be guaranteed. The *raison d'être* of the military, the impetus to annihilate the enemy, as well as its rigid discipline and hierarchically defined organisation are inappropriate elements for police institutions; at least for that part of the police that does preventive policing and is in direct contact with the public. Further, according to this argument, an authoritarian heritage with its military attributes has shaped the Brazilian police organisation and its techniques from their inception.

Contemporary analyses of Brazilian police activities are dominated by criticism of the military model that they have followed. The militarisation of police patrolling is usually perceived as an unbroken continuum in the process of implementing the country's police forces from the time of Brazil's political emancipation (1822), or more precisely since the consolidation of the legal police institutions in the 1830s. The military model that the police force has assumed in Brazil was thought to have been reinforced at the emergence of the Republican regime (1889), and especially after the military coup in 1964 (Dallari 1977, Fernandes 1974, Holloway 1993, Love 1980, Pinheiro 1991). This analysis associates a nefarious character with the military traditions of the forces that maintain public order, and blames the military model – anachronistic and inappropriate – for its recurrent violence and antidemocratic trajectory. In other words, there is a general perception that the military attributes of the police, in terms of its organisation, functionality and ethos, are irretrievably linked to the inability of the police agencies and their police officers to respond to democratic imperatives.

The aim of this discussion is not to deny the proverbial roughness and arbitrariness – to use a euphemism – of the Brazilian police throughout its history; it rather seeks to dispel the common association of the military model adopted in Brazil with the disregard for democratic principles and basic human rights. This chapter attempts to portray this relationship as not 'natural', and is based on an historical approach to the context in which the police forces were constituted. Whilst current debates are dominated by a preponderantly social-anthropological view, this

---

1 For more analysis of recent Brazilian pacification strategies and their role in trying to shift dominant imagery of policing in Brazil, see the chapter by O'Reilly later in this volume.

discussion takes a longer historical perspective and is founded in studies of important empirical material that have not previously been analysed. The objective of this chapter, more than to present possible *causes* and *origins* of the prevalent military model of Brazilian policing, is to expose the way that these military characteristics have been manifest over time and in light of historical contingencies. This discussion is interested in discovering the meanings taken on by militarism as regards the police forces in Brazil, with special attention to the São Paulo police, as well as the manner in which this militarism was incorporated by the professional organisation; in its institutional relations with governments, with the public, and also in the daily experiences of the police.

As a basic premise, we consider some fundamental characteristics which encompass the training and organisation of the Brazilian police forces in a military typology: the first is their relationship with the armed forces. During the Imperial period, for example, the General Commandant of the *Corpo Policial Permanente* (Permanent Police Corps) (CPP) of São Paulo (then the name of the present day military police), was an Army officer and despite enjoying autonomy, the CPP subordinated itself to the Ministry of War. During the First Republic, with the federalisation of administration, the prerogative of creating their own military police forces was conceded to the federal states; São Paulo enjoying broad autonomy vis-à-vis the national army and forming, *intramuros*, i.e. their own body of officers. A series of laws further reinforced the connection between the two institutions – the Army and the police force – and obliged the police to provide support to the Army in cases of serious public order disturbances or foreign attacks (Cotta 2012). It can also be said that the functional constitution of the military police also reproduced, on a large scale, the hierarchical-disciplinary scheme that was in place in the armed forces. The rigid rank system, inter-hierarchical relationships and the moulding of a cohesive *esprit de corps* were part of the aspirations of the top leaders and intrinsic to regimental norms.

However, what we want to discuss here are the contextual limits, the practical uses, the professional re-qualifications, and the meanings that the police, in its most varied ranks, gave to all these objective cases. The militarism of the Brazilian police cannot be taken as a static characteristic. It varies according to the contingencies and the way that the actors involved have articulated it. In other words, the *result* of the militarism that forged the Brazilian police forces is not an inevitability and should not be taken for granted.

The chronological approach that follows prioritises the latter part of the 19th century, when the military police became the primary institution with responsibility for ordinary policing until 1924, the year of the civilian-military 'revolution' in the state of São Paulo, which involved part of the São Paulo police force.

Policing Brazil in the 19th century

Legal and police institutions played an essential role in creating the legal framework for political emancipation in Brazil. Much of the public administration in the vast territory of Brazil was founded on the pillars of justice and the police

58 André Rosemberg

(Bretas 2011, Flory 1981). Consolidation of the legal framework for an independent Brazil involved adopting a dual system for the organisation of the police apparatus that prevails to this day. This system is based on the coexistence of two police institutions that inhabit the same territory and which often have convergent competencies: (a) the civil police (*Polícia Civil*), who are not uniformed and function as an ancillary instance of public authority, responsible for investigating and reporting criminal events; and, (b) the uniformed military police (*Polícia Militar*), responsible for patrolling and ordinary policing. Both police forces were historically established at the provincial state level in line with the legal prescriptions. Contrary to what has happened in the United States and England, police organisation at a local or municipal level is residual. In contrast to France, the national police – the Federal Police (*Polícia Federal*) – have limited authority.[2]

Although the rise of the police machinery can be traced back to the country's constitution, it is not possible to carry out a generalisable study of its formation, given the idiosyncrasies of each of Brazil's states. As a force with a provincial character, the development of the police is linked to the socio-economic realities of each locale. In São Paulo, the most evident impetus that launched the police force into a preeminent position came after the end of the War with Paraguay (1870), a period that coincided with the economic boom of the coffee trade, which connects to other important aspects that define the end of the Empire in São Paulo: the crisis of the slavery system, that called into question the subsistence of a slave society – it is important to note that Brazil was the last sovereign country to abolish slavery; the republican and abolitionist movements; debates about labour; and, the expansion of the agricultural frontier.[3]

Various social groups exerted a civilising pressure that permeated the official discourse with their political and ideological input. There was a clear demand that the rural province wrap itself with the accoutrements of modernity and progress that was emanating from Europe. In contrast to Rio de Janeiro, the city of São Paulo, the provincial capital, was demographically unimpressive until the beginning of the 20th century. Characterised by slave or rough rural populations hardened by a backward way of life, alienated from the benefits of progress and science, inhabiting the forgotten corners and remote *sertões* ('hinterland'), their barbarism had to be overcome (and dominated) by civilising forces. Interjected into this antinomic scenario, affirmed by the circulation of liberal and positivist ideals about 'order and progress' during the last quarter of the 19th century, the São Paulo police force came to embody the power and presence of the State in the farthest

---

2 The Federal Police Force was established relatively recently. It is regulated by the 1967 Constitution and according to the 1988 Constitution it has restricted functions. One of these is dealing with crimes and security issues that that have federal repercussions or that go against the Union and its enterprises; such as corruption, international drug and arms traffic, smuggling, immigration oversight, border policing and criminal activities that cross state lines. Primarily it does intelligence and investigative work.

3 For the development of São Paulo's economy in the context of the country, see Love (1980) and Morse (1958).

Militarism in the São Paulo police force 59

regions of São Paulo province. Even where other administrative entities were absent, the presence of a police squad was not uncommon – one or two rank and file members who represented the auspices of imperial government functioning as the last link in the hierarchical chain (Rosemberg 2010).

Public police patrols, although few in number, offered protection for life and property, or performed police services in the more precisely accepted definition of the term. Even more importantly, they were expected to function as the spearhead of civilisation, what Clive Emsley (1999) has defined as 'carrying the flag'; a pedagogical mission that was part of a tangled, intermittent, incomplete process of expanding the State's monopoly over legitimate power over regions more centrifugal to the centre of power (and of civilisation), whose main bastion was the city of Rio de Janeiro, then capital of the Empire (Mattos 2004, Needell 2006).

Organised along military lines, with the national army as its model and mirroring its regulations (ranks were the same and most of the police officialdom had originated there), one can say that the militarism of the São Paulo police force under the Empire represented the adoption of civilising ideas, much more than any bellicose or martial inclination. However, the functional, organisational and economic limitations ensured that the institution remained at a distance from its projected ideals.

From the outset, basic impediments prevented training a police force of excellence. These ranged from obsolete arms to ruined barracks, through non-existent training and instruction (whether for soldiers or officers) and a feeble selection process. Even the more reserved institutional discourse, exchanged in internal correspondence was disrespectful of the police force. The 'acculturation' of non-commissioned personnel and officers into the founding principles of the military was never completed. On the contrary, the *esprit-de-corps* was based on ambivalent alliances. A military ethic or culture was not part of the São Paulo police corps during the Empire. The longed-for sense of belonging came and went on the whim of the contingencies and immediate imperatives for the troops who were themselves recruited from among the same population upon which their civilising cudgel would fall. In contrast to what happened in Europe, the soldier base was not the 'respectable working class' (London Metropolitan Police) or veterans of the Armed Forces (*gendarmerie*), the São Paulo police force was largely composed of *pardos* (brown-skinned), *pretos* (black-skinned), illiterate Brazilians with no prior occupation, single, and without any physical traits – height or robustness – that distinguished them from the general population.[4]

Nevertheless, a military police organisational model, linked to the central political power, prevailed over contemporary alternatives that were proposing a civil model for organising policing. Thus, in São Paulo two further structures for uniformed, 'decentralised' policing coexisted. One was active on the local, municipal

---

4 For the composition of the gendarmerie, see Houte (2010); and for the London Metropolitan Police, see Shpayer-Makov (2002).

60 André Rosemberg

level (*polícia local*) and another, only in the capital (São Paulo), which expressly mimicked the parameters adopted by the London Metropolitan Police (this was called the *Companhia de Urbanos*).

Instituted in the municipality, the local police (*polícia local*) constituted an instrument of control by plantation owners with these private militias founded on the basis of cronyism, favours and patronage. Remunerated, armed and uniformed at the cost of the public treasury, they were promptly co-opted by private interests. These police organisations had an intermittent existence during the period of the Empire and were extinguished and resuscitated at the mercy of political arrangements. Consequently, they were always considered forces that were supplementary to the military police, the latter receiving the lion's share of the provincial budget. This superimposition of police institutions was never tranquil and also mimicked the dialectically entangled process of formalising a public liberal state whilst disguising a slaveholding society.

The police under the republic

The police model set out above was still in place in São Paulo when the Imperial Regime was replaced by the Republic in 1889, whose first constitution was approved in 1891, installing the first federalist regime *comme il faut*, decentralised, giving the federal units a large measure of autonomy vis-à-vis the Union, and invested with broad fiscal and legal powers that included the authority to legislate and organise the police corps.[5]

This shift in the axis of power – from the hands of the emperor to control by state oligarchies – and the recrudescence of federative principles drew police institutions, especially the public police force, closer to the new political centre. Institutional representation was under the charge of the federative state republican parties that governed without any significant competition at both the federal and local levels. Political and administrative decentralisation also had the potential to create tensions between federal and state governments. This was especially true in São Paulo which experienced both an economic boom and demographic growth from the start of the 20th century. Under the new political configuration and power distribution, inaugurated by the Republic, the army functioned as another vortex of power, maintaining itself in a critical position, and often, with interventionist eruptions (Stepan 1971, McCann 2004). According to some historians (Dallari 1977, Fernandes 1974, Love 1980), the competition with the central government and the ever- present threat of intervention by the national army led federal state governments to create their own minor armies, outstanding amongst which was the 'small São Paulo army' an epithet suggested by a governor in an excessively laudatory report.[6]

---

5 For the organisation of the Republican regime, see Love (1980) and Woodard (2009).

6 Mensagem Apresentada ao Congresso Legislativo do Estado de São Paulo a 14 de julho de 1909, p. 416. The message was delivered by São Paulo State Governor Albuquerque Lins.

Militarism in the São Paulo police force 61

Consequently, during the First Republic (1889–1930) the militarism of the uniformed police machine in São Paulo divested itself of civilising inclinations in order to take on an eminently martial appearance: the police force assimilated the role of troops, ready to defend local interests against any potential enemy incursion – whether from inside (Army and Union) or outside. The militaristic sprit of government rhetoric prevailed over any civilian perspective on the police function.

It is worth noting that the first years of the republican regime were especially tense with respect to their political composition. Even with the stability achieved by President Campos Sales from 1898–1902, diverse groups representing a variety of ideologies and aspirations regarding the republican project, managed to put the new government's viability into question (Lessa 1988). Governments were forced to face civilian revolts, such as the Federalist Revolt and Canudos, and military challenges (Revolt of the Armada) that turned into civil war. São Paulo's militarised police, subordinate to the legal government, actively participated in repressing these movements (Rosemberg 2012a).

In the first decades of the 20th century, the police were obliged to confront the nascent workers' movement, organised under the aegis first of anarchism and anarcho-syndicalism, and later, of socialism/communism. Exclusion from the public arena of debate over social rights as well as the impossibility of formal political representation for organised workers raised these 'social issues' to the sphere of private relations. The owner-worker relationship, the concession of benefits, took place under violent mediation, with police forces having interfered directly in the more dramatic episodes, mostly on the side of the dominant interests. Control over the labour market, the taming of worker recalcitrance and the alignment with the owners' demands were some of the 'missions' to be carried out by the police in the role of implementing governmental strategies and containing workers' demands. Even so, the partial autonomy enjoyed by the police as regards the government cannot be overlooked and their co-option was never absolute (Rosemberg 2013).

Another argument that attempts to explain the recrudescent martialism of the São Paulo police at the beginning of the Republican era was a deliberate policy of social control exercised over the lower income population to whom civil rights and citizenship had been extended after the end of slavery and the promulgation of the 1891 Constitution. This movement was expressed at the beginning of the 1890s in legal reforms that facilitated the aspirations of politicians and administrators to transform the police into an eminently military organisation, with a size and structure proper to an army division. For Silveira Junior (2006), the goals of the members of parliament in promoting such a profound alteration was to create a corps that would be able to confront and control the urban disturbances which devastated the city of São Paulo, and were caused by intense demographic pressures in the first years of the Republic.

In this way, the social pressure to be combated was the urban base: the agitation was attributed to indiscriminate urban growth, motivated by the waves of immigration and the recalcitrance of a population disaffected with the prevailing norms

62 André Rosemberg

and social standards. During the First Republic, the militarisation of the state police, especially in São Paulo, was manifest in its formal subordination to the political apparatus in a context of strong federalisation. Value was placed on bellicosity, especially after the arrival of the French military mission in 1906, which was commissioned by the São Paulo Government with the task to train the local police force. The Mission was active in Brazil up until 1924, with the exception of the years of World War I. At first, constituted by a captain, a lieutenant and a sergeant, the French Mission contributed to the São Paulo state's efforts to modernise the police apparatus in a more militarised framework. Upon the arrival of the foreigners, an Officer Preparatory Course was created and a systemised training schedule was formalised. A set of rules whose aim was to consolidate the hierarchical relations and intra-corporate subordination was promptly implanted. In parallel, new martial sections were created, such as the Machine Gun Company and an air force. The French Mission is a symbol of the intense exchange of information, know-how and diplomatic pressures in the police and military spheres during the 19th and 20th century.[7] It is also a clear display of the influence under which Brazil found itself at the moment of its declaration of independence from Portugal in 1822. The mould on which the Brazilian juridical institutions and police were founded had English and French characteristics.

During the First Republic, the military nature of the police was important in interjecting federal states' rights into the tenuous balance of power with the central government (Viscardi 2001); this reflected the political decentralisation enacted by the 1891 Constitution. It aspired to subordinate the police to the federal state governments, resulting in a Praetorian stance, whether against local dissidents or the interventionist inclinations of the federal government. Control of the labour market and of workers, who were increasingly organised at the beginning of the Republic, was a constant concern for São Paulo's federal state government.

Accommodating the mass of workers who swelled São Paulo state's population, whether liberated slaves or the growing number of European immigrants, became a challenging social problem. The political and economic elites used the police to enforce social controls, arrest vagrants, and force compliance with precarious and draconian work contracts, among other functions. In a typology proposed by the French sociologist Dominique Monjardet (1996), during the first years of the Republic, the states, and São Paulo in particular, armed themselves with 'sovereign police forces' in order to maintain the *status quo*, and the enforcement of political 'loyalty' emerged as their paramount function. Militarised features were to be the optimal action model in order to fulfil this instrumental role.

However, the gap between official plans and the pragmatic unfolding of policies in daily life was perceptible. Police loyalty to the political machinery and any notion of their instrumentality proved to be very tenuous. Material limitations became

---

7 There are only a few references about the French Mission in São Paulo (Câmara and Andrade 1931, Amaral 1968, Fernandes 1974, Carvalho 2001, Dallari 1977, Santos 2004, Souza 1998).

evident during the First Republic (1889–1930). Joining the police force was not a lasting career option for blue collar workers: the number of desertions and exclusions for disciplinary reasons was significant. Instruction by French military officials was also limited, and did not encompass the entire corps. An older sector of officialdom proved resistant to training and the restructuring of functions that subverted the traditional dynamics of the established hierarchy. Cases of corruption, embezzlement, abuse, and extortion were numerous, even among officers. A praetorian guard, which candidly defended the political situation due to ideology, was, in fact, a mere rhetorical tactic. In daily practice, more nuanced interests survived and were interwoven across several levels of the police organisation, subverting the twisted rectitude of the pure military spirit – of discipline, of honour and of hierarchy. Day-to-day survival, petty rivalries, improved placement within the still rigid social pyramid, a little extra money, even if it were the product of a lapse in conduct or illicit activity, caused the pillars of the untouchable 'small São Paulo army' to collapse.

In fact, the police force never functioned as a standing force, which was trained and ready to intervene to maintain the public order, as an important part of historiography might lead one to believe.[8] Although after 1906, the training, formation, and organisation of the police force stressed attributes similar to those of the armed forces, the penetration of a military ethos among the police and into the organisational culture was always ambivalent and patchy. In daily practice, the demands of the public and even institutional interests were not aligned with the military option. In this eminently rural context, in its main activity, in which only the capital had coalesced in its vocation for being a metropolis, the police force spread out over the São Paulo state in small squads and was obliged to confront situations and circumstances which contrasted with the martial spirit that adorned its ideology (Rosemberg 2012b). With the exception of the periods of political turbulence at the beginning of the 20th century, the soldiers had no real enemies to fight. War training within rigorous French standards had little practical use in the lethargic villages of the interior, in which 'common criminality' and more prosaic events – from horse theft to drunken disorderly conduct, to disputes among plantation owners and the ubiquitous presence of counterfeit currency whose circulation grew as the economy became more sophisticated. These were what disturbed the public peace. The São Paulo police force was thus in a paradoxical situation. Invested with a military character and spirit and instructed in martial leadership, in its everyday practice it managed to free itself to perform 'classic' policing tasks, for which immersion in a bellicose, martial environment forged by official rhetoric and by daily practices was of little use.

There did exist, however, the heraldic use of the police force as an instrument to impress foreign and national authorities. The assiduousness and care with which reviews and parades were organised for civic holidays and for receptions for foreign dignitaries, especially in the state capital, lent an indispensable lustre to

---

8 Among others, Fernandes (1974), Pinheiro (1991), Jaqueline Muniz (2001).

64 *André Rosemberg*

the São Paulo government, meant to mark its 'sovereignty' from the central government, other federal states and of course, before civilised nations. In the symbolic demonstration of strength in contained environments, with controlled risk, like a peacock showing off, the São Paulo military police displayed all the shiny veneer of its military propensity. At the close of the spectacle, battalions of police from the most varied ranks, took off their gala uniforms and returned to their daily ration of rice and beans not without a sigh of boredom.

Conclusion

To summarise, the process of militarising the police force in Brazil and especially in São Paulo, was not teleological, the inevitable unfolding of natural imperatives. During the Empire, the military model served a civilising proposal; in the First Republic, it summed up the political approximation with the dominant party and the formation of a federal state militia, a symbol of robustness and São Paulo's autonomy. At the same time the police found themselves entangled in social control policies to regulate the organised workers' movement, and last but not least, the symbolic and heraldic use of troops in civil pageants and public parades.

It is necessary to emphasise that 'policies' and strategies undertaken by the government and the heads of the police in appropriating military features into the police force were obligatorily tinged by material contingencies, organisations and professionals wills. The discrepancies inherent to the functioning of any organisation, since they are made up of individuals, are also responsible for the 'flaws' in the ideal functioning of the police. The policemen, in turn, interpreted and updated their superiors' prescriptions through different prisms.

Essentially, the military model assumed by Brazil's police forces, especially in São Paulo, from the time of the imperial period should not be automatically associated with arbitrary and violent police practices. A martial ethos, proper to the armed forces, was not necessarily infused into the institutional ideology of the military police. Brazilian style militarism took several forms and was moulded by diverse filters. If today after thirty years of a democratic regime, we still live with violent police forces disrespectful of basic citizenship rights, the causes must be identified, first in the broader historical context, in the origins that inform them and the professional and corporative interests that make up police culture.

References

Amaral, A.B. 1968. A Missão Francesa de Instrução da Força Pública de São Paulo, 1906–1914. *Separata da Revista do Arquivo Municipal.* São Paulo: Prefeitura de São Paulo.

Bretas, M.L. 2011. La policía de la capital del Imperio Brasileiro, in *Mirada (de) Uniforme – Historia y Crítica de la Razón Policial,* edited by D. Galeano and G. Kaminski. Buenos Aires: Teseo, 87–110.

Câmara, E. and Andrade, H. 1931. *A Força Pública de São Paulo. Esboço histórico (1831–1931).* São Paulo: Sociedade Impressora Paulista.

Militarism in the São Paulo police force 65

Carvalho, G. 2001. *Forças Públicas: Instrumento de Defesa da Autonomia Estadual e de Sustentação da Política dos Governadores na Primeira República (1889–1930)*. MA, USP, São Paulo.

Costa, A. and Medeiros, M.A. 2003. A desmilitarização das polícias? Policiais, soldados e democracia. *Teoria & Sociedade*, 11(1): 66–89.

Cotta, F.A. 2012. *Matrizes do Sistema Policial Brasileiro*. Belo Horizonte: Crisálida.

Dallari, D.A. 1977. *O Pequeno Exército Paulista*. São Paulo: Perspectiva.

Emsley, C. 1999. *Gendarmes and the State in Nineteenth-century Europe*. Oxford: Oxford University Press.

Fernandes, H.R. 1974. *Política e Segurança – Força Pública do Estado de São Paulo: Fundamentos Socioculturais*. São Paulo: Editora Alfa-ômega.

Flory, T. 1981. *Judge and Jury in Imperial Brazil, 1808–1871: Social Control and Political Stability in the New State*. Austin: Texas University Press.

Holloway, T.H. 1993. *Policing Rio de Janeiro: Repression and Resistance in a 19Th-Century City*. Stanford: Stanford University Press.

Houte, A.-D. 2010. *Le Métier du Gendarme au XIXe Siècle*. Rennes: Presse Universitaire de Rennes.

Larkins, E.R. 2013. Performances of police legitimacy in Rio's Hyper Favela. *Law & Social Inquiry*, 38: 553–575.

Lessa, R. 1988. *A Invenção Republicana: Campos Salles, as Bases e a Decadência da Primeira República*. Rio de Janeiro: Topbooks.

Love, J. 1980. *São Paulo in the Brazilian Federation*. Stanford: Stanford University Press.

McCann, F. 2004. *Soldiers of the Pátria – A History of the Brazilian Army, 1889–1937*. Stanford: Stanford University Press.

Mattos, I.R. 2004. *O Tempo Saquarema*. São Paulo: Editora Hucitec.

Monjardet, D. 1996. *Ce que Fait la Police – Sociologie de la Force Publique*. Paris: Édition la Découverte.

Morse, R.M. 1958. *From Community to Metropolis: A biography of São Paulo, Brazil*. Miami: Univesity of Florida Press.

Muniz, J. 2001. A Crise de identidade das Polícias Militares Brasileiras: Dilemas e Paradoxos da Formação Educacional. *Security and Defense Studies Review*, 1: 177–198.

Needell, J.D. 2006. *The Party of Order the Conservatives, the State, and Slavery in the Brazilian Monarchy, 1831–1871*. Stanford: Stanford University Press.

Pinheiro, P.S. 1991. Police and political crisis: The case of the military police, in *Vigilantism and the State in Modern Latin America – Essays on Extralegal Violence*, edited by M.K. Huggins. New York: Praeger Publisher, 167–185.

Rosemberg, A. 2010. *De Chumbo e Festim – Uma História da Polícia Paulista no Final do Império*. São Paulo: Edusp.

Rosemberg, A. 2012a. As Políticas de Segurança Pública Nos 'Primórdios': A Força Pública e a Lei em São Paulo (1870–1901). *Estudos de Sociologia*, 17(33): 353–373.

Rosemberg, A. 2012b. Prelúdio de Um 'Pequeno Exército'? A Força Policial Paulista nos Primeiros Anos da República (1890 & 1895). *História Unisinos*, 16(3): 333–345.

Rosemberg, A. 2013. A Greve Pelas Oito Horas em Santos (1908): Em Busca do 'Inimigo Imaginário'. *História e Perspectivas*, 26(49): 17–40.

Santos, M.A. 2004. *Paladinos da Ordem – Polícia e Sociedade em São Paulo na Virada do Século XIX ao XX*. PhD Dissertation, USP, São Paulo.

66   André Rosemberg

Shpayer-Makov, H. 2002. *The Making of a Policeman: A Social History of a Labour Force in Metropolitan London, 1829–1914*. Burlington: Ashgate.

Silveira Junior, O.J. 2006. A ordem antes do progresso. A militarização da Força Pública paulista e sua inserção na política estadual de segurança (1892–1905), in *História Económica – Agricultura, Indústria e Populações*, edited by E.B.B. Moura and V.L.A. Ferlini. São Paulo: Alameda, 121–141.

Souza, L.A. 1998. *Poder de polícia, Polícia Civil e Práticas Policiais na Cidade de São Paulo (1889–1930)*. PhD Dissertation, USP, São Paulo.

Stepan, A. 1971. *The Military in Politics: Changing Patterns in Brazil*. Princeton: Princeton University Press.

Viscardi, C.M.R. 2001. *O Teatro das Oligarquias: Uma Revisão da 'Política do Café Com Leite'*. Belo Horizonte: C/Arte.

Woodard, J.P. 2009. *A Place in Politics – São Paulo, Brazil, From Seigneurial Republicanism to Regionalist Revolt*. Durham: Duke University Press.

Comment

The Portuguese colonial policing mission in comparative perspective

Richard S. Hill

Introduction

The history of 'police and policing practices' in the Lusophone world has been neglected by scholars, and the concept of policing has been too prescriptively conceived, as Gonçalves and Cachado note. Similar assessments are valid for other empires, to a greater or lesser degree. But there is sufficient work to date to suggest that key characteristics of policing were shared across global empires, creating patterns that reflected the logical consequences of imperialism – of metropolitan powers occupying or dominating weaker polities to exploit their human and natural resources. In that sense, colonial policing was transnational policing.

Wherever outside powers conquered, or coercively entered or overstayed their welcome, people resisted. In response, the imperial state and its local agencies sought to bring them to submission, often through police agencies or institutions, or coercively sanctioned personnel acting as police (Duffy 1959: 357). The most persistent official term for the Portuguese Empire, even with regard to colonies acquired with little or no bloodshed, was appropriately 'The Conquests'.[1]

In the Lusophone world, as elsewhere, policing modes and systems resulted from both the imperatives of the decision makers at the various *loci* of power and the characteristics of the societies they were 'bringing to order' – the culture and religion of the people to be controlled, the composition and goals of the political and economic controllers, and so on. Of course, there were many variations from practices within other empires. Diego Palacios Cerezales in his chapter contribution, for example, points to the continuing importance of the role of magistrates in the Portuguese countryside in calling upon military policing, a practice which lasted considerably longer than in a number of other metropoles. The powers of the magistracy, moreover, tended to differ from those elsewhere, with detained persons handed over by the military to the judicial authorities – unlike in Spain – to take one example.

---

1 Refer to Boxer (1963: 2–3) and more generally Holloway (1993). For a discussion of Boxer's work, see Curto (2013). The various works of Rene Pélissier (1977, 1984, 1989) document numerous Portuguese invasions and raids into the African interior from 1841 to 1941.

68   *Richard S. Hill*

In turn, metropole-based political and policing characteristics led to transfers of specific and general practices and ambiences throughout the Lusophone world, albeit differentially, reflecting time and place. While metropolitan authorities in a number of empires increasingly interrogated the cost of holding onto colonies as pressure to decolonise strengthened, New State ideology saw retention of empire rise in significance. This in turn solidified militarised policing throughout the Portuguese Empire, presaging bloody retentionist wars well after other metropoles had begun to abandon the concept of empire. Despite such inter-imperial differences, the work of the four authors indicate how an examination of social control in Portugal and its spheres of influence can shed light on the fundamentals of imperial policing in general – and therefore of critical aspects of the world we live in today.

Policing

In the Lusophone past, as in most imperial systems, the authorities had multiple sources of coercion available to them. Most obviously, these were exercised by and on behalf of the political decision makers and the interests they represented in the metropole and peripheral centres of control. They also included legitimated coercive powers exercised by both indigenous authorities in colonies and power elites in neo-colonies such as Brazil. There was a massive amount of auxiliary power available for the state to call upon or franchise as well, both in emergency and routine circumstances – powers of compulsory appropriation of manpower, for example, or using concessionary governance and policing regimes as standing modes of controlling sectors of colonised territories. From orders emanating from the highest police official in Lisbon, right down to informal but state-sanctioned (or tolerated) disciplinary power enjoyed over indigenes by even poor peasants sent to colonise distant territories (Bender 1978), all such mechanisms embodied a high degree of potential or actual violence. Many of them reflected the centuries-long processes that were often called 'pacification', a term which usefully applies to numerous modes of 'exploitative ambitions delivered through military conquest and systematic control' (see O'Reilly in this volume: 403).

This was the case in all modern empires: the exploitative purpose underpinning empire led inexorably to highly coercive methodologies of social control. Policing, the first line of defence of the state, was a crucial component of these – arguably *the* major mode of state control through the lifetimes of entire empires. Within the paradigms of coercive control, in effect, the three chapters in Part One invite us to consider the ways in which successive metropolitan, colonial and neo-colonial regimes paid serious and ongoing attention to the most effective way to control their peoples.

However much operational flexibility they might (or might not) be able to muster, police forces were necessarily geared to the requirements of the governing regimes at various levels and the interests they represented. This was often overt enough, as Rosemberg reminds us with São Paulo's militarised police being viewed in the later 19th century by the dominant political and economic circles as their own 'little army', one expected to assist them retain as much power as possible vis a vis the colonial capital as well as to impose the types of order sought nationwide. For the latter, the work of the police engaged in the 'ostensive patrolling' of Rio de Janeiro's streets formed an example of the order requirements of the central ruling elite, with their open and brutal suppression of customary social life and their attempts to substitute the submissive behaviours sought by central government (Holloway 1993: 276).

State expectations in the Lusophone world, then, focussed on 'taming' the bulk of the population, peasant and indigene, and keeping the tamed sectors 'tranquillised' (to use a term popular in British colonial policing). The chapters invite us to reflect on how these difficult terms of reference required both the capacity to deploy daily coercion and gather main force in crises, and on the relationship between routinised and exceptional force. Certainly, the policing services outlined in the chapters all had, at very least, military resonance – and indeed, were often performed by the military itself. Coercion levels were high as the stakes were high – public order, private profit and, ultimately, the security of the state. Thus, when police forces failed to live up to the expectations of the authorities which employed them, they were liable to be unceremoniously replaced, as proved to be the case with the three Portuguese forces created in 1834 (see the contribution from Palacios Cerezales).

The coercion required to both impose the social conditions required by the authorities and maintain it once the populace had been subjugated and brought to order, was generally sanctioned by metropolitan and colonial law. Where it was not, police personnel routinely ignored what they, and the powerful in society, saw as 'senseless [legal] injunctions' which only supposedly guaranteed specified rights (Mecklenburg 1910: 165–167). Thus, the Rio de Janeiro police 'explicitly recognized terror as one of the several weapons at their disposal in their ongoing effort to force submission' (Holloway 1993: 12). Of course the degree and methods of terror differed from case to case, time to time. But what is clear is that, whether it be in the metropole, formal colonies or informal empire, whenever the law clashed with the requirements of order, the latter prevailed. For, to borrow from Carl Schmitt's (in)famous dictum, the sovereign power is that authority which has the strength and capacity to declare and enforce *the exceptions* to the law (Schmitt 1922). In one interpretative extension of this theory, colonies collectively constituted a gigantic exception to the metropolitan 'rule of law', territories where 'the rule of colonial difference' prevailed (Chatterjee 1993: 16–19). While this argument cannot be addressed here in detail, it forms a suitable backdrop to the topics raised by the four authors.

The exceptional element was, essentially, endemic extra-legal violence. Even after considerable social stabilisation in metropole as well as colony, the relationship between police authority and subject continued to remain inherently adversarial. This manifested itself in many ways, including in forced labour demands upon the populace (Nzula et al. 1933). A big-game hunter reported a typical incident in Angola after the Great War: villagers fled from his party, thinking it was an official expedition 'collecting labourers' for enforced work (Statham 1922:

70 Richard S. Hill

94–95). Such practices continued in the Lusophone world towards the end of empire, with repercussions to this day. As we can see from the preceding chapters, in the former imperial world the past has often transferred palpably to the present. Holloway aptly ends his work on the history of policing in Rio de Janeiro: 'Brazil lives with the results [of coercive social control] to this day' (Holloway 1993: 291).

As Captain Salgueiro Rego stressed in the 1930s, effective social control depended on close surveillance of the population (see the contribution from Gonçalves and Cachado). Portuguese administrations sought to penetrate every village, frequently through policemen and soldiers (or often, police-soldiers) reporting to the authorities. In the colonies, the reporting lines often included indigenous structures, whose political and policing personnel enjoyed a great deal of control delegated by the Portuguese officials to whom the chiefs reported.[2] This continued towards the end of the empire, when James Duffy – for example – reported that 'reliable chiefs in the midst of the African population [in Portuguese territories] have helped contain dissatisfaction and nascent sentiments of Africanism' (Duffy 1959: 303).

Officialised chiefs and their policing personnel often employed brutal techniques of discipline and detention, to which European officials tended to turn a blind eye so long as order was preserved and profits extracted.[3] As a result, indigenously-directed official violence remained endemic over large tracts of territory. While there were countless official denials of this, some practitioners acknowledged it privately or even publicly. In post Second World War Mozambique, Senior Colonial Inspector Captain Henrique Galvao testified, 'corporal punishment and physical violence are still the current practice' (Figueiredo 1961: 155). Soon after this report, police repression began to further embed itself as Portugal's authoritarian government sought to retain formal empire in the face of increasing resistance, eschewing the more accommodatory methods of some empires in some of their colonies (Holland 1985: 292–293).

But authorities at various levels also calculated that the degree of state violence was best minimised within parameters of effectiveness, in order to avoid provoking greater opposition to imperial occupation, to maximise the profits of empire, and to assist the task of coaxing the people into automatic obedience. While sustained resistance was always a possibility, this did not greatly matter so long as it remained small-scale or uncoordinated, and heavy handed police action did not escalate or unify it. Containment measures in the preceding chapters invite us to look elsewhere in the Lusophone world and beyond, and there are a myriad of circumstances where police forces 'had become adept at maintaining the level of repression deemed necessary to keep the myriad small and personal acts of resistance from becoming disruptive or generative' (Holloway 1993: 289).

---

2 See for example Col. Statham's observations during his hunting trip to Angola in 1920 (1922: 372).

3 This was reported extensively by travellers. In a typical comment, Statham, himself ruthless to indigenes, commented: 'every one who knows Africa will realise what delegation of authority means to such people, and what a tyrant a black in temporary authority can prove if given the chance' (1922: 372).

Comment: the Portuguese colonial   71

While colonial and neo-colonial control was suffused with exemplary coercion, then, it was generally a calibrated violence that was exerted (except where things went wrong, especially in heated situations or emergencies). In particular, the infliction of extreme terror, even where it was expressed in the 'controlled chaos' of randomised exemplary targets, needed to be carefully regulated lest it become counter-productive by driving masses of people beyond endurance. As a British governor of the Cape Colony had once put it, the method was that of 'a proper degree of terror' (Pithouse 2013: 2). Nevertheless, when mass resistance or armed rebellion broke out, the level of official force could be terrible indeed.

Knowledge circulation

While the deeply entrenched nature of violence in the Portuguese Empire derived from the same fundamental imperatives as in other empires, as noted above the nature of the endemic coercion in the Lusophone world responded to and reflected characteristics specific to central, regional and local culture and political economy. Within Lusophone parameters, as the preceding chapters note, both considerable cross fertilisation of police methods and transfer of policing personnel within empires took place through time. This perhaps occurred to a greater degree than in at least some other empires, given the more highly militarised and coercive policing characteristic of the metropole vis a vis non-Iberian imperial hubs, and in view of renewed attempts at tighter central control of much of the periphery than in other empires. There were strong incentives, especially from the 1880s, when Portuguese governments saw the pacification (in particular) of Angola, Guinea-Bissau and Mozambique as the key to greatly enhance the metropole's economic prospects and create a 'second Brazil' (Vandervort 1998: 34).

The preceding chapters invite further work on such inter-imperial comparisons, both across the board and within specific periods. As Palacios Cerezales notes, from the beginning of the 20th century a greater effort was made to integrate policing of the Lusophone colonies with that of the metropole, given the militarised nature of both operations. The Portuguese army, indeed, welcomed colonial experience for its men during that century, and this in turn assisted it to perfect quasi-military policing practices such as mobile-unit and flying-column policing. When the National Republican Guard was established in 1911, it was a fully militarised police force in which army officers continued to serve. In their contribution, Gonçalves and Cachado note that under its guidelines, control of policing from Lisbon grew the more powerful. With institutional reshaping and rationalisation of police (among other) services under the New State, and its emphasis on Lusophonism, metropolitan policing influence increased yet further in the colonies. Can comparisons with other empires help answer questions relating, for instance, to the degree to which the new regime altered or supplanted previous modes of control? We find some answers in the preceding chapters.

When Portuguese military officers arrived in colonies, for example, they not only brought policing knowledge gained from their home unit, but also (in many cases) from serving in civil, albeit paramilitarised, constabularies such as those

72   *Richard S. Hill*

of Lisbon and Porto. After Lisbon imposed stricter urban social controls, these were applied to Mozambican and other large Lusophone cities (see Gonçalves and Cachado). Understanding of knowledge transfer within Lusophone and imperial spheres of influence, however, needs to be tempered by examination of transfer of policing know-how (and sometimes personnel) *between* empires. As yet little is known about this, but all the authors' chapters provide examples. Thus, in early 19th century Brazil, British officers in the Portuguese army influenced its social control methodology. Mozambique took on significant numbers of British police personnel to improve its urban policing. With Brazilian independence in 1822, French policing influences joined British-inflected practices. The picture is complexified even more by the fact that such external influences were refreshed from time to time, as with the French mission to train police in militarised policing in São Paulo early in the 20th century.

Knowledge transfers between empires were not confined to practical assistance. Sometimes theory came to the fore. Thus, as Gonçalves and Cachado note, the military theoretician Marshall Gomes de Costa looked to the differing models of Germany and Britain, as well as that of the metropole, for guidance for policing in Mozambique; policing practitioner Rego reflected international influences in his 1930s works on policing in Portugal; and Rosemberg's case study of São Paulo notes that its city police used London Metropolitan Police modelling. All of the authors invite us, in effect, to further investigate such nexuses and interconnections in the intertwined realms of practice and theory.

Military

None of this, of course, is to dismiss the very real differences between French, German, English and other policing influences, many of which related to the *degree* of conflictualism involved in the police-public interface as well as to methods. Much more investigation is needed into the links between military and civil policing within both metropoles and their peripheries. Many historians have imagined that policing and soldiering are incompatible enterprises, but as André Rosemberg notes with regard to Brazil, they are integrally connected. One fruitful line of enquiry might be where best to place, and how best to interrelate, police and military factors along the continuum of measures available for coercive social control (Hill 2015).

The chapters show that, essentially, the military was central to policing both Portugal and its global spheres of influence, for decade upon decade, even if it has now forgotten this. Most prominently, Palacios Cerezales explores the 'army as police', tasked as it was with much of the day to day policing in the streets and villages of the metropole. Beginning his chapter with an historical quote on the soldierly worldview needed for policing in the period covered, he later cites an 1855 declaration that only a fully armed soldier can garner respect, and he concludes aptly in arguing that 'when military officers were put in charge of the colonial police forces, they already knew the business' (p. 51). Their militarised policing methods are resonant of the Royal Irish Constabulary's occupation-policing of the Irish countryside in a similar period, a 'model' which was adapted in various forms to many British colonies (Hill 2015).

To argue thus is not to deny or downgrade the obvious differences in both theory and practice between fighting and policing. Theoretical differences were important at the time. Thus, as we have seen, the Portuguese military provided what was deemed to be policing aid to the civil power, rather than comprising a gendarmerie *per se* (see the Palacios Cerezales chapter). But theory in such matters was never uncomplicated. In this case, the military's functions embodied what have been called 'high police' (Brodeur 2012) powers, with the ultimate responsibility that of defending the state.[4] Such responsibilities constituted, in effect, Costa's primary category of policing. Its echoes extended far and wide, including – as noted by our other authors – the tasks assigned to the militarised police of Brazil and Lusophone Africa. Moreover, when it sought military intervention, the metropolitan civil power, as a matter of course, needed to make formal arrangements at senior officer level.

But in real terms, while military leaders were not necessarily always happy about it (or about acknowledging it), policing was integral to their function both at home and in the colonies, *pace* official declarations that the military did no more than provide aid to the civil power (see the contribution from Palacios Cerezales). Whatever the benefits of using the (contested) terminology of 'high policing' to bring together police and military theory, policing practice remained policing practice – defending the state at all hours of every day was and had always been a police function. To whatever degree this was carried out by military, semi-military or quasi-military organisations, their tasks were conceptually interlinked. And of course, they would assist each other, including police aid to the military as well as the other way round, as Rosemberg notes with reference to Brazil.

Whether they were deemed military or police operatives, personnel conducting policing surveillance, analysis and operations always constituted the state's first line of defence. To be sure, these forces did generally need military-style discipline if they were to be successful and sustained. Thus, when private forces were incorporated into the state they would typically be injected with military discipline and know-how and prove satisfactory enough – as in Macau and Mozambique (see Gonçalves and Cachado). What is significant is that, while there were jurisdictional contestations, tensions and rivalries between and within police and military milieus, they were all involved in defence of the state. The means were many and varied, from preventive daily patrols through to the armed suppression of riot or rebellion, but the ultimate ends were the same – and these ends were essentially politically driven on behalf of those who held wealth and power. Thus, throughout the Lusophone world as elsewhere (e.g., Thomas 2012), strikes would frequently be put down by the combined might of civil and military forces, as Palacios Cerezales notes of the events in Portugal in 1903.

---

4 For a discussion of conflations of 'high police' and military functions, see Bruno Reis' chapter in this volume.

74   Richard S. Hill

Militarised action against workers and other subjects deemed to need disciplining would occur however civilianised routine policing had become. With the beginnings of a general (if highly uneven) stabilising of social order in the Lusophone world, policing reform took a civil direction from the 1860s onwards in the metropole, and from the 1880s in the colonies (see the contribution from Gonçalves and Cachado). In 1909 a traveller reported of the military who policed an area in Tete that, rather than a 'glorious life of conquest and battle', the men had the luxury of quietude, albeit still able to carry out any necessary remedial discipline from two local forts (Letcher 1913: 61–63).

The combined results of a general (if spatially and temporally uneven) movement towards social tranquillity, part of a global phenomenon, allowed policing to increasingly de-emphasise violence and oppression during its daily activities. In some cases, at least on a formal level, militarism was superseded, as in Mozambique (see Gonçalves and Cachado). So long as there was backup reserve force available in case of crisis, then, the degree of violence in social control would lessen – as would costs – as the populations became increasingly 'tranquillised'. But however much processes of demilitarisation might kick in, militaristic undertones to the police role, its organisation, capacity and ethos, continued. Because of this platform, punitive policing could be tightened whenever necessary, often at short notice – to combat mass-based decolonisation movements with military 'police operations' similar to those within other empires, not to mention countering the unrest among the masses who had become proletarianised (see: Palacios Cerezales in this volume; also, Thomas 2012).

This was an essential task of policing control in the Lusophone world in the 19th and 20th centuries. As in other modern empires, in the final analysis this was concerned with imposing state-defined order upon masses of people, and thereafter maintaining the ordered conditions which had been achieved. A 'crime control' or 'preventive policing' subset (in effect, Costa's second category as discussed by Gonçalves and Cachado) within the broad policing function was developing, but this was mostly concentrated in the cities of empire. The major urban areas, in particular, were host to economic elites, their political allies and the amassed wealth of colony and empire (Boxer 1963: 39–40). Once the bulk of the urban population had been tamed, these concentrations of 'orderly public behaviour' were depicted as showcases for the modes of conduct expected from the rest of the country or colony – as was explicitly the case for Rio de Janeiro, for example (Holloway 1993: 274).

None of this is to argue that there were not downstream beneficial consequences for the common people from an imposed 'state of order', even though policing targeted many aspects of the popular lifestyle – such as Brazil's *capoeira* (Holloway 1993: 9). Many subjects came to accept such intervention as a trade-off for safer lives and securer property. But such benefits for body and possessions do not alter the fundamental purposes of policing, and hence the predominance of military and military-influenced formations to conduct the state's major modes of coercive social control. The complications involved in police-state interaction, the temporally and spatially uneven application of force and its effects upon the populace, are among the most fruitful arenas of research for future scholarship.

Multilayered control

The complications of policing within each jurisdiction were intensified by another factor, one common in other empires and their spheres of interest: many and overlapping styles and organisations policed the Lusophone world. Sometimes there was a reasonably clear demarcation between two or more broad styles, functions or levels of policing: military and civil; central, regional and local; public and private; mobile and fixed-point; and rural and urban, as indicated by Gonçalves and Cachado with reference to Portugal. Many an essay on colonial policing has accordingly focused on either one or a handful of specific forces or categories.

Almost invariably, however, along the way other types and organisations need to be mentioned, even if only in passing. Before we can fully get to grips with the arrangements and procedures by which colonies were policed and held, research paths need to be opened up that aim to integrate the varied types of coercive control, that seek to examine the various layers of policing modes and forces and the interactions between them – the 'multi-layered resonances of pacification that stretch from the colonial to the contemporary', as Conor O'Reilly puts it later in this volume (p. 403). One crucial area of enquiry would be the complexities of the private policing regimes which existed alongside and overlapped with state-controlled or state-directed forces. In the chapters under consideration we can see such possibilities. One of the two major São Paulo policing modes was that of elite-controlled militarised police bodies, for example, and private rural forces are mentioned as well. The very existence (often short-lived) and *modus operandi* of such forces often depended on the purposes and needs of the likes of owners of industry, mines or plantations (see the contribution from Rosemberg).

In African colonies, private policing by concessionary companies running plantation or other extractive industries exerted a violence which was often more endemic (and even more horrific) than in state forces. In the Portuguese East African interior early last century, a traveller observed 'the prazo-owner [was] a virtual despot' in the concessionary regimes, employing extreme force to ensure order and discipline in the workforce (Letcher 1913: 150). It would take 'almost superhuman courage' for a worker to defy management, however legally justified, wrote investigators in 1907 after some two years of examining indentured labour in Portuguese West Africa.[5] 'What are laws and royal decrees compared

---

5 There were prior *exposés*, including by campaigning journalist Henry Nevinson, who published *A Modern Slavery* in 1906 and sought a boycott by British cocoa firms on purchase of raw materials from Portuguese West Africa. The 1907 Report, by J. Burrt and W. Horton, was reproduced in William Cadbury's influential *Labour in Portuguese West Africa*, which he published in 1910 after warding off legal action. The Portuguese government had promised to reform the indentured labour system after the original release of the report, but had failed to do so, causing Cadbury and fellow campaigners who also owned or were associated with cocoa companies to cease purchasing from São Tomé and Principe (see, e.g., Cadbury Brothers, letter to the editor of *The Spectator*, 20 March 1909). They were subject to much scepticism at the time, but the thrust and many details of their observations accord with those of many other contemporary eyewitness reports.

76   Richard S. Hill

with the proximity of the chicotte?' (Cadbury 1910: 112). It is possible to interpret the state's franchising or acceptance of such violent modes of indirect control as filling-in where the colonial forces were too weak to police properly (or at all), as set out by Gonçalves and Cachado in their contribution. Certainly, many companies would have preferred a state service, as maintaining their own policing regimes made significant inroads into profits. On the other hand, a state-provided service would have been unlikely (on cost grounds alone) to provide adequate *intensity* of policing within mine, plantation or factory compounds and their neighbourhoods, given that colonial or provincial administrators were tasked with at least breaking even on the costs of governance.

In effect, divesting concentrated or targeted policing duties (formally or informally) to the economic elites in whose interests they ruled was the logical solution to controlling large and unwilling work forces. Of course the concessionary regimes were accountable to political leaderships, but apart from the receipt of tax revenue the state required little more than workers and their social milieus being subdued and productive. Protecting their legal rights (insofar as these existed) had little to do with it, so that the 'rule of law' was undoubtedly systemically violated within private police regimes (Hill 2007). But this was generally the situation in the state-patrolled areas in any case. The important thing for the colonial state was order and cost, in that priority. It is not surprising then that Costa saw private policing not as an example of messiness and blurred lines between it and state policing, but as one of three clear and legitimate categories of policing (see Gonçalves and Cachado in this volume).

This is not to say that state and private categories were static or mutually exclusive. As Gonçalves and Cachado recount, for example, Macau abandoned private policing in 1861, and Portuguese territories gradually phased out concessionary policing (or at least gained greater control over it) through time and for a number of reasons. In particular, its 'excesses' became embarrassing for the imperial reputation once reformers had launched international campaigns exposing the horrors of forced or indentured labour schemes – such as the plight of Brazilian rubber collectors, or the virtual prisoners on cocoa and coffee plantations in São Tomé.[6] These, like their Angolan neighbours, were subject to the endemic discipline of the *palmatoria*, a 5-holed paddle, for minor offences, and whippings, 'beatings to the point of permanent injury', or worse for more serious issues (Figueiredo 1961: 96–97). Much of the violence was inflicted by indigenous police working for the companies, usually superintended at officer level by whites, and with hereditary or appointed chiefs in intermediary positions. In such circumstances, 'traditional' punishments, many of them falling well outside the letter of the law, were typical.

As non-concessionary colonial areas became more tranquil – or at least less tumultuous – in the 'settling down' which characterised significant parts of the globe by the early 20th century, state police resources could gradually replace private concessionary policing. But many of the authorities in Lusophone spheres

---

6 For a useful summary of the situation in São Tomé and Príncipe, see Shaw (1994: xvii–xix).

Comment: the Portuguese colonial   77

of influence continued to secure the services of chiefs to monitor and discipline their people through their policing retinues. Thus violence remained integral to the control techniques, including (and sometimes especially) in circumstances where white officers were involved in a supervisory capacity. Songs recorded in the Quelimane district of Mozambique show 'a bitter hatred of the state-appointed chiefs and headmen' and their police for rounding up of subjects for labour in places like the dreaded sisal plantations, for their brutal enforcement of oppressive laws and exactions, and for their sexual predations. Women forced into work might have their babies confiscated as ransom for harder work, as a song relating to policeman Muripata recounted; another policeman was nicknamed Blanket because he 'used to beat people all over' (Vail and White 1986: 200–209).

Legal slavery, with its attendant inflictions upon the body and the mind, continued into the 20th century in Portuguese Africa – with Angola, for example, being dubbed 'A Land of Slavery' – and many travellers reported extreme cruelty. Enforcement of the 'moral and legal obligation to work' (which lasted until 1961), however, meant that slave-type conditions continued in supposedly liberated areas and brutal control regimes were established in others (Nevinson 1925: 38–69, Newitt 1981: 107–109). In the so-called free plantations of Angola in 1905, Henry Nevinson reported that workers were kept in order, during more than 12 hours' labour from 5.30 in the morning, at the point of 8-foot sharpened staves: 'the difference between this system and slavery was only official; that is to say there was no difference'. Workers were watched over by armed patrolmen and their large mastiffs, and beaten with the *palmatoria* or flogged with the *chicotte* (hide whip), the universal tools of discipline in the territories (Nevinson 1925: 49–52, 65, 82–84). Elsewhere, for decade after decade, masses of people were forced to serve on public works and services of various types, including policing and soldiering, as well as to work for concessionary companies. This often took people far from their families, not necessarily with payment or means of return, and so resistance was inevitable – as was the violent response of the private police and, especially following violent mass resistance, the public forces.

In his chapter, Palacios Cerezales alludes to non-military layers of policing in Portugal which are as complex as the military policing mechanisms on which he focuses. These layers include, for example, municipal forces under locally based administrators to whom sheriffs from each parish reported. In turn, parish constables, obliged to provide policing service as a civic responsibility (as in premodern London), reported to the sheriffs. Newly independent Brazil continued a system inherited from the Portugal rulers, with civilian watchmen being hired by town councils and neighbourhood inspectors by local judges (Holloway 1993: 28, Boxer 1965). In early 20th century Porto, the Civil Police coexisted with the quasi-military Municipal and Customs Guards (see Palacios Cerezales). Rosemberg discusses Brazilian provincial forces at intermediary levels of political control; these operated in the spaces between local regimes and the high-police concerns of central government. Such references in our chapters, and more, provide a good starting point for further research into the complexities of policing in the Lusophone world.

78   Richard S. Hill

What we do know is that here, as elsewhere, the various and variegated police layers and levels operated far from exclusively of each other. Thus, for example, in Portugal 'civil policemen [would be] detached from the provincial capitals' (Palacios Cerezales in this volume, p. 47) to assist militarised policing in the countryside. In the rural areas, infantry remained in barracks ready for emergency or short-term deployment (such as to suppress riots or enforce tax collection), while cavalry squadrons routinely patrolled highways and mobile units travelled to wherever necessity took them. Such complementarism also occurred within forces. Here, while roles and types of policing could differ immensely, personnel engaged in disparate duties and functions would provide support for each other, sometimes routinely and often in emergencies. Complementary and overlapping policing within countries, colonies and forces reflected synergies in the nature and methods of police coercion as well as tailoring to meet specific needs. It points, essentially, to universal policing needs, and methods that were deployed globally – if adapted autochthonously.

Generally, humble rank and file police and soldiers were at the coercive heart of colonialism and metropolitan social control, throughout entire empires (Etemad 2007: 39ff, Stapleton 2011, Hill 2007). In colonies, they were generally indigenous, although reporting (often) to white NCOs and (almost always) white commissioned officers. Such reporting lines were a *sine qua non* for policing regimes devolved, to a greater or lesser extent, to indigenous authorities in Portuguese spheres of influence. Here, chiefs-of-post or liaison administrators often operated their social control systems through *regedores* – chiefs and other *regulo*s – and lesser indigenous authorities such as village headmen. These functionaries would gain their officially recognised (and often remunerated) positions through a number of means, such as traditional succession, tribal election or (especially in areas where tribal ties had loosened, often with official encouragement) skills useful for the colonisers – former indigenous soldiers, policemen or officials who had 'civilised' themselves and given good service, for example (Barns 1928: 159, Bailey 1969: 139).

The duties of such an agent typically included: 'to maintain public order, to assist in the collection of taxes, to try and convince his people to fulfill their labour obligations, either through contracting their services or working on their own account, and to keep the Portuguese authorities apprised of village happenings.' They could not conduct such duties without the services of their policemen. In the formal empire, official policing authority, perhaps more directly than in other empires, extended 'directly from the Overseas Ministry to the individual African in the hinterland village'. The indigenous authorities at village level were often specifically designated policemen, or were public officials tasked in part with policing duties, including liaising with the Portuguese police and other authorities (Duffy 1959: 287–288).

More broadly, as we have noted, in effect all non-indigenes within a colony acted as police personnel, including wealthy European tourists whose justifications for, say, beating villagers at will were legion: the 'negro is absolutely heartless' to animals, and so 'I beat them in my horror and anger' (Statham 1922: 212–213). When a travelling party's stores were pilfered in Angola in 1925, the leader decided that the 'raw savages' needed to gain 'a wholesome respect' for whites: 'it was very necessary, alone in that country many days from any other white man, that no native should think that he could dare to steal with impunity.' In a crude judging process, he detained a suspect but deemed him innocent the next morning because the man had returned when ordered to go and collect firewood. A local tribesman and his 'half-bushman satellite' were then taken on as 'C.I.D. policemen' to track down the stolen goods, and two alleged offenders were identified. Once local headmen had been induced to bring them in, a makeshift 'court' found them guilty. After a humiliating punishment, they were 'whipped out of camp by my own natives, not without a few hearty kicks added by my own boots' (Wienholt 1939: 38–42). This was a typical episode of empire, although the punishment was untypically mild for a colony.

Civilising mission

Like other metropoles, Portugal claimed to be subjugating indigenes for their own good, to turn them into civilised beings, to assist them on the stadial ladder to modernity. This was ideally achieved via suasion, albeit such processes were infused with repressive intent (Jeronimo 2015b). Colonial Minister F Vieira Machado declared in 1943 that '[i]t is necessary to inspire in the black the idea of work and of abandoning his laziness and his depravity if we want to exercise a colonising action to protect him' (Duffy 1959: 318). The colonial ideal was for indigenes to gain so much 'respect' for the colonisers that they automatically acted (and eventually thought) in accord with the metropolitan requirements and worldview, a respect initially extracted by inducing fear. This was often euphemised: 'we Portuguese regard the native as a child and like good parents we have to spank them from time to time', a senior Angolan official told James Duffy when he was collecting material for his influential book *Portuguese Africa* (Duffy 1959: 304).

But in reality, the modes of control were heavily coercive – the indigene would be *made* to civilise. In the most recent scholarly study of the Lusophone colonial civilising mission, Miguel Bandeira Jeronimo frames his assessment in terms of Henry Rowling's comments on the Portuguese endeavour: 'Theoretically, nothing can be better . . . Practically, nothing can be worse or more humiliating' (Jeronimo 2015a: 1). The enterprise may have involved altruism, but its major motivation was that of social control: colonial populations behaving and working as Europeans were expected to, leaving behind ways of life and labour which impeded Western order and profit order and opting for self policing within Western parameters. In the effort to procure such results from vast populations, as we have noted, coercive social control needed to continue, up to and including extreme violence when necessary, throughout the colonial period.

In Portuguese Africa the police in particular, and whites in general, wielded the *chicotte* and *palmatoria* profligately on indigenous bodies. The reason might be something like insubordination to an employer, or there might be no reason at all – an exemplary lesson in power relations. Of course, the degree and type of

80   *Richard S. Hill*

violence waxed and waned, and could defy international tends. Thus Salazar's New State added 'a police-state efficiency to an informal apparatus of terror' at a time when many other nations and colonies were ameliorating state violence in line with a general social quietening (Duffy 1959: 304).

But matters of state coercion and consent were always complex, with carrot and stick measures often intertwined. Thus the New State also strengthened the ideology of enlightened assimilation, seeking to 'civilise' through ideological persuasion. Metropolitan peasants and colonial indigenes alike were being pacified and cajoled at the same time in the state quest to bring them to specific types of order. They would (or should) *want* to become better people, casting off (among other things) the 'inborn dread of any compulsory, steady bodily exertion' that indigenes were supposed to have (Mecklenburg 1910: 165–167)[7] or abandoning the rural customs of the Portuguese countryside which so interfered with the desired state of order and rhythms of work. While suasion and coercion often coexisted, in the final analysis fear-based discipline had first to beat the 'primitive savagery' out of subjects before the various ideological apparatuses of state (which generally included policemen) could fully begin to reprogramme them into appropriate ways of doing, being, and working.[8]

On the surface, Portugal's 'civilising mission' in the colonies differed little from the claims of other Western imperial nations, but Lisbon made a particularly strident case for its approach to indigeneity being uninfected by racial prejudice. This 'mystique of Lusitanian identity' supposedly operated in two ways. Firstly, tolerance for indigeneity and its customs were said to prevail during the entwined processes of coercing and coaxing 'primitive' populations towards civilisation: 'understanding the African and exploiting him [were] often one and the same thing' (Duffy 1959: 157, 312).

However, the toleration extended only so far, even at the beginning of the processes. Only those African customs which were useful, harmless or ineradicable for the time being were allowed to survive without harassment. The goal remained, inexorably, that of the 'Portugalisation' of colonial life – the Lusophone equivalent of what has been termed cultural genocide (Hastings 1974: 111). Even where the official decrees showed some enlightened tolerance, they were often ignored in practice – if not necessarily by the police, certainly by the wealthy and powerful. One weighing up of difference between theory and practice in the colonies aptly highlights a 1913 indictment of 'Portuguese Slavery' (Harris 1913): 'Portugal may send a ship-load of regulations out of the Tagus every week and the planters will welcome them – as waste paper' (Newitt 1981: 102). Such qualified toleration of aspects of indigeneity was little different from that of other empires.

---

7 The alleged indigenous characteristics of laziness can be summed up in a typical heading, 'Indolence of Natives', in an early 20th century travel book (see Angier 1908: 103).

8 This process was the desired one in colonial territories, masquerading as humanitarianism; amidst the carnage of the late 19th century Congo Free State, a British apologist for the Belgian-run territory talked of the replacement of 'incessant savage inter-tribal warfare [by] a regime of peace [as in] the mother country': Boulger (1898: 256).

Secondly, and particularly in the concept of 'Lusotropicalism', Portugal claimed a special and uniquely non-racial 'civilising mission' in its tropics (Bender 1978). This was summed up in 1926 by Silva Cunho: 'We maintain for [indigenes] a juridical system consistent with the state of their faculties, their primitive mentality, their feelings, their way of life, but at the same time we continue to encourage them constantly, by all appropriate means, to raise their level of existence' (Duffy 1959: 293). Ultimately they would become Portuguese, even in colour as the result of miscegenation. In 1961, Portugal's' Foreign Minister Dr A. Franco Nogueira claimed before the United Nations that all peoples of the Portuguese Empire, including those of the *ultramar*, were of the same status, with colonies being the equivalents of home provinces (Bruce 1975: 54). The relative lack of a 'colour bar' in the Lusophone world has had some degree of academic support, as in Gilberto Freyre's work *The Portuguese and the Tropics*, published in the same year as the minister's plea for colonial legitimacy (Freyre 1961). In 1963 Charles Boxer, despite his growing disquiet with aspects of the Lusophone empire, canvassed formal removals of aspects of discrimination in Portugal's colonial history, even if caveating his discussion by noting that much social and legal prejudice – for example, in Brazil – had remained (Boxer 1963: 73, 117–126).

The official line, as delineated by Franco Nogueira and many others, argued that the assimilation project was working. In reality, by the time of his defence, meaningful progress towards assimilation had long been put on hold: for the imperatives of empire required focussing on low- or no-pay service to the interests of colony and metropole, rather than on education and general socio-economic improvement for the masses, whatever the official propaganda to the contrary. Lusophone indigenes remained, under the Native Statute/Estatuto dos Indigenas, wards of the administration – a condition convenient for exploiting African labour (Clarence-Smith 1985). By the beginning of the wars of liberation, fewer than 1% of *indigenos* had assimilated enough to be legally deemed *assimildos* (Bruce 1975: 58, Duffy 1959: 294).

The imperative to exploit the colonies through labour and other demands upon the people and their resources, then, meant that coercion and violence remained the foundational underpinning of the Portuguese Empire: indigenes remained heavily policed, by both the state and its franchisees, often under systems that paralleled or approximated those of slave regimes. As a 19th century Portuguese master said: 'if you keep slaves . . . you must degrade them by the whip . . . until, like dogs, they are the unhesitating servants of your will'. Late in that century a Portuguese soldier reported of his African experience: 'For the slightest fault [workers] were often cruelly punished by being beaten with hippopotamus-hide whip which cut their skin horribly. Very frequently one heard in the late hour of a warm mysterious African night piercing shrieks of pain' (Duffy 1959: 150, 154).

The systemic infliction of pain, on macro and micro level, sometimes exemplarily indiscriminate but more usually targeted, depended upon in-depth surveillance aimed at creating a situation in which '[t]here is hardly any place to escape from the Administration' – from the likes of the 'administrative policemen, dressed in khaki, [who] often came to bring [offenders] to the white *senhores chefes de posto*

82   *Richard S. Hill*

and *administradores* for disciplining (Figueiredo 1961: 97). Just as the British 'new police' had carried out the role of 'domestic missionaries' while penetrating the farthest corners of the land (Storch 1976), the 19th century São Paulo police sought to bring 'barbarous' ex-slaves into citizenly modes of seeing and doing by similar means (see the contribution from Rosemberg).

The preceding chapters invite us to ponder broad comparative issues of empire. Was the nature and composition of the civilising emissaries in Portuguese colonies different from other imperial spheres of influence? This might cogently be argued: the Lusophone emphasis on the civilising mission tended to *succeed* order-imposition by the military and by quasi-military police, for example, while elsewhere it was generally only when indigenes or peasants had been subjugated and subdued by main force that the process of winning 'the hearts and minds'[9] of the colonised, spearheaded by a rapidly demilitarising police, seriously began.

But as always there are complications in such sweeping assertions. In Portugal itself, as Palacios Cerezales recounts, despite the disapproval of social-control theoreticians, elite military officers continued to be tasked with ensuring their soldiers educated the rural poor as part of their policing routines. Through personnel and knowledge transfer, this 'civilising by soldiers' became complementary to 'civilising by policeman' in colony as well as metropole. When Portuguese soldiers went to the colonies, they took with them perspectives that saw peasants as children or savages in need of civilisation; it was an easy segue into viewing indigenes as peasants who were even more greatly lacking in ideas on how properly to behave and think – and work (see the contribution from Palacios Cerezales in this volume).

A late 19th century official report, which confirmed the need for forced labour, noted: 'The state, not only as a sovereign of semi-barbaric populations, but also as a depository of social authority, should have no scruples in *obliging* and, if necessary, *forcing* these rude Negroes in Africa, these ignorant Pariahs in Asia, these half savages from Oceania to work, to acquire through work the happiest means of existence, to civilise themselves through work' (Duffy 1959: 155). The requirement went beyond official labour. The traveller T. Alexander Barns noted in the 1920s that the policing of Angolan indigenes included regulations that 'all able-bodied males of between sixteen and forty-five are required to hire themselves out' to an employer; this required 'a certain amount of pressure' but it was 'absolutely necessary [in such] a semi-wild country' (Barns 1928: 176).

Winning hearts and minds, then, was to be done by rough-hewn metropolitan soldiers themselves born into the peasantry, *and* through the medium of the indigenes who numerically dominated colonial control (and who had imbued only the rudimentaries of 'civilisation' themselves), *and* by such formations as 'the little army of São Paulo' and hosts of other military policing units, large and small,

---

9   The Minister of the Overseas Provinces, Adriano Moreira, used such concepts in his vigorous defence of Portugal's plans for the colonies: Moreira (1962); see also the contribution from Palacios Cerezales to this volume.

throughout the world (see the contributions from Palacios Cerezales, and from Rosemberg). Amidst such complexities and complications, things might not be as one might expect. Thus Rosemberg argues that for some decades the Brazilian military police had gained the popular consent of the people – that martial ethos did not necessarily translate into oppression in the street, given that the police (however soldierly they might be) needed to get at least some support from the people to carry out their daily tasks. The partial autonomy that they managed to wrest from the dominant political and economic elites, even during the early 20th century working class upsurge which saw overtly politically-directed policing elsewhere (e.g. Hill 1995: 283ff, Thomas 2012), assisted their gaining of at least some degree of street-level and village-level support for their tasks (see the chapter from Rosemberg). Consent and coercion, then, are not necessarily binarised. The case studies of Brazil and Portugal which we have examined, together with the broader canvass of colonial policing from the 1870s, invite us to complexify these notions.

Professionalisation

Societal stabilisation in many a colony or metropole enabled demilitarisation of policing and facilitated its professionalisation. In the Lusophone world, however, professionalisation tended to develop within a militarised policing milieu. While modernisation of policing services in Portugal begun in the later 19th century went in tandem with developments in other metropolitan powers and settler colonies, then, it was arguably of discrete ilk. As Gonçalves and Cachado remind us, certain Lusophone colonies – essentially, those which could produce large profits – were prioritised for pacification, adding an extra coercive edge to the broad global trend towards professionalisation of policing.

Professionalisation would increase once pacification had been deemed successful in Mozambique by 1907 and in Angola a few years later (though in large parts of each it took longer). Administrative restructuring, including that of policing and governance systems, followed (Duffy 1959: 248–249). As our authors note, in less prioritised colonies such as Goa and Macau, professionalisation came much later and less comprehensively, while São Tomé did not gain separate detection services, a common characteristic of professionalisation, at any point. In Lorenzo Marques and other large colonial cities, urban-led police modernisation was assisted by an influx of police from Portugal late in the 19th century. The imperative to safeguard elite property and lives had led to the emergence of detection and mass surveillance capacities in Mozambique in the early 20th century. Here, as in the metropole and more important colonies, professionalisation and modernisation were spearheaded by civil policing developments in the cities, where patrolmen came to learn such things as the ability to use discretion in order to de-escalate problems; and, more broadly, to behave in such ways as to gain at least some degree of public trust. Certain major cities, such as Rio de Janeiro and Lisbon, were seen as policing models, from which the (interrelated) policing and civilising missions fanned out in efforts to better control the behaviour and

84   Richard S. Hill

'colonise' the minds of the masses in hinterland and, eventually, more remote rural areas.[10]

Even in Lusophone metropolitan and colonial-urban areas, however, the pace and extent of demilitarisation and professionalisation of policing should not be exaggerated; and the task of complexifying and de-binarising does not eliminate the usefulness of concepts clustered under the headings of 'coercion' and 'consent' respectively. São Paulo's police in the later 19th century not only remained militarised but were openly creatures of dominant ruling circles; if people benefited in the streets and in their homes from imposed order, this was only a by-product of the motivations for tighter social control. The official drive to 'civilise' the people, firmly ensconced by mid century, was seen as integral to economic progress and nation-building – and the profits and power of the wealthy and influential (Barman 1988: 235–242).

In Lisbon itself, for decades there was no professional training beyond that learned by new recruits out on patrol. As Palacios Cerezales notes, moreover, until 1937 policing handbooks were geared towards military personnel. Under New State institutional rationalisation, hopes of developing consent-based policing in the Portuguese centre and its peripheries had become all the more problematic. On the other hand, as we have seen from Rosemberg's São Paulo example, any neat equation between military policing and oppression needs to be interrogated case by case, with the means used and the ends attained placed under analytical scrutiny. Conversely, as a great deal of work on policing in other imperial jurisdictions indicates, one cannot necessarily equate civil policing with non-oppression. For now, what one can say of the Lusophone world, as our three cases studies emphasise, is that the processes of police modernisation and professionalisation were long-term, uneven in their development, and enormously complex.

Conclusion

It is scarcely an exaggeration to claim that the policing history of modern empires is one of the remaining academic frontiers whose exploration is in its early stages. Greater knowledge of policing within metropoles and their colonies, and more comparative work within and between empires, will help us better understand the imperial past and therefore the post-colonial present. The connections between the decision makers in the imperial capitals and the police patrolmen in the farthest corner of empire are far from imaginary. Institutions and personnel tasked with policing functions, often including the military, constituted the first line of defence of the imperial state at its centre, its periphery and the points in between.

Lusophone policing history involves issues familiar to historians of policing in other empires: the widespread use of poor or indigenous individuals to police the mass of the poor and indigenous, for example. There seem to be temporal,

---

10 For coverage of the points in this paragraph, see the contributions from Palacios Cerezales, and from Gonçalves and Cachado.

Comment: the Portuguese colonial   85

spatial and methodological divergences in Lusophone policing and that of other empires, however. The preceding three chapters suggest, for example, that overtly coercive policing lasted longer than in a number of other metropoles and their spheres of influence, especially in non-urban environments. In effect they point us to factors that need to be further explored for the purpose of comparativist scholarship.

To a greater extent than in other empires, for instance, Portuguese metropolitan policing may have been significantly influenced by that of the colonial periphery. The phenomena of both formal and extra-legal forced labour demands and the policing regimes (private and public) which enforced them, moreover, seems especially complex in Portuguese spheres of influence. On the other hand, there seem to be some universal policing tropes, including what colonisation meant for the colonised. These need to be explored not only in relation to the imperial period, but to what came before and what followed. How applicable to the masses of Lusophone Iberia, Asia, Africa and Latin America are the words reportedly spoken by Congolese subjects of the Belgians to the traveller Hermann Norden in the 1920s: 'What does it matter? The [previous oppressor] goes but the European comes. There is but a new oppressor.'? (Norden 1924: 63–64).

As Gonçalves and Cachado note, policing historians have a huge challenge ahead in examining both similarities and differences within the Lusophone world and between it and other imperial jurisdictions. In addressing some very big and under-studied questions – the vexed questions of imperial police professionalisation, the purpose and mechanisms of the civilising mission, and the interface between 'authoritarian' and 'military' (Rosemberg in this volume: 56) policing culture and consent-based policing and so on – Gonçalves and Cachado, Palacios Cerezales and Rosemberg have opened up significant lines of scholarly pursuit.

References

Angier, A.G. 1908. *The Far East Revisited*. London: Witherby and Co.
Bailey, N.A. 1969. Government and administration, in *Portuguese Africa: A Handbook*, edited by D.M. Abshire and M.A. Samuels. London: Pall Mall Press.
Barman, R.J. 1988. *Brazil: The Forging of a Nation 1798–1852*. Stanford: Stanford University Press.
Barns, T.A. 1928. *Angolan Sketches*. London: Methuen and Co.
Bender, G.J. 1978. *Angola Under the Portuguese: The Myth and the Reality*. London: Heinemann.
Boulger, D.C. 1898. *The Congo State, or the Growth of Civilisation in Central Africa*. London: W. Thacker and Co.
Boxer, C.R. 1963. *Race Relations in the Portuguese Colonial Empire 1415–1825*. Oxford: Oxford University Press.
Boxer, C.R. 1965. *Portuguese Society in the Tropics: The Municipal Councils of Goa, Macao, Bahia and Luanda, 1510–1800*. Madison: The University of Wisconsin Press.
Brodeur, J.-P. 2012. *The Policing Web*. Oxford: Oxford University Press.
Bruce, N. 1975. *Portugal: The Last Empire*. Newton Abbot and London: David Charles.
Cadbury, W.A. 1910. *Labour in Portuguese West Africa*. 2nd ed. London: Routledge.

86 Richard S. Hill

Chatterjee, P. 1993. *The Nation and Its Fragments: Colonial and Postcolonial Histories*. Princeton: Princeton University Press.

Clarence-Smith, G. 1985. *The Third Portuguese Empire 1825–1975: A Study in Economic Imperialism*. Manchester: Manchester University Press.

Curto, D.R. 2013. The debate on race relations in the Portuguese Empire and Charles R. Boxer's position. *E-Journal of Portuguese History* [Online], 11(1): 1–42. Available at: www.brown.edu/Departments/Portuguese_Brazilian_Studies/ejph/html/issue21/pdf/v11n1a01.pdf [accessed 7 August 2015].

Duffy, J. 1959. *Portuguese Africa*. Cambridge, MA: Harvard University Press.

Etemad, B. 2007. *Possessing the World: Taking the Measurements of Colonisation From the Eighteenth to the Twentieth Century*. New York: Berghahn Books.

Figueiredo, A. de 1961. *Portugal and Its Empire: The Truth*. London: Gollancz.

Freyre, G. 1961. *The Portuguese and the Tropics*. Lisbon: Grafica Santelmo.

Harris, J.H. 1913. *Portuguese Slavery: Britain's Dilemma*. London: Methuen and Co.

Hastings, A. 1974. *Wiriyamu*. London: Search Press.

Hill, R.S. 1995. *The Iron Hand in the Velvet Glove: The Modernisation of Policing in New Zealand, 1886–1917*. Wellington: The Dunmore Press.

Hill, R.S. 2007. 'The taming of wild man': Policing colonised peoples in the nineteenth and twentieth centuries, in *Empire, Identity and Control: Two Inaugural Lectures*, edited by R.S. Hill and S. Bandyopadhyay. Wellington: Treaty of Waitangi Research Unit.

Hill, R.S. 2015. Policing Ireland, policing colonies: The Irish constabulary 'model', in *Ireland in the World: Comparative, Transnational, and Personal Perspectives*, edited by A. McCarthy. New York and London: Routledge.

Holland, R.F. 1985. *European Decolonization 1918–1981: An Introductory Survey*. London: Macmillan.

Holloway, T.H. 1993. *Policing Rio de Janeiro: Repression and Resistance in a 19th-Century City*. Stanford: Stanford University Press.

Jeronimo, M B. 2015a. *The 'Civilising Mission' of Portuguese Colonialism, 1870–1930*. Basingstoke: Palgrave Macmillan.

Jeronimo, M.B. 2015b. Ordering Resistance: The Late Colonial State in the Portuguese Empire (1940–1975). Paper presented to the Practices of Order: Colonial and Imperial Projects Conference, University of Copenhagen, Denmark, 28–30 January, 2015.

Letcher, O. 1913. *The Bonds of Africa: Impressions of Travel and Sport From Cape Town to Cairo 1902–1912*. London: J. Long.

Mecklenburg, Duke O.F. 1910. *In the Heart of Africa*. London/New York/Toronto and Melbourne: Cassell and Co.

Moreira, A. 1962. *Portugal's Stand in Africa*. New York: University Publishers.

Nevinson, H.W. 1906. *A Modern Slavery*. London and New York: Harper and Brothers.

Nevinson, H.W. 1925. *More Changes More Chances*. London: Nisbet and Co.

Newitt, M. 1981. *Portugal in Africa: The Last Hundred Years*. London: Longman.

Norden, H. 1924. *Fresh Tracks in the Belgian Congo* London: H.F and G Witherby.

Nzula, A.T., Potekhin, I.I. and Zusmanovich, A.Z. 1933. *Forced Labour in Colonial Africa*. 1979 Edition translated by R Cohen. London: Zed Press.

Pélissier, R. 1977. *Les Guerres Grises; Résistance et Révoltes en Angola (1845–1941)*. Orgeval: Éditions Pélissier.

Pélissier, R. 1984. *Naissanace de Mozambique: Résistance et Révoltes Anticoloniales (1854–1918)* [2 vols]. Orgeval: Éditions Pélissier.

Pélissier, R. 1989. *Naissanace de la Guiné: Portugais et Africains en Senegambie (1841–1936)* Orgeval: Éditions Pélissier.

Pithouse, R. 2013. A hundred years after the 1913 land act [Online], *The Archival Platform*. Available at: www.archivalplatform.org/news/entry/a_hundred_years_/ [accessed: 25 June 2013].

Schmitt, K. 1922. *Political Theology. Four Chapters on the Concept of Sovereignty*. 2005 Edition translated by G. Schwab. Chicago: University of Chicago Press.

Shaw, C.S. 1994. *São Tomé and Príncipe: Vol 172, World Bibliographical Series*. Oxford: Clio Press.

Stapleton, T. 2011. *African Police and Soldiers in Colonial Zimbabwe, 1923–80*. Rochester, NY: University of Rochester Press.

Statham, J.C.B. 1922. *Through Angola: A Coming Colony*. Edinburgh and London: William Blackwood and Sons.

Storch, R. 1976. The policeman as domestic missionary: Urban discipline and popular culture in Northern England, 1850–1880. *Journal of Social History*, 9(4): 481–509.

Thomas, M. 2012. *Violence and Colonial Order: Police, Workers and Protest in the European Colonial Empires, 1918–1940*. Cambridge: Cambridge University Press.

Vail, L. and White, L. 1986. Forms of resistance: Songs and perceptions of power in colonial Mozambique. *Banditry, Rebellion and Social Protest in Africa*, edited by D. Crummey. London: James Currey.

Vandervort, B. 1998. *Wars of Imperial Conquest in Africa, 1830–1914*. London: UCL Press.

Wienholt, A. 1939. *In the Sand Forest: Lion-Hunting With the Maquengo Bushmen*. London: John Long.

Part Two

Policing at the end of Empire

4 PIDE's racial strategy in Angola (1957–1961)

Fernando Tavares Pimenta

Introduction

This paper deals with the role of the Portuguese political police, *PIDE* (*Polícia de Informação e Defesa do Estado*[1]) in repressing Angolan nationalism between 1957 and 1961. More precisely, it analyses the 'racial strategy' that PIDE used to weaken Angolan nationalist organisations that were initially characterised by their multiracial composition. This 'racial strategy' was aimed at dividing Angolan nationalists along racial lines by creating an atmosphere of suspicion and fear between blacks, mulattoes and whites. This divide to rule strategy (*divide et impera*) was used several times by the colonial political police, namely against the Angolan Liberation Nationalist Movement (MLNA) in Luanda (1959) and the Angolan United Front (FUA) in Benguela (1961).[2] The discussion that follows is divided into three parts. First, it discusses the highly racialised society created by Portuguese colonial rule in Angola under Salazar's dictatorship. Second, having established the colonial context it progresses to focus on the origins and key features of PIDE. Third, it explains the features of the repressive action undertaken by PIDE in Angola.

Racial segmentation in colonial Angola

In the 1950s Angola was part of a highly centralised and authoritarian imperial State, the *Estado Novo* ('New State'), 1926–1974, under the dictatorship of Salazar, which denied both Portuguese settlers and indigenous Africans any form of internal self government. In fact, from 1930 onwards, with the promulgation of

---

1 'International State Defence Police'. PIDE was responsible for political policing in Portugal and it was also the entity with primary responsibility for colonial policing in Angola after 1957.
2 Cleary, PIDE also repressed the activities of other national movements, such as MINA (Angolan National Independence Movement, 1960) and later MPLA (Angolan Liberation People's Movement, 1961). However, I have chosen to write on the MLNA and the FUA because these parties have had from the beginning a high number of white activists, which is an important specificity within the Angolan nationalism. The MPLA, although multiracial, only much later admitted the participation of whites in the nationalist struggle, preferring to maintain a primarily African militancy, ie, black and mulatto.

92 Fernando Tavares Pimenta

the Colonial Act (and subsequent legislation), Salazar concentrated all power in the hands of the Lisbon government. By centralising the administration, he completely excluded the white settlers from the decision-making process; and suppressed the white autonomist political activities in Angola (Colónias 1930). Salazar also enforced economic legislation that favoured metropolitan interests over settlers' interests. For example, white settlers were obliged to buy almost all the things that they needed from Portugal alone, whilst at the same time they were also obliged to sell their products to Portugal at low prices. Portuguese economic legislation also favoured the interests of foreign capital – American, Belgian, British, French and South African – which also exerted significant influence over the colony's economy. For example, the huge mineral resources of the colony – iron, diamonds and oil – were directly controlled by foreign capital without the participation of settler capital (Pimenta 2005a: 41–62).

Salazar's colonial dictatorship also practised a sort of racial discrimination against Angolan born whites, who were racially classified as Euro-Africans. Indeed, Angolan colonial society was permeated by heavy racial tensions and – contrary to official Lusotropicalist assumptions- racism was at the core of Portuguese colonialism in Angola (Castelo 1998). Racial discrimination legitimised the official demographic segmentation of Angolan population in three groups: whites, mulattoes and blacks. The former were divided into Europeans and Euro-Africans, whilst the latter divided into *assimilados* ('civilised') and *indígenas* ('uncivilised') (Angola 1947, Santos 1945: 41–42, Neto 1964: 241, Lemos 1969: 196, Pimenta 2006: 37–40). Until the abolition of the Indigenousness Status in 1961, only assimilados – never more than 1% of the entire black Angolan population – had the right to claim full Portuguese citizenship (Colónias 1926, Ultramar 1954, 1961). *Indígenas* were considered mere colonial subjects and could be recruited by the colonial authorities as forced labour (Colónias 1928, Moreira 1956). As such, Indigenousness Status was the legal instrument used by Portuguese colonialism to politically marginalise the majority of the black population whilst at the same time exploiting it economically. In turn, the *assimilados* constituted a small minority that was politically alienated from the rest of the colonised population and which was sometimes the victim of social contempt of both whites and mulattoes. This racial discrimination provoked resentment within the majority of the black population against the white community which was usually identified with Portuguese colonial rule. Thus, the racist policies practiced by the Portuguese colonial authorities contributed to the political division of Angolans along racial lines; creating a gap between blacks, mulattoes and whites.

Insofar as the white population was concerned, the colonial regime promoted racial prejudice against Angolan born whites, who like the mullatoes were considered second-class citizens. There is significant historical evidence of such discrimination against white Angolans. For example, Thomas Okuma, an American missionary in Angola during the 1950s, stated that:

Discrimination by the Portuguese against Angolan Europeans over a period of many years has made the ties to the mother country weaker for the Angolan

PIDE's racial strategy in Angola (1957–1961)   93

Europeans than for the new colonos or settlers from Portugal. Angolan Europeans resent the fact that metropolitans consider them second-class Portuguese. Prior to 1950 the bilhete de identidade (identity card) of Angolan Portuguese was not valid in the homeland. Restrictions on travel to Portugal applied to them as it did to non-Portuguese residents in Angola

(Okuma 1962: 59).

In 1961, the United Nations Sub-committee on Angola also remarked:

> It was stated that though the major line of distinction in social practices has been between the não-indígenas and the indígenas and in spite of the objectives of Government policy regarding a multi-racial society, in Angola race and place of birth had come to determine, in practice, many rights and privileges. It was said that in Angola there were in practice five categories of inhabitants. First the Portugal-born Portuguese; second, the Portuguese actually born in Angola; third in line was the mestiço (mulatto); next was the African assimilado; and finally, the great majority of the Africans.[3]

Simultaneously, probably as a reaction to Salazar's discriminatory policy, white settlers – especially the Angolan-born whites – developed a strong political attachment to Angola. This deep identification of settlers with Angola was underscored by the British Consul General of Luanda, J.C. Wardrop:

> It is not generally realised how deep are the roots of the European population in Angolan soil. Many were born here; many have come in the present generation with the intention of staying for good. You find them not only in the larger towns and plantations but dotted all over the map in innumerable tiny and remote villages. The majority are humble folk who could not afford to visit Portugal even if they wanted to. They belong here; they know no other home; to them Angola é nossa ('Angola is ours')! They have no parallel in any British colony that I know of. In our former West African possessions the British were administrators, soldiers or businessmen, the great majority of whom were based on, and retired to Britain. In Kenya and Rhodesia we have, it is true, settlers of longer standing. But in the main they are relatively well-to-do and still have their links with the home country. Only Algeria and South Africa are comparable in this respect with the Portuguese African Provinces.[4]

In this context, Salazar's authoritarian and racist government provoked both political and economic dissatisfaction with Portuguese colonial rule which contributed to

---

3 United Nations General Assembly, 16ª Session, Agenda Item 27 – *Report of the Sub-committee on the Situation in Angola* (22/11/1961).
4 PRO, FO: 371/161626 – *Internal Political Situation: Angola*, 1962 (J.C. Wardrop, British Consul General, Luanda, to British Embassy, Lisbon, 16/04/1962, p. 3).

94 Fernando Tavares Pimenta

the emergence of nationalist feelings amongst the white settler community. Euro-African whites felt that they too were victims of the Portuguese government's colonial policies, even feeling that they were now being colonised by Portugal, just like the black and mulatto populations before them (FUA 1963: 2). Consequently, the white settlers started to consider themselves as Angolan nationals rather than Portuguese expatriates and they began to reject metropolitan colonial rule and support the idea of Angolan independence (Santos 1945: 54, Dáskalos 2000, Carvalho 2001, Pimenta 2005a: 119–136, 2008).

After 1945, and especially during the 1950s, a small part of this new generation of Angolan born whites became engaged in anti-colonial politics, side by side with some mulattoes and Europeanised blacks. Almost all of them were left-wing intellectuals and some were in touch with the clandestine *Partido Comunista Português* (Portuguese Communist Party) and with other nationalists groups in other Portuguese colonies. Many of them were also members of cultural and academic associations that had been formed by Angolans both in the colony – *Sociedade Cultural de Angola* (the Angolan Cultural Society), *Associação dos Naturais de Angola* (the Angolan Natives Association) – and also in Portugal – *Casa dos Estudantes de Angola* (the Angolan Students' House), later *Casa dos Estudantes do Império* (the Empire Students' House). In the protected political environment of these associations, Angola's new white (and mulatto) generation collaborated for the first time with the Europeanised younger black generation, engaging through essays and literature characterised by notions of an Angolan national identity. They created the idea of *angolanidade* or in other words 'the idea that Angola had an individual cultural identity not only distinct and independent from the Portuguese one, but also free from any kind of racial, ethnic or religious prejudices' (Margarido 1980). Politically, they defended the independence of Angola under black majority rule, but with the political participation of the white minority.

PIDE

It was in this political context that PIDE established itself in Angola. However, it is important to first outline the origins and key features of PIDE. The Portuguese political police was created by Salazar in August 1933 under the original name of PVDE, *Polícia de Vigilância e de Defesa do Estado*.[5] It had two main sections: a) the Social and Political Defence Section, which was used to prevent and repress crimes of a political nature; and, b) the International Section, which was used to control the entrance of immigrants and refugees and to take care of counter-espionage and international espionage. In 1945, after the defeat of Fascism and Nazism in Europe, PVDE name was changed to PIDE.[6] However its power and repressive functions remained untouched. Indeed, PIDE remained as one of the cornerstones of the dictatorship until 1974. It had full powers to investigate,

---

5 'State Defence and Surveillance Police'.
6 In 1969 PIDE was named DGS – General Direction of Security.

detain and arrest anyone who was thought to be plotting against the State. Using a wide network of covert cells, which were spread throughout Portugal, PIDE infiltrated agents into almost every underground movement, including the Portuguese Communist Party, with the number of PIDE's agents growing from 400 in 1945 to 3000 in 1974 (Soares 1975, Ribeiro 1995). Furthermore, PIDE encouraged citizen informers – the so-called *bufos* (snitches) – to denounce suspicious activities, through the use of monetary and prestige incentives. This resulted in an extremely effective espionage service which was able to exert control over almost every aspect of Portuguese daily life. Thousands of Portuguese were arrested and tortured in PIDE's prisons, namely in Aljube, Forte de Caxias and Forte de Peniche. The political prisoners who were considered more dangerous by the regime were sent to the Concentration Camp of Tarrafal, in Cape Verde. There was a similar camp in the Desert of Moçâmedes, in Southern Angola. It was in the 1950s that PIDE extended its activities to the colonies, most especially to Angola and Mozambique (Raby 1988, Pimenta 2010: 71–72).

PIDE in Angola

PIDE's Delegation in Angola was formally created by the Portuguese government in 1954, but only became operative in 1957.[7] PIDE established its headquarters in Luanda, the colony's capital, where it opened two police stations, one at the airport and the other at the harbour. In 1961, at the beginning of the war of independence, PIDE established further police stations in the districts of Cabinda, Uíge, Huambo and Huíla. Between 1962 and 1966, PIDE extended this network of police stations to the remaining districts of the colony, also creating sub-delegations in the major towns, including Lobito. Under the command of São José Lopes, Luanda's delegation chief-inspector and then director, PIDE also came to perform an important intelligence service for the Portuguese army. Indeed, PIDE functioned as a sort of military intelligence, especially in the rural areas bordering Zaire and Zambia. Finally, PIDE also participated in the creation of elite military corps drawn from the black population, namely the *Flechas*. However, PIDE's military relations lie beyond the scope of this paper and will not be analysed here (Mateus 2004, Antunes 1995, Cann 1997). Rather, the discussion will focus on the repressive action undertaken by PIDE in Angola from 1957–1961.

Initially, PIDE maintained a low profile, emphasising the training of its first officers, who were recruited from the Public Security Police. It also began gathering information about the local political situation. Gradually PIDE created its own network of informants which allowed it to infiltrate the nationalists groups that were being formed in Luanda. Indeed, during the second half of the 1950s, some left-wing whites, mulattoes and blacks from Luanda organised themselves into several clandestine nationalist groups of Marxist inspiration, such as the *Partido Comunista Angolano* (PCA or Angolan Communist Party). In the

---

7 PRO, FO 371/125907, *Establishment of Police Forces From Portugal in Angola*, 1957.

96   *Fernando Tavares Pimenta*

beginning these groups were too small and politically unorganised to represent a true threat to the colonial State.[8] However, the Portuguese Presidential election of June 1958 favored the political articulation of some of these nationalist groups. In fact, the dictatorship did allow the opposition to present its own candidates, even if the electoral results were usually a fraud. During some months, Salazar even allowed a degree of political and press 'freedom' which permitted the opposition to express their point of views and grievances against the dictatorship. In Angola, many nationalists supported the campaign of General Humberto Delgado, the opposition candidate, who ran as an independent in an attempt to challenge the regime (Delgado et al. 1998, Madeira et al. 2007).[9] The electoral campaign thus provided them with the opportunity to present their criticisms of Portuguese colonialism, while also attempting to build a more structured political organisation.[10]

A group of white intellectuals tried then to create a multiracial nationalist movement under the leadership of Engineer Calazans Duarte, Professor Julieta Gandra and the Architect António Veloso. They were all left-wing and were also members of the Angolan Cultural Society. Initially they created a movement called the *Movimento de Libertação Nacional* (MLN or National Liberation Movement), which was formed only by whites. Shortly after, the MLN merged with the *Movimento de Libertação de Angola* (MLA or Angolan Liberation Movement), a group which was formed mostly by mulattoes. The new organisation was named the *Movimento de Libertação Nacional de Angola* (MLNA or Angolan National Liberation Movement) (Maugis 1962). Subsequently, other small nationalist groups that were mostly composed of mulattoes and blacks, also joined the MLNA thanks to the political mediation of Ilídio Machado who belonged to a well-known mulatto family from Luanda. In early 1959, the PCA, which was made-up mostly of young whites and mulattoes, also joined the MLNA (Pimenta 2006: 44–49).[11] Within the space of a few months, the MLNA had unified the majority of the nationalists groups from Luanda and started to make contact with other nationalist groups residing in other Angolan towns, namely Benguela, Lobito and Huambo.[12]

---

8 PRO, FO 371/125894, *Internal Political Situation in Angola*, 1957.

9 Admiral Américo Tomaz won the election in Portugal. However, the democratic opposition considered the electoral results a fraud. In this regard, Portuguese historiography has demonstrated the existence of fraud in several areas of the country. Nevertheless, Humberto Delgado actually won in the Benguela district, which was the second most important town of Angola, as well as in Lubango, a settler town in Southern Angola.

10 PRO, FO 371/131637, *Effect on Angola of Election Held in Portuguese Africa on 8 June 1958*, 1958.

11 AN/TT, Arquivo PIDE/DGS, Movimento de Libertação Nacional de Angola (MLNA), Processo 3474/59, 2968; AN/TT, Arquivo PIDE/DGS, Movimento de Libertação de Angola (MLA), Processo 3807/63, 3331; ANTT, Arquivo PIDE/DGS, Movimento de Independência Nacional Africana (MINA), Processo 863/61, 3078; AN/TT, Arquivo PIDE/DGS, Frente de Unidade Angola, Processo 515-Sr/61, 3059.

12 AN/TT, Arquivo PIDE/DGS, Movimento de Libertação Nacional de Angola (MNLA) – Processo 3474/59, 2968; AN/TT, Arquivo António Oliveira Salazar, Sociedade Cultural de

Racialised incarceration and divide to rule

PIDE recognised the political danger represented by the MLNA, in the sense that it could become a threat to the continuation of Portuguese colonial rule in Angola. Indeed, the MLNA could easily become the nucleus of a vast nationalist front involving whites, mulattoes and blacks under a single unified leadership. PIDE further understood that it was not enough to arrest the movement's members. Instead it was necessary to split whites, mulattoes and black nationalists along racial lines. Essentially, it would be easier to control Angolan nationalists if they were politically divided or, even better, in conflict with each other. Thus, PIDE devised a strategy to create an atmosphere of suspicion and tension between whites, mulattoes and blacks. This strategy consisted of importing the heavy racial tensions that permeated the colonial society into the nationalist movement, in order to destroy any chance of political collaboration between whites, mulattoes and blacks. In a certain sense this strategy was a logical one given the markedly racist character of Angolan colonial society. Racism was thus used as a weapon to detonate the Angolan nationalist movement. As such, PIDE defined a strategy of racial division through incarceration which had three main features and objectives: (i) incarceration as punishment; (ii) incarceration as containment of nationalist activity; and, (iii) incarceration as tactic to divide along racial lines.

This multi-dimensional strategy of imprisonment of nationalists was implemented for the first time by PIDE in 1959. Indeed, PIDE began making arrests of Angolan nationalists in Luanda in March 1959. There were three successive waves of arrests, which culminated in the elimination of MLNA as a political force in August 1959. The white leadership of the movement was arrested, as well as the majority of the younger generation of white and mulatto intellectuals from the Angolan Cultural Society, notably the writers Luandino Vieira and António Cardoso. A number of exponents of the Angolan intelligentsia were also arrested, including two famous mulatto writers: Mário António Fernandes de Oliveira and Aires de Almeida Santos. PIDE also detained some of the members of the most important native families in the capital, as well as several of the *assimilados* (Europeanised blacks). Altogether, PIDE arrested some two hundred people and almost completely destroyed the political structures being formed by Angolan nationalists in Luanda. Furthermore, PIDE, with the ambition of preventing any reorganisation of MLNA, deliberately introduced a racial dimension to the subsequent penal consequences. More specifically, PIDE used selective methods according to the prisoners' race. Normally, extreme violence was used against black nationalists from the lower classes. Many were beaten or subject to torture and some died whilst in prison. Mulattoes and middle class blacks on the other hand, whilst also beaten, were not subjected to torture. White prisoners were not subjected to any physical violence and were held in separate cells from the mulattoes and blacks.

Angola (SCA) – Processo 5551, 7397; PRO, FO 371/131635, *Internal Political Situation in Portuguese Africa*, 1958.

98   *Fernando Tavares Pimenta*

In a final act of racially differentiated treatment PIDE released the majority of the whites and the mulattoes but kept the majority of the blacks in prison. Those nationalists who remained prisoners were sentenced in the famous case known as the 'Case of the Fifty' (Medina 2003). Only seven whites were tried. The court sent almost all black and mulatto nationalists to the concentration camp of Tarrafal in Cape Verde, along with three Angolan-born whites. However, the court ordered the four other whites be deported to Portugal, from where they were released after having spent a period of time in prison.[13] From that moment onwards, white nationalists were treated with suspicion by blacks and mulattoes.[14] Clearly, this all had a remarkable effect on nationalist politics in the sense that PIDE's strategy ensured that they were determined by division along racial lines. More specifically, whites were excluded from some of the nationalist movements created by mulatto and black Angolans, this including the *Movimento Popular de Libertação de Angola* (MPLA) (Pacheco 1997, Tali 2001).[15]

The shantytown massacres

PIDE was also responsible for the explosion of racial tensions in Luanda during February 1961. These tensions occurred after attacks carried out by a group of black and mulatto nationalists on the colonial prisons in Luanda. The attacks had sought to liberate some nationalists who had been imprisoned in the previous years by PIDE, but their plan was unsuccessful and many of the attackers were actually killed by the prison guards with the Portuguese colonial police also suffering several casualties. Nevertheless, the attacks did serve to demonstrate that Portugal had lost control over the political situation in Angola and were a signal that Angolan nationalists no longer feared the Portuguese. Indeed, for the first time in many years, Angolans were fighting back against colonial rule and this had a tremendous effect on public opinion and on the Portuguese authorities. Furthermore, PIDE feared that the example of the attackers would encourage other nationalists or even lead to the formation of a well-organised political movement capable of unifying whites, mulattoes and blacks nationalists.

In this context, PIDE promoted a campaign of violence against the African population of Luanda's shantytowns, the aim of which was to dissuade nationalists from carrying out further attacks against the colonial rule. PIDE thought that the use of extreme violence against civilians would frighten nationalists and dissuade them from continuing their fight. As such, in the weeks that followed the attacks, PIDE encouraged the massacre of hundreds of blacks and mulattoes in Luanda's

---

13 Calazans Duarte, Julieta Gandra and António Veloso were deported to Portugal.
14 AN/TT, Arquivo PIDE/DGS, Delegação de Angola, MINA, MIA, MLA – P INF, Processo 11.20.C/4, 1841.
15 AN/TT, Arquivo PIDE/DGS, Movimento de Libertação Nacional de Angola (MLNA), Processo 3474/59, 2968; AN/TT, Arquivo PIDE/DGS, Delegação de Angola, MINA, MIA, MLA, P INF, Processo 11.20.C/4 1841; AN/TT, Arquivo PIDE/DGS, Frente de Unidade Angolana, Processo 515-Sr/61, 3059.

PIDE's racial strategy in Angola (1957–1961)   99

shantytowns by armed militias (Marcum 1969, Pélissier 1978).[16] The participation in the massacres of a number of white extremists under the command of PIDE officers fed the belief that the white community supported the colonial regime as a whole when in reality this was not the case. The majority of the white population opposed the massacres but lacked the power and the means to stop the repression. For example, the leaders of the settlers' economic and cultural associations demanded that the Portuguese Governor General put an end to the massacres. But their efforts proved ineffective and the massacres continued at least until April 1961. The massacres created a deep political rift between blacks and whites in Northern Angola, a situation that weakened the nationalist cause. From that moment onwards, any kind of political collaboration between white and black nationalists in Luanda become impossible.[17]

Combating the Angolan United Front (FUA)

PIDE used the same racial strategy in Central Angola against the *Frente de Unidade Angolana* (FUA or Angolan United Front), which was a nationalist movement founded by white and mulatto nationalists from Benguela. The FUA was led by a political commission, which consisted of liberal businessmen and intellectuals. Its President was Fernando Falcão, a second generation Angolan-born white, who was an important businessman, as well as the only elected member of Lobito city council. During the Portuguese Presidential elections of 1958, Fernando Falcão successfully led the political campaign of the opposition candidate in Central and Southern Angola. The elections had provided him with the opportunity to create a political network, under his leadership, that included some of the most influential businessmen and intellectuals from the white settler community (as well as some mulattoes). At the beginning of 1961, he used this political network to found FUA, which was rapidly established in several Angolan towns, including Benguela, Lobito, Huambo, Lubango and Moçâmedes.[18]

The FUA presented itself as a non-racial nationalist movement, open to all Angolans, but with special attention to the position of whites and mulattoes in Angola (FUA 1961).[19] In a certain way, it tried to represent an intermediate political position between the Portuguese colonial dictatorship and the armed opposition movements, namely the *União dos Povos de Angola* (UPA or Angolan People's Union) that had launched the war of independence in Northern Angola in March 1961. As such, the FUA condemned the use of violence and demanded

16 PRO, FO 371/155481, *UN Sub-Committee Report on Angola*, 1961.
17 AN/TT, AOS/CO/PC – 77, Pasta 225 – Situação política em Angola (1961).
18 AN/TT, AOS/CO/PC – 77, Pasta 70 (sbd.) – Criação em Angola da Frente de Unidade Angolana; AN/TT, Arquivo PIDE/DGS, Fernando Gonçalves Magalhães Falcão – Processo 841/47, 2600; AN/TT, Arquivo PIDE/DGS, Delegação de Angola, Fernando Gonçalves Magalhães Falcão – Processo 993, 1021 (1.º volume).
19 AN/TT, Arquivo PIDE/DGS, Sócrates Mendonça de Oliveira Dáskalos ou Onrani Amari – Processo 62, CI (2), 6954.

100   *Fernando Tavares Pimenta*

a peaceful resolution to the armed conflict. It also called for Angola's immediate political autonomy, which was to prepare the country for independence. This independence would signify recognition of the political participation of the mulatto and black population in the government of the country, but, at the same time, it would also assure the political rights and economic interests of whites in a future independent Angolan State. As such, the FUA was able to mobilise a substantial part of the white and the mulatto communities from Central and Southern Angola, as well as some blacks from the large Angolan ethno-linguistic group, the Ovimbundu. These Ovimbundu rejected both Portuguese colonial rule and the extreme violence of UPA; the latter having massacred many Ovimbundu workers in Northern Angola in March 1961. Because of this, a substantial number of Ovimbundu were open to an agreement with the FUA.[20]

Between February and June 1961, the FUA was able to take control of the local media, namely the newspaper *Jornal de Benguela* and the radio station, *Rádio Clube de Benguela*. In May 1961, it organised a demonstration of five thousand people in Benguela in favour of Angola's immediate political autonomy. The Portuguese Oversees Minister, Adriano Moreira, who was visiting Benguela, then received Fernando Falcão and some other members of the movement. The Minister promised to consider FUA's requests. Finally, FUA also made some contacts with the Brazilian government through a delegate of the Brazilian Embassy in Lisbon, who came to Benguela at the beginning of June 1961.[21]

It was clear to the Portuguese authorities that the FUA was becoming stronger every day. Although it was an unarmed political movement, FUA had become a threat to Portuguese colonial rule in Angola. Consequently, the colonial authorities decided to eliminate FUA. By the end of May 1961, a Portuguese military battalion was transferred to Benguela, where it took over control of the town's strategic positions. It was a measure of intimidation the aim of which was to prevent any attempt at rebellion by the FUA. On 4 June 1961, the Public Security Police, under the instructions of PIDE, launched a large-scale repressive operation, arresting the leaders of the FUA, including Fernando Falcão. In the following weeks, a substantial number of FUA's supporters were arrested in several other towns, namely Lobito, Huambo and Lubango. The prisoners were transferred to Luanda, were they were kept in prison under the custody of PIDE.[22] As in 1959, PIDE used the same racial strategy to divide the nationalist movement along racial lines. Whites, mulattoes and blacks were put in separate cells according to race. Blacks were beaten, while non-physical violence was used against the whites and the mulattoes. Furthermore, whites and mulattoes were released after some months

---

20 AN/TT, Arquivo PIDE/DGS, Frente Unida para a Libertação de Angola (FULA) – Processo 380/60, 2983.

21 AN/TT, AOS/CO/PC – 81, Pasta 1, 2.ª Subdivisão, Doc. 3 – Actividade política de Alberto Vasconcelos da Costa e Silva, 3.º Secretário da Embaixada do Brasil, durante a viagem a Angola (1961); AOS/CO/PC – 81, Pasta 1, 2.ª Subdivisão, Doc. 28 – Visita a Angola do Embaixador do Brasil em Portugal (1961).

22 AN/TT, Arquivo PIDE/DGS, Frente de Unidade Angolana (FUA) – Processo 515/61, 3059.

in prison, while the blacks were kept in jail without trial before later transfer to a concentration camp in the desert of Moçâmedes. Joahannes Sidolo, Paulino Cuanhama and some other black supporters of FUA disappeared after their arrest by the Portuguese police; it is most likely that they either died or were killed during their time in prison (Maugis 1962: 96–98).

As in 1959, PIDE's racial strategy destroyed any chance of collaboration between white, mulatto and black nationalists in Central Angola. The Ovimbundu became suspicious of the whites, who had been well treated by the police when the blacks had been victims of extreme violence. As a result, the Ovimbundu refused to collaborate with FUA, which tried to re-establish itself in Huambo in 1962. This 'new' FUA involved a significant number of mulattoes and settlers from Central Angola, including doctors, engineers, teachers, students, businessmen and railway workers. As such, FUA created several clandestine groups in the major towns and villages crossed by the Benguela Railway, especially Nova Lisboa (Huambo), Benguela and Lobito (as well as in Novo Redondo, in the Cuanza Sul district). FUA's supporters used the railway to disseminate their own propaganda and to extend their political activities to the interior of the colony.[23] However, without the political support of the Ovimbundu, the FUA did not have the strength to fight alone against Portuguese colonial rule. Thus, in May 1963 PIDE arrested the majority of the members of the FUA and the movement was crushed (Pimenta 2012: 177–198).[24]

Conclusion

In sum, PIDE's racial strategy was successful. PIDE managed to transport the racial tensions that existed within Angolan colonial society into its nascent nationalist movements. In other words, racism was used as a political weapon against Angolan nationalists. Thus, PIDE was able to prevent the formation of a unified multi-racial nationalist front and, as a consequence, to weaken the nationalist cause. Angolan nationalists remained divided along racial lines during the entire period of the independence war (1961–1974). In the long run, this division led to the political isolation of the white minority who never managed to present a political alternative to either the colonial regime or to the guerrilla's movements. This isolation of the white minority was one of the reasons for the weakness of those political movements founded by whites, including the FUA, whose aims were to unify the various nationalist tendencies and, at the same time, to ensure the participation of whites in the government of the country post-independence.

However, it should be noted that the failure of FUA was not solely induced by the repression of the colonial regime. Indeed, the hostility of African nationalists towards white nationalists was also decisive in weakening the FUA. In fact, even the

---

23 AN/TT, Arquivo PIDE/DGS, Movimento Afro-Brasileiro de Libertação de Angola (MABLA), Processo 435/61.
24 AN/TT, AOS/CO/UL – 30D, Pasta 5 – Diversos, actividade da FUA.

102 *Fernando Tavares Pimenta*

MPLA, who proclaimed the principle of multi-racialism, refused the admission of whites as militants during its First National Conference in December 1962 (MPLA 1962, Reis and Reis 1996).[25] Indeed, white Angolans were seen merely as Portuguese expatriates by the African guerrillas whose political vision of the Angolan nation did not include a white component. As such, the guerrillas did not accept the participation of whites in the independence war and, later, also denied whites the right to participate in the independence process in 1975. On the other hand, white nationalists, who had been heavily repressed by the colonial regime, especially by PIDE, did not have the political strength to present a viable alternative to the African guerrillas. In the final analysis, PIDE could not prevent the independence of Angola, but, paradoxically, it also made a decisive contribution to the defeat of white nationalism and its political exclusion from the decolonisation process in 1974/1975.

References

Archives

National archives/Torre do Tombo (AN/TT, Lisbon)

AN/TT, Arquivo PIDE/DGS, Movimento de Libertação Nacional de Angola (MNLA) – Processo 3474/59, 2968.

AN/TT, Arquivo PIDE/DGS, Sociedade Cultural de Angola (SCA) – Processo 5551, 7397.

AN/TT, Arquivo PIDE/DGS, Fernando Gonçalves Magalhães Falcão – Processo 841/47, 2600.

AN/TT, Arquivo PIDE/DGS, Delegação de Angola, Fernando Gonçalves Magalhães Falcão – Processo 993, 1021 (1.º volume).

AN/TT, Arquivo PIDE/DGS, Delegação de Angola, MINA, MIA, MLA – P INF, Processo 11.20.C/4, 1841

AN/TT, Arquivo PIDE/DGS, Sócrates Mendonça de Oliveira Dáskalos ou Onrani Amari – Processo 62, CI (2), 6954.

AN/TT, Arquivo PIDE/DGS, Frente Unida para a Libertação de Angola (FULA) – Processo 380/60, 2983.

AN/TT, Arquivo PIDE/DGS, Frente de Unidade Angolana (FUA) – Processo 515/61, 3059.

AN/TT, Arquivo PIDE/DGS, Movimento Afro-Brasileiro de Libertação de Angola (MABLA), Processo 435/61.

AN/TT, Arquivo António Oliveira Salazar, AOS/CO/PC – 77, Pasta 225 – Situação política em Angola (1961).

AN/TT, Arquivo António Oliveira Salazar, AOS/CO/PC – 77, Pasta 70 (sbd.) – Criação em Angola da Frente de Unidade Angolana.

AN/TT, Arquivo António Oliveira Salazar, AOS/CO/PC – 81, Pasta 1, 2.ª Subdivisão, Doc. 3 – Actividade política de Alberto Vasconcelos da Costa e Silva, 3.º Secretário da Embaixada do Brasil, durante a viagem a Angola (1961)

25 AN/TT, AOS/CO/UL – 30D, Pasta 3, Actividade do MPLA.

PIDE's racial strategy in Angola (1957–1961)   103

AN/TT, Arquivo António Oliveira Salazar AOS/CO/PC – 81, Pasta 1, 2.ª Subdivisão, Doc. 28 – Visita a Angola do Embaixador do Brasil em Portugal (1961).

AN/TT, Arquivo António Oliveira Salazar, AOS/CO/UL – 30D, Pasta 5 – Diversos, actividade da FUA.

AN/TT, Arquivo António Oliveira Salazar, AOS/CO/UL – 30D, Pasta 3, Actividade do MPLA.

Public Record Office (PRO, London)

PRO, FO 371/131635, *Internal Political Situation in Portuguese Africa*, 1958.

PRO, FO 371/131637, *Effect on Angola of Election Held in Portuguese Africa on 8 June 1958*, 1958.

PRO, FO 371/125894, *Internal Political Situation in Angola*, 1957.

PRO, FO 371/125907, *Establishment of Police Forces From Portugal in Angola*, 1957.

PRO, FO 371/155481, *UN Sub-Committee Report on Angola*, 1961.

PRO, FO: 371/161626, *Internal Political Situation: Angola*, 1962

United Nations General Assembly, 16ª Session, Agenda Item 27 – *Report of the Sub-committee on the Situation in Angola* (22/11/1961).

Bibliography

Angola, D.S.E.R.E.G.C. 1947. *Censo Geral da População 1940*. Luanda: Imprensa Nacional.

Antunes, J.F. 1995. *A Guerra de África, 1961–1975*. Lisboa: Círculo de Leitores.

Cann, J.P. 1997. *Counterinsurgency in Africa. The Portuguese Way of War, 1961–1974*. London: Greenwood Press.

Carvalho, A. 2001. *Angola. Anos de Esperança*. Coimbra: Minerva.

Castelo, C. 1998. *O Modo Português de Estar no Mundo. O Luso-tropicalismo e a Ideologia Colonial Portuguesa (1933–1961)*. Porto: Afrontamento.

Colónias, M. 1926. *Estatuto Político, Civil e Criminal dos Indígenas de Angola e Moçambique*. Decreto n.º 12.533, de 23 de Outubro de 1926.

Colónias, M. 1928. *Código do Trabalho dos Indígenas nas Colónias Portuguesas de África*. Decreto n.º 16.199, de 6 de Dezembro de 1928.

Colónias, M. 1930. *Acto Colonial*. Decreto n.º 18.570, de 8 de Julho de 1930.

Dáskalos, S. 2000. *Um Testemunho Para a História de Angola. Do Huambo ao Huambo*. Lisboa: Vega.

Delgado, I., Pacheco, C. and Faria, T. 1998. *Humberto Delgado. As Eleições de 58*. Lisboa: Vega.

FUA. April 1961. *À População de Angola* [Manifesto Político da FUA]. Benguela: FUA.

FUA. February 1963. A População Branca no Contexto Nacional. *Kovaso. Órgão da FUA*.

Lara, L. 1999. *Documentos e Comentários Para a História do MPLA Até Fevereiro de 1961*. Lisboa: Dom Quixote.

Lemos, A. 1969. *Nótulas Históricas*. Luanda: Fundo de Turismo e Publicidade de Angola.

Madeira, J., Pimentel, I.F. and Farinha, L. 2007. *Vítimas de Salazar – Estado Novo e Violência Política*. Lisboa: A Esfera dos Livros.

Manya, J. 2004. *Le Parti Communiste Portugais et la Question Coloniale, 1921–1974*. Bordeaux: Université Montesquieu-Bordeaux IV.

104 Fernando Tavares Pimenta

Marcum, J. 1969. *The Angolan Revolution. I: The Anatomy of an Explosion (1950–1962)*. Cambridge: MIT Press.

Margarido, A. 1980. *Estudos Sobre Literaturas das Nações Africanas de Língua Portuguesa*. Lisboa: A Regra do Jogo.

Mateus, D.C. 2004. *A PIDE/DGS na Guerra Colonial 1961–1974*. Lisboa: Terramar.

Maugis, M.T. 1962. Entretien Avec des Pied-Noirs Angolais. *Partisans*, n.º 7.

Medina, M.C. 2003. *Angola. Processos Políticos da Luta Pela Independência*. Luanda: Faculdade de Direito da Universidade Agostinho Neto.

Moreira, A. 1956. As Elites das Províncias Portuguesas de Indigenato: Guiné, Angola e Moçambique. *Garcia da Orta*, 4(2): 159–189.

MPLA. December 1962. *First National Conference of the Peoples's Movement for the Liberation of Angola (MPLA)*. s.l.: MPLA.

Neto, J.P. 1964. *Angola: Meio Século de Integração*. Lisboa: [s.p.].

Okuma, T. 1962. *Angola in Ferment: the Background and Prospects of Angolan Nationalism*. Boston: Beacon Press.

Pacheco, C. 1997. *MPLA: um Nascimento Polémico*. Lisboa: Vega.

Pélissier, R. 1978. *La Colonie du Minotaure. Nationalismes et Révoltes en Angola (1926–1961)*. Orgeval: Éditions Pélissier.

Pélissier, R. 1979. *Le Naufrage des Caravelles. Etudes sur la Fin de l'Empire Portugais (1961–1975)*. Orgeval: Editions Pélissier.

Pimenta, F.T. 2005a. *Brancos de Angola: Autonomismo e Nacionalismo, 1900–1961*. Coimbra: Minerva.

Pimenta, F.T. 2005b. Angola's Whites: Political behaviour and national identity. *The Portuguese Journal of Social Science*, 4(3): 169–193.

Pimenta, F.T. 2006. *Angola No Percurso de um Nacionalista. Conversas com Adolfo Maria*. Porto: Edições Afrontamento.

Pimenta, F.T. 2008. *Angola. Os Brancos e a Independência*. Porto: Edições Afrontamento.

Pimenta, F.T. 2010. *Portugal e o Século XX. Estado-Império e Descolonização (1890–1975)*. Porto: Edições Afrontamento.

Pimenta, F.T. 2012. Angola's Euro-African nationalism: The United Angolan Front, in *Sure Road? Nationalisms in Angola, Guinea-Bissau and Mozambique*, edited by E. Morier-Genoud. Leiden: Brill, 177–198.

Raby, D.L. 1988. *Resistência Antifascista em Portugal, 1941–1974*. Lisboa: Edições Salamandra.

Reis, M.C.C. and Reis, F.C. 1996. O MPLA e a crise de 1962–64 como representação; Alguns fragmentos, in *III Congresso Luso-Afro-Brasileiro de Ciências Sociais*. Lisboa: ICS.

Ribeiro, M.C.N. 1995. *A Polícia Política no Estado Novo 1926–1945*. Lisboa: Estampa.

Santos, A.C.V.T. 1945. *Angola. Coração do Império*. Lisboa: AGC.

Soares, F.L. 1975. *PIDE/DGS. Um Estado Dentro do Estado*. Lisboa: Portugalia.

Tali, J.M.M. 2001. *Dissidências e Poder de Estado. MPLA Perante si Próprio, 1962–1977*. Luanda: Editorial Nzila.

Ultramar, M. 1954. *Estatuto dos Indígenas Portugueses das Províncias da Guiné, Angola e Moçambique*. Decreto-lei n.º 39.666, de 20 de Maio de 1954.

Ultramar, M. 1961. *Revogação do decreto-lei n.º 39666, que promulga o Estatuto dos Indígenas Portugueses das Províncias da Guiné, Angola e Moçambique*. Decreto-lei n.º 43893, de 6 de Setembro de 1961.

5   Knowing 'Mozambican Islam'

The Confidential Questionnaire on Islam and colonial governance during the liberation war

Sandra Araújo[1]

Introduction

Previous research on the colonial governance of Islam discloses that the British, Dutch, French and Portuguese Empires devoted particular attention to the study, surveillance and control of Muslim populations (Robinson and Triaud 1997, Thomas 2008, Ferris 2009, Maussen and Bader 2011). Although there were diverse political approaches, and each occurred in different colonial and historical contexts, there is a degree of commonality in their strategies towards Muslims. The 'Orientalist' (Said 1978) approach to Islam upheld notions of European superiority and legitimised colonial rule. Its representations and concerns led to the production of similar discourses that focused on both real and imaginary political implications of the religious beliefs and practices of Muslims, conceiving them to be potentially subversive and a colonial security concern (Hallet 1976, Robinson and Triaud 1997, Harrison 2003, Luizard 2006, Simpson and Kresse 2007, Thomas 2008, Ferris 2009, Trumbull IV 2009). The transnational character of Muslim societies and indeed of Islam itself that had no regard for colonial boundaries deepened these anxieties (Maussen and Bader 2011: 14).

European colonial administrations placed a premium on data-collection and surveillance, albeit that there were usually problems in understanding the cultural and social dynamics of subject populations. Despite arising from different colonial and historical contexts, the insights that were garnered regarding Muslims were inevitably a reflection of those political strategies that targeted them (Thomas

---

1   PhD candidate CRIA/FCSH – UNL (*Centro em Rede de Investigação em Antropologia/Faculdade de Ciências Sociais e Humanas – Universidade Nova de Lisboa*). This research was initiated during the research project '*Muçulmanos sob Pressão: das microscopias locais às dinâmicas geopolíticas do sistema-mundo colonial e pós-colonial*' (PTDC/ANT/71673/2006), financed by FCT (*Fundação para a Ciência e Tecnologia*) under the supervision of Susana Trovão, Mário Machaqueiro and Gabriel Bastos, whom the author would like to thank the insights and guidance; and further developed with the support of FCT (*Fundação para a Ciência e Tecnologia*, SFRH/BD/70531/2010). The author would equally like to thank Conor O'Reilly for his comments and help editing this chapter and the valuable comments of the anonymous referees.

106 Sandra Araújo

2008, Grandhomme 2009, Trumbull IV 2009). It is generally the case that knowledge on Islam in colonial history remained flawed and for most of the time was confidential. It also took a wide range of forms, spanning from intelligence analysis to academic studies (Grandhomme 2009: 178–179, Ferris 2009: 57–58).

This pursuit of knowledge regarding Islam often had an impact upon the institutional apparatus of the colonial powers with the creation of departments, or sections within them, that were exclusively dedicated to the study and surveillance of Muslim groups (Harrison 2003, Robinson and Triaud 1997, Thomas 2008, Trumbull IV 2009, Laffan 2011). There were a number of agents and mediators who extended this web of colonial control through data collection. This broad spectrum of experts encompassed administrator-ethnographers, scholars, clerics and missionaries, as well as police and intelligence officers. Beyond violence and repression, European rulers also pursued policies that sought to anchor their authority within local societies through strategies of co-option. Whilst often claiming not to interfere with local customs, colonial authorities did engage in acts such as: establishing alliances; using divide to rule strategies; and, attempting to control religious education and Muslim transnational connections (Bader and Maussen 2011: 243–244).

In the discussion that follows, this chapter focuses upon one specific strategy of pursuing knowledge of Islam conducted by a Portuguese colonial agency. It centres on the *Serviços de Centralização e Coordenação de Informações de Moçambique* ('Mozambique Information Centralization and Coordination Services') – hereafter referred to by its acronym SCCIM – and explores the interplay between one of its knowledge devices, the *Confidential Questionnaire on Islam*, and Islamic colonial governance, during the liberation war (1964–1974). However, its significance, goals and outcomes were already highlighted by several researchers (Alpers 1999, Bonate 2007, Cahen 2000, Macagno 2006, Machaqueiro 2012, Vakil 2004, Vakil et al. 2011); so far the *Confidential Questionnaire on Islam* was not object of a detailed and systematic study.

The knowledge that was gathered through this data-collection instrument was hybrid and speaks to governance strategies of surveillance and control. It echoed the entanglement of intelligence with scientific procedures while also operating as a mode of authority through which 'human beings are made subjects' (Foucault 1982: 777–778). The fact that it was conducted by an administrative agency such as SCCIM also reinforces the close relationship that existed between 'intelligence gathering and the colonial state' (Thomas 2008: ix). Although knowledge and intelligence were not themselves powers, they did represent its manifestation. Intelligence was required in order to maintain political and social control. It was strategic knowledge, born from epistemic delirium, not necessarily being an objective, verifiable or accurate truth (Horn and Ogger 2003: 60, 63–64, 66). Even though these features were closely linked to the preservation of the colonial state, they have received minimal academic attention within the analysis of Portuguese colonialism.

The questionnaire records that comprise the SCCIM collection disclose both illusory and concrete information (Stoler 2009: 106). Examining the content and contexts of documentary production uncovers colonial analytical grids, categories, images and representations, which were strategic and fundamentally ambivalent;

Knowing 'Mozambican Islam' 107

i.e. they shed light on the duality and opposing perceptions and dimensions of discourses on Muslims (Bhabha 1994, Heald 1996: 92, Trovão 2012: 262, Roque and Wagner 2012: 11). The survey was influenced by 'Orientalist' assumptions, being the outcome of a particular 'will to know' (Foucault 2011) that stemmed from the colonizers' need for information (Bayly 1993: 19). It was also an instrument of governance that had the '. . . potential to generate actions, forge ontologies, and shape relations . . .' (Roque and Wagner 2012: 14), revealing an interaction between culture and policy-making (Jackson 2009: 3).

It is also important to note that these documents are the result of encounters within which Muslims had a potentially interactive role, providing information and also acting as an important interface for the production of strategic colonial knowledge (Bastos 2008: 80–94, Roque and Wagner 2012: 3). Nevertheless, these documents remain the outcome of epistemic violence and are a product of the unequal power-relations that characterised colonialism, where coercion and repression were ever-present. The information that was collected also reveals inconsistent data-collection procedures as well as serious linguistic obstacles as the information-gatherers were unprepared for the task and were largely dependent on translators as mediators; an element of the process that is beyond the scope of this study but which merits greater attention. However, revealing the frailties of the questionnaire and its responses still retains importance for those who wish to gain a better understanding of the colonial governance of Islam as it provides situated, circumstantial and contingent descriptions of these interactions (Bonate 2007: 26).

The case study presented in this chapter relies upon SCCIM records, secondary sources and interviews with Fernando Amaro Monteiro.[2] Adopting a qualitative approach, it sheds light on the design and implementation of SCCIM's *Confidential Questionnaire on Islam* as well as exploring its impact upon colonial politics. The chapter itself is divided into five parts: the first establishes the context of colonial governance of Islam in Mozambique; the second addresses SCCIM and its features as an administrative intelligence service; the third proceeds to analysis of the *Confidential Questionnaire on* Islam; the fourth examines its implementation; and, the fifth examines the outcomes of this instrument of colonial governance.

Colonial governance of Islam in Mozambique

The Islamic presence in Mozambique goes back to the 8th century (Bonate 2007: 7). Muslims were both a religious and an ethnic minority, albeit one with transnational links that have had an enduring influence in East Africa. During the colonial period, their number increased and by 1960 it was estimated at 1.2 million, roughly 18% of the Mozambican population (Morier-Genoud 2002: 123). However, to

---

2 Fernando Amaro Monteiro (1935-. . .) worked as a SCCIM analyst between July 1965 and August 1970. After that he continued to act unofficially, as a local government consultant regarding Islamic policy, until 1974. The trajectory of his colonial activities ensure that he is an interesting historical figure for academic attention and a long interview providing a detailed biographical account was published in 2011 (Vakil and Monteiro and Machaqueiro 2011).

108   Sandra Araújo

speak of a single Mozambican Muslim community is misleading. The Muslim population displayed significant diversity, consisting of an African majority and a minority of mixed-race descendants from earlier Indian immigrants, as well as Indians from (former) British and Portuguese India. *Sunni Muslims* were preponderant and Sufism was widespread, with *Sufi* brotherhoods becoming the leading religious organisational frame in the region from the 1930s (Bonate 2007: 180–181). There were also Muslims of *Deobandi* and *Wahhabi* revivalist persuasions, both *Sunni*, as well as a small *Shia* group: the *Ismailia* community (Monteiro 1972: 23, Alpers 1999: 167, Bonate 2007: 13, 181, Bader and Maussen 2011: 236).

Muslims appear in Portuguese colonial records mostly as the targets of surveillance and for several reasons, were enduringly perceived as a threat to colonial rule (Alpers 1999: 167, Cahen 2000: 585, Vakil 2004: 20). However, those policy measures that specifically focused upon them were, for much of the colonial period, erratic and unsystematic. They also occurred somewhat late within colonial history when compared with those deployed by the British, French and Dutch Empires (Bader and Maussen 2011: 233). Even still, the Portuguese initiatives for the governance of Mozambican Muslims were operationalised and mediated by a range of actors that included a small group of individuals from within the central and local administrators, the Catholic Church, and a plethora of informal and formal civil and military intelligence services, as well as being influenced by the agency of these colonial subjects.

In the 1930s and 1940s, there were few experts familiar with Islam. There was no tradition of Islamic studies and the institutional apparatus specifically dedicated to this task was, for most of the Portuguese colonial period, scarce or non-existent – as indeed was knowledge of Islam (Vakil 2003a: 271, 2004: 28, Macagno 2006: 90, 92–93). From the 1950s onwards, central and local authorities began to sponsor academic studies as well as missionary and intelligence activities in order to deepen their knowledge of colonial subjects; the study of Islamic communities was embedded within these efforts (Macagno 2006). It was during the liberation war, that the need for this information became even more acute. This stemmed from the fact that this was a counterinsurgency (Cann 2005); one in which most Africans were considered potential enemies (Souto 2007: 32).[3] Consequently, the study of, and the policies directed at, Muslims, arrived somewhat late in the Portuguese colonial project and were predominantly a reaction to conflict (Bonate 2007: 14, Machaqueiro 2012: 1099).

The Portuguese *Estado Novo* ('New State' 1933–1974) regime, a police state constituted by a dictatorial, nationalist and authoritarian core, developed a patriotic rhetoric against pernicious denationalising influences and threats to colonial rule (Rosas 1994). Within this context until the mid-1960s, Islam was largely regarded through a negative frame, as an expansionist and transnational religion, an anti-Portuguese and anti-Catholic force, the presence of which could become a menace to colonial rule. Furthermore, whilst formally secular, the Portuguese regime privileged its relationship with the Catholic Church (Cahen 2000: 551).

---

3   On counterinsurgency see Bruno Reis' chapter in this volume.

The Concordat and Missionary Accord (1940) and the Missionary Statute (1941) helped to establish a bond between Catholicism and nationality that was to play a significant role in the persistence of a 'crusade spirit' towards Islam (Vakil 2003a: 257). Consequently, Muslims were depicted as 'infidels' with a sinister influence over the animist natives (Macagno 2006: 89).

Portuguese colonial representations of Muslims were also embedded within wider racial discrimination towards Africans. Islam was perceived to be an 'Asian' importation (Arabic, Persian and Indian) that was nonetheless amenable to African mentalities, permeable and adaptable to their ways, as well as a potential path to social mobility and identity promotion. The Portuguese followed the French-West African 'Islam Noir' approach, distinguishing *black Islam* that was considered to be superficial, faulty, ignorant and syncretistic from *Arab/Asian/Indian Islam* that was considered to be genuine but more threatening (Alpers 1999: 165, Vakil 2004: 24, Bonate 2007: 9–11, Machaqueiro 2011: 41–42, 46). During the 1950s, the diffusion of socialist, anti-colonialist and pan-Islamist ideologies and sentiment increased longstanding Portuguese anxiety as regards its external enemies and their conspiracies to overthrow the colonial empire (Alexandre 2000: 181). Within this context, Islam was viewed as a political danger that provided Muslims with a transnational identity that had the potential to undermine Portuguese power and eventually to promote a counter-establishment. This was a fear that was acutely felt as regards Indian Muslims in Mozambique (Bastos 2008: 85).

Repression was one of the methods that the Portuguese authorities employed to deal with these concerns and several violent episodes occurred during the *Estado Novo*, notably between the 1930s and 1960s as well as following the outbreak of the liberation war in 1964. Indeed, between 1965 and 1968, the Portuguese colonial authorities, namely the civilian administrators and the political police, PIDE (*Polícia Internacional e de Defesa do Estado*), adopted a repressive approach, commonly known as the 'PIDE purges' that consisted of the identification, imprisonment and assassination of Muslims who were suspected of collaborating with FRELIMO (Alpers 1999: 175–176, Bonate 2007: 235, 240).[4] Even so during the colonial war, the *psy-ops* strategy that was followed by the Portuguese was wrapped in Luso-Tropicalist ideology (Castelo 1999), as well as being inspired by Second Vatican Council (1961–1965) ecumenism. From 1968 onwards this resulted in an official paradigm change regarding the discourse and relations between colonial authorities and Muslims. This *rapprochement* witnessed strategic realignment towards co-opting Muslim leaderships to restrict their support for FRELIMO as well as parallel objectives that sought to cut its connections with foreign Islamic centers. Mozambican Muslims were to become 'Portuguese Muslims' and '*allies*' against anti-colonial forces (Machaqueiro 2011: 53). Hence, the traditional bond between the Catholic religion and Portuguese nationality was strategically and officially broken (Cahen 2000: 552). However, this change was tainted with distrust and ambivalence as targeted repression, suspicion and negative

---

4 Frente de Libertação de Moçambique ('*Mozambican Liberation Front*'), created 25 July 1962.

110   *Sandra Araújo*

images persisted despite official colonial public representations on Islam becoming more positive (Cahen 2000, Vakil 2003b, 2004, Machaqueiro 2011).

The strategy that was adopted to cope with Muslims in the course of the war, although not fully accomplished or systematically implemented (Bonate 2007: 201–202), had four formal stages: (1) *detection*: data-collection about local cultural context, Muslim leaderships and their foreign connections; (2) *attraction*: propaganda acts that officially and symbolically portrayed respect towards Islam; (3) *commitment*: the persuasion of Muslim religious leaders to give their public support to the Portuguese; and, (4) *mobilisation*: the wider involvement of Muslim populations in the counter-subversive war against the liberation movements by harnessing the influence of their leaderships (Monteiro 1989b: 84–89). Furthermore, Muslims were also the targets of divide to rule strategies. The aim was to control Muslim transnational connections and to preserve the distinction between African and Asian Muslims, thereby restraining any empathy that could emerge from their common religious faith as well as preventing the development of an Asian Muslim leadership in Mozambique (Machaqueiro 2012: 1104). This strategy for the colonial governance of Islam was developed by SCCIM and empirical knowledge rested at its core. In the following sections the discussion progresses towards a more focused analysis of both SCCIM and its *Confidential Questionnaire on Islam*.

The Mozambique Information Centralization and Coordination Services (1961–1974)

Whilst it is beyond the scope of this chapter to provide a detailed account of the Information, Centralisation and Coordination Services, or SCCI, it is important to highlight some key details.[5] First, these administrative agencies were created on 29 June 1961, in both Angola and Mozambique.[6] These services were also established in Macau (December 1961) and in Guinea (1969).[7] Mozambique Information Centralization and Coordination Services, or SCCIM, shares some of the features of a 'high policing' organisation (Brodeur 1983, Marx 2014). Its actions were conducted on behalf of the political system with the ambition of maintaining

---

5 The SCCIM are addressed in detail in my ongoing PhD research and Araújo 2017: 137–158; and the following paper is currently being adapted for publication: 'The Mozambique Information, Centralisation and Coordination Services 'Eyes and Ears': Exploring Transnational Intelligence Exchanges and Informants Networks', presented at the *International Seminar On Transnational Connections in Southern Africa (1950–1990)*, convened at the University of Évora, 29 April 2014.

6 Decree no. 43761, DG, I, no. 1490, 29 June 1961, 767–768.

7 15 May 1965, *Secret Information no. 1240, Fialho Ponce, GNP, PT/AHD/MU/GM/GNP/ RNP/0566/02753, 7 fos.; 1969, Confidential, Normas para o funcionamento do SCCI da Guiné e para a actividade coordenada dos vários Serviços de Informações Militares e não Militar da Província (NISCCI), República Portuguesa, Província da Guiné, Serviço de Centralização e Coordenação de Informações da Guiné (SCCIG), ADN, F2, 2.ª Repartição, no. 4341, 3, 30 fos.;* see also Reis' chapter in this volume.

Knowing 'Mozambican Islam' 111

the *status quo* of the colonial order with little care for the interests of colonial subjects. This agency was under the jurisdiction of the general-governor and its assignment was to gather, study, coordinate and disseminate all information vis-à-vis colonial politics, administration and defense, in order to ensure the continuity of Portuguese colonial rule. Its methods, which were often swathed in secrecy, consisted of intelligence gathering and its analysis, achieved through a wide net of information suppliers.

From 1962 onwards, SCCIM served and reported both to the general-governors and also to the commanders of the armed forces.[8] Located in local administrations, its activities sought to extend over all Mozambican territory.[9] Although it especially focused on African populations, the entire Mozambican population were its target, regardless of race, colour or geographical origin.[10] It at once co-existed, collaborated and competed with other branches of civilian and military intelligence.[11]

Despite aiming to be a key-player during the conflict, namely to coordinate the intelligence policy in Mozambique, SCCIM's ambitions were not realised. The service was in fact, a secondary, local civilian actor in the Portuguese colonial intelligence apparatus as it did not have a direct role in military operations, maintaining order, law enforcement, imprisonment or mass repression. Although, it did concur with and advise upon the operationalisation of such strategies, it was essentially an administrative intelligence agency. Through a complex and entangled web of methods it focused upon the development of strategic intelligence on Mozambican populations in order to act as a political

---

8　Legislative Act no. 2205, BOM, I, no. 7, 21 February 1962, 225–226.

9　Decree no. 43761, DG, I, no. 1490, 29 June 1961, 767–768.

10　23 July 1962, Information no. 55/962, from A. Ferraz de Freitas, SCCIM Director, to Mozambique General Governor: SCCIM Instructions, ANTT/SCCIM no. 30, fo., 260–261.

11　It is important to note that SCCIM's intelligence activities took place within an extensive web of Portuguese intelligence actors. The dominant actor was the State Defense International Police (*'Polícia Internacional e de Defesa do Estado'*), commonly known as PIDE and created in 1945. In 1969 its designation was changed to General Security Direction (*'Direcção-Geral de Segurança'* – DGS). PIDE/DGS was in charge of intelligence gathering, political policing and repression during the *'Estado Novo'*, and from 1954 onwards it established colonial branches. However, the intelligence architecture also included: (i) in the Colonial/Overseas Office (*'Ministério das Colónias/do Ultramar'*), since 1936, the 4th Section (Political Affairs) of Colonial Office Political and Civilian Public Administration, General Direction (*'4.ª Repartição (Negócios Políticos da Direcção-Geral de Administração Política e Civil do Ministério das Colónias'*) and since 1959, the Political Affairs Cabinet (*'Gabinete dos Negócios Políticos'*); (ii) in the Foreign Office (*'Ministério dos Negócios Estrangeiros'*), the Political Affairs General Direction (*'Direcção Geral dos Negócios Políticos'*); (iii) since 1950, the National Defense General Bureau 2th Section (*'2.ª Repartição do Secretariado Geral da Defesa Nacional'*), had the Military Information Service (*'Serviço de Informações Militares'* – SIM); (iv) finally, in Mozambique it is important to add the non-state-agent intelligence activities led by Jorge Jardim (1919–1982) that had a private intelligence branch the Intervention and Information Special Services (*'Serviços Especiais de Informação e Intervenção'*), with its headquarters in Beira (Mozambique) (Antunes 1996: 21, 417, Mateus, 2004: 20, 377–378, Cardoso, 2004: 129, Souto, 2007: 112, Garcia 2004: 235, 237, 239).

112   Sandra Araújo

advisor to the Mozambican General Government as well as to provide intelligence to the military, the political police and the metropolitan Overseas Office (Garcia 2003: 239–240, Cardoso 2004: 138–139, Mateus 2004: 377–378, Cann 2005: 113–114, Souto 2007: 111–112). This branch of the colonial intelligence architecture sought to gauge future risks and disseminate the intelligence that it had accumulated to a range of actors. The specific type of colonial knowledge that it developed, secret intelligence and counterintelligence, generated strategic predictions that had the ambition of colonial governance at its core.

Consequently, SCCIM's creation and its activities must be framed within Portuguese counterinsurgency doctrine where empirical knowledge was required to achieve other objectives: to obtain operational and strategic information; to shape governance; and, to prevent and repress insurgency. Furthermore, from 1966 to 1969, the military established

> . . . a strategy in which low-intensity population-centric counterinsurgency and psychological warfare were preferred to more aggressive counter-guerrilla operations . . . particularly among the Macua, who were traditional enemies of the Maconde, the northernmost tribe and the one providing the backbone of the FRELIMO insurgency.
>
> (Reis and Oliveira 2012: 87).

Indeed, Northern Mozambique was severely affected by the war and was also where the majority of African Muslims were located. Although, according to Liazzat Bonate '[. . .] it is difficult to apply to the northern Mozambican context the concept of 'ethnicity' in a sense of a 'homogeneous cultural unit, geographically and socially isolated from other such groups' [. . .]' (Bonate 2007: 2). The Makua were the largest linguistic group in the colony – spreading through the Cabo Delgado, Mozambique, Nyasa and Zambezi districts – also sharing a common religious identity, as most of the Makua were Muslims (Bonate 2007: 113–114, Cahen 2013: 284). Living in the region of the Mueda Plateau in Cabo Delgado district, the Makonde were fewer in numbers. They shared a common language, resisted the Swahili in the 19th century and were under the influence of the Dutch Catholic Church (Bonate 2007: 2, Cahen 2013: 284). At this light it is clear how knowledge was instrumental to win Muslim *hearts and minds* became especially important during the war. Additionally, the implementation of the *Confidential Questionnaire on Islam* (1966–1968) – the SCCIM 'detection' phase – and the 'PIDE Purges' (1965–1968), occurred almost simultaneously. According to Amaro Monteiro, the repressive operations of PIDE ended up preparing the ground for the co-option policy that was to follow.[12]

In reality, SCCIM developed several wide ranging studies and knowledge devices that shared the common goal of seeking to know the populations and the enemy within as well as to assess their influence over African natives and the presence of any foreign connections. The following table presents the surveys that were conducted by SCCIM.

---

12 21 June 2013, interview with Fernando Amaro Monteiro.

Knowing 'Mozambican Islam' 113

Table 5.1 SCCIM Surveys[13]

Date	Designation
23/05/1963	Index of Witchdoctors (*'Relação de Feiticeiros'*)
1964	Questionnaire Situation Study (*'Estudo da Situação'*), Traditional African Authorities (*'Regedores'*)
18/12/1965	Questionnaire on Anglican Churches and Missions (*'Questionário Missões Protestantes'*)
19/02/1966	Confidential Questionnaire on Islam (*'Questionário Confidencial Islamismo'*)
24/02/1966	Questionnaire on the Elements of Catholic Missions (*'Questionário Elementos sobre Missões Católicas'*)

This is not an exhaustive list and only presents those SCCIM studies that possessed certain common attributes; essentially, their implementation scope covered the whole Mozambique territory, they were conducted on SCCIM's own initiative and supervised by staff officially working in its service. Exception made to the Index of Witchdoctors, which had a very incipient structure, these were hybrid knowledge devices that echoed the cross-fertilisation and entanglement of scientific methodologies with political and religious intelligence-led data collection. However, scientific knowledge and its procedures were only to be used if they had operational value.[14] Whilst at first glance the type of data that was collected by SCCIM – encyclopedic, historic and ethnographic – had limited operational value, these studies retained a distinct high policing rationale in that the core ambition of strategic knowledge accumulation was all-encompassing and had a long-term focus as they sought to get a systemic sense of the big picture.

Although constructed upon biased and preconceived ideas, these surveys disclose SCCIM's epistemic aspirations. However, those studies often failed to live up to its ambitions. Amongst the governance aims for which SCCIM gathered operational and strategic data were: (i) the creation of a picture of the Mozambique population, understanding its dynamics, especially as regards internal divisions and transnational connections; (ii) the identification of native leaders to appraise their prestige and influence over the general population whether due to economic power, religious authority or familial connections with traditional authorities; (iii) the evaluation of the potential to use natives for political objectives; (iv) the assessment of the extent of their *contamination* by liberation movements and the degree of animosity towards Portuguese rule in order to prevent insurgency and act repressively if required; and, (v) the detection of any *subversive symbiosis* that could connect traditional authorities and native/religious leaders

13 Table 6.1 compiled with data that from ANTT/SCCIM no. 1447, fo. 8; ANTT/SCCIM no. 2, fos. 23–25; ANTT/SCCIM no. 140, fo. 17; ANTT/SCCIM no. 139, fo. 135; ANTT/SCCIM no. 408, 12–21; 831.

14 7 July 1965, Letter from Renato Marques Pinto, SCCIA Director, to A. Ferraz de Freitas, SCCIM Director, ANTT/SCCIM no. 32, fo. 2.

114   Sandra Araújo

with liberation movements.[15] Consequently, the study and surveillance of Muslims fits into a broader pattern of colonial governance and the ambition to *know* the whole population and identify the enemy within.

SCCIM had a degree of influence within the colonial political decision-making process. Through operations that included intelligence gathering, the use of informers, hybrid studies, other reports and assessments, it developed strategic knowledge about the colonial subjects. This knowledge was both concrete and imagined, ultimately shaping an empire of predictions. Nevertheless, its activities and political strategies did not result in a finished or comprehensive achievement. Its actions were flawed and the outcomes were diminished by the disturbances of war, insufficient time and staff resources to complete the work, a lack of coordination, overlapping responsibilities and disputes between the various intelligence agencies operating in Mozambique which increasingly led to turf wars.

Knowing 'Mozambican Islam': the *Confidential Questionnaire*

Turning the discussion towards the *Confidential Questionnaire*, the SCCIM analyst who developed it, Fernando Amaro Monteiro, was to follow a route that had previously been established by two SCCIM operatives: Afonso Ferraz de Freitas,[16] the SCCIM director (1962–1966)[17] and his brother Romeu Ferraz de Freitas, who was a SCCIM analyst, since 1962 (Freitas 1965: 184–185).[18] Although the support of the Mozambique General Government was at first reluctant, the Overseas Office sustained the initiative (Monteiro 1989a: 79–80, Machaqueiro 2011: 52). During November and December, 1965, Monteiro designed the *Confidential Questionnaire on Islam*, that was sent to the District Governors on 19 February 1966 and then disseminated to all Mozambican *Administrações de Concelho, Circunscrições e de Posto* ('County, Circumscription and Post Administrations') who were instructed to return the data as soon as possible. SCCIM also requested information on Islamic expansion, Muslim economic activities and the geographic locations of these groups.[19] During 1966–68, the local authorities – *Administradores de Posto* ('Administrative Post Commissioners') – conducted the data-collection, questioning 707 *Sunni* Muslim dignitaries. Although Muslims of

---

15 9 September 1966, SCCIM Secret Situation Report regarding Cabo Delgado District from 1 April–31 July 1966, no. 13, ANTT/SCCIM no. 410, fo. 306.

16 Information no. 56/962, 23 July 1962, Afonso Ivens-Ferraz de Freitas, SCCIM Chief, ANTT/SCCIM, no. 31, fo. 323.

17 BOM, II, no. 32, 10 August 1963, 1530. BOM, II, no. 5, 29 January 1966, 220.

18 BOM, II, no. 49, 10 December 1962, 2202.

19 Interview with Fernando Amaro Monteiro, 11 November 2009; 19 February 1966, Confidential Questionnaire and Notes – Islam in Mozambique, ANTT/SCCIM no. 408, fos. 12–21; Confidential Letter no. 346, 19 February 1966, from Eugénio Spranger, SCCIM Director Substitute, to Mozambique District Governors, Questionnaire Dissemination. ANTT/SCCIM no. 412, fo. 831.

Knowing 'Mozambican Islam' 115

Indian origin responded to the survey, the sample was largely composed of African Muslims, who were considered to be influential (Monteiro 1992: 132).

The survey excluded the *Ismaili*, who had been viewed as 'good elements' since the end of the 1940s with the colonial authorities expecting their 'disparition-assimilation' (Cahen 2000: 574, Bastos 2008: 92). This was also a small, cohesive group of Indian and Pakistani origins that did not mix with Africans, who were socially integrated with considerable economic resources due to their commercial activities (Monteiro 1972: 23) and who also did not seek a political role in the wider community. Additionally, as has previously been indicated, the *Sunni* Muslims were targeted for data-collection as they were the majority in Mozambique, whilst the *Ismaili* were too few in numbers for Portuguese strategic purposes although they were also targets of colonial surveillance during the war.[20]

Amongst the objectives of the questionnaire was the identification of African Muslim leaderships, to know about their hierarchies, their internal and foreign networks, their religious beliefs and practices as well as their permeability to Christian influence. The aim here was to explore the political and strategic potential of Muslim groups in the context of the war, to find pathways to stimulate connections rather than ruptures with the Portuguese rule and also to explore internal fractures within the Muslim populations and potentially increase the proximity between Islamic and Christian belief systems.[21] The questionnaire was also a double-edged power manifestation: with knowledge aimed to achieve co-option as well as to detect where to strike, in order to repress and prevent insurgency (Monteiro 1989b: 87).

The questionnaire was quite extensive with five sections, thirty questions and several sub-questions. The fifth section consisted of a general evaluation of the Muslim respondents made by the data-collectors. This was particularly important, since it provided, for example, information regarding perceptions of Muslims' loyalty to Portuguese power. It also reveals how limited the data-collectors' knowledge on Islam actually was (Bonate 2007: 26), exposing their prejudices, fears, anxieties and suspicions. It is also a precious tool through which to obtain a glimpse of the atmosphere amid Muslims, 'Animist' and Christians.

The set of questions discloses Monteiro's Orientalist approach as well as an uncommon degree of doctrinal knowledge and acquaintance with the internal dynamics of Islam in Mozambique. Through the questionnaire his aim was to get a detailed account of: respondent identity; familial dynamics; secular and religious education; language skills, occupation and income; *Sunni* Islam ritual-legal tradition, doctrine and ritual practices; religious and linguistic syncretism; respondents'

---

20 According to a 1968 military study, there were about 3500 Ismaili in Mozambique. SUPIN-TREP no. 23, Confidential, Mozambique Religious Panorama, ANTT/SCCIM, no. 105, fo. 186; Interview with Fernando Amaro Monteiro, 11 November 2009. 19 February 1966, Confidential Questionnaire and Notes – Islam in Mozambique, ANTT/SCCIM no. 408, fo. 12; Confidential Letter no. 1379, 11 August 1966, Eugénio Spranger, SCCIM Analyst, to Zambézia District Governor, Ismaili Community Control. ANTT/SCCIM, no. 412, fo. 820.

21 Interview with Fernando Amaro Monteiro, 3 February 2010.

116 *Sandra Araújo*

authority and prestige; religious geography, authority, hierarchies and networks within Mozambique and abroad; the location and physical description of Mosques and *Qur'an* schools; itinerant Muslim dignitaries; the possession, acquaintance and circulation of holy books and religious propaganda.[22]

Monteiro has since admitted that whilst the survey had the goal of 'interrogating individuals without frightening them', its length and structure made it difficult to carry out.[23] Its design betrays how interrogation strategies were used to detect contradictions and attempts to circumvent answering questions. Consequently, the order of the questions and their various formulations were far from innocent. This was evident in relation to subjects that included leaderships, hierarchies, networks, religious books and the circulation of individuals (both within Mozambique and abroad) which reflected both the anxieties of the Portuguese authorities as well as their desire to understand Mozambican Muslims' religious and geopolitical dynamics in addition to their transnational connections. The Portuguese intended to know, amongst other issues: Who was the leading Muslim dignitary in Mozambique? Who were the most important Muslim leaders and why? Would they be able to influence Muslim populations? Did Mozambican Muslims still acknowledge Zanzibar Sultan authority, or instead did they recognise other foreign Islamic centers? Did they want to be represented through a Mozambican Muslim committee?

Within the document sensitive questions on communal land and *Jihad* were also located next to ethnographic questions on doctrine and rituals to conceal the political rational of the survey. This was also a tactic to uncover internal fractures within Muslim populations, such as *Wahhabi* trends and religious syncretism regarding Christian and African religions. To provide two demonstrative examples of such attempts to extract information on issues that the Portuguese felt could be exploited by FRELIMO: the question about *Jihad* was positioned after a section on religious interdicts (Vakil and Monteiro and Machaqueiro 2011: 139); and, the question about communal land was located just before others covering funerary rituals, which despite its apparently neutral character was actually a way to identify *Wahhabi* trends.[24] In the questions regarding the belief and performance of magical rituals to obtain protection and immunisation against diseases and animal attacks, the subjacent goal was to know more about the possession of *Hirizi*s or *Irisses* – talismanic objects with Arabic writings that were traditionally used in the region for personal protection against animals and diseases, as well as in times of political unrest. These objects were considered to be items of political propaganda and indicators of subversive political activities, or at least a more passive form of resistance to colonialism (Bonate 2007: 77).[25] Mosques and *Qur'anic* schools were also perceived to have

---

22 19 February 1966, Confidential Questionnaire and Notes – Islam in Mozambique, ANTT/ SCCIM no. 408, fos. 19–21.

23 Interviews with Fernando Amaro Monteiro, 11 November 2009, 2 June 2010.

24 Interview with Fernando Amaro Monteiro, 2 June 2010.

25 Confidential Note no. 437/A/44, 7 December 1964, João Granjo Pires, Interim Administrator of the Information Commission of Mozambique District, to the SCCIM Director, *Distri-*

Knowing 'Mozambican Islam' 117

subversive potential: they could diffuse anti-Portuguese ideas without the control or awareness of the colonial authorities (Alpers 1999: 167) and were a de-nationalising influence because of their use of Arabic and Swahili languages and teachings. Finally, Muslim reading materials also provided information on their transnational networks as they originated from important Islamic cultural centers in East Africa (the Comoro Islands and Zanzibar) as well as Egypt, India and Pakistan (Macagno 2006: 125). These are some of the key features that were scrutinised through the survey.

The questionnaire implementation

In principle the data-collection process was to be conducted with objectivity and impartiality in order to obtain accurate and unbiased information.[26] However, as it was carried out during the war there was a significant impact upon the information gathering process; data-collection was delayed due to the disturbances of conflict such as military operations and population movements.[27] Administrative apathy, insufficient time and the lack of requisite skills to perform consistent data collection were also present and there were also other wide-ranging surveys going on at the same time.

Furthermore, the records of the questionnaire disclose inconsistent criterion in the data-collection process. Different local administrators with dissimilar standard patterns recorded the questionnaire responses, this disparity being particularly evident in the general assessment section. The answers varied from developed accounts to almost telegraphic registration and local administrators also often simply replicated Muslims answers and the general assessment in the numerous questionnaires that they conducted. Such discrepancies within the answers given appear, therefore, to be an outcome of the local administrators' own agency. Finally, whilst the majority of the local administrators were unaware of local languages and Arabic, most questionnaire respondents similarly had little aptitude with the Portuguese language; this inevitably impacted on the accuracy of the information gathered and required a third mediator, the translator (Macagno 2006: 95).

The survey was disseminated along with notes on Islamic doctrine and culture that betrayed the mediators' lack of relevant know-how to accomplish consistent data-collection.[28] This was highlighted in several letters sent to SCCIM by the mediators, where they emphasised that there were insufficient resources to conduct the survey, to understand the answers, and also insufficient time in which to perform it accurately.[29] In contrast, the Inhambane district governor informed SCCIM about his intention

---

buição de Irisses pelo Mualimo Cuereria (Abudo Carimo), ANTT/SCCIM no. 408, fo. 31.

26 19 February 1966, Confidential Questionnaire and Notes – Islam in Mozambique, ANTT/SCCIM no. 408, fo. 12.

27 11 November 1966, Communication, no. 529/A/20, from Fernando Bastos, Lago Circumscription at Niassa District, to SCCIM Director, ANTT/SCCIM, no. 408, fo. 465.

28 19 February 1966, Confidential Questionnaire and Notes – Islam in Mozambique, ANTT/SCCIM no. 408, fos. 12–21.

29 11 November 1966, Letter, from António Furtado, Bajone Administrative Post at Zambézia District, to SCCIM Director, ANTT/SCCIM, no. 415, fo. 117; 10 October 1966, Confidential

118 *Sandra Araújo*

to produce one *autêntica dissertação* ('genuine dissertation') on the subject.[30] The response was harsh and instructions were clear: his task was to gather and send the responses; the analysis was a SCCIM assignment, a confidential survey beyond the attributes of the administrator.[31]

The validity of the information gathered and its limitations were also related to the Portuguese colonial system's authoritarian and repressive core. Revealing this rationality, the questionnaire was often referred as an 'interrogation'. In fact, local administrators, who interacted with colonial subjects on a daily basis (Freitas 1957: 19), were the most visible faces of colonial rule and often acted in a coercive and repressive manner (Rita-Ferreira et al. 1964: 53). However, Monteiro denies that coercive practices were used in order to obtain information throughout the survey implementation. On the contrary, he has stated that the selection of Muslim dignitaries to respond to the questionnaire was often perceived by them as a mark of prestigious distinction. Although he has acknowledged that to be 'invited' to go to the administrative post headquarters was perceived as a humiliation by Muslims as well as a cause for apprehension; not least because the behavior of administrative post commissioners was often discretionary and could result in coercion, physical violence and imprisonment.[32]

In relation to the delays in data-collection, in May 1966, all District Governments were requested to urgently send their questionnaire responses.[33] The delay persisted and on 1 September 1966 the urgent remittance of the responses to the district governments was requested once again.[34] On 27 October 1966, most still had not been returned, especially those responses from the North Mozambican Districts – Mozambique, Niassa and Cabo Delgado – the areas where the majority of African Muslims were concentrated and also the areas that were most severely affected by the war.[35] Almost one year after the dissemination of the survey, on 9 February 1967, SCCIM were still pressing local authorities to return their questionnaire responses. SCCIM underscored the impact of this situation upon their capacity

---

Communication no. 757/SDI/1/3, from Salvador Peralta, Inhambane District Governor, to SCCIM Director, ANTT/SCCIM, no. 409, fos. 19–20.

30 10 October 1966, Confidential Communication no. 757/SDI/I/1/3, from José Peralta, Inhambane District Governor, to SCCIM Director. ANTT/SCCIM no. 409, fos. 19–20.

31 20 October 1966, Confidential Communication no. 1674, from Eugénio Spranger SCCIM Director Substitute, to Inhambane District Governor, ANTT/SCIM, no. 409, fo. 14.

32 Interview with Fernando Amaro Monteiro, 11 November 2009; November, 1968, Secret Report, Fernando Amaro Monteiro, ANTT/SCCIM no. 412, fos. 364–365.

33 10 May 1966, Confidential Communication no. 930, Eugénio Spranger, SCCIM Analyst, to Mozambique District Governors. ANTT/SCCIM no. 412, fo. 822.

34 1 September 1966, Confidential/Urgent Communication no. 1469, Eugénio Spranger, SCCIM Director Substitute, to Zambézia District Governor; 1 September 1966, Confidential/Urgent Communication no. 1470, Eugénio Spranger SCCIM Director Substitute, to Mozambique District Governors; 1 September 1966, Confidential/Urgent Communication no. 1471, Eugénio Spranger, SCCIM Director Substitute, to Mozambique District Governor, ANTT/SCCIM no. 412, fos. 819, 818, 817.

35 27 October 1966, Information no. 6/66, Eugénio Spranger, SCCIM Director Substitute, ANTT/SCCIM no. 412, fos. 813; 815.

Knowing 'Mozambican Islam' 119

to define a governance strategy as well as the fact that the information already gathered could lose its validity in light of the delays.[36] Indeed, in July 1968, according to Monteiro, some one year and seven months after the dissemination of the questionnaire, SCCIM still had not received all of the responses despite multiple insistences.[37]

According to Bonate, the questionnaire records '. . . contained historical and ethnographic material, and details on localized Islamic conceptions and practices . . .' (2007: 26). Whilst for Vakil, such documents disclose an insurmountable inability of the Portuguese colonial authorities to understand Islam (2004: 29–30). Alongside these two interpretations remains an even more critical one: that the survey reveals the Portuguese Administration's anxieties, fears, assumptions, information (and voids within it) as regards Islam generally and the Muslim population in Mozambique in particular. Overall it provides a picture of the Portuguese colonial administration and discloses its preconceived and long-lasting negative images and threat-centric perceptions regarding Muslims in Mozambique. The accuracy and value of the information, whilst sometimes uncertain, still impacted and shaped governance strategies and as such had a concrete outcome upon the lives of Mozambican Muslims.

In significant numbers, the local authorities reported to SCCIM that Muslims displayed scarce and superficial knowledge of Islamic doctrine, also stating that they were unable to properly answer the questionnaire.[38] The Head of the Mopeia Administrative Post informed SCCIM that there were no Muslims in that region, stating: '. . . *na área desta divisão administrativa não existem felizmente, quaisquer indivíduos nas condições indicadas.*' ('. . . in this administrative division, fortunately there do not exist, any individuals with the conditions indicated . . .'.[39] The use of the expression 'fortunately' is particularly noteworthy, with the administrator's relief reiterating both negative representations of Muslims as much as contentment with not having to fulfill this hard and time-consuming task. In Tete District, the administrator did not report the questionnaire answers, although he did make a general evaluation of the resident Muslims: '. . . *conhecendo-se apenas quatro indivíduos que se dizem crentes maometanos mas que parecem não levarem muito a sério a religião que professam.*' ('. . . there are only four individuals that describe themselves as Muslims, however it seems that they do not take their religion seriously').[40]

---

36 9 February 1967, Confidential Information no. 3/967, Fernando da Costa Freire, SCCIM Director, ANTT/SCCIM, no. 408, fo. 5–10.

37 26 July 1968, Fernando Amaro Monteiro, Report on Foreign Service, ANTT/SCCIM no. 412, fo. 442.

38 20 September 1966, Confidential Communication (copy), no. 68/A/10, Francisco Torrezão, Vila Macia Circumscription, to Gaza First Assistant of the Psychosocial Action Services in João Belo. This document was sent to the SCCIM of Gaza District. ANTT/SCCIM no. 411, fo. 22; 3 June 1966, Confidential Communication no. 270/E/7/3, Manuel Amaral, Zambézia District, to SCCIM director, ANTT/SCCIM no. 415, fos. 20–21.

39 14 April 1966, Confidential Communication no. 177/E/7/3, Álvaro Melo, Provincial Inspector in Mopeia, to SCCIM director, ANTT/SCCIM no. 415, fo. 25.

40 17 June 1966, Communication no. 19/A/21, António Santos Tete Circumscription Administrator Assistant, to Tete District Governor, ANTT/SCCIM, no. 416, fo. 2.

120   *Sandra Araújo*

As an illustration of the suspicion towards Muslims, many administrators stated that ignorance of Islamic doctrine was merely a method of concealing sinister Muslim intentions (Vakil 2004: 29) or a response to fear of the local authorities.[41] As a result of their responses, some were assessed as loyal to the Portuguese and others were considered willing to cooperate with them.[42] Others were recommended for surveillance or were, according to the authorities, already under investigation.[43] A vague Portuguese national identity was attributed to some Muslims, due to the denationalising influence of their religion.[44] Finally, others were simply referred to as opportunistic, viewing Islam as a path for social promotion.[45] The local administrators also provided a picture of the respondents' attitude. They informed that some 'behaved well', whilst others showed fear and distrust towards the survey.[46] However, the ambivalence regarding the representation of Muslims was there all along as it was stated 'one cannot have an excessive trust'.[47] Furthermore, revealing ambivalence and suspicion, the Metuge Post Administrator (at Cabo Delgado district) recorded:

> '*Não é por o interrogado jurar lealdade à soberania portuguesa e na presença das autoridades mostrar-se submisso que vamos julgá-lo leal. Os seus actos ocultos, ainda desconhecidos [. . .] falarão, quando se tornarem patentes.*' ('It is not because the respondent swears loyalty to the Portuguese power, and in the presence of the authorities show obedience or respect, that we will consider him loyal. His hidden actions, yet unknown . . . will speak, when they became known').[48]

It was not unlikely that Muslims were unaware of Arabic language, Islamic doctrine, ritual practices, hierarchies and leaderships. Although, if the colonial authorities were seeking to measure their reactions when questioned on sensitive issues, the ignorance displayed by Muslims could also be considered as a defensive strategy or epistemic resistance. In this sense, the knowledge that was displayed is an important finding but

---

41 *Shaykh* Momade Braímo, ANTT/SCCIM no. 418: 324–327.

42 *Shaykh* Selemane Carone, ANTT/SCCIM, no. 409, fo.217. *Mwalimu* Noormamade Agi Abdula, ANTT/SCCIM, no. 411, fo. 32.

43 *Shaykh* Cade Caisse, ANTT/SCCIM, no. 409, fo. 421. *Mwalimu* Buana Inusso, ANTT/ SCCIM no. 409, fo. 490–493. *Imam* Nordim Mussa, ANTT/SCCIM, no. 415, fo. 40, *Imam* Juma Abreu, ANTT/SCCIM, no. 415, fo. 52.

44 *Imam* Muadine Abdul Karimo; Assane Amad Esmail, Nova Lusitânia Village Mahommedian Comunity President, Búzi Council; *Mwalimu* Safurdine Issufo; *Mwalimu* Antumane Abdulmagide, ANTT/SCCIM, no. 409 fos. 35; 130; 138; 400.

45 *Shaykh* Muquela Rufino, *Shaykh* Ajuda Mupsal, *Shaykh* Ussen Cusupa, *Shaykh* Rodrigo Socoheia, *Shaykh* Daniel Muculelia, *Shaykh* Amade Imparoe; *Sajada* Mussagy Agy Sacugy and *Sajada* Issa Muhunze Aquital Ibraimo, ANTT/SCCIM no. 411, fos. 142; 143; 152; 166.

46 For example, the local administrators highlighted the *good behavior* of the *Imam* Canate Jaja (Ussene Jaja), *Imam* Ali Salimo, *Imam* Pedro Assane and *Imam* Mussa Essumaila, ANTT/ SCCIM, no. 411, fos. 70; 73; 76; 79; and the distrust of *Imam* Muadine Abdul Carimo regarding the survey, ANTT/SCCIM, no. 409, fo. 35.

47 *Mwalimu* Noormade Agi Abdula, ANTT/SCCIM no. 411, fo. 32.

48 Jahama Amed (Muhamade, Halifa)ANTT/SCCIM, no. 409, fo. 234.

silence is also a significant indicator as it mainly occurred when issues such as leaderships and transnational connections, *Jihad* and common property were raised.

During 1968 and 1969, in order to overcome the delays and deficiencies in the survey, Monteiro led three field missions to gather additional information, as well as to have individual conversations with Muslim leaders in their home environment. He acknowledged that it was necessary to meet with Muslim leaders without the interference of local administrative authorities in order to gain their confidence as he sought to circumvent the problems with the application of the questionnaire.[49] This was SCCIM's second phase of detection: (i) 6–23 November 1968, Mozambique and Cabo Delgado Districts; (b) 22 January–7 February 1969, Inhambane, Lourenço Marques, and Gaza Districts; (c) 10 July–2 August 1969, Niassa, Mozambique, Zambézia, Tete, and Manica and Sofala Districts.[50]

Remarks on the questionnaire outcomes

According to Monteiro the outcome of the questionnaire was successful as through the survey he got a glimpse of the ethnical differentiations and sensibilities within the Muslim population, their religious leadership's and communication networks. Furthermore, the survey disclosed the centrality of Sufi Brotherhoods in Northern Mozambique. Accordingly, he was able to confirm the three areas where the Muslim population was concentrated: (i) northern Mozambique Cabo Delgado, Nyasa and Mozambique districts (now, Nampula, Nyasa and Cabo Delgado), where *Sunni* Muslims followed the *Shafi'i* ritual-legal tradition under the authority of African dignitaries and with adherence to *Sufi* Brotherhoods; (ii) in the Zambezi district, where African Muslim dignitaries (*Shafi'i* ritual-legal tradition) coexisted with Asian and mixed-Asian Muslims (*Hanafi* ritual-legal tradition); and, (iii) the remaining areas, where Muslim notables were largely of Asian origin and followed the *Hanafi* ritual-legal tradition (Monteiro 1989a: 79–80, 82–83). The existence of twenty-one prominent Muslim dignitaries (ten African, nine mixed African-Arabic or African-Asian and two Asian) with transnational connections was also identified and corresponded to the following pattern: from the Zambezi to the South, through Lourenço Marques to Durban and Pakistan; in the remaining areas, through Mozambique Island to the Comoro Islands and Saudi Arabia (Monteiro 1972: 26, 1989a: 83–84).

From the 707 respondents interviewed, 92 openly recognised the authority of the Zanzibar Sultan and 176 made statements that allowed Monteiro to deduce that although they did not speak openly about the subject or misinterpreted the questions, they equally acknowledged this authority (from Cabo Delgado, Nyasa,

---

49 November, 1968, Secret Report, Fernando Amaro Monteiro, ANTT/SCCIM no. 412, fos. 363–364.

50 28 December 1968, Confidential Information no. 28/968, Fernando Amaro Monteiro, ANTT/SCCIM no. 412, fos. 332–333; November 1968, Secret Report, Fernando Amaro Monteiro, ANTT/SCCIM no. 412, fos. 363–371; 20 February 1969, Secret Report, Fernando Amaro Monteiro, ANTT/SCCIM no. 412, fos. 318–322; 9 August 1969, Secret Report, Fernando Amaro Monteiro, ANTT/SCCIM no. 412, fos. 153–166.

122   Sandra Araújo

Mozambique and Zambézia districts).[51] A changing pattern in Mozambican *Sunni* Muslims' transnational links was also identified. Following Zanzibar's independence from the British Empire (December 1963) and the Zanzibar Revolution (January 1964), the *Ibadi* Zanzibar Sultan, Sayyid Sir Jamshid bin Abdullah Al Said (1929-. . .), was deposed and exiled to the United Kingdom, losing his long-lasting influence and authority in Mozambique (Monteiro 1989a: 76–79).[52]

Although considered 'Catholic wishful thinking' by Alpers (1999: 173), Monteiro equally noticed a local Islamic cultural specificity: 60 African Muslims who, in contrast with the *Qur'an*, declared their belief in the Passion of the Christ and the Resurrection, as well as expressing devotion to the Virgin Mary with very heterodox versions of the Immaculate Conception (Monteiro 1972: 26–27). Indeed, the links between Islamic and Christian belief systems were to be exploited in several messages that the Mozambican General-Governor addressed to Muslims.[53]

The questionnaire provided the Portuguese Administration with information that was then strategically deployed to shape its governance strategy (Vakil 2004: 29). It is within this frame that the project of creating an *Ijma* (the Arabic word for consensus) was to be located – later referred to as the *Conselho de Notáveis* ('Council of the Notables') – which other than facilitating the translation of the *El-Bokhari Hadiths* into Portuguese never came to have a practical impact or influence.[54] This gathering of Islamic leaders occurred on the island of Mozambique between 7–15 August 1972.[55] In fact, according to Monteiro, the approval of the translation text of the *Hadiths* was the pretext used to engage the Muslims leaders in talks with the Portuguese authorities. It was a starting point in order to establish who exactly was in charge and what the power dynamics amongst these leaders were.[56] Additionally, the gathering served as a symbolical message of compromise with Muslim dignitaries by the Portuguese Administration that was to assist in framing Muslim identity as being under the control of the colonial authority during the war. This was to advance its integration into a *pluricontinental*, *multi-racial* and *multi-religious* Portuguese nation. This strategy, along with the failed attempt to promote, control and frame *Qur'anic* education (Monteiro

---

51 Secret Report, 12 September 1968, Fernando Amaro Monteiro, Metropolis Service Report, ANTT/SCCIM no. 412, fo. 412.

52 This is another branch of Islam (as with *Sunni* and *Shia*).

53 The messages were radio broadcasted on 17 December 1968 and 24 November 1969 (Baltazar Rebelo de Sousa), 1 December 1970 (Eduardo Arantes e Oliveira), and 12 March 1972 (Manuel Pimentel dos Santos) (Monteiro 1989b: 85, Cahen 2000: 575, Macagno 2006: 97).

54 A selection of texts about the actions and words of the prophet Muhammad, written by Abu Abdallah Mohammed Ben Ismail Ben Ibrahim El-Bokhari (b.810-d.870). In 1972, it was translated and published by Fernando Amaro Monteiro, in Mozambique, with the support of the General Government: *Tradições Muçulmanas. Adaptada da Tradução Francesa de G.H. Bousquet.*

55 Secret Information no. 11/71, 29 May 1971, Fernando Amaro Monteiro, Lourenço Marques University researcher, ANTT/SCCIM no. 412, fos. 121–127.

56 Secret Report, 9 August 1969, Fernando Amaro Monteiro, ANTT/SCCIM no. 412, fo. 154.

Knowing 'Mozambican Islam' 123

2004: 108–109), was expected to facilitate the dissemination of the Portuguese language amongst Muslims.[57]

Monteiro has argued that the failure of the Council of the Notables was attributable to the divisions and inadequacies of the Mozambican local government (Monteiro 1989a: 81) despite the fact that at that time *Sufi* Muslims opposed, contested and competed with the *Wahhabis* located in southern Mozambique. The containment of the *Wahhabis'* influence was a powerful driving force behind the leaders of the *Sufi* brotherhood's connection with the Portuguese authorities (Monteiro 2004: 110). Consequently, after this meeting, when Monteiro became aware of these tensions amongst the Muslims, he discouraged the installation of a Muslim Council of the Notables.[58] In essence, this demonstrates how up until this meeting, the Portuguese colonial authorities had been unaware of this significant fracture within the Muslim community and its impact upon their governance strategy.

Furthermore, on 12 December 1969, Monteiro identified, selected and proposed to the Mozambique General Government that the Muslim dignitaries would travel on a state sponsored pilgrimage to Mecca, which was planned to take place in 1970.[59] The participants were selected according to three main criteria:

> . . . *receptividade demonstrada aos contactos com eles efectuados em 1969, poder de accionamento que detêm e circunstância de nunca terem efectuado a peregrinação.* (. . . their demonstrated receptiveness to the 1969 contacts, their influence, and the fact that they had never made the pilgrimage.)[60]

Both Monteiro (1989b: 84–85, 2004: 109–110) and Bonate (2007: 14, 201, 240) agree that the ongoing colonial conflict generated an atmosphere that reinforced sentiments of suspicion and repression. Indeed, in northern Mozambique a significant number of Muslims were engaged with FRELIMO and adopted either passive or active attitudes of resistance towards the Portuguese. Albeit that from 1968 onwards, Muslim dignitaries became increasingly receptive to Portuguese co-option. The accommodation of Muslims was due to: the support granted by the Portuguese to the *Sufi* brotherhoods; the containment of the *Wahhabi* influence; the PIDE repression; and also, to the radical Marxist ideology adopted by FRELIMO which discouraged Muslim co-operation with the liberation movement (Bonate 2007: 240).

---

57 I would like to acknowledge Mário Machaqueiro who called my attention to the following document: 18 August 1973, Secret Information no. 564/73, Fernando Amaro Monteiro, AHD-MNE/ PT /MU/GM/GNP/RNP/0456/07178, fos. 1–4.

58 18 August 1973, Secret Information no. 564/73, Fernando Amaro Monteiro, AHD-MNE/ PT /MU/GM/GNP/RNP/0456/07178, fo. 3.

59 Secret Information no. 26/969, 12 December 1969, Fernando Amaro Monteiro, ANTT/ SCCIM n.º 412, fos. 93–97. 5 January 1970, Letter, Fernando da Costa Freire, SCCIM Director, to Armed Forces Chief Command, ANTT/SCCIM no. 412, fo. 43.

60 26 December 1969,Communication no. 865/5, Baltazar Rebelo de Sousa, Mozambique General-Governor, to the General Overseas Agent, ANTT/SCCIM no. 412, fos. 57–58.

124 *Sandra Araújo*

Conclusion

During the liberation war, the Portuguese colonial administration endeavoured to study, control and co-opt the *Islam Noir* in Mozambique. Empirical knowledge was at the heart of this strategic *rapprochement* towards African Muslims and information was required to both shape a governance strategy and also to prevent insurgency by all means necessary. However, the knowledge and political strategy that was adopted to cope with this religious minority was flawed, and came somewhat late in the colonial process. The *Confidential Questionnaire on Islam* and the SCCIM strategy, conducted by the Mozambican General Government with the support of the Overseas Office, did not result in a finished or comprehensive product. The ongoing conflict, bureaucratic apathy and poorly prepared data-collectors delayed the implementation of the questionnaire and resulted in inconsistent information-gathering, delayed political measures and the loss of strategic information.

In spite of these failings, the *Confidential Questionnaire on Islam* still remains a valuable manifestation of colonial governance, providing guidelines that were aimed at advancing political control and propaganda initiatives. Additionally, the questionnaire presents distinctive characteristics, specifically related to its extent, its scope and the circumstances of its implementation. Carried out by SCCIM, a civilian secondary player and local administrative intelligence agency, during an ongoing counterinsurgency war that hastened the need for information, it retained a wide territorial scope that covered the whole Mozambique colony and was a study specifically addressed to *Sunni* Muslim dignitaries. SCCIM also developed other knowledge devices that shared common goals of aiming to know the whole population and the enemy within as well as their transnational connections that were also carried out due to colonial insurgency. Therefore, this initiative also fits into a broad pattern of the perception of threats to the colonial project that was driven by a pervasive condition of epistemic delirium.

The intelligence knowledge that was accumulated included the concrete and the imagined. As such, SCCIM's *Confidential Questionnaire on Islam* produced facts, narratives and predictions. Moreover, the nature, structure, goals and outcomes of the survey show that this was also a knowledge device in which there was a patent entanglement and cross-fertilisation of scientific methodologies with politically-directed intelligence gathering. Within the composition of the questionnaire, there were questions with an ethnographic outlook that co-existed beside politically oriented questions as well as with interrogation strategies. Through all of these devices, SCCIM sought to obtain information on Islam in Mozambique, especially as regards its leaderships, internal divisions and transnational connections. It also assessed the influence of Islamic dignitaries over the Muslim population, the possibility of their co-option as well as trying to find bridges between Christian and Islamic beliefs that could be politically exploited. Whilst SCCIM equally wished to measure the Muslim animosity regarding the Portuguese rule, to detect their collaboration with liberation movements, the questionnaire also disclosed a set of preconceived ideas that linked Islam to political subversion.

Certainly the information about Islam and Muslim populations within the questionnaire records should be treated with caution. However, it does still provide

Knowing 'Mozambican Islam' 125

important information concerning the Portuguese images, representations, categories, concerns and patterns of suspicion as regards Islam. One of the most important features that was disclosed is the persistence of negative imaginary even when official discourse was spreading positive images in order to co-opt Muslims and turn them into *Portuguese Muslims.*

Whilst the questionnaire implementation suffered from many flaws, the operation itself provides a valuable window on to strategies of colonial governance and indeed their limitations. While the success in achieving their aims may have been limited, this exercise in administrative intelligence lays out the workings and ambitions of colonial governance as well as the frantic, yet ultimately futile, endeavours of late colonialism to win the war of liberation through the conquest of its colonial subjects' *hearts and minds.* Finally, looking at the questionnaire in this manner also opens up new research pathways such as the role of mediating native informants within the coloniser-subject relation or the information flow between several intelligence branches. Both have significant potential to provide novel insights regarding the connection between subject populations, intelligence-collection and governance.

References

Primary sources

(ANTT/SCCIM) Arquivo Nacional da Torre do Tombo/Serviços de Centralização e Coordenação de Informações
(AHD-MNE/MU/GNP) Arquivo Histórico Diplomático do Ministério dos Negócios Estrangeiros, Gabinete dos Negócios Políticos do Ministério do Ultramar

Interviews

Fernando Amaro Monteiro (Lisbon): 11 November 2009, 3 February 2010, 31 March 2010, 2 June 2010, 21 June 2013.

Printed sources

(*BOM*) *Boletim Oficial de Moçambique*, I/II Series, Mozambique: Imprensa Nacional.
(*DG*) *Diário do Governo*, I Serie, Lisbon: Imprensa Nacional.
El-Bokhari, A. 1972. *Tradições Muçulmanas. Adaptada da Tradução Francesa de G.H. Bousquet*, Lourenço Marques: Mozambique General-Government.
Freitas, A. (1957). *Seitas religiosas gentílicas: província de Moçambique.* Confidential, 3 vols, Lisbon: Junta de Investigações do Ultramar – Centro de Estudos Políticos e Sociais, no. 19.
Freitas, R. 1965. *Conquista e Adesão das Populações*, Lourenço Marques, Serviços de Centralização e Coordenação de Informações.
Pedro, A. 1961. *Influências Político-Sociais do Islamismo em Moçambique (Relatório Confidencial), Missão para o Estudo da Missionologia Africana*, Lisbon: Centro de Estudos Políticos e Sociais da Junta de Investigações do Ultramar, no. 49.
Rita-Ferreira, A. 1964. *Promoção social em Moçambique*, Lisbon: Junta de Investigações do Ultramar – Estudos de Ciências Políticas e Sociais, no. 71.

126 *Sandra Araújo*

Bibliography

Alexandre, V. 2000. *Velho Brasil Novas Áfricas. Portugal e o Império (1808–1975)*. Porto: Edições Afrontamento.

Alpers, E. 1999. Islam in the service of colonialism? Portuguese strategy during the armed liberation struggle in Mozambique. *Lusotopie*, 1999. Paris: Karthala: 165–184.

Araújo, S. 2017. Shaping an Empire of Predictions: The Mozambique Information Centralization and Coordination Services (1961–1974), in *Policing in Colonial Situations. Cases, Connections, Boundaries* (ca. 1850–1970), edited by E. Blanchard, M. Bloembergen and A. Lauro. Bruxelles, Bern, Berlin, Frankfurt am Main, New York, Oxford, Wien: P.I.E. Peter Lang, 137–158.

Bader, V. and Maussen, M. 2011. Chapter 12: Conclusion, in *Colonial and Post-Colonial Governance of Islam*, edited by M. Maussen, V. Bader and A. Moors. Amsterdam: Amsterdam University Press, 233–248.

Bastos, S. 2008. Ambivalence and Phantasm in the Portuguese colonial discourse production on Indians. *Lusotopie*, XV(1): 77–95.

Bayly, C. 1993. Knowing the country: Empire and information in India. *Modern Asian Studies*, 27(1): 3–43.

Bhabha, H. 1994. *The Location of Culture*. London/New York: Routledge.

Bonate, L. 2007. *Traditions and Transitions: Islam and Chiefship in Northern Mozambique ca. 1850–1974.* PhD Thesis, Cape Town University.

Brodeur, J.-P. 1983. High policing and low policing: Remarks about the policing of political activities. *Social Problems*, 30(5): 507–520.

Cahen, M. 2000. L'État Nouveau et la diversification religieuse au Mozambique, 1930–1974 – II. La portugalisation désespérée (1959–1974). *Cahiers d'Études africaines*, XL-3(159): 551–592.

Cahen, M. 2013. Review essay. Un Islam au service de l'empire? *Social Sciences and Missions*, 26: 275–289.

Cann, J. 2005. *Countersinsurgency in Africa. The Portuguese Way of War (1961–1974)*. St Petersburg, FL: Hailer Publishing.

Cardoso, P. 2004. *As Informações em Portugal*. Lisboa: Gradiva.

Castelo, C. 1999. *'O Modo Português de Estar no Mundo'. O luso-tropicalismo e a ideologia colonial portuguesa (1933–1961)*. Porto: Edições Afrontamento.

Ferris, J. 2009. The internationalism of Islam: The British perception of a Muslim Menace, 1840–1951. *Intelligence and National Security*, 24(1): 57–77.

Foucault, M. 1982. The subject and power. *Critical Inquiry*, 4(8): 777–795.

Foucault, M. 2011. *Leçons sur la volonté de savoir: Cours au Collège de France (1970–1971) suivi de Le savoir d'Oedipe*. Paris: Gallimard.

Garcia, F. 2003. *Análise Global de uma Guerra (Moçambique, 1964–1974)*. Lisbon: Prefácio.

Garcia, F. 2004. A importância das informações na condução da guerra em Moçambique (1964–1974), in *Informações e Segurança. Estudos em Honra do General Pedro Cardoso*, edited by Adriano Moreira, Lisbon: Prefácio, 233–255.

Grandhomme, H. 2009. Connaissance de l'Islam et Pouvoir Colonial: L'exemple de la France au Sénégal, 1936–1957. *French Colonial History*, 10: 171–188.

Hallet, R. 1976. Chapter 13: Changing European Attitudes to Africa, in *The Cambridge History of Africa, From c. 1790 to c. 1870*, Vol. 5, edited by J. Fage, J. Flint and R. Oliver. Cambridge: Cambridge University Press, 458–496.

Knowing 'Mozambican Islam' 127

Harrison, C. 2003. *France and Islam in West Africa 1860–1960*. Cambridge: Cambridge University Press.

Heald, C. 1996. Is there room for archives in the postmodern world? *American Archivist*, 59: 88–101.

Horn, E. and Ogger, S. 2003. Knowing the enemy: The epistemology of secret intelligence. *Grey Room*, 11: 58–85.

Jackson, P. 2009. Introduction, in *Exploring Intelligence Archives*, edited by R. Hughes, P. Jackson and L. Scott. London and New York: Routlegde, 1–11.

Laffan, M. 2011. *The Makings of Indonesian Islam: Orientalism and the Narration of a Sufi Past*. Princeton and Oxford: Princeton University Press.

Luizard, P. (ed.). 2006. *Le Choc Colonial et l'Islam. Les Politique Religieuses des Puissances Coloniales en Terres d'Islam*. Paris: La Découverte.

Macagno, L. 2006. *Outros Muçulmanos: Islão e Narrativas Coloniais*. Lisbon: Imprensa de Ciências Sociais.

Machaqueiro, M. 2011. Ambivalent Islam: The identity construction of Muslims under Portuguese colonial rule. *Social Identities*, 18(1): 39–63.

Machaqueiro, M. 2012. The Islamic policy of Portuguese colonial Mozambique, 1960–1973. *The Historical Journal*, 55(4): 1097–1116.

Marx, G. 2014. High policing, in *Encyclopedia of Criminology and Criminal Justice*, edited by G. Bruinsma and D. Weisburd. New York: Springer, 2062–2074.

Mateus, D. 2004. *A PIDE/DGS na Guerra Colonial (1961–1974)*. Lisbon: Terramar.

Maussen, M.; Bader, V. 2011. Chapter 1. Introduction, in *Colonial and Post-Colonial Governance of Islam*, edited by M. Maussen, V. Bader and A. Moors. Amsterdam: Amsterdam University Press, 9–26.

Monteiro, F. 1972. *Traços Fundamentais da Evolução do Islamismo com vista à sua incidência em Moçambique*, Universidade de Lourenço Marques, Lourenço Marques.

Monteiro, F. 1989a. As Comunidades Islâmicas de Moçambique: Mecanismos de Comunicação. *Africana*, 4: 65–89.

Monteiro, F. 1989b. Moçambique 1964–1974: As Comunidades Islâmicas, o Poder e a Guerra. *Africana*, 5: 83–125.

Monteiro, F. 1992. *O Islão, o Poder e a Guerra (Moçambique 1964–1974)*. PhD Thesis, Universidade Técnica de Lisboa – Instituto Superior de Ciências Sociais e Políticas, Lisbon.

Monteiro, F. 2004. Moçambique, a década de 1970 a corrente Wahhabita: uma diagonal, in *O Islão na África Subsariana – Actas do 6.º Colóquio Internacional Estados, Poderes e Identidades na África Subsariana*, edited by A. Gonçalves. Porto: Faculdade de Letras da Universidade do Porto, 107–113.

Morier-Genoud, E. 2002. L'Islam au Mozambique après l'independace. Histoire d'une montée en puissance. *L'Afrique Politique*, 2002. Paris: Karthala, 123–146.

Reis, B. and Oliveira, P. 2012. Cutting heads or winning hearts: Late colonial Portuguese counterinsurgency and the Wiriyamu Massacre of 1972. *Civil Wars*, 14(1): 80–103.

Robinson, D. and Triaud, J. (eds). 1997. *Le Temps des Marabouts. Itinéraires et stratégies islamiques en Afrique occidentale française v. 1880–1960*. Paris: Karthala.

Roque, R. and Wagner, K. 2012. Introduction, in *Engaging Colonial Knowledge: Reading European Archives in World History*. Basingstoke: Palgrave Macmillan, 1–32.

Rosas, F. 1994. *História de Portugal: O Estado Novo (1926–1974)*, Vol. VII, s.l. Círculo de Leitores.

128 Sandra Araújo

Said, E. 1978. *Orientalism: Western Conceptions of the Orient.* London: Routledge and Kegan Paul.

Simpson, E. and Kresse, K. (eds). 2007. *Struggling With History: Islam and Cosmopolitanism in the Western Indian Ocean.* London: Hurst & Company.

Souto, A. 2007. *Caetano e o Ocaso do 'Império'. Administração e Guerra Colonial em Moçambique durante o Marcelismo (1968–1974).* Porto: Edições Afrontamento.

Stoler, A. 2009. *Along the Archival Grain: Epistemic Anxieties and Colonial Common Sense.* Princeton/Oxford: Princeton University Press.

Thomas, M. 2008. *Empires of Intelligence: Security Services and Colonial Disorder After 1914.* Berkeley/Los Angeles/London: University of California Press.

Trovão, S. 2012. Comparing postcolonial identity formations: Legacies of Portuguese and British colonialisms in East Africa. *Social Identities,* 18(3): 261–280.

Trumbull IV, G. 2009. *An Empire of Facts: Colonial Power, Cultural Knowledge, and Islam in Algeria, 1870–1914.* Cambridge: Cambridge University Press.

Vakil, A. 2003a. Questões Inacabadas: Colonialismo, Islão e Portugalidade, in *Fantasmas e Fantasias Imperiais no Imaginário Português Contemporâneo,* edited by M. Ribeiro and A. Ferreira. Porto: Campo das Letras, 255–293.

Vakil, A. 2003b. O 'Portugal Islâmico', o 'Portugal Multicultural' e os Muçulmanos Portugueses: História, memória e cidadania na construção de novas identidades, in *Minorias Étnicas e Religiosas em Portugal: História e Actualidade,* edited by G. Mota. Coimbra: Instituto de História Económica e Social, Facultade de Letras da Universidade de Coimbra, 409–451.

Vakil, A. 2004. Pensar o Islão: Questões Coloniais, interrogações pós-coloniais. *Revista Crítica de Ciências Sociais,* 69: 17–52.

Vakil, A., Monteiro, F. and Machaqueiro, M. 2011. *Moçambique: Memória Falada do Islão e da Guerra.* Coimbra: Almedina.

6 Intelligence-centric counterinsurgency as late colonial policing
Comparing Portugal with Britain and France

Bruno Cardoso Reis

Introduction

The aim of this chapter is to analyse the relationship between the military and policing in the counterinsurgency campaigns of the late colonial period. Comparing doctrinal guidelines and practices in the Portuguese wars of decolonisation with those of Britain and France my main argument is that there was much convergence that has often been overlooked or denied by a focus on national ways of war to the detriment of a more transnational perspective.

There seems to be, in fact, an enduring trend in the international literature to point to a Portuguese colonial *Sonderweg*, a uniquely brutal way of doing things overseas that stemmed from the authoritarian nature of the *Estado Novo* political regime, as opposed to the democratic nature of the British and French metropolitan polities. References to the 'well-known case of the comparatively anaemic and brutal Portuguese empire' (Lewis in Lewis, Branche, Edgerton, Imlay, Stanard, Thomas 2013: 3) as a peculiar example of 'very repressive and yet "successful" empires (in terms of longevity)' (Stanard in Lewis, Branche, Edgerton, Imlay, Stanard, Thomas 2013: 16) need to be revisited and at least partly revised. As Thomas (2012) argues, resorting to massive force was seen as a marker of failure by the men on the spot in charge of the late colonial state. I would argue that this also applies to the case of the late colonial Portuguese state, as illustrated by the rapid replacement of those in charge in Angola when the insurgency started in 1961.

It is important to underline that this is not the same as claiming that Portuguese colonialism was particularly benign, or that Portuguese late colonial counterinsurgency was especially population-friendly – as some seem to believe (Cann 1997: 187–194, CECA 1988)[1] – but rather that it lacked both the means and the will to use substantial force effectively before the early 1960s. Moreover, other European colonial powers were democratic in the metropolis, but were far from benign in their colonial dependencies, especially during security emergencies.

---

1 This difference of views does not detract from the great usefulness of these pioneering works.

130 *Bruno Cardoso Reis*

Those that argue for the unusual repressiveness of the Portuguese colonial State should also account for contradictory evidence, such as the absence of the death penalty in the Portuguese colonies. Even if we take into account extra-judicial executions that occurred during the Portuguese wars of decolonisation – even if by their nature they are difficult to quantify – such atrocities were also present in other late colonial campaigns; including in British late colonial counterinsurgency which until recent revisions was often portrayed as the supposed paragon of minimum force (Anderson 2005, maxime 173, 307).

Portugal, I would argue, is less of an exception to, rather than a variant of, Western patterns of late colonial rule and late colonial counterinsurgency in terms of violent repression and policing. The latter did vary but to a degree that was primarily dependent upon the different level of intensity of these late colonial campaigns, a point in which the insurgents had a crucial impact (namely in terms of their access to modern weaponry and external support more widely). To pursue this argument, this chapter adopts a comparative approach between Portugal and the two other major colonial powers in Africa that were also involved in major late colonial counterinsurgencies, Britain and France.

The comparison between Portuguese and other late colonial counterinsurgencies assesses guidelines and practices to not only determine whether Portuguese late colonial policing, in the context of counterinsurgency was significantly different from those of Britain and France, but also to ask why were military actions characterised as imperial policing and operations to maintain law and order, and not as wars? In addressing these questions I argue that the Portuguese approach to late colonial policing and counterinsurgency was not fundamentally different from that of the British or the French. Furthermore, framing counterinsurgency as policing was not just a matter of propaganda. It was both natural given longstanding discourses and practices regarding suppression of colonial insurgencies and also a result of the intelligence-centric nature of this far from conventional armed conflict and the fact that police forces were important in this vital dimension of counterinsurgency.

The text is divided into four sections. The first briefly considers the challenges posed by trying to place the Portuguese case within the wider context of imperial policing during the late colonial period. The second addresses the questions of why these late colonial campaigns against armed independence movements were framed as policing operations. The third analyses the central role of intelligence as a form of high policing in these late colonial campaigns. The fourth and concluding section links my main claims with larger debates regarding minimum force, the nature of a colonial intelligence community and of the late colonial state.

Locating Portuguese colonial policing

Scholars of colonial policing have often pointed out that this field of study has been relatively marginalised and under-developed. This can be seen as part of a wider problem identified three decades ago by Howard (1984: 34–35) as an 'almost taboo' eclipsing the violent dimension of imperial history. Arguably the advantage

Intelligence-centric counterinsurgency **131**

that conventional and nuclear warfare have had over colonial small wars – in terms of scholarly attention – has now been partly overcome. The work of authors like Bayly (1996) on British intelligence gathering in colonial India have helped to raise the academic profile of policing-related issues in the imperial context. Some will probably feel progress has been too slow, others will point to recently published work – to be cited further bellow – as evidence that this is now being overcome.

Insofar as the study of colonial policing in Portugal is concerned, what Blanchard and Glasman (2012: 11) have written seems to apply: colonial policing has remained 'the poor relative of the renewal of imperial studies'. Both themes – policing and empire – were, of course, politically out of bounds before the end, in 1974, of the Portuguese *Estado Novo*. After the fall of this authoritarian regime, its violent repressive dimension naturally became first a focus of political denunciation rather than of in-depth analysis. Portuguese historians have also tended to first direct their research attention towards high political policing in metropolitan Portugal rather than in the overseas territories (Pimentel 2007: 19–21). The history of policing in metropolitan Portugal is therefore also relatively scarce, even if some existing publications have made important contributions to our understanding of the theme (see Palacios Cerezales 2011, and his contribution to this volume).

When searching the catalogue of the National Library of Portugal using 'colonial policing' as a keyword, a single book is listed by Dalila Mateus (2004) that moves this focus on high political policing from the metropole to the colonies. Broadening the scope of the research at the catalogue of the National Library of Portugal uncovers, for the most part, semi-official publications with revealing titles about how blurred the line was between policing and military action in a Portuguese colonial context (e.g. Sôtto 1943).

Portugal was, of course, distinct from Britain and France, being ruled as a military dictatorship from 1926–1933, and then as an institutionalised authoritarian regime, the *Estado Novo* (1933–1974), led by António de Oliveira Salazar from 1933–1968. Yet despite some differences – in terms of high political policing – there are important convergences with Britain and/or France in the trajectory in terms of policing (in particular, but not exclusively, in the case of colonial policing). Two main reasons for this relative convergence seem to emerge from the existing literature.

First, there was a transnational standard of policing professionalism. And the *Estado Novo* was closely aligned with the West during the Cold War, as demonstrated in 1949 when Portugal became a founding member of NATO. Therefore it was natural for Portuguese police leadership to aspire to emulate Western policing standards to reinforce their professional standing.[2] This meant that in more developed urban areas – including a few rare ones in the colonies – there was already a distinction, even if not a permanently irrevocable one, between civilian policing responsible for normal law enforcement using graduated force; and the military, deployed rarely in urban areas and only in response to more serious or violent

---

2 Palacios Cerezales (2011: 274). On the concept of police professionalism cf. Charlan (2007).

132   *Bruno Cardoso Reis*

internal threats. It is true that Portugal had militarised police units even in the metropole, the *gendarmerie* or *Guarda Nacional Republicana* (GNR), as well as special anti-riot regiments of the *Polícia de Segurança Pública* (PSP). However this was normal in other Western European democratic countries like Italy or France, even in the United Kingdom there was the Royal Irish/Ulster Constabulary.

The PSP special anti-riot mobile units, the *Companhias Móveis* (CPs), established from April 1960, sought to emulate the French *Compagnies Républicaines de Sécurité*. The CPs deserve a special mention because one of these mobile police units was quickly moved to Luanda in 1960 in anticipation of serious internal security problems. Eventually twelve such mobile police companies would be sent overseas during the Portuguese late colonial counterinsurgency campaigns (Palacios Cerezales 2011: 308).

Even in terms of high policing, there was some effort by PIDE/DGS to emulate to some degree the professional standards of other Western intelligence services after 1945. With the CIA, cooperation was belated (after 1956) and always limited by strong suspicion given US support for decolonisation in general, and UPA/FNLA in particular. But there was very close cooperation with the SDECE and *Sureté*, the French security services (Pimentel 2011: 112–126). Created in 1933 as the *Polícia de Vigilância e Defesa do Estado* (PVDE) from the fusion of different intelligence units of the police, it enjoyed significant extra-judicial powers in the metropole. From 1945 onwards it was renamed PIDE (*'Polícia Internacional de Defesa do Estado'*), and from 1969 to 1974, DGS (*'Direção Geral de Segurança'*), but these changes in name changed little of substance. However, it is interesting to note that the 1945 decree creating PIDE explicitly mentioned the British example of a Special Branch (Cardoso 1995: 826). And DGS replicates *ipsis verbis* the formal designation of the French *Sûreté*. This had an obvious political intent of providing a respectable Western cover for a violent form of high political policing. Needless to say, this did not turn PIDE into a model intelligence agency and certainly not in exactly the same model of a Western liberal democracy. However, it does provide further evidence of the importance, after 1945, for all aspects of Portuguese policing, including high policing, of the attempt to emulate or at least appear to emulate to some degree Western European professional models of policing.

The second reason why Portugal was less unique than some have argued is because empires, even those of States that were liberal democracies in the metropoles, are by definition undemocratic, not least in terms of policing models and methods in their overseas dependencies. The development of new, less coercive guidelines of law enforcement took place in an increasingly more liberal Europe – first with the emergence of the norm of minimum necessary force in Britain from 1819 onwards (Townshend 1988, Babington 1990). At the heart of this was an increasingly strong feeling of shared identity between the governing elite and the rest of the population, between police officers and their fellow citizens in an increasingly liberalised and democratised Europe. Yet, even in Europe the process was not without important nuances, namely in how the police dealt with '"respectable" and "not so respectable" classes' (Wright 2002: 6–16). This led some to argue that there is a missing but important dimension of internal colonialism to the story of policing in Europe, illustrated for instance by the transfer of skills from French policemen in Algeria to France itself (Brogden 1987a, 1987b).

The dynamic towards more democratic forms of policing by consent, that was not homogenous, absolute or irreversible even in Europe, was therefore much weaker or non-existent in Western colonies. In colonial dependencies the management of a hierarchy of difference remained *de facto* at the heart of the colonial power system. This was especially the case in colonised Africa that was still, in the late 19th and early 20th centuries, in the process of being militarily occupied.

It is surely significant that even Britain with the oldest tradition of policing based on minimum necessary force and unarmed civilian community policing, turned instead to the armed paramilitary Royal Irish/Ulster Constabulary as a school for colonial policing. Colonial police, even in the late colonial period, often used lethal force to deal with various forms of colonial unrest (Anderson and Killingray 1991, Sinclair 2006: *maxime* 15–19, 146–160).

That there was some interpenetration of the military and policing is also clear in the French case: 'the professionalization of the police took place in different periods from region to region, it is still the case that colonies [. . .] were still marked by the visible support of the army to the small police forces' (Blanchard and Glasman 2012: 16).

It is hardly surprising, therefore, that even a preliminary historical analysis of the under-researched history of Portuguese colonial policing shows how, for a very long time, the distinction between the military and police forces overseas was blurred. I will offer two examples of this. After the triumph in Portugal of the First Republic in 1910, a cavalry unit of the new *gendarmerie* or GNR was created from the company of Dragoons that were part of the military garrison of Lourenço Marques, the capital city of colonial Mozambique. But this unit was turned again, in 1924, into a 'normal' military unit, with much the same duties of internal security (Neves 2001: 545). The second example is that of PIDE/DGS. It managed to survive in the overseas territories the fall of the Portuguese authoritarian regime, in April 1974, by being rebranded as PIM, *Polícia de Informação Militar* i.e. Military Intelligence Police. Even the leftist military leaders of the coup believed that this was 'indispensable, since most of the intelligence of the Armed Forces [. . .] was provided by DGS' and therefore as long as no firm ceasefire was in place the military 'could not survive without it' (Costa Gomes 1998: 214–15). As a consequence this very special branch of the civilian police was, for a very short period, taken-over by the Armed Forces – despite its close attachment to the worst of the fallen authoritarian regime, and the fact that it had sometimes been in conflict with the military. The relationship between policing, intelligence and the military is precisely the central subjects of analysis of the following section.

Framing late colonial counterinsurgency as policing

I do not deny or ignore that there was an element of propaganda in framing these late colonial conflicts as imperial policing and not as a war. But I would underline that this framing cannot be dismissed as merely propaganda. In this most political

134 *Bruno Cardoso Reis*

of all types of warfare, there is no such thing as *merely* propaganda. Propaganda played a major role. The very concept of counterinsurgency is a reflection of this, being aptly and briefly defined (O'Neill 1990: 13) as: 'a struggle between a non-ruling group and the ruling authorities in which the non-ruling group consciously uses political resources (e.g. organisational, expertise, *propaganda*, and demonstrations) and violence to destroy, reformulate, or sustain the basis of legitimacy of one or more aspects of politics'. The effort in terms of doctrinal and organisational change, and the resources invested by the Portuguese as well as by the British and French late colonial state in order to win the hearts and minds of locals and wage psychological warfare – regardless of whether these aims were achieved or not – makes clear that propaganda was indeed central (Carruthers 1995, Villatoux 2005, CECA 1990). But, above all, I would claim that this framing was about much more than propaganda, important as the latter was.

First, we should recognise that to frame late colonial counterinsurgency as policing was to a certain degree natural. There was a tradition of framing colonial conflicts, especially small wars after the initial period of occupation as policing operations aimed at maintaining law and order. The militarised nature of policing and the paramilitary nature of police in the colonial setting, moreover, made this formula of imperial policing seem all the more natural.

For instance, in the case of Britain, the quintessential imperial power, generic doctrine on how the military should deal with unrest in the colonies was normally labelled as imperial policing and as an aid to the civil power; this was the title of an influential book on the subject by General Sir Charles Gwyn (1939) as well as of the 1949 doctrinal manual (e.g. Moreman 1997: 110–111).[3]

In the French case there was also a long and prestigious tradition of distinguishing colonial conflicts aimed at pacification from conventional war, which went back to Gallieni and Lyautey, who had famously argued for a *tache d'huile*, a gradual ink-spot approach that went beyond spectacular military offensives. It was aimed not just at clearing a territory of armed opponents but also at providing conditions for holding it permanently, namely by effective policing (Porch 1986: maxime 395–98, Le Révérend 1983, Michel 1989). In French late colonial counterinsurgency in Indochina and, especially, in Algeria, this eventually resulted in the military being given a number of typically civilian powers, including police powers as well as control over the civilian police forces – first in certain areas, then in all of Algeria after the May 1958 military *pronunciamento*. It is interesting to note that within the guidelines of the main training centre for counterinsurgency in Algeria there was a distinction between pure combat operations and internal security missions or *opérations de maintien de l'ordre* ('operations to maintain order'). Combat operations were aimed at the 'systematic destruction' of the 'enemy' by 'using all kinds of weapons and firing at any target'. Internal security

---

3 A revised edition was been issued when post-Second World War late colonial insurgencies started WO, *Imperial Policing and Duties in Aid of the Civil Power*, London: HMSO, 1949. But I argue this had at the most a marginal impact in high intensity counterinsurgencies.

Intelligence-centric counterinsurgency 135

missions were aimed at dispersing the 'demonstrators' and therefore 'firing' at them should be 'exceptional' and 'strictly limited'. A table contrasted these two approaches in two parallel columns.[4] However, since the military deployments in Indochina and Algeria were not officially described as a war the manual does not adjudicate as to which should apply, even if in practice there can be little doubt that, in practice combat operations and their respective guidelines prevailed.

In the case of Portugal, Colonel Mouzinho de Albuquerque – one of the key figures of the Portuguese military occupation of the African hinterland – put it very clearly when he stated that: 'colonial forces are not organised and maintained only to engage in operations against native insurgencies, but primarily to avoid them, by policing [*policiando*] the territory' (cit. in Neves 2001: 477). A very influential Portuguese intelligence officer, General Pedro Cardoso (1995: 831), made clear that he considered it obvious that 'the thirteen years of war overseas were basically operations for the maintenance of law and order by the police' but he added, significantly, to the list 'and the Armed Forces.'

Second, *framing late colonial counterinsurgency as policing also reflected the fact that this was indeed a very different type of conflict from conventional warfare.* The unconventional challenges posed by this form of violence also meant that what role the police and the military should play was a matter of serious debate.

Many decision-makers, and even senior military officers, believed that whilst this would be a demanding role for the police, it should still be primarily a mission for it rather than the military. In the initial years of counterinsurgency in Malaya, for example, both the top British civil authority, High Commissioner Sir Henry Gurney, and the Police Commissioner, Colonel William Gray, were determined that the Malayan Communist Party insurgency should remain firmly under control of the civilian police. Significantly they had the support, not only of the local military commander in Malaya from 1948–50, Sir Charles Boucher, but also and more importantly, of Marshall Slim, Chief of the Imperial General Staff. The latter reported back to London after a tour of Malaya that this was primarily a question of maintaining law and order and therefore 'much more a matter for civil rather than military action'.[5] It took an increasingly obvious failure of this approach, which placed the military under civilian and police control in most areas, to put a stop to an escalation of the insurgency, made spectacularly manifest by the assassination of the British High Commissioner Gurney in an ambush in October 1951, for a fundamental change of approach to take place. True, this change had already started with the appointment of General Briggs as Chief of Operations, in 1950, but culminated in the doctrinal reforms forcefully implemented under General Sir Harold Templer, who replaced both Gurney and Briggs as a new all powerful civil-military supremo (Coates 1992: 109).

The British police in Malaya had arguably become too militarised to be effective in normal law enforcement but never enough to become an effective fighting

---

4 SHD 1H 1115, XRM – CIPCG, *Dossier d'Instruction*, 110.
5 TNA CO 537/4374 Field-Marshal Sir W. Slim, 'Note on Tour of SE Asia' (October 1949).

136 *Bruno Cardoso Reis*

force against well-organised guerrillas, and eventually returned to more traditional duties. The British military, formally under the police, had in fact maintained their organisational autonomy by conducting its 'own war' away from civilian areas through vast, largely futile, sweep operations that became known as 'jungle bashing'. In the new British approach that emerged between 1950–1952 – the so-called 'Briggs Plan', revised and implemented by Templer against previous resistances – the police still had an important role, but primarily in terms of ordinary police helping to hold areas previously cleared by the militarily and of the crucial role of the special branch in providing vital intelligence for military operations (see Cloake 1985, Gregorian 1994, Nagl 2002, Comber 2008).

The Portuguese military leadership, when faced with their first major late colonial insurgency in Angola in February-March 1961, also resisted political pressure to focus the Armed Forces entirely on counterinsurgency. They argued that this was no more than a 'war of *machetes*' and was consequently one that local police units (helped by local military units) should be able to deal with.[6] Both the Army Chief-of-Staff and the Chief-of-the-General-Staff, after touring Angola in March 1961, 'kept insisting that all was well, there were only some small uprisings that were totally under control' (Costa Gomes 1998: 113). The resistance by Portuguese military leaders to full engagement in this unconventional form of conflict went as far as a failed *pronunciamento* to try to force the replacement of Salazar and force a change of policy, led by the Minister of Defence, General Botelho Moniz, stopped *in extremis* in April 1961.

The Portuguese police was, on the contrary, eager to take a leading role in fighting the insurgency in Angola in early 1961. This was, in all likelihood, at least partly explained by the fact that colonial police – both the intelligence special branch (PIDE) and paramilitary anti-riot units (PSP) – were the first targets of insurgent attacks in Luanda in February 1961, and policemen were among the first casualties of this anti-colonial insurgency. When it quickly became clear that police, even with the help of military units in Angola, were not enough to deal with the problem, metropolitan police units joined the first wave of reinforcements. And these paramilitary units of the police were not useless in this initial stage of counterinsurgency. In fact, their utility was recognised by one of the few top generals critical of a lack of a more forceful initial military response who argued that: 'what is necessary is troops with guns' to recover control of the situation in Angola 'even if it is the *Guarda Fiscal* [Fiscal Gendarmerie]!'.[7]

The Portuguese regular police, especially via its paramilitary units did play a role in late-colonial Portuguese counterinsurgencies that deserves an in-depth study in the future. Still, in the absence of further research, it seems that these special police units played a secondary role in Portuguese late colonial counterinsurgency by acting

---

6 General Viana de Lemos cit. in J.F. Antunes (1992: 204). General Lemos was part of this mission.

7 Letter from General Albuquerque de Freitas to General Pinto Resende (16 April 1961) cit. in Valença (1981: 248).

as a deterrent and a source of basic intelligence to a spread of the insurgency into the main urban areas and of releasing the military from garrison duties in these areas.

Third, crucially in *framing these late colonial conflicts* not as a war *but as* a form of (high) policing, this also meant *denying the insurgents the status of lawful combatants. The latter would have exempted them from any kind of interrogation*, evidently including the 'enhanced interrogation' that was a euphemism for the torture to which real or presumed *insurgents were often subject in the pursuit of actionable intelligence* in all three cases examined in this text.

Torture is hardly ever officially recognised, but historians can and have started pointing to doctrinal principles of late colonial counterinsurgency that enabled it (see Branche 2001, Reis 2011, French 2012). For instance, British doctrine in Malaya made it clear that one of the main sources of intelligence were the insurgents themselves, thus making them 'extremely valuable.'[8] It was also emphasised to the military that, if possible, it was more important to apprehend terrorists than to kill them, in a logic similar to that of the policemen. But in an imperial context in which emergency regulations granted the British colonial authorities and also the military, extraordinary police powers of search, arrest, control and interrogation as well as powers of deportation, expropriation, imposition of collective curfews, fines and capital punishment.[9]

Portuguese doctrine made clear that while soldiers engaged in counterinsurgency, they should know and observe the law, as a policeman would. But it went on to note that 'ordinary law can be modified' by special legislation, in each colony, adapted to a 'state of siege', and even less strict in terms of the guarantees of basic rights than Portuguese metropolitan law under an authoritarian regime.[10] Insofar as the treatment of prisoners was concerned, a generic principle of 'humane treatment' was affirmed, in line with Western standards, but it was also explicitly underlined that, unlike in conventional warfare where the Geneva Convention applied, 'it is very hard in subversive warfare to establish the exact status of captured combatants.'[11] The order of priorities that is then set to govern the treatment of a prisoner is revealing: 'make sure he does not escape or is released'; 'obtain the maximum of information'; 'turn them for future use'; and, 'avoid resentment from innocent prisoners'.[12]

What was unique about French late colonial counterinsurgency was how militarised the whole effort was – making it much harder for the military to disclaim responsibility for abuses, later. In fact, French officers seemed uniquely willing to engage in this public controversy providing a 'Cartesian rationale for the use of torture' in Bernard Fall's apt formulation in his introductory preface to the English

---

8 HQ-MC, *ATOM*, pp. XIV/3; Similarly in Kenya EA-HQ, *A Handbook of Anti-Mau Mau Operations*, Nairobi, EA-HQ, 1954, p. 10.

9 HQ-MC, *The Conduct of Anti-Terrorist Operations in Malaya* [*ATOM*], Kuala-Lumpur, HQ-MC, 1954, 2nd rev. ed., chap. IV.

10 EME, *O Exército na Guerra Subversiva* [*EGS*], Lisboa, EME, 1963, Vol.4, pp. I/3.

11 EME, *EGS*, Vol.5, pp. I/8–9.

12 EME, *EGS*, Vol.5, pp. I/8–9.

138   *Bruno Cardoso Reis*

translation of the work of Colonel Trinquier (1964: XV). The latter was the key intelligence officer during the battle of Algiers in 1957. For Trinquier (1964: 20–21, 48) insurgents were part of a deadly organisation that because of its secret nature could only be dealt with effectively through intelligence obtained from capture insurgents making, in his revealing words, 'some brutality inevitable'. This was part and parcel of the kind of rationale made explicit by Chief-of-the-General-Staff, General Ély, in his preface to the official *Reglement de l'Action Psychologique*: 'we do not accept any other limits [in counterinsurgency] except the ones that the enemy accepts for himself'.[13] In my view, the French were more open about this – for reasons discussed elsewhere (Reis 2011) – but were not that different in their generic intelligence-centric approach from the other two cases of late colonial counterinsurgency considered in this chapter.

But what else did this intelligence-centric dimension mean in terms of late colonial counterinsurgency?

Diffusion of counterinsurgency as high policing – the intelligence-centric dimension

The military in these three cases of late colonial counterinsurgency had to be made aware of how central intelligence was in this type of conflict, much more than in ordinary warfare. In all three cases this was done through very clear doctrinal guidelines. In the Portuguese case it is also clear that there was a strong attempt, at least initially, to emulate foreign doctrinal principles. But this process of emulation faced significant limitations, not least given the highly political dimension of high policing.

Briefly put 'low policing consists in law enforcement and high policing in political surveillance' (Brodeur and Leman-Langlois 2006: 171, see also O'Reilly 2015, Brodeur 2010, L'Heuillet 2001). More specifically high policing 'was defined by [. . .]: (1) it was absorbent policing, hoarding all-encompassing intelligence [. . .]; (2) it conflated legislative, judiciary and executive or administrative powers [. . .]; (3) its goal was the preservation of the political regime ("the State") and not the protection of civil society; (4) to this end, it made extensive use of informants'. This was 'combined within a police paradigm where the protection of the political status quo was the primary goal of policing and where furthermore the interests of the regime were not seen to be coterminous with the interest of civil society' (Brodeur and Leman-Langlois 2006: 171). Intelligence work in colonial counterinsurgency would therefore seem to be, not surprisingly, the paradigmatic fit to this description of high policing.

The British manual for counterinsurgency in Malaya – the first set of guidelines developed specifically for these late colonial counterinsurgency campaigns – underlined that the insurgents 'are essentially an underground organisation', and

---

13 General Paul Ély 'Preface', Reglement de l'Action Psychologique, EMGFA (1958), cit. Faivre (1998: 14).

therefore 'the main counter to this technique is a first class intelligence organisation.'[14] The first generic – i.e. non-theatre specific – British manual at the very end of the period of late colonial counterinsurgency summarises these lessons by arguing that: 'good intelligence is the key to successful operations.'[15] The question therefore was not if intelligence as a special kind of policing was central in this type of conflict but rather *who* was best suited to collect it? More specifically, should this be done by an existing or reconstituted and augmented military intelligence structure or by reinforcing a special branch of the civilian police and improving its coordination with the military?

The dominant trend in British doctrine – the actual practice is always more complex but is nonetheless strongly conditioned by the norm – was to insist on the need for a coordinated well-organised intelligence apparatus at all levels but also to install a division of labour whereby some kind of civilian special branch of the police had prime responsibility for the gathering and handling intelligence. In the case of Kenya, military guidelines dictated that the interrogation of captured insurgents 'should be rapid and confined to establishing terrorist locations' and they should be handed over after a day for 'deliberate interrogation' by the 'Special Branch.'[16] In the case of Malaya, the principle in military guidelines was that 'the fewer people who question' a prisoner 'the better' and, again, civilian intelligence should have primary responsibility.[17]

The very serious difficulties for British counterinsurgency when this intelligence-centric model did not work, for some reason, were made clear in the retreat from Palestine in 1948. Or in the now largely forgotten but largely failed late colonial British counterinsurgency in Aden/South Arabia that ended in another humiliating retreat in 1967. In identifying lessons from the latter campaign Julian Paget (1967: 163), who had been deeply involved as an officer there, stated that one of the key requirements of counterinsurgency success was: 'skilled interrogators, since they may often be the main source of intelligence.' However in Aden they were either not skilled enough, or their skills were inadequate. They resorted to abuses that were eventually denounced in Britain. This resulted in a scandal and an official enquiry which concluded that complaints of torture and other abuses were largely true. Still the enquiry found that the massive local pressure on the interrogators to get results partly explained these abuses and recommended no prosecutions (Bowen 1966). This is but one example – and others are likely to appear given the still recent and ongoing opening of the so-called 'migrated

---

14 HQ-MC, 'Intelligence', *The Conduct of Anti-Terrorist Operations in Malaya* [*ATOM*], Kuala-Lumpur, HQ-MC, 1954), 2nd rev. ed., pp. XIV/3; Similarly in Kenya EA-HQ, *A Handbook of Anti-Mau Mau Operations*, Nairobi, EA-HQ, 1954, pp. 10, XIV/1–25 [8 practical appendixes].

15 MoD, *Land Operations. Volume III. Counter Revolutionary Operations. Part 3. Counter Insurgency, Army Code 70516 (Part 3) [Counter Revolutionary Operations. Part 3]*, London: HMSO, 1970, pp. 4, 11.

16 EA-HQ, Intelligence Organization, *Handbook*, p. 10.

17 HQ-MC, *ATOM*, pp. XIV/3–4.

140 *Bruno Cardoso Reis*

archives' relating to the more repressive side of British late colonialism – of the growing trends towards the demolishing of the myth of British minimum force in the wars of decolonisation (Bennett 2011, Anderson 2005).

In the French case, one of the central official lessons of the very costly French campaign in Indochina that culminated in Dien-Bien-Phu, in 1954, was that it was impossible to win a counterinsurgency if the insurgents had the upper-hand in intelligence.[18] The guidelines of the main French training centre for the counterinsurgency that immediately followed in Algeria stated that in a counterinsurgency 'everyone' accepts both the 'need' for intelligence given the 'clandestine' nature of the enemy and its 'fluidity.'[19] Timely intelligence for effective military operations was vital, meaning that 'intelligence gathering and its tactical exploitation have to be connected as if in a chain reaction.'[20] But no less characteristic of French late colonial counterinsurgency as a result of the latter was the fact that all intelligence gathering was done either by the military directly or under military authority. This is very clear in French military guidelines: 'the military authority is in charge of restoring order [. . .] therefore it has under its orders all the intelligence gathering institutions.'[21] The militarisation of intelligence was therefore a central aspect of French late colonial counterinsurgency, and the Battle of Algiers, in 1957, became paradigmatic of this, with French military intelligence led by Colonel Trinquier literally taking over the Algiers police, including its archives, and effectively side-lining the few senior policemen who opposed them. It is not insignificant that this was subsequently presented by the French military leadership in Algeria as an example to be followed of the 'need for unity of intelligence gathering and unity of [operational] action' with 'the organisation of intelligence is therefore directly linked at each level to the [military] command structure.' In fact, the priority given to intelligence within the military went so far that that it led to complaints from French troops that they were being reduced to *mere* policemen. One of the most prestigious French officers, Colonel Bigeard, felt obliged to issue a directive to his paratroopers stating that: 'we *are policemen now* because that is what it takes [to win].'[22]

Particularly significant was the eventual establishment of small specialised teams of intelligence and interrogation officers known as *Dispositifs Opérationnels de Protection* [DOPs] (Faivre 2006: 41). However, even this specialisation within the military of these disagreeable tasks, inappropriate for the military, was not enough for some French officers, who would have preferred something closer to the British model. This feeling, amazingly, is given voice in a French professional military journal: 'send to Algeria a special branch [*police spéciale*] if you will and it will be

---

18 SHD 10 H 983 EMAT, *Enseignements de la Guerre d'Indochine*, s.l., s.n., 1955, Vol.2, pp. 28–31.

19 SHD 1H 1115, XRM – CIPCG, *Dossier d'Instruction*, p. 101.

20 SHD 1H 1115, XRM – CIPCG, *Dossier d'Instruction*, p. 106.

21 SHD 1H 1115, XRM – CIPCG, *Dossier d'Instruction*, p. 102.

22 Col. Bigeard, Directive to 3 RPC (28.01.1957), in *Contre-Guérilla*, s.l., 3 R.P.C., 1957, p. 108 [emphasis added].

Intelligence-centric counterinsurgency 141

with relief that we [the military] will give up that task.'[23] In all likelihood, it was not merely a dislike at doing a policeman's job that was being expressed here, but also at the generalised practice of 'enhanced interrogation' i.e. torture in pursuit of actionable intelligence. Even if it is important to note that both the testimonies of French military officers and the analysis of historians indicates that the practice of torture in Algeria predated the militarisation of policing during counterinsurgency, being present before in the local colonial police (Branche 2001, Thénault 2004; for a testimony all the more significant because the officer in question does not deny his involvement in these violent practices see Aussaresses 2005).

What about the Portuguese case? As has been made clear Portuguese late colonial counterinsurgency was less distinct than has often been claimed. One reason is the importance of transnational networks facilitating counterinsurgency knowledge transfer also at the level of intelligence and (high) policing. In my research it became clear that a great deal of importance was explicitly placed upon emulation of British and French doctrinal lessons in the development of Portuguese late colonial counterinsurgency doctrine. This was mentioned in the testimonies of the privileged few Portuguese officers sent directly to Britain and French Algeria for training, who then had a leading role in teaching and developing late colonial counterinsurgency doctrine in Portugal. Even more significantly, the main Portuguese counterinsurgency manual included in its initial couple of pages an exhaustive list of foreign sources, despite the fact that it arguably was somewhat innovative, not least in combining two main sources of foreign lessons, British and French doctrines. This was a way to legitimise via emulation of more prestigious foreign armies the novelty of counterinsurgency.[24] Nevertheless, such evidence has paradoxically co-existed with enduring claims about the uniqueness of late colonial Portuguese counterinsurgency, for either positive or negative reasons, that have already been cited.

The remarkable sudden growth of Portuguese colonial intelligence since the late 1950s and early 1960s was, in sum, part of a very active effort to emulate best practices, primarily drawing from the other two major Western colonial powers, France and Britain. The study mission sent to French Algeria, in 1959, produced a very influential report summarising the guidelines of the French army counterinsurgency training centre in Arzew, among them that 'making prisoners is vital [. . .] as an excellent source of vital information' in this type of warfare.[25] Specifically regarding military intelligence, a few selected staff officers were sent to Britain to attend a course in Field Security/Counter-Intelligence that they saw as 'entirely based on the challenges of Malaya, Kenya, and the Soviet threat, wherever it might manifest itself.' All the main British manuals available in the late 1950s that we have been citing were then brought in and 'quickly translated'

---

23 Simplet [Col. Langlois], Guerre Révolutionnaire, guerre psychologique, ou guerre tout court?, *Revue Militaire d'Information*, Vol. 309, 1959, p. 101.
24 EME, *EGS*, Vol. 1, see 'Foreword' and list of 'Sources'.
25 Pinheiro et al., Relatório da Missão à Argélia-Arzew (Lisboa 20.5.1959) in Antunes J.F. (1995), 207.

142   *Bruno Cardoso Reis*

into Portuguese. Among those sent for training in Britain was General Pedro Cardoso (1995: 829), who became a key figure in the history of Portuguese intelligence, before and after the April 1974 coup, eventually becoming the head of the Portuguese equivalent of the British Join Intelligence Committee.

The officers sent on training missions to France and Britain were then made part of the team at the Staff College that, between 1961–1963, first taught and then wrote Portuguese counterinsurgency guidelines, resulting in the manual *O Exército na Guerra Subversiva* [*The Army in Subversive Warfare*].[26]

What can we gather from all this regarding intelligence-centric policing as part of Portuguese late colonial counterinsurgency? Portugal is one paradigmatic example of the pre-eminence of a civilian police special branch in intelligence matters. Portuguese military guidelines ordered the quick delivery of prisoners to PIDE after a basic preliminary interrogation.[27] And in this very generic aspect Portuguese late colonial counterinsurgency was closer to the British model. True, it is important to note in this respect that PIDE only started to grow significantly in the Portuguese colonies from 1954/1957 onwards, in the expectation of a violent insurgency, and it was from 1961, once the latter had started, that the number of PIDE agents exploded.

The process started in August 1954 with a decree reforming PIDE and setting an aim of having fifty-two personnel in total in the main Portuguese colonies in Africa – Angola, Mozambique and Guinea. Given how small PIDE's presence overseas was, initially, it is only natural that its agents in the colonies worked closely with the 'ordinary' police (PSP) and from within police stations. This was not entirely novel. British intelligence in the Empire, notably in sub-Saharan Africa, also developed relatively late, mostly after 1945, and were strongly reliant upon liaising the MI5 metropolitan intelligence apparatus with local intelligence units of the police in different colonies – but the latter were much more developed and autonomous, unlike in the Portuguese case (Walton 2013).

This close initial linkage in the Portuguese case between high colonial policing and ordinary colonial policing, between PIDE and PSP in fighting anti-colonial activists was dramatically illustrated by the first wave of anti-colonial attacks. In reaction to PIDE-led repression of nationalist networks in Luanda by PSP, Angolan nationalists targeted PSP police stations and a prison in their initial uprising of February 1961. But after that event, PIDE rapidly took-over an increasing leading role and grew significantly. The end result was that in 1974, at the end of late colonial Portuguese counterinsurgency PIDE had 800 personnel in Angola, 630 in Mozambique and 81 in Guinea. This means that in small Portuguese Guinea alone PIDE had more men in 1974 than it had initially planned to have

---

26 For the official history of the process cf. CECA (1990). See also alongside *EGS* cited in full in fn 10 – EME, *Guia para o Emprego Táctico das Pequenas Unidades na Contraguerrilha*, Lisboa, EME, 1961; EME, *Instruções para o Emprego das Forças Armadas em Apoio da Autoridade Civil*, Lisboa, EME, 1962.

27 EME, *EGS*, Vol. 5, pp. I/8–9.

Intelligence-centric counterinsurgency   143

for the whole of Portuguese Africa in 1954. This expansion was often achieved by recruiting *in loco* amongst those military officers and police officers perceived to have shown some aptitude for intelligence work. This may have been the best option available, and may have favored the development of a relatively cohesive colonial intelligence community, but did not prevent some institutional tensions between PIDE and the military (Mateus 2004: 24–25).

The British counterinsurgency approach provided one possible solution for these institutional tensions by the creation of committees for the coordination and dissemination of counterinsurgency related intelligence, from different administrative, police and military entities. Emulation of Britain was indeed the solution pursued to some degree by Pedro Cardoso, who, from 1959 onwards, was put in charge of reforming the intelligence section of the General Defence Staff, almost re-creating it from scratch. After all, according to all the British and French doctrine he and others had been reading, intelligence was a vital requirement for the military to be effective in dealing with an elusive insurgency. Still, military historians tend to agree that the Portuguese 'armed forces did not have a real intelligence service' and therefore 'this core task was performed mainly by PIDE/DGS' (Afonso and Gomes 2001: 234–41).

Pedro Cardoso was then asked by General Deslandes, who was appointed, in April 1961 as Angola's *supremo* to recover control of the territory, to deal with the matter *in loco*. Cardoso created the *Serviço de Centralização e Coordenação das Informações* (SCCI) in the British committee model. This was meant, as its name clearly signals, to both gather and analyse intelligence centrally, and to coordinate intelligence gathering efforts by the civil administration, the ordinary police, the military and PIDE to ensure effective sharing of information. From Angola, in 1961, SCCIs slowly spread to the two other theatres of operations in Portuguese Africa. In fact in Guinea it took so long that Pedro Cardoso was there himself when it was being installed in 1970. Cardoso was then in charge of all 'civil' matters as secretary-general appointed by the local *supremo* General Spínola. Despite his expertise, it is noteworthy that Cardoso was not made responsible for high policing, intelligence remained a preserve of PIDE and General Spínola. Cardoso was also to have a role in reforming intelligence in Mozambique as head of the intelligence section of the General Staff between 1968–1970. The role of Cardoso and the solutions he promoted, influenced by the British model, show the importance but also the potential obstacles faced by foreign emulation and transnational networks of intelligence in counterinsurgency.

Cardoso himself was the first to recognise that his efforts had not gone very far, largely because PIDE feared losing its power and autonomy – namely direct access to the supreme civilian authority. And in this PIDE had the support of the regime strongman, Salazar, who was not willing to give up control over intelligence to anyone. If SCCIs where not completely useless, still according to Cardoso (1995: 834 passim; 2004: 129–136) they developed into something narrower and more limited than originally intended, closer to a form of civilian administrative intelligence. This resulted in some additional capacity to gather information and produce analysis, even if with some limitations (see Araújo's chapter in this book

144   *Bruno Cardoso Reis*

in relation to Mozambique). What the three SCCIs clearly never managed was to really coordinate intelligence, least of all to subordinate PIDE. The emulation of British institutionalisation of intelligence-sharing and coordination by committee was therefore limited.

More effective coordination and *de facto* subordination of PIDE in Africa ended up being a more informal affair. First at lower levels, where things always seemed to have worked better based on personal rather than institutional relations (Afonso and Gomes 2001: 234–235). Later at the top level, once Salazar was gone from power, due to illness, in 1968. The process was driven by powerful military leaders with great political weight of their own. This was especially the case with Generals Spínola in Portuguese Guinea and Costa Gomes in Angola. Both were not only charismatic counterinsurgency military leaders but also were so politically relevant that they would eventually be the leaders of the military coup that overthrew the *Estado Novo* in 1974.

The case of Angola can be seen as paradigmatic in that it presents both extremes: PIDE at its most autonomous and then at its most subordinate. In the late 1960s PIDE felt powerful enough in Angola to turn, in 1967, the so-called *Flechas* (Arrows) – i.e. local tribesmen recruited as PIDE's scouts – into a fully-fledged paramilitary force that engaged in special operations quickly exploiting intelligence and gathering more (Mateus 2004: 173–175, Cann 2014). When, in 1970, General Costa Gomes became Commander-in-Chief in Angola, he felt strong enough to inform the head of PIDE/DGS in Angola that the latter 'could continue to fight, but it could no longer fight its own war, it had to fight *my* war' (cit. Rodrigues 2008: 81). In other words it had to become directly subordinated to him.

PIDE, in other words, regardless of more or less colonial expertise, had for a long time enjoyed the political support that gave it the necessary authority, resources and numbers to be the prime mover in high policing during the Portuguese late colonial wars. Indeed, if PIDE had marginalised the colonies until relatively late in the colonial process, the Portuguese military had marginalised intelligence even more and until even later. By the early 1970s the most that the Portuguese military wanted was greater control over PIDE. This was a result of the Portuguese military's realisation of its own limitations in the field of intelligence *and* that this unconventional and irregular type of conflict had to be intelligence-centric. Emulation of British and French counterinsurgency doctrinal lessons left no room for doubt about this, later confirmed through direct experience.

But what are the implications of the points analysed above for wider debates about intelligence and the late colonial State? This will be the focus of my concluding section.

Late colonial counterinsurgency as policing – some wider implications

In this concluding section three main claims will be made relating my arguments to wider debates in the field of counterinsurgency and the late colonial state. First, the recent revision of the literature on British counterinsurgency away from minimum force makes a crucial contribution, both in terms of allowing a more rigorous comparison with other cases, and because it corrects a mistaken reading of the connection between these counterinsurgency campaigns and imperial policing. There is a connection but it does not result from traditional aid to the civil power doctrine being applied in counterinsurgency. Second, there was in these three cases some sort of colonial intelligence community, but its cohesion cannot be exaggerated or taken for granted. Third, this final show of force by the late colonial state in fact showed both its persistent weaknesses and a paradoxical reinforcement of it in its dying days.

A correct understanding of minimum force issue is crucial if we are to analyze correctly the linkage between the military and policing in the context of late colonial counterinsurgency. Minimum force has been given until recently a central role in the history of British late colonial counterinsurgency, contrasting it with similar campaigns by France and other colonial powers like Portugal. In fact, it is not mentioned at all in British military manuals dealing specifically with counterinsurgency between 1945 and 1970 – the Malaya and Kenya manuals, and the first British generic manual on counterinsurgency. This means that British minimum force in late colonial counterinsurgency was a myth not just in practice, but even in terms of doctrinal principles, as I have argued at length elsewhere (Reis 2011). Crucially for the theme of this book, this was the result of a *misreading* of *the fact that insurgencies were framed in official discourse as internal security problems,* for a number of reasons that have been addressed above, ignoring the fact that the military developed specific counterinsurgency guidelines ignoring traditional aid to civil power and, therefore, minimum force. The most recent literature on British counterinsurgency and late colonial policing have correctly pointed out that, in fact, the trend was for such operations to become increasingly militarised and use lethal even exemplary force (Sinclair 2006: 136 passim, Reis 2011, French 2012, Bennett 2001.

What makes this comparison between Portuguese and British late colonial counterinsurgency especially interesting in this respect, is that Portuguese military guidelines of the early 1960s do contain an explicit reference to minimum force, but in the volume on aid to civil power, not in the volumes focused on counterinsurgency proper. This is not exactly what the traditional contrast between benign British and ruthless Portuguese late colonial counterinsurgency would make us expect. Rather it reflects emulation by the Portuguese military of British doctrinal texts, in line with a Portuguese professional policing tradition of trying to align itself with the rest of the West. There was also a specific Portuguese legal norm prescribing that shooting at rebellious crowds had to be preceded by three clear warnings that lethal force was about to be used.[28] But even this and even when it was applied – in areas away from actual active insurgency – of course, meant minimum *necessary* and *legal* force, two key, often forgotten qualifiers, which could mean the use of still quite a lot of deadly force, particularly in a colonial setting.

28 EME, *EGS*, Vol. 4, pp. II/22.

146   *Bruno Cardoso Reis*

Regarding the French case what is most relevant is not the absence of minimum force in its late colonial counterinsurgency guidelines but rather the militarising of all the vital policing aspect of counterinsurgency – namely intelligence. This led to the French military being held directly responsible for abuses in interrogating prisoners that in the other cases were attributed to a special branch in charge of high policing. But this should not make us think that this systematic use of abusive force in pursuit of intelligence was an exclusive problem of the French military. What is most relevant from the point of view of our analysis is that these systematic abuses during interrogations were closely linked to the nature of counterinsurgency as an intelligence-centric conflict greatly dependent upon high policing. And with the fact that intelligence was being gathered in a colonial context where policing, even in normal times, was not exactly bound by ordinary democratic rule of law.

The second concluding point is directly related to pursuing the point rightly raised by Martin Thomas (2005: 1042–1043) when he highlights the importance of a 'cohesive imperial "intelligence community"'. British general Frank Kitson (1977: 285), who had a very long career fighting insurgencies from Kenya to Northern Ireland, often as an intelligence officer, did underline that it would be harder in a post-colonial future to achieve coordination of different aspects of state power vital for an effective counterinsurgency because in colonial contexts a lot of discretionary power was already concentrated in a small closely connected community of senior colonial officials and military and police officers. Yet Kitson himself provides a good example of how the existence of this community cannot be confused with a monolithic identity of views, for instance on how best to organise intelligence to fight an insurgency. Kitson (1960: 92–94) makes clear that his controversial experience in developing so-called counter-gangs of pseudo-insurgents in Kenya, was only possible because of support from the very top military leadership because 'so many people were opposed to our ideas'.

As I have tried to show in the Portuguese case, convergence on some key points vital for colonial state security did not avoid serious tensions about issues such as hierarchy, coordination and even whether the approach to intelligence should be more enemy-centric or more population-centric, more the PIDE approach versus the SCCIs' approach. General Cardoso's (Cardoso 2004: 135) complaints about how PIDE had 'covertly worked against' his intelligence reforms present an interesting parallel with Kitson's complaints.

In the French case this was manifest in even more dramatic fashion in the opposition of some to the militarisation of all police work during the intelligence-centric Battle of Algiers and the brutal methods being used – most famously with the resignation in protest of Paul Teitgen, the head of the police department in French Algiers, in 1957.

In sum, a degree of rivalry between civilians and military actors, and between different branches of the military and the police is probably inevitable, even in a colonial war setting. And if fighting an insurgency made intelligence more vital, it also made it potentially more contentious.

Third, the development of an intelligence-centric imperial high policing played an important role in the post-1945 trend towards a stronger late colonial State. In the British, French and Portuguese doctrinal guidelines developed in reaction to the threat of anti-colonial insurgencies the weaknesses of the colonial State in general and of policing in particular were implicitly or explicitly recognised. For instance the main Portuguese late colonial counterinsurgency manual – far from the idea of a very effectively brutal Portuguese colonial state – includes among the priority 'missions of the Armed Forces' for successful counterinsurgency 'those that have as their aim keeping or regaining the support of the people, i.e., psycho-social action and control of the population' because 'in the overseas provinces the density of administrative authorities and police forces is very small.' The Portuguese military, in other words, felt it had to be responsible for some belated colonial state-building.[29] Still, a *caveat* is in order. This trend could provoke a backlash: 'far from bringing the colonizers closer to the people, security service efforts to develop an information order' and to enhance colonial rule often 'increased popular antagonism to the mechanisms of state surveillance and colonial rule' (Thomas 2005: 1055). The events of February 1961 in Luanda – now increasingly seen as an improvised violent reaction to police repression of anti-colonial networks, more than a planned uprising – provide a paradigmatic example of this.

Conclusion

In sum, the colonial state arguably always had the aim of being some sort of police state (on the latter definition see Hoffman 2012: 1004–1008). The intelligence-centric nature of counterinsurgency and the significant resources it required ensured that the late colonial state certainly acquired some characteristics of a police state. We can find support for this potentially controversial view even in official guidelines. French counterinsurgency made clear that high policing, intelligence, should be a 'permanent' effort aimed not just at the 'armed insurgent' but at the 'whole of the population', the 'whole of the country' and a whole range of 'military, economic, political' issues, in what might be qualified as a very *Brodeurian* statement.[30] Even in the public apologia of British counterinsurgency in Malaya in a book published by one of its leading figures Sir Robert Thompson, we can find evidence of this. The first of Thompson's (1966, 50–53, 55, 70–83) principles for success in counterinsurgency was the need for an 'an overall plan' that included 'all political, social, economic, administrative, police and other measures which have a bearing on the insurgency'. He went on to make the case that while a state should not break its own laws in order to win a counterinsurgency, it could enforce very harsh laws like Britain had done during counterinsurgency in Malaya, and he gives examples: 'strict curfews, a mandatory death penalty for carrying arms, life imprisonment for providing supplies or other support to the terrorists'. In other words, being a colonial police state was, clearly, not exclusive to Portugal. Not because Portuguese colonialism was especially benign, but

---

29 EME, *EGS*, Vol. 1, pp. II/19.
30 SHD 1H 1115, XRM – CIPCG, *Dossier d'Instruction*, p. 101.

148 *Bruno Cardoso Reis*

because no form of colonialism was. Indeed we might argue that Portugal developed later than the British or French colonial states the means to be more ruthlessly effective, namely in terms of high policing.

It is important to emphasise, however, that this was, in my view, the result of the fact that the colonial state remained to a remarkable degree a foreign state to the colonised societies it ruled over. After centuries in coastal areas, many decades in the hinterland, of Portuguese colonisation – the oldest European colonial power in Africa – a leading military intelligence expert, like Pedro Cardoso (1995: 834), was still forced to concede that 'we did not know well the ethnic-linguistic and religious communities' in the overseas territories, as is well illustrated by the efforts to fill this gap by the SCCI in Mozambique (see Araújo's chapter in this volume).

Colonial states may have been like police states in their discretionary use of powers of surveillance, control and repression of the local population. But in most cases, and in most colonies, they were limited by their lack of basic knowledge about native societies as well as by their lack of repressive capabilities. This was true at least until something as serious as a major insurgency arose, and to a certain degree even after that. A great deal of discretionary power for violent repression by the colonial state was an ever-present threat for the colonised people. But this was tempered by an acute awareness on the part of the colonial authorities of how limited their resources really were. And also a realisation of how unpopular colonial officials, namely those in charge of policing, would become with the government at the metropole if they were held responsible for something as politically messy and financially costly as a major insurgency. Anti-colonial insurgencies, in other words, represented a defeat of the late colonial intelligence state from the moment that they started. After all what greater intelligence failure could there be than to fail to prevent a major insurgency? The paradox is that the last days of colonialism in Africa witnessed a major expansion of the colonial state, namely in terms of high policing, in what was an ultimately vain attempt to respond to the challenge of *finding* the anti-colonial insurgents in vast territories and amongst diverse civilian population in order to be able to *fight* them effectively.

References

Afonso, A. and Gomes, C.M. 2001. *Guerra Colonial*. Lisboa: Editorial Noticias.

Anderson, D. 2005. *Histories of the Hanged: Britain's Dirty War in Kenya and the End of Empire*. London: Weidenfeld & Nicolson.

Anderson, D. and Killingray, D. (eds). 1991. *Policing and Decolonisation: Nationalism, Politics and the Police, 1917–65*. Manchester: Manchester UP.

Antunes, J.F. 1992. *Kennedy e Salazar: O Leão e a Raposa*. s.l.: Círculo de Leitores.

Aussaresses, P. 2005. *Battle of the Casbah: Counter-Terrorism and Torture*. New York: Enigma.

Babington, Anthony. 1990. *Military Intervention in Britain: From the Gordon Riots to the Gibraltar Incident*. London: Routledge.

Bayly, C.A. 1996. *Empire and Information: Intelligence Gathering and Social Communication in India, 1780–1870*. Cambridge: CUP.

Intelligence-centric counterinsurgency 149

Benett, H. 2012. *Fighting the Mau Mau: The British Army and Counter-Insurgency in the Kenya Emergency*. Cambridge: CUP.

Bennett, H. 2011. Soldiers in the court room: The British Army's part in the Kenya emergency under the legal spotlight. *The Journal of Imperial and Commonwealth History*, 39(5): 717–730.

Blanchard, E. and Glasman, J. 2012. Le Mantien de l'Ordre Dans l'Empire Français: Une Historiographie Émergente, in *Maintenir l'ordre colonial: Afrique et Magagascar, XIXᵉ- XXᵉ siècles*, edited by J.-P. Bat and N. Courtin. Rennes: Presses Univ. de Rennes.

Bowen, R. 1966. *Report on Procedures for Arrest, Interrogation and Detention of Suspected Terrorists in Aden*. London: HMSO.

Branche, R. 2001. *La Torture et l'Armée pendant la Guerre d'Algérie (1954–1962)*. Paris: Gallimard.

Brodeur, J.-P. 2010. *The Policing Web*. Oxford: Oxford UP.

Brodeur, J.-P. and Leman-Langlois, S. 2006. Surveillance Fiction or Higher Policing in *The New Politics of Surveillance and Visibility*, edited by K.D. Haggerty and R.V. Ericson. Toronto: University of Toronto Press, 171–198.

Brogden, M. 1987a. The emergence of the police – The colonial dimension. *British Journal of Criminology*, 27(1): 4–14.

Brogden, M. 1987b. An act to colonise the internal lands of the island: Empire and the origins of the professional police. *International Journal of the Sociology of Law*, 15: 179–208.

Cann, J. 1997. *Counter-Insurgency in Africa: The Portuguese Way of War, 1961–1974*. Westport: Greenwood Press.

Cann, J. 2014. *The Flechas: Insurgent Hunting in Eastern Angola, 1965–1974*. Solihull: Helion.

Cardoso, P. 1995. Poder de Saber, in *A Guerra de África*, Vol. 2, edited by J.F. Antunes. s.l.: Círculo de Leitores, 828–834.

Cardoso, P. 2004. *As Informações em Portugal*. Lisboa: Gradiva.

Carruthers, S. 1995. *Winning Hearts and Minds: British Governments, the Media and Colonial Counterinsurgency, 1944–1960*. London: Leicester UP.

CECA. 1988. *Resenha Histórico-Militar das campanhas de África: 1961–1974*. Lisboa: EME, 4 vols.

CECA. 1990. *Subsídios para o Estado da Doutrina Aplicada nas Campanhas de África*. Lisboa: EME.

Charlan, Ph. 2007. Professionalism, in *The Encyclopedia of Police Science*, edited by Jack R. Greene. New York: Routledge, 1063–1065.

Cloake, J. 1985. *Templer: Tiger of Malaya: The Life of Field Marshal Gerald Templer*. London: Harrap.

Coates, J. 1992. *Suppressing Insurgency: An Analysis of the Malayan Emergency 1948–1954*. Boulder: Westview.

Comber, L. 2008. *Malaya's Secret Police 1945–60: The Role of the Special Branch in the Malayan Emergency*. Singapore: Institute of Southeast Asian Studies.

Costa Gomes, F. 1998. *O Último Marechal*, with M.M. Cruzeiro. Lisboa: Notícias.

Faivre, M. 1998. *Le Général Paul Ély et la Politique de Défense (1956–1961)*. Paris: Economica.

Faivre, M. 2006. *Le Renseignment dans la Guerre d'Algérie*. Panazol: La Vauzelle.

French, D. 2012. *The British Way in Counter-Insurgency, 1945–1967*. Oxford: OUP.

150 Bruno Cardoso Reis

Gregorian, R. 1994. 'Jungle bashing' in Malaya: Towards a formal tactical doctrine. *Small Wars & Insurgencies*, 5(3): 338–359.

Gwyn, Ch. 1939. *Imperial Policing*. 2nd rev. ed. London: Macmillan [orig. ed. pub. 1934].

Hoffman, D. 2012. Police states, in *The Encyclopedia of Police Science*, edited by J.R. Greene. London: Routledge, 1004–1008.

Howard, M. 1984. The military factor in European expansion, in *The Expansion of International Society*, edited by H. Bull and A. Watson. Oxford: Clarendon Press, 33–43.

Kitson, F. 1960. *Gangs and Counter-Gangs*. London: Barrie and Rockliff.

Kitson, F. 1977. *Bunch of Five*. London: Faber & Faber.

Le Révérend, A. 1983. *Lyautey*. Paris: Fayard.

Lewis, M., Branche, R., Imlay, T., Stanard, M., Thomas, M.[0] 2013. Review of violence and colonial order police, workers and protest in the European Colonial Empires, 1918–1940. H-Diplo Review Roundatable [Online], 15(5). Available at: www.h-net.org/~diplo/roundtables/PDF/Roundtable-XV-5.pdf [accessed: 11.12.2013].

L'Heuillet, Hélène. 2001. *Une approche historique et philosophique de la police*. Paris: Fayard.

Mateus, D. 2004. *A PIDE/DGS na Guerra Colonial: 1961–1974*. Lisboa: Terramar.

Michel, M. 1989. *Gallieni*. Paris: Fayard.

Nagl, J. 2002. *Counterinsurgency Lessons From Malaya and Vietnam: Learning to Eat Soup With a Knife*. London: Praeger.

Neves, O. 2001. Moçambique, in *Nova História da Expansão Portuguesa. XI. O Império Africano 1890–1930*, edited by A.H. Marques. Lisboa: Ed. Estampa, 469–584.

O'Neill, B. 1990. *Insurgency and Terrorism: Inside Modern Revolutionary Warfare*. Washington, DC: Brassey's.

O'Reilly, C. 2015. The pluralization of high policing: Convergence and divergence at the public – Private interface. *British Journal of Criminology*, 55(2): 1–15.

Paget, J. 1967. *Counterinsurgency Campaigning*. London: Faber & Faber.

Palacios Cerezales, D. 2011. *Portugal à Coronhada: Protesto e Ordem Pública nos séculos XIX e XX*. Lisboa: Tinta da China.

Pimentel, I. 2007. *A História da PIDE*. s.l.: Círculo de Leitores.

Porch, D. 1986. Bugeaud, Gallieni, Lyautey: The development of French colonial warfare, in *Makers of Modern Strategy*, edited by P. Paret. Oxford: Oxford UP: 1986, maxime 395–398.

Reis, B.C. 2011. The myth of British minimum force in counterinsurgency during the campaigns of decolonization. *Journal of Strategic Studies*, 34(2): 245–279.

Rodrigues, L. 2008. *Marechal Costa Gomes: No Centro da Tempestade*. Lisboa: A Esfera dos Livros.

Sinclair, G. 2006. *At the End of the Line: Colonial Policing and the Imperial Endgame*. Manchester: Manchester UP.

Sôtto, Major A. 1943. *Operações Militares de Policia para Repressão das Tribos Mucubas Insubmissas na Colonia de Angola em 1940–1941: Breve Noticia*. Lisboa: s.n.

Thénault, S. 2004. *Une Drôle de Justice: Les Magistrats dans la Guerre d'Algérie*. Paris: La Découverte.

Thomas, M. 2005. Colonial states as intelligence states: Security policing and the limits of colonial rule in France's Muslim territories, 1920–40. *The Journal of Strategic Studies*, 28(6): 1033–1060.

Thomas, M. 2012. *Violence and Colonial Order: Police, Workers and Protest in the European Colonial Empires, 1918–1940.* Cambridge: CUP.

Thompson, R. 1966. *Defeating Communist Insurgency: Experiences From Malaya and Vietnam.* London: Chatto & Windus.

Townshend, Charles. 1988. *Britain's Civil Wars: Counter-Insurgency in the Twentieth Century.* London: Faber & Faber.

Trinquier, R. 1964. *Modern Warfare: A French View of Counter-Insurgency.* London: Pall Mall Press [orig. French ed. 1961].

Valença, F. 1981. *A Abrilada de 1961: as Forças Armadas e as Crises Nacionais.* Mem-Martins: Europa-América.

Villatoux, P. and Villatoux, M. 2005. *La Republique et son Armée Face au Peril Subversif: Guerre et Action Psychologiques en France, 1945–1960.* Paris: Les Indes Savantes.

Walton, C. 2013. *Empire of Secrets: British Intelligence, the Cold War and the Twilight of Empire.* London: Harper Press.

Wright, A. 2002. *Policing: An Introduction to Concepts and Practice.* Cullompton: Willan Pub.

Comment

Reflections on Portuguese late colonial policing

Martin Thomas

Let's begin, in reflecting on these three fascinating chapters, with the general factors typically identified as setting Portuguese decolonisation apart. Six are perhaps most commonly cited. First is the existence of the Lisbon dictatorship. Increasingly unpopular and geriatric to be sure, its declining position at home tended, if anything, to increase its political investment in empire. This phenomenon might be described as a late 20th century variant of the social imperialism thesis once applied to Wilhelmine Germany. In both cases, according to this interpretational line, a socially conservative, highly militarised regime laid greater stress upon imperial attachments in a desperate bid to deflect domestic societal pressure for democratisation (Costa Pinto 2003: 19–20).

Linked to this first factor is a second: civil-military friction. The contest for supremacy between the institutions of the Salazarist state and the security forces called upon to do its bidding proved instrumental to the final outcome of Portugal's decolonisation from Africa. While the remit of Portuguese military action might be imperial and global, this second factor is, once again, primarily metropolitan in focus. Salazar's regime, and Caetano's gerontocracy that succeeded it, could not survive without the support or, at minimum, the acquiescence of Portugal's armed forces. Domestic and colonial loathing for the regime's secret police ran deep, as evidenced in the preceding three chapters. Yet the military's social standing set it apart from the regime's internal security services, helping to conserve popular respect for the army despite – or even perhaps because of – its immersion in three decolonisation conflicts. For all that, as was the case with France and Algeria from 1956 onwards, public support for involvement in these theatres eroded once large numbers of national service personnel – young conscripts rather than volunteer professionals – were sent to fight their country's colonial wars.

Put differently, the constituent elements of this second factor – the military's position – must be disaggregated. Professional commanders and long-service professional units became alienated from a Lisbon regime whose backing for the three discrete campaigns being fought in Portuguese Africa they found both perilously inadequate and politically self-serving. More to the point, it became clearer over time that the regime might deflect personal responsibility for ultimate defeat onto commanders *in situ*. There was, after all, a painful precedent for this in the punishments meted out to senior officers following Portugal's humiliating eviction from Goa in 1961 (Robinson 2003: 4–9). For all that, Generals and Colonels tended to vent their frustration behind closed doors. Frontline cadres and their dependents were less reserved. A more vocal source of opposition to these protracted wars emanated from conscripts, their junior officers, and their families back home, none of which considered the price of keeping empire worth paying.

Here again, there are links with our third factor, the last with a metropolitan edge. For the discontent fed by costly colonial war was harnessed to the more pervasive Portuguese public animosity to the dictatorship. Portuguese society was changing fast. Urbanisation and attendant housing pressures rendered Lisbon's fast-expanding population in particular harder to govern and to control. Changing patterns of migration brought more Portuguese into contact with more prosperous Western European societies. Closer trade relationships with the European Economic Community promised greater rewards to Portugal's export producers than a captive, but impoverished African colonial market. As a result, so the argument goes, unending colonial wars assumed a doubly negative aspect. On the one hand, they were out of step with Portugal's societal modernisation. On the other hand, they held back that modernisation to the detriment of the country's long-term prosperity (Clarence-Smith 1985: 193). In simple terms, the pressures of decolonisation catalyzed the regime's collapse amidst the Carnation revolution of 1974. Central to this line of thinking is the Armed Forces Movement (*Movimento das Forças Armadas* – MFA), which, despite drawing its numerical strength from service personnel fighting reluctantly in Africa, was always primarily concerned with ejecting the Salazarists from power back home to release the country's true potential (Ramos Pinto 2013: 105).

Another compelling metropolitan explanation for the co-terminal collapse of Portugal's dictatorial regime and its overseas empire comes from political scientist Hendrick Spruyt. He points out that the rapid withdrawal from Lusophone Africa after the April 1974 revolution was closely linked to the absence of political pluralism at home. Logically enough, most commentators have focused on the regime's opponents to explain its downfall. But, in Spruyt's analysis, the underlying reasons for the dictatorship's overthrow were more systemic. Having denied political space to civil society groups over so many decades, the regime silenced not just the opponents of imperial attachments, but their supporters as well. Aggrieved settlers were unable to petition effectively for any continuation of the wars in Angola and Mozambique once the army – the sole organisation powerful enough to challenge state power – turned against both regime and empire. Having proscribed multiparty politics and containing civil society activism the regime sealed its own fate. Even pro-imperialist settlers were stifled, leaving the regime isolated when the military turned against it (Spruyt 2005: 195–201).

Moving from metropolitan considerations to broader colonial or transnational factors, three more might be singled out. First is the obvious point that Portuguese Africa was engulfed by three conflicts at once. More than coincidental, the origins, development and outcome of the anti-colonial wars in Angola, Mozambique and Guiné-Bissau were connected in multiple ways. For one thing, the principal

154   *Martin Thomas*

movements involved were transnationally networked. Some shared common ideologies. The senior leadership cadres of others were connected by their elite backgrounds, which afforded access to advanced education and, later, administrative service. A good number of these people shared similar experiences of exile and imprisonment. Still others were conjoined by their adhesion to broader anti-colonial and pan-Africanist movements at regional, continental, or global level. Clearly problematic insofar as leftist elites were often ignorant of rural lives and concerns, the transnational ties between nationalist leaderships were strategically significant even so (Nugent 2004: 282–286). Indeed, these anti-colonial connections helped generate similar practices of insurgent warfare. And while the internecine quality to the conflicts in Angola and Mozambique impeded joint inter-colonial action against the Portuguese, offensives launched in one colony nonetheless assisted the prosecution of war in the others.

The second local consideration often stressed is the role of settler colonialism in Mozambique and, above all, Angola. Regime efforts to encourage colonisation saw tens of thousands of Europeans migrate to both colonies in the 1950s especially. Nominally part of the Lusotropical enterprise, most of these settlers were determined to conserve their relatively privileged position within late colonial societies. Few were wealthy. Fewer still were substantial landowners, despite the generous terms offered for land acquisition, usually at African expense (Bender 1978: 127–131). Instead, their urban concentration and predominantly artisanal backgrounds were strongly redolent of French Algeria's *petits colons* or the 'poor whites' of British East Africa.[1] The sociology of Lusophone settler society aside, the point to emphasise here is that the presence of such large numbers of migrants was bound to affect security planning. From the mass departures of Europeans from Luanda in the first stages of Angola's war of independence to the final, larger evacuations of settlers at the end of the conflicts in Portuguese Southern Africa, the fate of white minorities was emblematic of the wider course of these wars. If the presence of large numbers of Europeans helped sustain the foundational myths of Portuguese colonialism, their ultimate removal surely signified the definitive abandonment of Portugal's colonial project. The fact that approximately 75% of Angola's 335,000 white settlers left the colony for good in the final years of the Caetano administration offered incontrovertible evidence that Portuguese defeat was perceived as imminent by those likely to be most immediately affected by it. Much the same could be said for the similar proportion among Mozambique's 200,000 whites that opted to go (Clarence-Smith 1985: 213). Tellingly, their rate of departure accelerated markedly in the years 1971–1973 (Bowen 2000: 45).

---

1 For the 'poor white' phenomenon and the transgressive behaviour ascribed to poor white urban settlers in Kenya, see Will Jackson, 'Bad blood, psychopathy and politics of transgression in Kenya Colony, 1939–1959,' *Journal of Imperial & Commonwealth History*, 39:1, 2011, 73–94; and, more generally, *idem, Madness and Marginality: The Lives of Kenya's White Insane*, Manchester: Manchester University Press, 2013.

Comment 155

The third and last colonial factor that must surely be considered is the civil war dimension to contested decolonisation in Angola and Mozambique. The analytical implication here is that Portuguese actions were increasingly secondary to the internecine conflicts played out between local rivals for power. To be sure, as our authors have demonstrated, the Portuguese colonial authorities lent support to favoured clients, delegating much of the dirty work of war to paramilitary militias and other irregular forces. But the key issue of who was manipulating whom became harder to untangle as clashes between local rivals intensified and the Portuguese grip over the rural interior weakened. The benefit of hindsight also makes apparent the extent to which the support offered by Cold War outsiders to their local proxies in Lusophone Southern Africa was prefigured in the external aid garnered by contesting insurgent movements in their fight against Portuguese colonialism. Again, there are echoes of such foreign interventionism in other decolonisations from French Indochina to the Belgian Congo. But nowhere did the poisonous combination of paramilitarism, foreign sponsorship, and internecine rivalry have such enduring consequences in decades of civil war.

Each of the three chapters, in different ways, has much of say about the singularities of Portuguese decolonisation. For Bruno Reis, this is the central issue, his argument being that Portugal pursued strategies of late colonial governance, counterinsurgency, and psychological warfare analogous with its French and British counterparts. Any singularities of regime ideology are thus outweighed by the commonalities of military doctrine and repressive practice on the ground. Sandra Araújo is equally careful to situate her assessment of the SCCIM (*Serviços de Centralização e Coordenação de Informação de Moçambique* or 'Mozambique Information Coordination and Centralisation Services') within a comparative framework. As she makes plain, its information-gathering exercises about Mozambique's Muslim minority population were rudimentary and riddled with stereotype. SCCIM information gathering was, in this sense, comparable to the surveillance and psychological warfare operations of the colony's secret police. Whether through coaxing or coercion, each sought to convince northern Mozambique's Muslims to rally to the regime in opposition to the Godless Marxism of FRELIMO. Neither enjoyed much success (Alpers 1999: 171–183). Few SCCIM questionnaires seem to have reached the highest tiers of government.

For all that, the SCCIM was symptomatic of structural changes in imperial administration, whose increasing professionalisation brought intelligence specialists to the fore. Indeed, the expansion of the security bureaucracy in Portugal's Southern African territories ran in parallel with the growth of the colonial administration in Lisbon. Particularly noteworthy was the 1959 creation of the Overseas Ministry's Political Affairs Department (Gabinete dos Negócios Politicos – GNP), which, as Miguel Bandeira and António Costa Pinto have demonstrated, became the metropolitan hub for the analysis of colonial intelligence (Bandeira and Costa Pinto 2015: 54, 57–58). The point is an important one, not least because it helps explain why colonial secret police agencies accrued such authority and influence over the repression of nationalist movements and other civil society groups within Portuguese Africa. Fernando Tavares Pimenta's rich analysis of PIDE operations against Angola's most prominent anti-colonial groups in the rebellion's crucial

156   *Martin Thomas*

preparatory phase is immensely revealing in this regard. His conclusions are also consistent with Araújo's. Determined to sow dissent among nationalist movements that it could not otherwise contain, the PIDE's violence actors used markers of racial difference and social status to claim that these groups were self-serving and unrepresentative. Unabashed in their pursuit of divide and rule, PIDE officers inadvertently acknowledged that the regime was anything but colour-blind. The supreme irony here was this: the reality of Angola's racial segmentation – a colonial phenomenon – was mobilised against the very anti-colonial forces that contested it. In Pimenta's pithy phrase, 'Racism was thus used as a weapon to detonate the Angolan nationalist movement.'

In conclusion, these three chapters remind us why Portugal's colonial withdrawal from Africa was so protracted and so painful. State security forces and, in many instances, the settler communities that backed them, grew increasingly repressive as their strategic position worsened. This apparent paradox – of greater violence in response to growing weakness – was, in fact, no paradox at all. It was, rather, a by-product of a form of asymmetric warfare in which imperial security forces' numerical and technological superiority confers minimal advantage in the absence of sustained control over local populations. It is this strategic calculation as much as any distinctively Salazarist colonial repression, which explains both the official preoccupation with human intelligence gathering and the belated efforts made to 'understand' the internal dynamics of local communities.

As the three chapters demonstrate, this intelligence work was consistently stymied by three factors. One was essentially a problem of resources, human and material. Although the numbers of secret police and intelligence analysts deployed to Angola and Mozambique increased markedly in the latter stages of Portugal's colonial wars, they were insufficient to accomplish the gargantuan tasks assigned to them. A second, deeper problem confronting these state agents was that of cognition; in other words, less a matter of accumulating information than of processing it – of reading intelligence right. Loaded with presumptions about the ways in which dependent populations and their political leaders might react to external pressures and state inducements, intelligence analysis was the victim of the colonialist mindsets that produced it.[2] Little more than a counterinsurgency variant of classic Orientalism, this barrier to understanding was compounded by a third and final factor. This was the shortage of detailed knowledge about the colonial communities that the Portuguese professed to administer. That the sociological basis of colonial authority remained superficial is well evidenced by the preceding chapters. The reliance on translators and other local intermediaries and the limited understanding of religious and kinship affiliations among Muslim communities explained by Sandra Araújo each exposed the gaps in colonial knowledge production. Colonial administration was neither administratively rooted

---

2 This is a point I've pursued in an earlier historical context in *Empires of Intelligence: Security Forces and Colonial Disorder After 1914*, Berkeley, CA, University of California Press, 2007, especially Chapter 1.

within colonial society nor culturally attuned to its foremost concerns as a result. For all that, as Bruno Reis reminds us, this was by no means a uniquely Portuguese imperial shortfall. It was merely a Lusophone iteration of the knowledge gaps and repressive actions of colonial counter-insurgencies in general.

If there is much to be said for abandoning any idea of Portuguese colonial exceptionalism, certain other factors should give us pause. One is the distinct role of the military. The army's mounting antagonism to the Lisbon regime and its growing dependence on local paramilitary auxiliaries were each highly combustible politically (Wheeler 1976, Henriksen 1977). The first augured the army protest movement that was so pivotal to the end of the Portuguese dictatorship at home and overseas. The second typified a descent into inter-communalist violence and dirty war methods. The consequences were grim indeed. Appalling violence against civilians, a hardening of ethnic, communal and religious animosities, and the greater likelihood of civil war once the old colonial masters were gone. Here, too, Bruno Reis is surely right in seeing echoes of British and, even more so, of French colonial experiences elsewhere. A volatile officer elite and reluctant conscripts will be familiar to any student of French Algeria (Alexander 2002: 246–259). The excesses of loyalist militias, hiding their pursuit of local advantage beneath a thin veneer of government sanction, are redolent of the civil war conditions of Kenya's Mau Mau Emergency (Branch 2007, 2014). Moreover, the violence involved was less discretely colonial than characteristic of societal breakdown. As political scientist Stathis Kalyvas notes, historians have been at pains, especially in recent decades, to emphasise that the 'real' dynamics of apparently political or ideological violence in civil wars lay in the less immediately visible context of ethnic tensions, material conflicts or community rivalries. Viewed from this perspective, much of what might appear to be political, or was indeed claimed to be political by the actors at the time, would appear to have been motivated by pre-existing social tensions or to have been a by-product of the more immediate stimuli of envy or acquisition (Conway and Gerwarth 2011: 141, Kalyvas 2006).

In other respects, though, the decolonisation process hit Portuguese Africa differently. Its relatively late timing guaranteed a louder chorus of criticism from interested outsiders that were already mobilised for action by other, earlier anti-colonial contests. For one thing, there were more independent African states to lead that chorus, whether in pan-Africanist forums, at the United Nations or elsewhere. For another thing, revulsion at systems of colonial governance built on discrimination and exclusion was more widespread. Portugal's military operations in Southern Africa disquieted NATO allies, although not enough initially to prevent them supplying weaponry and advice to the regime. In similar vein, the promise of a distinctly pro-nationalist turn in US African policy under John F. Kennedy's administration was neither fulfilled by Lyndon Johnson's successor team nor replicated by other European partners. The decisive turn in NATO opinion thus came later, from 1968, after which former imperial and Cold War allies abandoned the regime (Muehlenbeck 2012: 97–111, 199–205, Nuno Rodrigues 2015: 246–256). In practice, this was less in deference to the moral outrage of their voters than in anticipation of the need to find stronger local

158 *Martin Thomas*

proxies to resist the Communisation of Southern Africa. Whatever the motivation, a reckoning of UN Security Council votes on Portuguese Africa during Marcello Caetano's term of office speaks volumes. At no stage between July 1969 and July 1973 did the United States, France or Britain endorse the Portuguese position in any of the sixteen votes taken (MacQueen and Oliveira 2010: 31).

Changing international alignments were equally significant at a regional level. The warring parties in all three Portuguese colonial conflicts in Africa relied on cross-border sanctuary and external aid. This proxy war dimension to Portuguese decolonisation, often remarked upon, was devastating in its longer-term consequences, particularly along the frontiers of Angola and Mozambique where the Cold War frontlines became bound up with the older, even more intractable enclaves of white minority rule (Westad 2007: 224–227, Henriksen 1980, Jackson 1995). Angolan and Mozambican communities were left with no respite between the violence of decolonisation and the ravages of civil wars in which external proxies – South African, American, Cuban, Chinese and Soviet – played almost as decisive a role as the Portuguese had done previously (Gleijeses 2003, Jaster 1988: Pt III, Schneidman 2004).

References

Alexander, Martin S. 2002. Seeking France's 'Lost Soldiers': Reflections on the Military Crisis in Algeria, in *Crisis and Renewal in France, 1918–1962*, edited by Kenneth Mouré and M.S. Alexander. Oxford: Berghahn, 242–266.

Alpers, Edward A. 1999. Islam in the service of colonialism? Portuguese strategy during the armed liberation struggle in Mozambique. *Lusotopie*, 171–183.

Bandeira Jerónimo, Miguel, and António Costa Pinto. 2015. A modernizing empire? Politics, culture, and economy in Portuguese late colonialism, in *The Ends of European Colonial Empires: Cases and Comparisons*, edited by Miguel Bandeira Jerónimo and António Costa Pinto. Basingstoke: Palgrave, 51–80.

Bender, Gerald J. 1978. *Angola Under the Portuguese. The Myth and the Reality*. London: Heinemann.

Bowen, M. 2000. *The State Against the Peasantry: Rural Struggles in Colonial and Postcolonial Mozambique*. Charlottesville: University of Virginia Press.

Branch, Daniel. 2007. The enemy within: Loyalists and the war against Mau Mau. *Journal of African History*, 48(2): 291–315.

Branch, Daniel. 2014. Violence, decolonisation, and the Cold War in Kenya's North Eastern Province, 1963–1978. *Journal of East African Studies*, 8(4): 642–657.

Clarence-Smith, G. 1985. *The Third Portuguese Empire, 1825–1975*. Manchester: Manchester University Press.

Conway, Martin and Robert Gerwarth. 2011. Revolution and counter-revolution, in *Political Violence in Twentieth-Century Europe*, edited by Donald Bloxham and Robert Gerwarth. Cambridge: Cambridge University Press, 140–175.

Costa Pinto, António. 2003. The transition to democracy and Portugal's decolonization, in *The Last Empire: Thirty Years of Portuguese Decolonization*, edited by Stewart Lloyd-Jones and António Costa Pinto. Bristol: Intellect, 17–35.

Gleijeses, Piero. 2003. *Conflicting Missions. Havana, Washington and Africa, 1959–1976*. Chapel Hill: University of North Carolina Press.

Henriksen, Thomas H. 1977. Some notes on the national liberation wars in Angola, Mozambique and Guinea-Bissau. *Military Affairs*, 41(1): 30–37.

Henriksen, Thomas H. 1980. Angola, Mozambique and Soviet intervention: Liberation and the quest for influence, in *Soviet and Chinese Aid to African Nations*, edited by Warren Weinstein and Thomas H. Henriksen. New York: Praeger.

Jackson, Steven F. 1995. China's third world foreign policy: The case of Angola and Mozambique, 1961–1993. *China Quarterly*, 142: 388–422.

Jackson, Will. 2011. Bad blood, psychopathy and politics of transgression in Kenya Colony, 1939–1959. *Journal of Imperial & Commonwealth History*, 39(1): 73–94.

Jackson, Will. 2013. *Madness and Marginality: The Lives of Kenya's White Insane*. Manchester: Manchester University Press.

Jaster, Robert Scott. 1988. *The Defence of White Power: South African Foreign Policy Under Pressure*. London: Macmillan.

Kalyvas, Stathis. 2006. *The Logic of Violence in Civil War*. Cambridge: Cambridge University Press.

MacQueen, Norrie and Oliveira, Pedro Aires. 2010. 'Grocer meets butcher': Marcello Caetano's London visit of 1973 and the last days of Portugal's *Estado Novo*. *Cold War History*, 10(1): 29–50.

Muehlenbeck, Philip E. 2012. *Betting on the Africans: John F. Kennedy's Courting of African Nationalist Leaders*. Oxford: Oxford University Press.

Nugent, Paul. 2004. *Africa Since Independence*. Basingstoke: Palgrave-Macmillan.

Ramos Pinto, Pedro. 2013. *Lisbon Rising: Urban Social Movements in the Portuguese Revolution, 1974–75*. Manchester: Manchester University Press.

Robinson, Richard A.H. 2003. The influence of overseas issues in Portugal's transition to democracy, in *The Last Empire: Thirty Years of Portuguese Decolonization*, edited by Stewart Lloyd-Jones and António Costa Pinto. Bristol: Intellect, 1–16.

Rodrigues, Luís Nuno. 2015. The international dimension of Portuguese colonial crisis, 1961–1968, in *The Ends of European Colonial Empires: Cases and Comparisons*, edited by Miguel Bandeira Jerónimo and António Costa Pinto. Basingstoke: Palgrave, 243–267.

Schneidman, Witney W. 2004. *Engaging Africa: Washington and the Fall of Portugal's Colonial Empire*. Dallas, TX: University Press of America.

Spruyt, Hendrick. 2005. *Ending Empire: Contested Sovereignty and Territorial Partition*. Ithaca, NY: Cornell University Press.

Thomas, Martin. 2007. *Empires of Intelligence: Security Forces and Colonial Disorder After 1914*. Berkeley, CA: University of California Press.

Westad, Odd Arne. 2007. *The Global Cold War: Third World Interventions and the Making of Our Times*. Cambridge: Cambridge University Press.

Wheeler, Douglas. 1976. African elements in Portugal's armies in Africa (1961–1974). *Armed Forces and Society*, 2(2): 233–250.

Part Three

Post-colonial, transitional and transnational policing dynamics

7 Post-war police reform in Mozambique

The case of community policing

Helene Maria Kyed

Introduction

A growing body of literature on transnational policing has waged a welcome critique of Community Oriented Policing (COP) as a one size fits all 'solution' to establish 'democratic policing' in transitional and post-conflict societies (Bayley 2001, Brogden and Nijhar 2005, Ellison 2007, Murphy 2007). As the current 'official gospel of international police reform' (Murphy 2007: 248), COP is heralded as a panacea to a whole range of problems such as instability, crime, and unaccountability, violent and corrupt police forces. Critics, however, highlight that there is little evidence of success. Studies show that COP has reproduced local power imbalances, enhanced the politicisation of policing and reproduced police violence and exclusion (Buur and Jensen 2004, Ruteere and Pommerolle 2003, Brogden and Nijhar 2005). According to Murphy (2007) this is not simply due to poor implementation. COP is a transnational export commodity that is transplanted from the Global North to the Global South, without due consideration for contextual differences and structural constraints. While it praises decentralisation and citizen participation, COP presumes the existence of democratic governance, effective state policing and homogenous communities. These conditions do not exist in societies moving from authoritarian to democratic rule or from war to peace. Murphy (2007: 253) consequently proposes the 'professional policing model' as a more suitable initial reform response to the problems of transitional police reform. Professionalisation and de-politicisation of the state police, enabling the police to effectively and autonomously enforce law and order, should precede COP.

In this chapter I critically examine the internationally supported police reform process in post-war Mozambique since the mid-1990s, which in fact adhered to the 'professional policing model'. In line with Murphy's (2007) description this model implied a state-centric approach to police reform aimed at professionalising the state police legally, technically and managerially. I contrast this official process with developments in everyday policing through an empirical analysis of a homegrown 'community policing' initiative.[1] Although inspired by international ideas of COP,

---

1 This chapter is based on ethnographic fieldwork from 2005–2010 in the rural district of Sussundenga, Manica Province, and the neighborhood of Chasana A in Maputo. This included participant observation among the community policing groups, and at three Police Stations.

164   *Helene Maria Kyed*

community policing in Mozambique was, in contrast to other post-conflict settings (Ellison 2007, Murphy 2007), never a significant component of the official UNDP-led police reform program. It was an underfunded and partly informal program, initiated by personnel from within the Ministry of Interior (MINT) with a very small source of funding. Although 'Community Policing Councils' (CPCs) were expanded to the whole country in 2005, they were never supported by any legislation. In practice, however, the CPC initiative has had a major impact on everyday policing in poor urban and rural neighbourhoods. Community policing has existed, so to speak, in the shadow of the professional reform model.

Mozambique constitutes a particularly interesting case for current debates about transnational policing, because of this peculiar co-existence of two different international policing models. While my empirical research confirms much of the current critique of COP in transitional contexts, I argue that the 'professional policing model' is equally at risk of downplaying context-specific politics and histories of policing. The model is just as much an export commodity as COP is, developed as Murphy (2007: 253) himself asserts, in the United States in the 1930s–1940s. In fact, the parallel community policing initiative in Mozambique can be seen as a response to the failure of the 'professional policing model' to reduce crime and to deal with weak state police capacity and legitimacy, because of its inherently technical focus. The model disregarded Mozambique's long history of civilian and non-state actors' involvement in policing, and consequently that many government and police officials believed that the state police needed civilian alliances to be effective after the war. Ideas from internationally circulating models of COP (Brogden and Nijhar 2005), like police-citizen partnerships, appealed to, rather than contradicted, the state-building agenda of the government. The 'professional policing model' also omitted any direct consideration of context-specific notions of justice and security. As I detail through ethnographic descriptions in this chapter, community policing was appropriated in practice to dispense informal justice as well as to allow the police to continue some of those practices that post-war reforms had made illegal, but that were still viewed as effective. As such community policing became the invisible counterpart of official police reform. It allowed the informalities of everyday policing to continue in the shadow of rule of law programming and professionalisation. Yet this was done according to the belief that community policing would boost the capacity and legitimacy of the state police.

These observations resonate with another recent body of literature on customary justice and non-state security provision (Baker 2008, Albrecht et al. 2011, Baker and Scheye 2007, and Isser 2011). International rule of law reforms and their state-centric focus are seen as problematic, because they undermine local justice needs and are unrealistic about what the state can achieve in the short to medium-term. This is because such an approach ignores the fact that policing is

---

I also made a large 'user survey' among the residents of the areas, including questions about their opinions of justice, security and punishments.

already decentralised and plural in post-conflict societies, and that many citizens prefer to turn to non-state security and justice providers to settle crimes and disputes. As an alternative to the professional model, Baker and Scheye (2007) therefore suggest a multi-layered approach, which links up the police with existing non-state security providers and civilian bodies, much in line with the COP model. Such an approach is also believed to enhance state police legitimacy. Missing in this literature, however, is a discussion of the politics involved in the inclusion of non-state actors. As I illustrate in this chapter, not only were the civilian community police used to boost state police authority and to reproduce extra-legal police practices, they also became subject to frequent politicisation by the ruling party.

Consequently, I suggest that the Mozambican case calls for a critical re-examination of both the 'professional' and the 'community oriented' policing models from an empirical as well as a politically grounded perspective. Neither of these models were implemented in any pure form, but became superimposed upon each other in rather informal and politicised ways. The empirical analysis of community policing clearly resonates with the critique of COP made by scholars like Murphy (2007) and Ellison (2007), but it also questions the professional policing model as necessarily an adequate alternative or as devoid of the political pitfalls of the COP model. These observations, I suggest, go to the heart of some of the core dilemmas of police reform in transitional and post-war countries like Mozambique where the quest for reforming the police co-exists with major capacity deficiencies and a deep history of a politically partisan police and a plurality of policing actors.

I begin this chapter with an analysis of the internationally-driven police reform process, and the challenges that the international donor-community faced vis-à-vis the political agenda of the Frelimo government and the state of policing in the country at the end of the war. Initiating the reform was a contested process, which ultimately ended up ignoring the very politics and realities on the ground that had challenged the agreements on police reform in the first place. In the next section I turn to the emergence of the community policing initiative 'from the backdoor' and as an implicit critique of the official reform failures. While clearly drawing on international COP ideas, I show in the third and fourth sections how the initiative in practice was implemented in an *ad hoc* and rather informal manner that quickly became politicised. I do so by drawing on two in-depth case studies: first, Sussundenga District in central Mozambique, which is a rural, former war-zone and oppositional stronghold, and; second, Chasana a poor urban neighbourhood and ruling party stronghold in the capital city of Maputo.

The contested police reform process

When Mozambique attained peace in 1992 the 16-year war between Frelimo and Renamo had shattered the state's limited capacity to provide security and justice to its people. Officially police reform had to adhere to the new liberal-democratic constitution of 1990, which marked a shift from a one-party, Marxist-Leninist socialist state, to a multiparty democracy, including emphasis on human rights, the rule of law and the separation of powers. While this political shift fitted well with the

166   *Helene Maria Kyed*

international donor template at the time, police reform faced major practical as well as political challenges. This caused severe delays in the reform process. Indeed, it was not until 1997 that an internationally supported police reform process took off.

The police force (the Police of the Republic of Mozambique (PRM)) lacked physical outreach and was defined by observers as an operational and managerial disaster. The police performed reactively rather than proactively, had poor equipment, very low levels of education, and they were confined to maintaining presence in the provincial capitals. Officers' knowledge of, and respect for, citizens' rights was very limited (Lalá and Francisco 2006: 165). Instead the police had operated as a military force, concerned principally with the defence of national security (Baker 2002). While these issues posed practical challenges to police reform the process was delayed also for clear political reasons that were deeply embedded in the dynamics of war and the control of territory and populations.

During the war the rebel movement Renamo, which was initially supported by the white minority regimes of Rhodesia and South Africa, was gradually able to gain internal support in the central and northern parts of the country. Renamo took control of large parts of the rural territories, which was partly facilitated by Renamo's collaboration with local traditional authorities, who had been banned by Frelimo after Independence from Portugal in 1975. When the Peace Agreement was signed Renamo turned into a political party, yet was still very much seen by Frelimo as a military threat. This was supported by a *de facto* dual administration, which rendered state sovereignty highly contested. Even after the first elections in 1994 when Frelimo won the majority, there were still areas in the central provinces that were *de facto* governed by Renamo and where the state police could not enter. Here a plurality of non-state policing actors operated, including: chiefs; Renamo soldiers now acting as local administrators; remnants of the *mujhibas*, Renamo's local police during the war; and traditional healers (*wadzi-nyanga*). Large sections of the rural population also distrusted the state police, because they were associated with militarised state governance.

Against this background, the Frelimo government was very sceptical towards police reform. Frelimo feared that as the military was downscaled and Renamo combatants were integrated within its ranks, as part of the UN-demobilisation effort, the Frelimo party and state apparatus would be left without secure protection (Chachiua 2000). Due to the inherent distrust between Renamo and Frelimo, the latter thus saw the police as its major security force. Indeed, until 1996 the government resisted any involvement of external actors in police affairs. During the implementation of the peace agreement, the police issue was non-negotiable, as the Frelimo government alleged that some kind of sovereignty should be maintained. It largely jeopardised the ability of the UN-led civilian police (CIVPOL) during the peace mission to contribute to police reform despite its 1,144 members and some $30 million of expenditure (Lalá and Francisco 2006). Also the National Commission for Police Affairs (*Commissão Nacional dos Assuntos Policias* – COMPOL), which was established with international support to oversee police activities, got very little response from the government. Outside the purview of the international community, Frelimo instead began a process of

Post-war police reform in Mozambique   167

transferring weaponry and personnel from the army to the police (Chachiua 2000). This reflected not only the militarised but also the inherently partisan history of the police. The police had served the interests of the Frelimo-state rather than the wider public.

Between 1992 and 1994 security policies were very much a reflection of the narrow political interests of the warring parties. Efforts to curb crime were postponed or crime was used as the legitimising reason for militarising the police in defence of the Frelimo-State. In the Renamo controlled areas the military-trained Rapid Reaction Force was employed to curb civilian and Renamo opposition to the re-establishment of police posts and Frelimo party representations. In the first part of the 1990s, as Chachiua (2000) notes, concern regarding Frelimo's political survival largely kept security policies detached from the security needs of the population. This was despite a perceived skyrocketing of violent crime. The main preoccupation of the Frelimo government, it seems, was to regain territory in the many rural areas were the police had ceased to exist due to Renamo occupation. Yet as Frelimo's confidence in the peace process grew and crime established itself as the most challenging security threat, a slow process of reform started.

International involvement – the UNDP-led process

When the Spanish *Guardia Civil* first arrived in 1995, to assist the UNDP police reform program as technical advisors, they were met with deep suspicion by the Mozambican police (Lalá and Francisco 2006: 169). In response to the stalemate, a Police Donor Group (PDG) was formed in 1996, which under the management of UNDP engaged in a year-long negotiation before an agreement was signed with the government in 1997. The result was laws 17/97 and 18/97. These implied major shifts for the police: from a defence of national unity to the protection of individual rights, property and liberties; police impartiality; prohibition on torture; and legal prosecution of law-offending police officers.

The UNDP-led reform program consisted of three phases over a ten-year period (1997–2007) and a total expenditure of 33.7 million US dollars. It focused on professionalising the national police by investing in training, equipment, infrastructure, and eventually in managerial changes (Lalá and Francisco 2006). The main aim was to modernise the service. As the government chose to keep the old force, this initially took the form of retraining existing officers at a newly established police academy (ACIPOL) and at training centres (Baker 2002). Over the first two phases (1997–2003) 46% of the total force was retrained. The first new cadets graduated in 2004. These were integrated with the old force at 'model unit' police stations where it was expected that the exchange of operational experience with new police knowledge would modernise the service (Lalá and Francisco 2006: 169–170). However, while UNDP training focused on human rights and rule of law aspects, the government overall chose the more militarised model of the Spanish *Guardia Civil*. This model had a natural appeal, because most of the high-ranking officers had a military background in the liberation guerrilla army. It also fitted well with the government's main concern to build a stronger state apparatus.

168   *Helene Maria Kyed*

A common characteristic for these two co-existing approaches was nonetheless a narrow focus on the state police officer. This had two implications. Firstly, there was no coordination with changes in the wider criminal justice sector. Only in phase three (2004–2007) did talks begin about integrating the police into a new system of 'public order and security' (Lalá and Francisco 2006: 168), but as Alar (2012) asserts, alignment with the justice system was not achieved in practice due to resistance within the Ministry of Interior. UNDP on its part largely addressed judicial and police reform as separate activities. It did not have a holistic approach to Security Sector Reform (Lalá and Francisco 2006: 175–176). The state police was by and large treated as an isolated institution. This created a strong separation between the police and the judiciary with significant consequences for case handling, corruption and also for the prosecution of officers who violated the law (Lalá and Francisco 2006: 173–174).

Secondly, whereas the UNDP emphasised citizen safety and security, the isolated focus on the state police omitted a consideration of non-state involvement in policing and largely left out citizen perceptions of justice and security. It was only in 2002 that police performance surveys were conducted in three cities. Until then there had been no effort in the UNDP-led program to identity citizen needs and priorities (Lalá and Francisco 2006: 17). No similar assessment was, however made of the wide range of non-state policing actors that operated 'on the ground', often informally in collaboration with the state police. This included remnants of the neighbourhood leaders, popular vigilantes and civilian militias that were established in 1970s to assist Frelimo's party-state structures in local crime control (MINT 2005a). It also included those traditional leaders and healers who, outside state regulation played a significant role in policing rural areas (Kyed 2007a). The key objective was to modernise the state police. Non-state institutions were perceived as an impediment to developing a state monopoly on policing, and initially this also appealed to the government's concern to reclaim state governance in the contested territories. Implicitly it was assumed that non-state policing actors would cease to be significant once the state police system was in place. However, this did not happen in practice. In fact, a range of alternative initiatives took place outside of the UNDP-led police reform program.

By 2000 few positive changes were visible in everyday state policing. It was still partisan and paramilitary. The media and human rights organisations reported human rights violations, irregular detentions, extrajudicial killings, participation in criminal activity and corruption (Baker 2002: 112–118). Simultaneously, the police proved incapable of handling the rising urban crime, which also bolstered mob-justice, which underpinned high mistrust in the state police. In rural areas reform was incapable of substituting non-state with state policing. In Manica province for instance the police's fear of creating antagonism in areas dominated by Renamo and chiefs, meant that police posts were only set up in 2001 (Kyed 2007a).

This state of affairs instigated a number of responses drawing towards a 'return' to civilian and non-state involvement in policing and dispute resolution. In 2000 the Decree 15/2000 led to state recognition of traditional chiefs, who – amongst other administrative tasks – had to assist the police in reporting crimes. Yet they were regulated by the Ministry of State Administration, not part of the police reform. In the justice sector there was a renewed emphasis on strengthening the non-judicial community courts, which in 2004 culminated in the constitutional recognition of legal pluralism (Kyed et al. 2012). Finally, forces within MINT's public relations department instigated a community policing initiative, which eventually got funding through the urban planning and governance program of the German GTZ. This initiative was not integrated under the UNDP-led police reform program, which continued to have a state-centric focus.

Although community policing is mentioned in the Strategic Plan for the Police (2003–2012), produced during phase two of the UNDP program, this was not accompanied by any funding. In fact, the Strategic Plan states that 'an organized strategy of crime prevention as such does not exist' and refers to the efforts to strengthen police-community links as 'sporadic actions' (MINT 2003: 42). This reflects, I suggest, how community policing emerged as a parallel response to the failure of the first years of UNDP-led police reform to reduce crime and change the public image of the police. In stark contrast to other post-conflict settings community policing was therefore not the result of a donor-driven process or part of donor conditionality (Ellison 2007). The initiative was a home-grown adaptation of an international policing model. It sought to rectify the problems of state police capacity and legitimacy, which the 'professional policing model' had failed to adequately address. The police needed civilian assistance to regain territory. Outside the police reform program, community policing has *de facto* served as a tool to try to 'save' the authority of the state police amidst efforts to professionalise and modernise the service. Before turning to how this was played out in practice let me first introduce MINT's community policing model and how it evolved nationally.

The Mozambican community policing model

The main person behind community policing in Mozambique was the late General Macamo, who was head of the public relations department in MINT. He was one of those old generation police who was retrained at the new ACIPOL. Through exchange visits to South Africa, as part of this training, he heard about and was inspired by community policing. His incentive, he told me, was a frustration with the incapacity of the police to deal with rising crime and the large mistrust between police and the people. In 1999 he developed an idea that was clearly inspired by international models of COP, especially from the UK and the US, which he cited generously in the MINT guidelines. The 'philosophy' was that 'public order, security and peace should not alone be the function of police authorities', but require 'active citizen participation in and responsibility for local community security' (MINT 2005b: 5). In 2000 he received a small source of funding from GTZ to pilot the project.

Internationally COP represents an almost endless range of possible initiatives (Ellison 2007, Brogden and Nijhar 2005), rendering it open to various translations. Macamo's focus was not on police officer training or problem-solving techniques, but on the setting up of Community Policing Councils (CPCs) staffed by voluntary citizens of smaller administrative areas. The emphasis was thus on the

170 *Helene Maria Kyed*

direct inclusion of citizens in policing and on police-citizen partnerships, akin to the South African Community Policing Forums (Baker 2002). The members should be approved by the populations of their area, and include community leaders and other persons with an important social position (MINT 2005a: 10). The CPCs were envisioned to fulfil three rather ambitious objectives, strongly resembling COP ideas elsewhere (Brogden and Nijhar 2005): to reduce crime by involving citizens in identifying security problems and solutions and by bringing the police closer to local communities; to democratise policing by diminishing human rights violations and by fostering a transparent police service, accountable to the citizens, and; to strengthen the internal coherence of local communities and their trust in the police through collective resolution of problems and legal education (MINT 2005b).

The CPCs should not substitute the state police, but assist officers by being forums for discussing security problems and solutions affecting the community (MINT 2005b: 10). They can also mediate minor conflicts and facilitate patrols in public spaces. However, they cannot settle criminal cases or carry any instruments of force, and may only arrest people caught in the act of committing a crime under the ordinary powers of 'citizens' arrest'. CPCs also have the responsibility to forward information about criminals to the police as well as to put pressure on the police to respond to community crime problems, for instance by recording unacceptable behaviour by police officers (MINT 2005b: 11–16). Thus the CPCs were envisioned as mediators between citizens and the police, and as a kind of police oversight body. This role, it was hoped, would both transform the police to service local communities and nurture law-abiding citizens. In short, the CPC model promised a comprehensive transformation of the police, in line with the UNDP-led program, yet it went far beyond the state police.

National expansion and pilot projects outside official reform

The CPC project was piloted first in 2001 in a poor, crime-inflicted Maputo suburb, and then in 2002 expanded to three towns in Manica Province. These pilot projects were closely supervised by MINT representatives, and assisted by GTZ with awareness raising meetings, exchange visits to Germany, and equipment to CPCs and police stations (bicycles, whistles, t-shirts and mopeds) (GTZ 2002, MINT 2005b). Workshops were also conducted with 1,200 police officers and 250 civil society representatives, who were introduced to the community policing concept. The budget was small (€200,000) when compared with the UNDP-led program's spending of USD 15.7 million in the same period (Lalá and Francisco 2006). Yet according to MINT and GTZ's own assessments it had major impact.

In late 2002 MINT and GTZ concluded that in the neighbourhoods with CPCs crime had diminished, active community participation was high, and trust between the police and communities had increased (MINT 2005b, GTZ 2002).[2]

---

2 It should be noted that no independent evaluation was made of the pilot project. Only in 2007 did the NGO FOMICRES and the ACIPOL make independent assessments, but these were

Subsequently, CPCs were expanded to other provinces. By 2004 there were a total of 1,113 CPCs in urban and semi-urban areas (MINT 2005b: 14). In 2005 the new Guebueza-led Frelimo Government included the aim of expanding CPCs to the whole country in its five-year plan (2005–2010), including now rural areas. By 2008 there were 2,710 registered CPCs. This expansion, with political support from the government, has not, however, been supported by any law or national strategy, and after 2005 it received no further funding.[3] GTZ's appeal to continue funding for 2005–2006 was turned down, and several attempts by General Macamo and Maputo-based CPC members to get a law approved was stalled in MINT and later in the Council of Ministers. This stalemate reflects, I suggest, how the initial CPC concept failed to be incorporated into the wider donor-supported police reform process. When the UNDP-led program ended in 2007, and police assistance was taken over by the EU commission and the Portuguese, the focus also remained state-centric.[4] Ultimately, I would further suggest that the legal stalemate also hints at divided opinions within MINT and the government about the inclusion of civilians in policing. These are political matters.

In 2012 the MINT official, who became responsible for community policing after General Macamo passed away, explained to me that a law on CPCs is unlikely to ever pass. His explanation was that 'community policing is an institution of the community, not of the police', and therefore should remain a voluntary community association.[5] Conversely, the Maputo coordinator of community policing, Snr. Mbanguini, told me that forces within MINT had gotten cold feet, because the draft law that was produced in 2009 by General Macamo and selected CPC members had a strong focus on the setting up of provincial and national CPCs, which would perform a watchdog role over the police. This fear within MINT reflected more broadly how community policing in practice had shifted from being predominantly an instrument of the state police to taking on a life of its own. Snr. Mbanguini, explained that 'community policing has now grown so strong that it can reveal the corrupt practices of the police and how they neglect poor citizens'

---

not in-depth, nor part of any effort to improve the program. This resonates with Ellison's (2007) observation about the lack of thorough independent assessments of COP in other places too, which allows community policing to be left as an unquestioned good policing model for transitional societies.

3 The legal basis of community policing is confined to Art.61 in the Constitution on the right of citizens to participate in civil defense (República de Moçambique 1990).

4 The explanation for this exclusion of COP from police reform in Mozambique – as opposed to most other transitional contexts – can only be speculative. One answer could be that when the UNDP program began in 1997, as Lalá and Francisco (2006) suggest, the holistic SSR approach that dominates today, and which has a clear COP component, was still not developed within the UNDP. The current EU-led reform program did, according to my personal communications with the coordinator, consider community policing, but the coordinator was not a strong personal supporter of COP and her excuse was that there needed to be a law before donors could move forward.

5 Interview, Snr. Boavida, Maputo, November 2012.

172   *Helene Maria Kyed*

security needs'.[6] Yet there was also a more negative side to this autonomy, which opponents could use. Reports on community police using vigilante-style violent tactics supported those MINT officials and police officers who opposed community policing and saw it as a threat to police authority. Proponents within the police, who viewed the civilian community police as a necessary supporter of the police, conversely highlighted that these violent practices were a core reason why a law was needed. In short, the police were split on the issue.

Politically it is harder to comprehend why the Frelimo government has not pushed for a law on community policing – and subsequent donor support – given its strong commitment to expand the CPCs in 2005. Also Frelimo in its 2009 party program listed community policing as one of its important achievements in its 2005–2009 government period. My empirical analysis suggests that the answer to this apparent paradox is to be found in the political instrumentalisation of the CPCs by Frelimo. By keeping the CPCs outside of formal regulation and the donor reform-program, the government and the police could use the CPCs for ends that were not necessarily in accordance with official reform agenda. In the following sections I will show how this was played out in practice in one rural and one urban area.

Due to the lack of project funding and regulation, the implementation of CPCs after 2004 was done by Station Commanders without any direct supervision from MINT. What they had were Macamo's guidelines and their notes from the one-day GTZ workshop that they had attended (MINT 2005b: 14). This left considerably room for translation of the original, internationally-inspired COP ideas, and also allowed community policing to serve political agendas. Yet CPC members were also in some instances able to turn this room for manoeuvre to their own advantage. I begin with the rural district of Sussundenga in Manica province.

Rural case-study: new civilian agents of the state police

Community policing in Sussundenga District began in 2004 when the Station Commander ordered the local traditional chiefs to each choose eight 'clever, trustworthy and physically strong persons' to work with the police.[7] It was only after the selection of these individuals, who were locally called *communitários*, that the population was invited to a meeting where they were expected to approve of them. As asserted by one participant: 'we did not say anything against that, because they were chosen by the chief and the government agreed'. Also a *communitário* claimed that he had no choice but to join, because 'we have to obey the orders of the government.'[8] In short, despite the involvement of chiefs, the formation of CPCs was seen locally as a 'state order'. The general opinion was that the members were recruited to work for the police, and this was confirmed

---

6 Interview, J. Mbanguini, Maputo, November 2012.
7 Interview, District Station Commander, August 2005.
8 Interview, community policing member, September 2005.

by the fact that the *communitários* were trained by the police to perform arrests and searches so that they could assist the police in their daily work. There was no deep sense of community ownership. This was reflected in statements like:

> The comunitários work for the police to help control the zones . . . to patrol and arrest people who are thieves and beat up people, because the police cannot be in all of the territory [. . .] They are with the police, because the police give them instructions.[9]

The state police appropriation of the CPC initiative also had political underpinnings. For example in a locality strongly dominated by Renamo, all but two of the chosen members refused to 'work for the Frelimo police'. A police officer intervened and obligated six new persons to be members, including two Renamo supporters, while trying to convince people that 'community policing is not a Frelimo police.' The resistance to join community policing reflects the aforementioned association of the police with serving Frelimo interests against Renamo (Kyed 2007b). The CPC initiative was conversely appropriated by police officers to reverse this situation, by deliberately trying to win over Renamo supporters to the police.

The result of the process was a massive recruitment of young men, amounting in one administrative post to 18 units (144 members) within an estimated population of 46,000 and with eight police officers. In everyday policing it became clear that the *communitários* were indeed recruited to strengthen the capacity of the police.

Everyday policing: state outsourcing and autonomous actions

The *communitários* had to assist the police posts on 24-hour weekly shifts. Here they were given batons and handcuffs and a heavy workload. When cases appeared outside the immediate vicinity of the police posts, the police sent out the *communitários* to arrests suspects on foot. With no available transport for police officers, this eased their work considerably. Another regular task of the *communitários* was night patrols, which often involved extra-legal arrests of persons caught without ID. Some spent the night in the cell and did 'public' work for the police. When an interrogation took place it was also the *communitários* who beat the suspects until they 'talked'. They cooked for the officers, cleaned the premises, and brought suspects from the cell to interrogation.

In short, the police outsourced not only the physically hard work of everyday policing, but also the methods that are illegal under post-war legislation such as torture and irregular arrests. Officers in this way could continue the use of violent practices without personally breaking the law. Many officers believed that the use of force and control of movement was still necessary to enforce 'law and order',

---

9 Interview, Female resident, Sussundenga District, August 2005.

174 *Helene Maria Kyed*

not least, they said in the rural areas where people had lived under Renamo control. This view reiterated the discourse of the Frelimo government in justifying the necessity of militarised policing, as discussed earlier. Yet outsourcing was also associated with problems of state police capacity such as lack of means of transportation, human resources, and physical outreach to areas where the police had no physical presence. As such, the *communitários* could help not only to reduce crime levels, but also to boost state police control.

This way of appropriating community policing was strongly influenced by the particular rural context of plural policing and politically contested state authority. These were contextual factors that were clearly undermined in the official police reform process and its exclusive focus on the state police. Already the state recognition of chiefs in 2002 had helped to increase the police's capacity to deal with crime through different forms of collaboration. Yet chiefs still posed a threat to the police's claim to be in charge of criminal matters (Kyed 2009). Many rural residents preferred to bring their cases to chiefs due to the alternative kinds of justice they dispense (Kyed 2009). Because chiefly authority is partly based on their capacity to handle even severe forms of crime, chiefs often disobeyed police orders. This made the police look weak. The *communitários* added further strength to the police in this competitive plural landscape, and was therefore welcomed by local police commanders.

Yet the police's command over the *communitários* was far from secure. Outsourcing was risky. A number of the members took matters into their own hands, ranging from overt illegal and indeed illegitimate acts in the eyes of rural residents, to more subtle forms of case handling. For example, rural residents complained that *communitários* extracted excessive sums of money from persons they arrested or threatened to take people to the police or beat them up if they did not pay. When such complaints reached the police, the *communitários* were expelled or punished with several days in the cell. In the majority of cases, however, the *communitários* acted in more subtle and legitimate ways outside the purview of the police. This included solving cases 'on the spot' without the required police involvement, because victims preferred this. *Communitários* also at times forwarded criminals to the chiefs' courts, rather than to the police. In these cases, they had a good chance of receiving a small amount of cash as an act of gratitude for not bringing people to the police. While these acts were clearly a defiance of police orders, they were also driven by the individual members' quest for personal survival and future status.

The *communitários* were all unemployed and had low levels of education, so income from police work was significant. They sustained their livelihoods by cultivating small plots or through informal trading, yet by spending time on police tasks they had less time for such income-generation. Most of them hoped for some sort of state subsidy or salary in the future. This reflected how they saw themselves as working for the state – not as persons who volunteered to serve the security needs of their 'communities'. Some also hoped that the role they played in community policing could grant them enough authority to advance their social status – for example, to one day become a local leader – or to get a paid job. Yet MINT's

CPC model did not meet this aspiration, due to the principle of voluntarism and the idea that CPC members would be persons of some status and position. Working for an authority like the police could help to achieve these aspirations, but so could the help they gave to rural residents. It gave them local legitimacy and prestige. For this reason they also at times bypassed the police.

From the perspective of the police officers the circumvention of police orders highlighted the inherent dilemmas of outsourcing policing tasks to civilians in a context like Sussundenga. In light of capacity deficiencies outsourcing could boost the authority of the state police, but since the police could not offer any official compensation in return, outsourcing could also turn against them. For this reason, the Station Commander in Sussundenga began to help some *communitários* to obtain salaried jobs as private security guards so as to motivate them and to recruit new members. Although this was an entirely informal arrangement, the Commander did it because he depended on the *communitários* to do the police job and to show crime prevention results for his district. It was, in his view, a necessary adaptation of the CPC model to the particular contextual circumstances. Although not as explicitly articulated the same kind of reasoning was used for outsourcing violent methods to the *communitários*. The result was a decentralised reproduction of the militarised forms of policing from the past, which starkly diverted from the democratising promises of MINT's CPC model. These observations resonate well with the scholarly critique of transplanting COP models to transitional societies where state police capacity is weak and democratic governance is not in place (Murphy 2007, Brogden and Nijhar 2005). Yet the superimposition of the CPC initiative upon the official police reform also brings to attention the pitfalls of a 'professional policing model' that ignores the challenges that police officers face in inherently plural policing landscapes. Here the state police cannot be treated as an isolated institution. Much the same can be said of the urban suburb of Maputo city to where I now turn. However, here the community police members took matters even more into their own hands and were more intensely politicised.

Urban case-study: a new neighbourhood court

In the Chasana neighbourhood (*bairro*) a CPC was formed in 2002. Its implementation adhered more or less to the criteria set out by MINT, involving the admission of voluntary members from among persons with social status. Rather than the police, it was the local 'structure of the *bairro*' that was in charge of forming the CPC. This structure includes the *secretário do bairro* – the lowest level state administrator – the Secretary of the Frelimo party branch as well as the group of people organised around these two figures. In this sense the process was more locally owned, yet it was also inherently politicised. The CPC members were not approved by the whole population, only by the local members of the ruling party.

This political anchoring of community policing was also prevalent when I conducted fieldwork in the *bairro* in 2009 and 2010. At this point the CPC had dissolved due to internal leadership disputes. Because the CPC had considerably contributed

176 *Helene Maria Kyed*

to a reduction in crime, its coordination had also become a pathway to authority and prestige, which sparked leadership conflicts that had roots within the ruling party. What remained in 2009 were eleven young men between the age of 22 and 35, who were called *agentes de policiamento comunitário* or community police agents. They were coordinated by a middle-aged female, Dona Sara, who was a Frelimo hardliner. She was supported by the *secretário do bairro* and the Frelimo Secretary. The young community policing agents were also expected to be Frelimo members.

In contrast to Sussundenga, the community police was less under the command of the state police and more integrated with the *bairro* structure. The young agents operated from the *circulo* of the *bairro* – the name for the central governance site of a *bairro*, which houses the *secretário* and the Frelimo party branch. The state police had little say inside this local Frelimo-based structure. Yet when police officers were present in the neighbourhood the agents did serve them. The Commander of the nearest Police Station had also given the agents their first batons and handcuffs, and had trained them for instance in where and how to beat 'offenders' with the baton. As in Sussundenga, the community police were a strong part of everyday state policing.

Everyday policing: legal defiance and political instrumentalisation

One Sector Police officer was attached to the *circulo* and when he was present the community police agents helped him with all sorts of police work: patrols, arrests of suspects, control of people for IDs, searches, investigations, and recuperation of stolen goods. They also walked suspects to the police station and on several occasions I observed the Sector Police officer ordering the agents to beat suspects during interrogation. As in Sussundenga, the local police relied extensively, yet unofficially, on the community police to do their job. The sector police officer saw the young agents as having contributed significantly to his capacity to handle crimes. Their manpower was important to him, because being only one officer in the *bairro* could be very risky for his personal security. To the community police agents, the police offered a significant source of authority and inspiration. When officers were present they obeyed their orders and viewed themselves as under the command of the state police. Many also aspired to become police officers, and presented this as a key motivation for their work.

However, the agents also frequently operated autonomously. The sector police officer was only present two to three days a week and seldom stayed the whole day at the *circulo*. When he was not there the agents continued the police work, essentially by copying what they had learnt from the officer. They also went beyond this. Inside the *circulo* they developed their own court-like set-up where cases of all sorts came in – from crimes like rape and mobile phone thefts to family disputes. They had their own case register and also detained suspects for hours, sometimes tied up. The agents were also very active in the streets. They became famous for direct, immediate actions against the thugs and for their use of physical force as punishment. They were good at bringing back stolen goods. They also resolved social disputes using reconciliatory and compensational justice mechanisms, while copying state police ways of recording and hearing. They even gave themselves different police titles. When comparing their own case register with those cases that the Sector Police Officer reported to the station, the agents resolved by far the highest number of crimes.

In short, the community police had turned into a new kind of neighbourhood court with its own patrol officers and were frequently praised for having drastically reduced crime. Although this result was partly nurtured by the state police, who trained them and gave them equipment, the autonomous actions also challenged police authority. The relationship between state and community police was characterised by a mixture of interdependence and competition over the power to handle cases. On several occasions the community police agents kept information from the police so they could resolve their own cases. When discovered, the police officers got furious, but they never explicitly complained about the agents to the Commander. The reason was that the officers depended on the agents to do their work. Conversely, the agents also knew things about the officers that would harm them if it reached their superiors – such as frequent incidences of police corruption. This ambiguous relationship informed ongoing negotiations over who had the authority to decide cases and distribute information. There were lots of concealment and covert games going on. The agents and the officers engaged in webs of exchanges and favours that often blurred the boundary between law enforcement and illegality. The power games between them were partly motivated by the potential 'incomes' and favours that surrounded everyday policing, such as rewards from recuperating stolen goods or from negotiating with law-breakers to avoid prosecution. Yet they were also strongly influenced by the quest for popular legitimacy in the neighbourhood. Popular notions of justice, punishments and police effectiveness continuously shaped everyday policing practices, including those that are rendered illegal in post-war legislation.

The community police agents often bragged to me about being quicker at recuperating stolen goods than the police. It was also common that they beat up criminals before they dragged them to the police station. This, the agents told me, was to ensure that perpetrators got punishment, because with the police one is never sure of prosecution. With the community police, the victims could always count on immediate punishment. While this emphasis on immediate punishment, outside the legal system, fed into the power-games between the agents and the police, it was also supported by the *bairro* leadership and by most of the neighbourhood residents that I interviewed.

The beating of criminals before they were sent to the police was related to a common mistrust of the police since the reforms of the 1990s. It was widely believed that the police station often released suspects who had been arrested before they were prosecuted due to bribes. While such acts of corruption cannot be ruled out, there were also many occasions were release after 48 hours was, in fact, due to a lack of evidence and thereby an act of compliance with the law. Yet even when this was explained to victims, there was still a feeling that in the official system perpetrators had impunity. Most residents that I surveyed preferred

178   *Helene Maria Kyed*

immediate resolutions in the form of punishments and compensation. The community police agents gained popularity by using such methods and by contrasting themselves to the slow and complicated legal processes that most residents associate with the official justice system. When cases end up in this system there is meagre guarantee that people get compensated for their loss of stolen goods or for injuries related to assaults. The official system is therefore not associated with justice and effective crime prevention.

Intriguingly, this view was shared by many of the police officers that I spoke with at the Police Station when I did fieldwork there in 2010. Among them there was a strong idea that the post-war reforms and their emphasis on human rights and the rule of law had rendered the official system incapable of punishing criminals. The reforms had also made it more difficult for the police to do their job. Especially the protection of the rights of the suspects and the prohibition on the use of force had, it was believed, reduced the police's capacity to bring down crime and protect the citizens against the most dangerous criminals. The Station Commander explained to me:

> The population knows better how to punish the criminals, so that they will not do it [the crime] again. Here at the police station we have to follow the law . . . it is very complicated today. We can just listen and register and then we have to involve PIC [criminal investigation police], the attorney and the court. It is much easier out there [in the neighbourhoods]. They can do more and punish as they like.[10]

Statements like this help to explain the outsourcing of violence to the community police by the state police, and also why this Station Commander did not interfere in the autonomous actions of the agents in Chasana. More generally, such views also underpin why a lot of police work is informal or takes place in the shadow of the law despite massive investments in reforming the police. Transgressing the law is not simply about police corruption, but also due to a discrepancy between new legislation and popular perceptions of effective policing. Neither the 'professional policing model' nor MINT's 'community policing' initiative took into consideration such popular perceptions. This is because, I suggest, such imported models focus strictly on fixed rules and rights, rather than on the context-specific notions of justice and capacity constraints that everyday policing and experiences of insecurity face in poor urban neighbourhoods.

MINT's idea that community policing would reduce human rights abuses by the police ran counter to local appropriations of the concept, because ideas about human rights did not fit well with police and popular perceptions of effective policing. Consequently, community policing was used to try to save some of the authority that the state police felt they had lost due to the reforms of the post-war period. They did so by reinforcing the policing practices of the past, yet in an outsourced and informalised manner. While widely believed to reduce crime, there were two

---

10 Interview, Station Commander, Maputo, May 2010.

Post-war police reform in Mozambique 179

significant consequences of this appropriation of community policing. To the police the critical aspect is that they cannot always control the actions of community policing agents, who often take matters into their own hands. Another outcome is the ease with which community policing can become politicised.

In Chasana the community police were in the hands of the ruling party: they got protection from it, but only in exchange for political support. During the 2009 elections the agents were compelled to provide security for the Frelimo brigade and to cover opposition posters with those of Frelimo. This was supported by the *secretário*. When a group of Renamo members complained, he replied: 'these Renamo people are not serious . . . they are thieves and drunks who Renamo has mobilised to disturb public order'. One of the agents also warned the Renamo members that if they did not stop creating confusion, they would be arrested for physical aggression. These reactions reflect the deeper political discourse of Frelimo, which equates the political opposition with crime and disorder. On a smaller scale, community policing was therefore also appropriated to consolidate the powerbase of the Frelimo party-state, just as the state police have been on a larger scale since the end of the war. These politics of policing have happened in the shadow of the official police reform process.

Conclusion

Civilian community police members in Mozambique have at least as far as popular perceptions are concerned contributed more to the reduction in crime than the state police have. Such perceptions may seem surprising given the fact that the many millions of dollars that the international community has spent on post-war police reform in Mozambique since 1997 have not covered community policing. Instead, the official reform process has focused on professionalising the state police. The focus has been state-centric with very little concern for citizen inclusion and decentralisation. Community policing councils were in this set-up introduced from the 'back door' as an underfunded and rather informal initiative. It was clearly inspired by international ideas about Community Oriented Policing (COP), but it was not the result of donor pressure as in many other similar contexts (Ellison 2007, Brogden and Nijhar 2005). Rather the donors in Mozambique adhered to what in the police literature is referred to as the 'professional policing model', and which by critics of COP is now held out as a more viable alternative to COP in transitional and post-conflict situations (Murphy 2007).

The Mozambican case contributes with valuable insights to the debate about transnational policing and the export of policing models from the Global North to transitional societies, because of its unique combination of export models. Currently this debate is concerned with a critical examination of the COP model, which today is regarded as the most dominant international model. Emphasis is on this model's failure to produce effective policing and to do away with police violence, exclusion and politicisation, because it ignores the context-specific politics and structural constraints of transitional societies (Murphy 2007, Wood and Font 2007, Ellison 2007, Ruteere and Pommerolle 2003). Murphy (2007)

180 *Helene Maria Kyed*

consequently argues that before any implementation of COP, international agencies ought to invest in professionalising the state police, which will make the police accountable to the law rather than to the local communities, thereby freeing the police from political control. This perspective resonates with the official reform model that was adopted in Mozambique in 1997 under UNDP coordination. Yet empirical analysis of everyday policing suggests that we equally need to scrutinise this model.

While my ethnographic fieldwork of community policing confirms much of the critique of COP, it also draws attention to some of the pitfalls of the 'professional policing model'. At least as far as Mozambique is concerned the very technical and rule-of-law based approach of this model, did not pay due attention to the politics, history and reality of policing in Mozambique and it did not consider popular (as well as police) notions of justice, punishment and effective policing. In fact, as I have suggested in this chapter the community policing initiative was implemented in a locally-adapted form to fill the gaps left by the narrow focus on professionalising the police. This included three main gaps.

Firstly, policing in Mozambique was already plural and decentralised in the post-war period, and many police officers and government officials firmly believed that the strengthening of state police capacity to deal with crime depended on civilian alliances. This was not least the case in Renamo strongholds, like Sussundenga district, discussed in this chapter, where the police had meagre physical outreach and were associated with Frelimo. Here non-state actors like chiefs had collaborated with Renamo in policing rural society, severely challenging state authority. In this context, the community policing initiative was appropriated as a welcome strategy to recruit civilians and outsource functions to them so as to 'save' the authority of the state police amidst the official reform efforts to modernise and professionalise the service.

Secondly, post-war reforms emphasising the rule of law and human rights were seen by many citizens and police officers as incapable of punishing wrongdoers and compensating victims. While these views partly reflect that reform of the legal system as a whole is a long-term process, it also underpins how the UNDP-led police reform did not rely on assessments of citizens' needs and priorities, but on an international police-training model. The localised adoption of community policing allowed everyday policing to adhere to popular and police notions of effective policing, yet in inherently informal ways. The flipside of this was a reproduction of many of those violent policing practices that official reform sought to address. Without any funding, supervision and legal regulation community policing opened up for various forms of manipulation and personal strategies that were sometimes in accordance with popular demands and the reduction of crime and sometimes not. Yet both the positive and negative effects of community policing were largely rendered invisible in the official reform process, because of its narrow focus on the state police institution.

Thirdly, the technical optic of official reform underpinned a failure to fully consider the political dimensions of post-war policing. It was clear to the international donors in the mid-1990s that Frelimo was reluctant to embark on police reform for political reasons, because it wanted to use the police to regain power and protect Frelimo vis-à-vis Renamo in the former war-zones. However, once the reform agreement was signed in 1997 such politics were ignored. Instead the police continued to be used politically to re-expand Frelimo-state power in the shadow of reform. Non-state policing became instrumental in this respect, first through the recognition of traditional chiefs, and then through the community policing initiative. As shown in this chapter, community policing members were drawn into micro-level Frelimo party politics. What this reflects is not only that community policing is susceptible to politicisation in transitional societies, as the critical literature on COP rightly argues. It also suggests that by ignoring politics and the histories of plural policing in countries like Mozambique the 'professional policing model' can create gaps and loopholes that reinforce a politicisation of policing from the 'back door', while also downplaying local notions of justice and effective policing. This calls for a critical examination of both COP and the professional policing model as transnational export commodities. Each of these needs to more firmly consider context-specific politics of policing and popular notions of justice and security to be successful.

References

Alar, F.I. 2012. The police strategic plan and its implementation, in *The Dynamics of Legal Pluralism in Mozambique*, edited by H.M. Kyed J.P.B. Coelho, A. Neves de Souto and S. Aráujo. Maputo: Kapicua, 167–185.

Albrecht, P., Kyed, H.M., Harper, E. and Isser, D. (eds). 2011. *Perspectives on Involving Non-State and Customary Actors in Justice and Security Reform*. Rome: International Development Law Organisation.

Baker, B. 2002. *Taking the Law Into Their Own Hands. Lawless Law Enforcers in Africa*. Burlington and Hampshire: Ashgate.

Baker, B. 2008. *Multi-Choice Policing in Africa*. Uppsala: Nordic Africa Institute.

Baker, B. and Scheye, E. 2007. Multi-layered justice and security delivery in post-conflict and fragile states. *Conflict, Security and Development*, 7(4): 503–528.

Bayley, D.H. 2001. Democratizing the police abroad: What to do and how to do it. *Issues in International Crime*, US Department of Justice, Office of Justice Programmes.

Brogden, M. and Nijhar, P. 2005. *Community Policing. National and International Models and Approaches*. Devon, UK: Willan Publishing.

Buur, L. and Jensen, S. 2004. Introduction: Vigilantism and the policing of everyday life in South Africa. *African Studies*, 63(2): 139–152.

Chachiua, M. 2000. Internal security in Mozambique: Concerns versus policies. *African Security Review*, 9(1): 1–20.

Ellison, G. 2007. Fostering a dependency culture: The commodification of community policing in a global marketplace, in *Crafting Transnational Policing: Police Capacity-Building and Global Policing Reform*, edited by A. Goldsmith and J. Sheptycki. Oxford and Portland: Hart Publishing, 203–242.

GTZ. October–December 2002. *Special Report: Community Policing* (unpublished).

Isser, D. 2011. *Customary Justice and the Rule of Law in War-Torn Societies*. Washington: United States Institute for Peace.

182 Helene Maria Kyed

Kyed, H.M. 2007a. *State Recognition of Traditional Authority: Authority, Citizenship and State Formation in Rural Post-war Mozambique.* PhD Dissertation, Roskilde University.

Kyed, H.M., 2007b. The politics of policing: Re-capturing 'zones of confusion' in rural post-war Mozambique, in *The Security Development Nexus. Expressions of Sovereignty and Securitization in Southern Africa*, edited by L. Buur, S. Jensen and F. Stepputat. Uppsala: Nordic Africa Institute. South Africa: HSRC Press, 132–151.

Kyed, H.M. 2009. The politics of legal pluralism: State policies on legal pluralism and their local dynamics in Mozambique. *Journal of Legal Pluralism and Unofficial Law*, 59: 87–120.

Kyed, H.M, Coelho, J.P.B, Neves de Souto, A. and Aráujo, S. (eds). (2012) *The Dynamics of Legal Pluralism in Mozambique.* Maputo: Kapicua.

Lalá, A. and Francisco, L. 2006. The difficulties of donor coordination: Police and judicial reform in Mozambique. *Civil Wars*, 8(2): 163–180.

Ministry of Interior (MINT). 2003. *Strategic Plan of the Police of the Republic of Mozambique – SPPRM*, Vol. 1. Maputo: MINT.

Ministry of Interior (MINT). 2005a. *Policiamento Comunitário e Serviços Provinciais de Bombeiros, Reunião Com os Municípios*, Manica, 25–27 July 2005.

Ministry of Interior (MINT). 2005b. *Políciamento Comunitário. Segurança e Ordem Pública, Seminário Nacional dos Administradores Distritais*, October 2005.

Murphy, C. 2007. The cart before the horse: Community oriented versus professional models of international police reform, in *Crafting Transnational Policing: Police Capacity-Building and Global Policing Reform*, edited by A. Goldsmith and J. Sheptycki. Oxford and Portland: Hart Publishing, 243–262.

República de Moçambique. 1990. *Constitução da República.* Maputo: Imprensa Nacional de Moçambique.

Ruteere, M. and Pommerolle, M.E. 2003. Democratizing security or decentralizing repression? The ambiguities of community policing in Kenya. *African Affairs*, 120: 587–604.

Wood, J. and Font, E. 2007. Crafting the Governance of Security in Argentina: Engaging with Global Trends, in *Crafting Transnational Policing. Police Capacity-Building and Global Policing Reform*, edited by A. Goldsmith and J.W.E. Sheptycki. Oxford: Hart Publishing, 329–355.

8 Transformation of Macau policing

From a Portuguese colony to China's SAR

Lawrence K. K. Ho and Agnes I. F. Lam

Introduction

This chapter provides an overview of a transformation in policing as Macau shifted from Portuguese colonial rule to becoming a Special Administrative Region (SAR) governed by the People's Republic of China (PRC). Macau was originally a fishing village located in the Pearl River Delta in Guangdong Province, Southern China. It is now a small city, with a permanent residential population of about half a million, known primarily for its gambling and tourism industries (Statistics and Census Service 2013). Macau was ruled by Portugal until sovereignty reverted to the PRC on 20 December 1999; it followed Hong Kong in becoming the PRC's second SAR[1] (Mendes 2013: 28–29).

During Portuguese rule, government-society relations were relatively harmonious and only limited socio-political confrontations emerged. Cantonese-speaking citizens in Macau criticised ineffective Portuguese governance and expressed distrust towards the public administration system, but did not usually take action.[2] The exception to this was the so called '12–3 [December 3rd] Incident' in 1966 in which politically inspired masses demonstrated against the imperial, colonial government. Social, political, and economic conditions underwent rapid change just before Macau reverted to China. At that time, there was limited street-level violent crime and occasional public demonstrations, though few with more than a thousand participants. Under Portuguese rule, citizens of

---

1 After the Portuguese revolution in 1974, the new government was inclined to abandon the sovereignty over its overseas colonies. The 'Macau Organic Law' approved by the Council of Revolution in Lisbon came into effect in February 1976. It stipulated that the territory of Macau would have a high degree of legislative, administrative, economic, and financial autonomy. The Portuguese Constitution of 25 April 1976 stated that Macau was a 'territory under Portuguese Administration' (Mendes 2013: 28–29).

2 The only official language in Macau was Portuguese until after the 1985 Sino-Portuguese Joint Declaration, which recognised written Chinese as a second official language.

184   *Lawrence Ho and Agnes Lam*

Macau considered the police force as having 'nothing to do with the general public' (Interviewees A and H).[3]

Except for the period of turbulence immediately prior to the sovereignty retrocession and criminal activity associated with gambling and casino operations, there is usually an acceptable level of public order in Macau and violent crime remains uncommon. Grassroots political groups are relatively unpopular despite the presence of an anti-establishment camp.[4] The only major confrontation with police was when unemployed workers and right-of-abode claimants organised demonstrations.[5]

Following the sovereignty retrocession, several events triggered changes in policing in Macau. The first was Chief Executive Edmund Ho's decision in 2002 to de-franchise gambling licenses, which resulted in phenomenal economic growth in the Macau SAR (MSAR). Social conflict emerged out of the economic boom. Polarisation of income, high inflation rates, and public dissatisfaction with governance brought new challenges to police authorities in Macau. Large demonstrations began occurring annually on Labour Day and MSAR Establishment Day, but the Macau police had little experience with crowd management and control. For example, when a scuffle broke out between protestors and police on Labour Day in 2007, a detective opened fire to 'ensure law and order' (Government Information Bureau 2007). The ensuing chaos attracted international media to Macau. People then began debating Macau police strategies for handling demonstrations.[6]

Although the number of registered civic groups is surprisingly large, public concern with social and governance issues seems limited.[7] Most civic groups in Macau have a collaborative relationship with the SAR leadership and generally

---

3   Interestingly, both interviewees A and H used the same words in unequivocally stating that the police did not actually safeguard the public under Portuguese rule. See Appendix Table 8.1 for table listing the policing backgrounds of interviewees and dates of the interviewees.

4   Dissident groups tend not to overtly challenge SAR leadership. They avoided taking 'too radical action' to confront the SAR government after its establishment, although they disagreed with the first Chief Executive Edmund Ho's administrative philosophy (Hung and Choi 2012). Dissident groups claimed that problems in Ho's governing strategy would be revealed over time as crises developed because the institutional setup would be unable to keep pace with economic development (Interviewee E).

5   The massive clash ended after the police released tear smoke to disperse the demonstration.

6   In a press release issued by the Macau Special Administrative Region Government Information Bureau, the government declared its intolerance toward 'any act [intended] to wreck the rule of law and Macau's stable development' and its determination to 'trace responsibility for any attempts to do so'.

7   Hung and Choi (2012) explain the consistently low rate of civic participation in Macau but surprisingly high number of membership in associations as the result of a 'participation explosion.' They argue that real civil society has failed to develop in Macau and the volume of associations is a result of 'social group politics, interest group politics, or informal politics developed by a specially designed state corporate mechanism [based on the] colonial Portuguese government since the 1970s' (p. 5).

Although Macau policing is a unique fusion of Chinese and Anglo-Saxon cultures of criminal justice, very little has been written about it. Social scientists have evidently considered the policing system and social development in colonial and SAR Macau insufficiently attractive research topics. Macau is a small enclave; its governance and civil society do not represent a significant agenda for academics in the fields of Chinese or Asian Studies. Historians and scholars of criminal justice have ignored Macau; even Asianists have shown limited interest in selecting it as a platform for comparison with other parts of Asia. Local scholars have also not focused on Macau, perhaps because the first private university in Macau (University of East Asia) was not established until the 1980s and only a handful of publications on Macau society and politics were available before 1999. For example, the only comprehensive introduction to Macau policing was Blackburn's (1992) 'Police and Policing in Macau,' a graduate thesis for a Master's Degree Program at the University of Hong Kong that has limited analytic implications (Hung and Choi 2012).[9]

This chapter addresses this gap in the literature on policing in Asia by examining police attempts to maintain social order during the transition from Portuguese to Chinese governance in the 1990's. It is not difficult to collect public accusations of unsatisfactory governance and ineffective policing during this transition. We analyse the features and changes in Macau policing following the 1974 Portuguese revolution based on multiple sources of data, including: newspaper reportage, government news bulletins, academic literature in Chinese and English, and interviews conducted with retired and serving police officers of varying seniority and citizens involved in civil society associations.

This study organises the criticism of late colonial policing around three features under the colonial system that we argue contributed to the chaos during the transition: 1) the existence of two independent police forces which failed to integrate or coordinate their operations; 2) the minimal interactions between law enforcers and citizens, largely because police forces were not headed by locals; and 3) limited professional police training, resulting in public scepticism over the capacities and reliabilities of the police. As a contribution to the wider literature on colonial and post-colonial policing, the Macau case illustrates that coercive

---

8 For example, two key social groups in Macao, the Macau Federation of Trade Union (*Federacao das Associacoes dos Operarios* de Macau, AGOM) and Macau Union of Kaifong Associations (*União Geral das Associações dos Moradores de Macau*, UGAMM), usually tender their support to the MSAR government in policy debates.

9 Hampered by Portuguese illiteracy, Blackburn got help from a Portuguese friend to translate source texts and describe the Macau policing system.

colonial policing is not the only factor contributing to the relative inefficiency of post-colonial social order management.

This chapter concludes with a discussion of the challenges that remain for police authorities in the MSAR. We argue that these challenges are a result of the effect of the post-colonial transition on the policing context. Increasing economic activities and population mobility across the border, the localisation of leadership in both of Macau's policing forces, and the prevalence of violent and syndicated crime associated with the gambling industry all exerted structural pressures on police reform during the late colonial period. After 1999, internal social conflict intensified due to the economic boom brought by the rapidly expanding casino industry. The policing context has been further shaped by a growing public demand for transparency and accountability, the presence of more critical local and overseas media, and the emergence of social activists unwilling to compromise with the new social order. Our research suggests that these ongoing contextual changes are likely to trigger future waves of reform in the organisation, staffing, and management philosophy of Macau police agencies.

Three key organisational features of colonial Macau policing

The policing literature and analyses of formal social control systems based on research in Western democracies tend to follow two major discourses (Brogden 1987). The first might be called 'policing by coercion.' This suggests a governmental emphasis on force and control in its attempts to ensure peace and order of the nation (Statistics and Census Service 2013). To achieve this objective, the government develops a strong law enforcement apparatus to manage public order. The police tend to operate as a military or paramilitary force, using violence to control those who intend to disrupt the social order established by the government. Autonomous civil society organisations are not present and there is segregation between the police and the policed. Thus, genuine police-citizen interactions are quite limited.

The second approach is known as 'policing by consent' (Alderson 1979). Partnership between police and citizens is the main emphasis. Police are understood as agents providing a service to the public. The police are not a military force but a civic department that works closely with citizens to ensure the smooth community operations. Violence is avoided and firearms are not considered necessary for police discharging general duties.

Colonial policing has usually been assumed to follow the 'coercive policing' paradigm. Colonial leaders tend to make use of both hard power (physical force) and soft power (autocratic legislation) to secure the metropole's interest in the colony (Sinclair 2006). Some recent research has started to demystify this perception as rather overdone and based on automatic prejudice against colonialism. Scholars are suggesting that some colonial leaders may not have been overly coercive when managing their indigenous subjects. For example, some colonial authorities used 'divide and rule' tactics to avoid confrontation with local communities and

Transformation of Macau policing 187

maximise the effectiveness of colonial governance (Sinclair 2006). After the 1970s, colonial Macau policing apparently fit this more 'conciliatory' model, since no major state-society confrontation took place.

The next subsections describe the three key features of colonial policing in Macau between the 1970s and 1990s: 1) dual police forces; 2) Portuguese police leadership distant from the Cantonese communities it served; and 3) limited capability and professionalism amongst Macau police. These three legacies of Portuguese colonial policing explain the limited legitimacy of the police forces and the colonial government in the eyes of the Cantonese public before 1999.

Dual police forces

The system of policing in colonial Macau mirrored that in Portugal, which followed a model adopted by many European countries (Mendes 2013). Colonial legislation established two distinct, independent law enforcement agencies to handle internal security: the Judiciary Police (JP) and the Public Security Police (PSP). The PSP were responsible for daily management of law and order, immigration, customs, and even fire services, while the JP concentrated on criminal investigation. The Secretary for Security, a position established in 1990, headed the Public Security Police, Marine Police, and Immigration and Customs. The Secretary for Justice presided over the Judiciary Police. Each Secretary was responsible directly to the governor of the colony.[10] The separation of the two police forces led to inter-agency distrust, suspicion, and rivalry. Their lack of cooperation was well known to the public (Blackburn 1992).[11]

Both forces were headed by expatriate commanders drawn from military or legal professions, while the rank and file was composed mainly of local Chinese. This administrative hierarchy, combined with the *laissez-faire* policing philosophy adopted by colonial leaders, resulted in segregation between the policing agencies and the community. Citizens avoided interacting with police, who they viewed as unprofessional and incapable of upholding the law or maintaining order.

10 Macau's colonial governor was appointed by the President of the Republic of Portugal. He was assisted by a number of departmental secretaries, such as the Secretary for Justice, the Secretary for Economic Affairs, Transport and Public Works and the Secretary for Education, Health and Welfare. The governor appointed his secretaries, but the appointments had to be approved by the authorities in Lisbon, who could override the governor.

11 As of December 2012, Macau Public Security units were organised as follows: The Secretary of Security oversees both Public Security Forces *(Forcas de Segurança de Macau)*, the Judiciary Police *(Polícia Judiciaria de Macau)*, Macau Customs (evolved from the Marine Police which was formerly under the command of the PSP) and Macau Prisons. Under the Public Security Forces, there are the Public Security Police, Public Security Forces Affairs Bureau, Public Security Tertiary Institute *(Escola Superior das Forcas de Segurança de Macau)*, and Fire Service Bureau. The PSP has several departments, including Immigration and the Police Tactical Unit, Macau Police Department, Islands Police Department, Police Training School, and Transport Department (Macau SARG 2013).

188   *Lawrence Ho and Agnes Lam*

Following the practice in Portugal, the PSP and JP were separately staffed and had different ranks and remuneration mechanisms. This transplantation of a European model to Macau resulted in numerous operational problems. In 1990, the colonial government attempted to reform the commandership and integrate the operations of the two police forces, with limited success. An interviewee who served in the Portuguese military and JP explained the failure of reform as follows:

> Macau was very small and thus the criminal justice system, characterized by a clear division of labour [imported from] Continental Europe, seems not [to have been] very appropriate for Macau. In my view, the feasible operation of such a well-established and sophisticated criminal justice system would [have to have] heavily relied on the availability of legal and law enforcement professionals. Transformation of Macau policing 421 this regard, Macau was totally lacking. And the leadership also lacked the determination to introduce necessary reforms to integrate the state and society during the colonial era.
>
> (Interviewee A)

The next subsection covers the history and structure of the Public Security Police, one of the two police agencies operating in Macau under Portuguese colonial rule.

The Public Security Police (PSP) or Corpo de Polícia de Segurança Pública (CPSP)

The PSP operated for over 400 years in Macau (Government of Macau SAR 2010). On 14 March 1691, the Portuguese government promulgated an order deploying soldiers to patrol the city at night. This date is regarded as the 'Establishment Day of the PSP' (Government of Macau SAR 2010). At that time, the colony was ruled by military personnel deployed from Portugal or other Portuguese colonies. The head of the PSP was normally a military colonel. The Portuguese heads and their expatriate subordinates led a group of locally recruited Cantonese constables. These constables were generally not very well educated and received only minimal, military-style training before assumption of police duties.

The PSP was not institutionalised until 1857. On 29 September 1857, Governor Isidoro Francisco Guimaraes issued a decree creating the '*Polícia do Bazar* [Police Ordinance]' (Government of Macau SAR 2010). In October 1861, Governor Guimaraes established the *Corpo de Polícia de Macau* (Police Corps of Macau), a body of regular police officers tasked to combat crime and maintain the peace in Macau. In 1914, under Governor Maia, the Head of the Police Service, Daniel Ferreira, separated police service from the auspices of the military and established the *Polícia Civil* (Civilian Police). In 1937, the service was renamed the *Corpo de Polícia de Segurança Pública da Colonia de Macau* or the Security Police Force of the Colony of Macau. In 1975, the civilian security forces and the military were re-united, retaining the name '*Polícia de Segurança Pública*' (Government of Macau SAR 2010).

The PSP was expected to defend public interests and guarantee security (Government of Macau SAR 2010). As stipulated by PSP regulations, public security police performed all the normal duties associated with a uniformed police force, as well as some unusual duties such as firefighting and handling immigration. These officers could be seen throughout Macau, patrolling the streets, standing guard duty outside banks and casinos, and operating traffic and enforcing traffic legislation. They also were expected to secure and maintain public order by preventing, investigating, and combating crime.

The training of the PSP officers was conducted in Portuguese by military trainers with the assistance from Macanese bilingual in Portuguese and Cantonese.[12] After completing 6 months basic training and swearing allegiance to the Portuguese government, PSP officers assumed duty. The Portuguese Code of Military Justice, known among the PSP personnel as 'Macau Government Order No. 6694,' was applied to govern PSP officers.[13] Violations could lead to disciplinary hearing and court martial by the Security Forces. Initial investigation of crimes committed by PSP officers were conducted by a judge from the Court of Criminal Instruction, who directed Judiciary Police officers to make enquiries. Court martial proceedings were presided over by two military judges along with a senior judge from the civil and criminal benches. The military judges had to have higher military rank than the accused.

The Judiciary Police (JP) or polícia judiciária de Macau

The Judiciary Police were formed in Portugal in 1945 at the end of the Second World War.[14] The Judiciary Police of Macau was not established until 1960, coincident with a loss of faith in the Macanese PSP by Macau's governor and the Portuguese government.[15] The military dictatorship of Portugal set up the JP to operate independently of the PSP. The JP reported directly to Macau's governor and thereby to the Director of Prosecution in Portugal.

---

12 Macanese is the term for Eurasians born in Macau, who usually speak both Portuguese and Chinese.

13 The Military Personnel Standing Order No. 66/94/M of Macau is similar to the Police General Order (PGO) of the Hong Kong police. It states the organisation, command structure, duties, and jurisdictions of different PSP police units, police operational procedures, and even the salary bands and points of police officers.

14 The JP was founded partly in response to criticism of the existing system of criminal investigation in Portugal, as at that time each investigation was directed by the same judge who would later here the trial.

15 According to the Judiciary Police website (www.pj.gov.mo/Web//Policia/history.html?lang=en), the JP was formally established on 19 August 1960, but was first named the 'Inspectorate of Macau Judiciary Police.' It was established following enactment of Decree-Law No. 43125 by the Macau-Portuguese Government, which consolidated overseas (including Macau) investigative procedures and handling of preliminary hearings. The JP was intended to support protection of the society against criminal activities in line with the Constitution of the Portuguese Republic and the Portuguese Code of Criminal Procedures.

190 Lawrence Ho and Agnes Lam

Now overseen by the MSAR Secretary for Security, the Judiciary Police in Macau was established primarily as a department of crime prevention and to provide investigative support to judicial authorities. They also liaised with Interpol and other overseas security agencies. Unlike the leaders of the PSP, who were mainly military officers from Portugal, the JP was run by civilians with strong legal backgrounds. JP Officers not only investigated crime, they also prosecuted and even adjudicated. Because of their secondary duties as judges, it was widely speculated that JP Officers were actually 'imperial crown agents' sent to gather intelligence on Macau. These rumours isolated JP Officers from the mainstream population, especially local Cantonese communities (Judiciary Police of Macau SAR of the People's Republic of China 2013).

Operational conflicts between PSP and JP

There has been considerable debate about the working relationship between the Judicial Police and the Public Security Police. The two forces were set up to operate independently, since they were under the jurisdiction of two different government bureaus. The Public Security Police were subject to the authority of the Secretary for Security, whereas the Judiciary Police reported to the Secretary for Justice. This meant that Judiciary Police could not be subordinated to the Public Security Police despite their civilian status. If any JP Officers required assistance of uniformed personnel, they were empowered to call upon PSP security units (including any of the sub-units who normally dealt with immigration, fire services, and so on) to provide manpower.

PSP commanders could only request the support of their JP counterparts in assisting with criminal cases. In accordance with Government Order No. 6694, any criminal cases involving valuables worth MOP\$500 or above had to be passed to the JP for subsequent investigation and prosecution. Since the size of the JP force has always been much smaller than that of the PSP, this relatively low threshold for demanding JP involvement accounts for some of the conflict that arose between the two forces (Macau SAR Administrative and Public Service Bureau 2012: 119).[16] One of our informants explained:

> Quite commonly, PSP officers hold the opinion that they are perfectly competent to conduct investigative work, but the law prohibits them from doing so. In some residential burglary cases, we have to wait for 1 to 2 h for the arrival of JP colleagues for follow-up work. From time to time, many PSP counterparts feel annoyed about the inefficiency of the JP and thus develop some kind of discontentment towards their partnership agency. The situation worsened stepping into the 1990s after living standards improved. I can say that all theft, even pickpocket cases, require intervention from JP as they are all over the MOP\$500 threshold!
>
> (Interviewee H)

---

16 The JP had only 400 personnel in 1999, which increased to 969 by 2011. There were 3,000 PSP personnel in 1999 and 4,489 in 2011.

Transformation of Macau policing 191

Apart from the unequal size of the two agencies and unreasonable arrangement of duties, the contentiousness between the two forces can be understood as a consequence of separate recruitment, training, and pay mechanisms. The two forces were not centrally staffed. The JP had (and still has) its own staffing exercises; post recruitment training was conducted by its own departmental training officers. Compared to the PSP, the JP set relatively high entry criteria for the candidates. Enrolees entered at the rank of 'Technician,' a professional rank widely used among different governmental departments in Macau. According to several of our informants (A–D), JP personnel perceived themselves as professionals and assumed an air of superiority over other security forces in Macau.

Separate from the JP, PSP recruitment was coordinated by a recruitment office under the Security Bureau. Graduates of a degree program offered by the Public Security Tertiary Institute were automatically enrolled as Deputy Superintendents. Rank and file junior police were publicly recruited through a mass selection exercise. To be appointed Police Constable (PC), recruits only had to have attended primary school and they did not have to meet any Portuguese language proficiency requirements. Most of the PSP PC recruits had weak writing skills and little understanding of the legal system and its rationale in Macau, although they were taught about this in Police Training School. There was not any formal vetting of new PSP recruits.

These factors made it difficult for the PSP to establish collegial relationships with the JP and the communities they served, let alone recruit and retain high quality personnel. Interviewee A, who served in the JP for three decades, described the PSP of the 1970s:

> The quality of the PSP was unbelievably low. It was totally chaotic in terms of organization and we actually did not know what the top Portuguese commanders were doing, as they seldom showed up to explain their police work in public. On the frontline, we had lots of contact with Cantonese policemen, but most of them had only received primary schooling. Some even held concurrent appointments with casino companies and associated with syndicated criminal activities. There was no vetting exercise before the policemen got their formal appointments. Do you think that the public would trust such a force, comprised of some members with Triad Society backgrounds? [Being] hired by [the PSP] was not satisfactory, not an excellent job when compared to appointments in casino-related businesses. [There was only] a primary schooling [requirement], no vetting exercise.
>
> (Interviewee A)

The difference in terms of quality of education and training between the JP and PSP generated mutual suspicion. JP officers doubted the competence of their PSP counterparts; PSP constables felt discriminated against. Indeed, they were discriminated against in terms of the remuneration packages for officers in the two forces. Newly recruited JP technicians entered at 260 points on the Macau government's civil service pay scale, but new PSP enrolees started at 190 points. In 2010, 1 point was equivalent to about MOP\$60, but even before 1999, a

192 *Lawrence Ho and Agnes Lam*

70-point difference meant much larger salaries for JP personnel. This discrepancy in pay scale led to the perception that even new JP recruits were 'senior' to PSP officers. Being treated as 'juniors' further demoralised PSP constables. Interviewees C and H both mentioned that PSP constables felt discriminated against as they had duties outdoors in all weather conditions, while their JP counterparts could work in an air-conditioned environment.

Non-local police forces distant from the community

The second important feature of colonial Macau policing was the social distance between its non-local, military leadership and the local community.[17] Senior PSP and JP personnel were all either Portuguese or Macanese who rarely interacted with the local Cantonese-speaking Chinese. Before 1966, mainstream Chinese communities distrusted the police, saw them as an expatriate force staffed by poorly educated and unreliable local constables, and assumed they only served the Portuguese people.

Some people suspected that the police were primarily in Macau to safeguard expatriate interests, even to the point of gathering intelligence for the colonial government (Interviewee A). This suspicion was not without foundation. Portugal was under military dictatorship after WW-II. After the Portuguese government set up Macau's Criminal Investigation Department (CID) under the Public Security Police, it was widely speculated that CID officers were actually spies for the Portuguese government (Interviewees A, B, F, G).[18]

The Chinese public did not even trust the PSP's frontline Cantonese constables, who were poorly educated and shared in a culture that rationalised illicit and corrupt policing practices. The misbehaviour common among the Chinese police in Macau's security forces further ruined their public image. Interviewee C, who joined the PSP in the 1970s, remarked on the public's perception of the police:

> The public saw the police force as not very trustworthy, not well-established, and lacking any capacity to effectively deal with conflict and possible violence arising from clashes among the triad societies. Instead, they [the triads] claimed the importance of policing themselves and some underground orders were established in which the Macau police authorities played a limited role. I think all of this was embedded in a more general cultural ideal of keeping one's affairs and person away from government agencies, a deep-seated belief among the conservative local community in Macau. As the traditional Chinese proverbs put it, 'No entry to the government offices,' and 'Good men

17 The first non-military police commander was not appointed in Macau until 1996.
18 All criminal investigations were carried out by the PSP CIDs before the JP was formed in 1960. Afterwards, the PSP and JP had some overlapping jurisdiction since they could both conduct criminal investigations. Theoretically, cases involving less than MOP $500 are dealt with by the PSP; cases involving more than that amount are handled by the JP.

Transformation of Macau policing 193

do not take up police work.' [These proverbs] were often invoked to describe the attitude of Macau citizens towards their police agencies.

The gap between the general public and law enforcement agencies was also created because many of the laws were never translated from Portuguese to Chinese and there were few academically qualified legal professionals originating from Macau working in the JP or PSP who could explain the law to the general population.[19] Since ethnic Chinese in Macau could not understand the laws, they preferred informal mechanisms for resolving dispute (i.e. negotiation and consensus formation). When local Chinese needed assistance, they sought help from people in mainland China. They turned to clan associations and trade unions to settle problems that were not emergencies rather than contact local police authorities. This reflected the Portuguese government's own segregationist approach in managing Chinese subjects in Macau. Thus, the nature of the Portuguese regime, combined with Chinese customs for handling disputes, prevented the police force of Portuguese Macau from gaining any measure of trust from its colonised population.

When China prepared to resume control over the territory in 1999, Macau citizens and Beijing government administrators favoured de-militarisation and localisation of police leadership in Macau. There was only lukewarm progress on both fronts, however. Still headed by Portuguese military specialists, the PSP attempted to recruit more local Cantonese. The postings failed to attract quality candidates. Several factors discouraged local high calibre candidates from joining the police force. First, only locally born citizens were eligible; Chinese from the mainland were not. Second, potential candidates were put off by the military-style training. Third, and most important, was the notorious reputation for corruption and scandal in the PSP. The insufficiently institutionalised organisation, the communication gap between commanders and the rank and file, and the lack of leadership experience amongst the newly promoted Chinese officers (most of whom were only in their forties), all made a career in the police force unattractive (Jim 2000).

Limited capacity and professional ability

A third key feature of colonial Macau policing was the incapacity of both the PSP and the JP to cope with public demand for the maintenance of law and order. By the late 1990s, police constituted nearly 1% of the population.[20] This seems like a reasonable number for a small city, but the police force was dealing with an

---

19 Police effectiveness was undermined by the simultaneous application of Portuguese and local Chinese laws even after the MSAR government was established. Maintaining public security was hindered by lack of progress in translating relevant legal codes from Portuguese to Chinese. The Chinese did not adopt the Codified Law and Criminal Law until 1998, even though these law codes were to become the basis for legal hearings and proceedings in the MSAR (Interviewee A; Jim 2000).

20 The Macau population was around 400,000 in 1999; 3,184 people worked at the PSP (a third were Marine Police) and the JP had 340 established posts.

194   *Lawrence Ho and Agnes Lam*

extremely complicated environment. In addition to ongoing public distrust of the police, society was in turmoil as Macau's economy became increasingly integrated with that of mainland China (Jim 2000). The police were given very few resources for handling crime. A former officer of the JP (Interviewee B) recalled the lack of resources and training available to JP leadership at the time:

> I was appointed head of the Forensic Science Division in the Judiciary Police. In fact, I received no formal training beforehand, but just had an attachment to the Royal Hong Kong Police for 2 weeks. How could I handle the cases and even design a training program for my subordinates?

Criticism of the Portuguese authorities intensified during the transitional period of the 1990s. It was widely noted that the departing Portuguese government showed no enthusiasm for reforming either police agency.[21] The passive, uncompromising attitude of the Portuguese government hindered any movement to modernise the police forces and undermined any capacity of the JP and PSP to prevent crime during the 1990s. This seemed to encourage the proliferation of gang fights and street violence, especially amongst people involved with the casinos (Jim 2000, Mendes 2013, Scott 2011).

The issues of succession and localisation certainly influenced Macau policing for the worse during the transitional period. The Sino-Portuguese Joint Declaration concluded in 1986 stipulated that the principal officials of the MSAR government be Chinese, excluding those holding overseas citizenship. This stipulation made the localisation of police forces an acute problem, as most of the commanding officers in the PSP were Portuguese military officers, while JP heads were principally Portuguese legal professionals trained in Lisbon. There were only a few Macanese personnel working for the police and even fewer Macau-born ethnic Chinese. Unlike their British counterparts in Hong Kong, the Portuguese government did not work out a comprehensive plan for turning over Macau to China. Up until 1999, most of the prominent positions in the colonial government, including the police chiefs, remained occupied by Portuguese. The PSP got their first Chinese commander only in March 1998; the JP was commanded by Portuguese until December 1999, the eve of sovereignty retrocession. A police officer recalled his frustration at the attitude of the Portuguese:

> I told my boss that there was a lack of monetary and human resources to handle the cases. His reply was so disgusting. [He said] that you may seek help in Hong Kong or Mainland China or the communities would have their informal mechanisms for successfully dealing with the issues. "This will not be our piece of land," [he told me].
>
> (Interviewee A)

---

21 Mendes (2013) argues that the lack of commitment to maintaining order in Macau can partly be attributed to domestic Portuguese party politics, as the President and the Prime Minister had conflicting approaches towards dealing with the Sino-Portuguese relationship.

A Portuguese officer born in Macau concurred:

> I was asked to think about localization and succession in 1998 by my boss. I found that there were just one or two Chinese personnel with limited managerial exposure who might succeed in managing our forces. We had to depart soon, but obviously the leaders cared nothing about the future development of the forces.
>
> (Interviewee A)

The chaotic situation arising from lack of adequate preparation for sovereignty retrocession had an unquestionably negative effect on the already limited competencies of the two police forces.[22] However, a transformation in Macau policing has gradually taken place following the departure of the colonial government at the end of 1999. The next sections discuss factors pushing reform and changes that have taken place.

Transformation of policing in the MSAR

The need for localisation in both policing agencies, increasing economic activities and cross-border population mobility, and rising violent crime associated with the flourishing gambling industries have all pushed the desire for reform of policing in Macau. The policing context has been further shaped by growing public demands for transparency and accountability, the presence of more critical local and overseas media, and the emergence of social activism under the new social order. These contextual changes have triggered waves of reform in Macau's police agencies.

Triggers for police reform after 1999

De-monopolisation of the gaming industry

Under Portuguese rule, Macau suffered from a generally weak economy and serious crime problems. However, the MSAR government under Chief Executive Edmund Ho's leadership won positive regard from the general public and the blessings of the PRC government for remarkable economic achievements during his first term from 1999–2004. For example, the Free Individual Travel (FIT) scheme for mainland Chinese wanting to visit Macau was introduced in 2003 to boost the tourism industry (Wu and Hao 2013).[23] Gaming is closely related to

---

22 In 1999, the PRC government in Beijing declared that People's Liberation Army (PLA) troops stationed in Macau were available to Ho to assist in maintaining public order. The presence of the PLA in Macau was generally perceived as a way for the Central People's Government in Beijing and the MSAR government to boost public confidence in the Macau police and thus Macau SAR governance.

23 Visitor arrivals increased by 1.9% each year, reaching 2,382,156 in April 2012. An annual 9.5% increase in visitors from Mainland China reached 1,391,119 (58.4% of the total) by

the tourism industry. The most far-reaching economic policy introduced by the MSAR government was the decision to end the *Sociedade de Turismo e Diversões de Macau* (STDM, 'Macau Tourism and Entertainment Company') monopoly over the gaming industry. The MSAR government terminated STDM's 40-year-old monopoly over Macau's gaming industry in 2002, which opened the gaming sector to two new gaming corporations from Nevada in the United States: the Las Vegas Sands Corporation and Wynn Resorts.

Total revenue from gaming activities grew from a MOP\$42,306 million in 2004 to a whopping MOP\$55,884 million by the end of 2006. Taxes on gaming activities supplied 47% of the government budget in 1999; by 2006 it accounted for 76% (Statistics and Census Service 2013). By 2011, the Gross Domestic Product (GDP) had reached MOP\$2,921 billion, with unemployment at just 2.6% (Statistics and Census Service 2013).[24]

The reorientation of Macau's economic development policy has had an adverse effect on small and medium enterprises (SMEs). Ever since new casinos started operating in 2004, the demand for labour has kept growing. Casinos and hotels, the most dynamic economic sectors, require large staffs. There is a very limited pool of local workers to feed the needs of the new economy. Imported workers are required to fill the gap, but only the casinos and sectors with foreign investment are allowed a quota of imported workers. SMEs are not eligible to employ imported workers, which adds to their grievances. They perceive the government as favouring the rich and powerful. SME employees' monthly wages range from MOP\$6,000–8,000. By contrast, a croupier working in a casino earns double that, from MOP\$12,000–14,000 a month (Wu and Hao 2013). Many reports have shown that SMEs experience difficulty recruiting staff since they are unable to match the salaries paid to workers in the gaming industry.

The economic boom has thus polarised Macau society. Although those working in the tourism and gambling sectors have benefited from development, a considerable number of people have not. Lower class families have instead been harmed by the rising price of goods. In 2006, the inflation rate reached 5.15% and it has consistently been over 5% since 2011 (Wu and Hao 2013, Statistics and Census Services 2013).

Those working in the public sector also don't appreciate the changes. The soaring inflation rates not only degraded their previously comfortable existence, there have also been increasing demands for better service from government servants. One legislator described the worsening life of public servants: 'In Macau the vast

---

2012. Most of the visitors came from the Guangdong (641,433), Fujian (72,755), Zhejiang (50,776), and Hunan (49,920) provinces. Nearly half (541,551) the visitors from mainland China travel to Macao under the FIT scheme.

24 The GDP expanded by 18.4% in real terms by the first quarter of 2012 over a year earlier. Private investment increased by 21.2%, of which construction investment and equipment investment went up by 22.3% and 19.2% respectively (Wu and Hao 2013). Throughout this period the Macanese pataca has been pegged to the Hong Kong dollar, holding an exchange rate of about eight pataca per US dollar.

majority of the civil servants under regular contracts want to leave the civil service because their career is stagnating. In the past, the middle class was composed of the civil servants. But now it is the civil servants who ask for public housing because they can no longer afford real estate' (Interviewee D). Civil servants demonstrated during the Labour Day Rally in 2007 for the first time since the 1999 handover (South China Morning Post 2007). The suffering middle class, together with low-skilled, poorly educated workers, constitutes burgeoning groups of aggrieved people in Macau.

Internal social conflict thus intensified along with the economic boom brought about by the rapidly expanding casino industry. The honeymoon ended in 2005, at the beginning of Edmund Ho's second term. The Macau SAR government has since been confronted by an increasingly polarised community and corruption scandals among principal government officials. Reduced public support for the government and greater social turbulence have emerged (Public Opinion Programme, The University of Hong Kong 2007).[25] With a sort of grim irony, Macau's spectacular economic growth has eroded the quality of life among the middle and lower classes and triggered a panoply of social and economic problems. These contextual changes threaten to gradually de-legitimise the Macau SAR government. The police are presented with novel challenges as they confront newly unhappy civilians and the emergence of autonomous interest groups, discussed next.

Emergence of new civil groups

Despite the dissatisfaction of some, participation in civil society activities and associations remains quite weak in Macau. Most people are still inclined to support their government. Civic groups generally establish a collaborative relationship with the Macau government and seldom overtly challenge public policies (Hung and Choi 2012). While dissident groups do exist in Macau, their voices are weak and underrepresented in the legislature.[26] The standing orders of the legislature prevent elected officials from exercising much power to check their Chief Executive. For example, legislators do not have the right to monitor public expenditures and they have no way of questioning the government's executive decisions (Yu 2011).

What had previously been a relatively harmonious corporatist partnership between the government and civil groups has started to fray in recent years. Interviewee E described the new political terrain:

> Before 1999, the total vote for the liberal camp against the pro-Beijing camp was 1 to 4. After 1999, the proportion is 1 to 1. Indeed, now the pro-Beijing

---

25 The rate of support towards Ho's leadership dropped by 15% between December 2004 and January 2007, from 84.7% to 69.3% in January 2007.

26 Only 12 of the 29 members of Macau's Legislative Assembly are directly elected. Ten other members are indirectly elected through functional constituencies and the remaining seven are appointed by the Chief Executive.

198 *Lawrence Ho and Agnes Lam*

camp faces the challenge of governing ability. Corruption has been there for many years. But today the new environment of economic adjustment and increasing social inequalities allow the corruption cases to be revealed to the public.

New socio-economic conditions have led more people to voice their discontent, resulting in the emergence of new autonomous interest groups. More than 50 such new groups were registered in the first-half of 2007 (Yu 2011). Most of their members were low skilled workers who had been marginalised from the labour market (Cheng and Ng 2007). These new civic groups are unlike their old counterparts in that they tend to take a more aggressive approach and even adopt street-level strategies such as holding demonstrations to intervene in certain policy debates. The 2007 Labour Day Rally (discussed below), for example, revealed that organisers could not rely on self-policing to maintain the peace, because protestors came from a heterogeneous background of different civic groups. The main organiser was powerless to control the radicals and extremists who joined the rally because they were not among its members.

Emergence of outspoken media and the 2007 Labour Day Rally

Traditionally, the media in Macau lacked independence from the government and refrained from criticising its policies. The MSAR government owns the only television station, *Teledifusao de Macau*. The two biggest newspapers, the Macau Daily News and *Jornal Va Kio*, are both owned by pro-China people in sympathy with the government (Hu 2007). Recent socio-economic conflict had already degraded the accommodating relationship between the government and media before the 2007 demonstration; since then, Macau's media have become more critical of government policies. Topics related to the necessity to protect Macau workers against external competition now appear frequently in the local media, including calls for repressing the flow of illegal labourers into Macau, restricting non-residents from access to certain types of jobs, imposing taxes on imported labour, and establishing a minimum wage.

Macau media became a lot more outspoken about criticising the police following the incidents at the 2007 Labour Day Rally. Riot police blocked demonstrators attempting to march into the central business district. The confrontation escalated to clashes between the two groups. One policeman attempted to disperse the crowd by firing five times into the air, but hit a passer-by with a stray bullet. The rally ended with the arrest of ten marchers and hospitalisation of 21 police officers (South China Morning Post 2007). The performance of the police in trying to control the crowd exposed the weakness and unprofessionalism of the police agencies in the new MSAR.

The MSAR government later denounced the minority among the protestors who had tried to use violence for political ends (Government Information Bureau 2007). There was also controversy about the policeman who had shot into the air despite the Macau government's claim that its police force had taken appropriate measures to maintain public order and the gunshots were necessary in the emergency (Government Information Bureau 2007). There were ongoing queries from the public on whether the police had made tactical errors and the appropriateness of firing shots near a crowd.[27] Many civic groups paid for advertisements in their local newspapers censuring the 'unlawful and violent crowd' that had failed to comply with police instructions on the rally route; they suggested it was a deliberate attempt to trigger chaos and disrupt Macau's stable development (Jornal San Wa Ou 2007b).

The confrontation between the police and Macau citizens at the 2007 Labour Day Rally also drew attention from international media, which had previously ignored Macau politics. The shooting incident was televised and photographed overseas soon after the demonstration (Jornal San Wa Ou 2007b). While under the spotlight of local and overseas reporters, the police continued to take relatively coercive action to disperse and arrest the protestors. The widespread debate about the shooting incident and the level of police professionalism in Macau society contributed to a push for reform.

Attempts to reform Macau police agencies and policies

As discussed earlier, there were many arguments about the inability of Macau police agencies to meet the demand for public security in a fast-changing society. The combination of increased social polarisation and the introduction of public sector reform by the Macau SAR government also increased the public demand for government accountability. These demands have gradually expanded into expecting a more transparent and responsive police force. Public opinion and media scrutiny challenge police chiefs in both agencies. Several actions have been taken in an attempt to transform different aspects of police management, including: establishing the Unitary Police Services (UPS), adjusting salary scale and amount, upgrading police professionalism, and increasing transparency.

Establishment of the Unitary Police Services (Servicos de Polícia Unitarios) in 2001

Chief Executive Ho introduced the first notable step in response to the request for police reform in 2000. He established a new government bureau, the Unitary Police Services (*Servicos de Polícia Unitarios*), to coordinate the JP and the PSP, which formerly operated under separate policies and bureaus. This structural change was intended to rationalise the roles and functions of the police in Macau.

---

27 Legislative Councillor Jose Pereira Coutinho made verbal inquiries to the Government on the crowd control arrangements planned by the police for that Labour Day He issued three substantive questions to the security authorities concerning excessive use of police force. See Macau Legislative Council Document No. 286/III/2007, Available at: www.al.gov.mo/ interpelacao_oral/2006/07-286c.pdf [accessed: 8 July 2007].

200　Lawrence Ho and Agnes Lam

Before the sovereignty retrocession, people in the community had attributed the problems in public order to the poor collegiality of the two separate forces. The UPS was established on 29 October 2001 in response to these criticisms. It is responsible for commanding the two subordinate police agencies in executing their duties. The UPS also allocates operational resources; manages criminal investigations (without contradicting the leading role of the judicial authorities); collects, analyses, processes, and releases significant information when needed; and supervises the operations of the two police agencies (Macau SARG 2013: 9).

Adjustment of salary scale and amount

Steps were also taken to standardise the entry salaries of the most junior enrolees in the two police agencies, such as PSP Police Constables and JP Technicians II. All were set at 260 points and given the same allowances for overtime, night shift, and armed duty (adding about 50 to 100 points each). Police had their personal income tax rates fixed at 7–11% according to their rank and received an MOP\$140,000 income tax allowance, equivalent to five to six months of basic salary. Standardising the entry salary, providing annual increases in salary points, and reducing income taxes on police was meant to alleviate tension between the two forces and make a career in law enforcement more attractive. These measures indeed made the remuneration package competitive even in a gloomy private market and increased the attractiveness of police work.

Interviewee H explained that the salary increase was also an attempt to stop the exodus of human resources from police agencies during the economic boom:

> In fact, the government needed to retain human resources after the economic boom. Around 2004 to 2005 there was a very high dropout rate among new police recruits and even experienced police officers, as they found that working for casinos as security officers or even croupiers could earn them 50% more or even double their prevailing salaries. A report from a newspaper that year said there were only a thousand candidates for the PSP PC recruitment exercise. So the government quickly adjusted the salary to stabilize the police forces.

Recruitment standards for PSP constables were also raised; individuals seeking a position with the PSP now had to have graduated secondary school, not only primary school. This initiative provided a new career path to junior police officers in the PSP as they could now advance to the Superintendent level, whereas formerly the rank and file officers were prevented from being promoted to any command position.

Upgrading police professionalism

The protest in 2007 demonstrated that rule-based policing had yet to develop in Macau. No clear written orders were available to front-line police about how to

Transformation of Macau policing 201

handle disorderly crowds at the time (Macau SAR Legislative Council 2001, 2012).[28] Dealing with crowds of protestors who are neither criminal nor violent is an ambiguous situation for police. After the Labour Day shooting incident, some senior government officials insisted that all the police officers involved had exercised reasonable force although they were not following orders. Mr. Cheong Kuoc Va, Secretary for Security, stated that the front-line police officers were never told to suppress the demonstrations, but that opening fire was a necessary move to restore order (*Jornal Cheng Po* 2007). Chief Executive Ho further clarified that opening fire was an on-the-scene judgment of the situation made by one officer to prevent demonstrators from trampling one another.

There is a set of written regulations governing the use of ammunition for all police officers in Macau. However, these rules seem to be ambiguous. The rules read, 'An officer is allowed to use his gun only if he and others are in danger, but should not open fire in a place where there is a danger of hurting a third person' (Hu 2007). When compared with the Police General Order developed by the Hong Kong Police, the Macau regulations are overly general. The Hong Kong Order more explicitly describes the appropriate use of firearms. It states that an officer can discharge his firearm while protecting himself or any other person from serious injury or death or if he suspects a person has committed a serious or violent crime and is evading arrest.

Also in contrast to Hong Kong police practice, Macau police are not required to write any reports of gunshot incidents and nor are there psychological assessments of police officers who have discharged their firearms (*Jornal San Wa Ou* 2007a).

The shooting incident also indicated a systematic weakness in Macau policing as an inadequately institutionalised internal security structure. It seemed that the Macau anti-riot squad could not effectively deal with large-scale protests. A Tactical Police Unit (*Unidade Tactica de Intervencao da Polícia*, 'UTIP') had already been established in 1995, but its main duty was to protect VIPs visiting Macau (Statistics and Census Service 2013). Members of this unit received specialist training on riot control and were expected to manage civil disturbances as well. However, the squad was under-staffed, comprised of only about 500 officers (Macau Daily 2006). Having a relatively small squad of anti-riot specialists may have made sense in the past in the absence of large-scale demonstrations, but it was inadequate for dealing with social disturbances in the mid-2000s.

---

28 Revisiting the official Chinese documents on the laws governing protests, demonstrations and public assemblies, there were only two booklets published by the Legislative Council of Macau SAR publicising the legislations governing the freedom of petition and freedom of assembly and protests. The booklet published in 2001 titled 'Exercising the Rights to Petition (*Exercicio do direito de peticao*) listed all the laws governing the behavior of petitioners and the law enforcers on this regard. The second book titled 'Rights to Assembly and Protests– Second Edition' (*Direito de Reuniao e de Manifestacao*) listed all the laws in this regard as well as the proceedings of legislators' debates on its revision. However, no publicly accessible government document was available except of the Government Order No. 6694/M which mentioned some procedurally adjustments on the public order policing.

202 *Lawrence Ho and Agnes Lam*

Following the shooting incident at the Labour Day Rally, it was reported that more tactical training in managing public demonstrations and protests would be provided to PSP officers. The PSP emulated the Hong Kong police in adopting 'soft' crowd control tactics. Female officers were deployed to the frontline. Superintendents were sent to Portugal for language lessons and to mainland China for vocational training.

Public relations

Since 2002, a number of tactics have been adopted to 'repackage' the image of Macau police. Two police emergency hotlines were publicised: 999 connects to the PSP and 993 to the JP. Public announcements were posted asking the general public to cooperate with the police. After the Labour Day incident, press conferences were held to address community concerns over police performance. This was also an attempt to deflect the emergence of more aggressive critiques in the MSAR media.

Assessing reform

During the colonial period, only limited documentation of police activities was available to the public, police salaries were low, and staffing was not institutionalised. The reform initiatives were undertaken in response to the changing contexts of policing and new public demands in the MSAR. Policing in Macau has certainly become more transparent, but the effectiveness of these reform measures remains to be seen. Despite the abundant supply of monetary resources and determination of MSAR leaders, the absence of independent media in Macau, the existence of civic associations unwilling to compromise with the government, and the shortage of qualified legal professionals undermines further professionalisation of Macau policing.

One of our interviewees described the public's attitude toward the police since the reform measures were instituted:

> I agree that the Macau police have performed far better than in the Portuguese colonial era. Now most police officers have got a good salary and we would generally not discriminate against the policemen. However, we [civic groups] still do not consider the police to be trustworthy, as their leadership has yet to display professional qualities in [dealing with] some policing issues and scenarios. For example, we still don't know what the work of the Unitary Police Service is. Which police force should I approach in an emergency, as they gave me two hotline telephone numbers? Meanwhile, police chiefs seldom satisfactorily explain some controversial policing decisions. Some of the commanders are still very conservative and their mind-set is still far from internationally accepted values.
>
> (Interviewee D)[29]

---

29 Interviewee E made similar comments on this topic.

This suggests that some of the underlying dimensions of public distrust toward the police still need to be addressed.

Conclusion: further change ahead

This article has described the transformation in police-society relations before and after reversion of Macau's sovereignty to China. The colonial system was characterised by a segregation of police from the mainstream community. The MSAR inherited a Portuguese-style police force that was strictly hierarchical, militarised, and under expatriate command. Many of our interviewees commented that the local Chinese community distrusted the police (especially between the 1960s and 1990s), who they regarded as akin to legitimised gangs given to extorting the public and abusing their power. Interestingly, some of the retired police officers we interviewed admitted that the public looked down on them and accused them of being motivated not by the desire to fight crime fighting and maintain order, but rather by the somewhat legitimised pursuit of bribes. This accusation may have been overstated, but it does reveal that the public held a strongly negative image of the police.

Macau's policing context remains quite complicated, so effective policing is difficult. Unlike the colonial situation in Hong Kong, locally born Chinese elites were never co-opted into the circle of governance in Portuguese Macau (King 1975: 422–439).[30] Interactions between police and the policed were instead organised in a relatively indirect manner through corporatised 'patriotic associations' that had strong connections to the Beijing regime (Hung and Choi 2012). These institutions even operated with the blessings of the colonial government, since their members received monetary support and public appointments (e.g., in the Legislative Assembly in Macau).[31] More significant for the 'web of policing' discussed by Brodeur (2010), these organisations sometimes acted as agencies involved in maintaining law and order. The government's institutionalised police force, by contrast, suffered from a lack of resources and a language barrier. Its role was relatively insignificant within the wider pattern of a politicised civil society generated by the participatory aspects of corporatist colonial governance.

This arrangement suited the Portuguese government and its representatives in Macau who were inclined to avoid intervening in any issues that arose in Macau and any troubles such might create for the home leadership. The existence of a

---

30 The 'administrative absorption of politics' was a strategy adopted by British colonial administers in Hong Kong before the 1970s to create a degree of participatory governance in the colony. In addition to so called 'Positive Non-Interventionism' by the MacLehorse regime, which had noted the increasing government presence in infrastructural and social policy involvement, this co-option strategy successfully brought the government and community together in Hong Kong despite the absence of democracy.

31 Members of the Legislative Assembly in Macau were not all democratically elected. The Legislative Assembly was presided over by the Governor, who appointed the majority of its members. Only 12 out of 29 members were directly popularly elected in 2009.

lame-duck government with conflicting policy orientations in turn suffocated Macau's policing agencies and added to public discontent and social turbulence during the countdown to the end of Portuguese colonial rule. Mendes (2013) argues that Portuguese colonial leaders were not mandated to properly govern Macau in the 1990s because by that time Macau had ceased to be of economic value to Portugal. Whatever the reason, internal and external accountabilities were absent from Macau's policing system before 1999.

The situation changed abruptly after Macau became the second Special Administrative Region of the PRC. Internal social conflict intensified due to the economic boom brought by the expansion of the casino industry after 2002. The Macau Police were confronted by new challenges and came under greater scrutiny by both local and international media agencies. As in much of the developing world, this new context posed significant problems and necessitated the reinvention and modernisation of policing in Macau. Declining government legitimacy due to administrative scandals after 2002, the emergence of civic groups coordinated by young, well-educated, but uncompromising activists, and the internationalisation of Macau brought about by external investors all posed increasing challenges to the old policing establishment and conservative police officers.

The new MSAR leadership attempted to redefine the state-society relationship by strengthening the interface between the government and the communities it serves. The new government worked at replacing the fragile, non-institutionalised, social control network with formal arrangements in which state police authorities would play a more prominent role in the communities. Increasing police capacity, making the police publicly accountable, and rationalising the commandership by establishing the Unitary Police Bureau were all done in order to build public trust in the policing system. We argue that it also was intended to legitimise the MSAR government. We expect that subsequent changes in Macau policing will continue to provide an important entry point for future research on state-society relationship in Macau in the 21st Century.

Appendix

Table 8.1 Informant profiles

Code	Background	Connection to Macau Policing	Interview dates
A	Macau born Portuguese (Male)	Joined JP in 1972 after finishing Portuguese military duties in Macau: served in JP for 32 years; retired 2004	21 Feb 2010 23 Feb 2012
B	Macau born Portuguese (Male)	Joined JP in 1968 as Acting Inspector; served in JP for 25 Years; retired in 1993	21 Feb 2010 23 Feb 2012
C	Macau born Cantonese (Male)	Joined PSP in 1976 as Police Constable	21 Feb 2010 23 Feb 2012
D	Macau born Portuguese (Male)	Legislative Councillor, advocated the interest of Portuguese and Civil Service communities in Macau in his political platform	4 Jun 2007
E	Macau born Cantonese (Male)	Legislative Councillor, advocated democratisation and accountability in MSAR governance in his political platform	5 Jun 2007
F	Macau born Cantonese (Female)	Service Professional; active in a civil society association	16 Mar 2012
G	Macau born Cantonese (Male)	Service Professional; active in a civil society association	16 Mar 2012
H	Macau born Cantonese (Female)	Joined Youth Adventure Programme* organised by PSP 1999–2000; university graduate in criminology	30 Jun 2013 4 Jul 2013

*The Youth Adventure Program is similar to the Junior Police Call and Outreach Program for Youth Members organised by Hong Kong Police.

206 *Lawrence Ho and Agnes Lam*

References

Alderson, J. 1979. *Policing Freedom*. Plymouth: Macdonald and Evans.

Blackburn, A. 1992. *Police and Policing in Macau*. Unpublished PhD Thesis. The University of Hong Kong, Hong Kong.

Brodeur, J.P. 2010. *The Policing Web*. Oxford: Oxford University Press.

Brogden, M. 1987. The emergence of the police: The colonial dimension. *British Journal of Criminology*, 27(1): 4–14.

Cheng, M.C. and Ng, C.K. 2007. The May-first rally: Organized by newly emerged civic groups composed of low skilled labour. *Hong Kong Economic Times*, 2 May, A21, Social News. (in Chinese).

Government Information Bureau. 2 May 2007. MSAR government denounces violation of law during demonstration [Online: *Government Information Bureau of the Macau SAR*]. Available at: http://www.gcs.gov.mo/showNews.php?DataUcn=25273&PageLang=E [accessed: 9 July 2007].

Government of Macau SAR, Public Security Police Force. 2010. History, structure, organization of CPSP [Online: *Corpo de Polícia de Segurança Pública*]. Available at: www.fsm.gov.mo/psp/eng/main.html [accessed: 30 July 2013].

Hu, F.Y. 2007. Protesters reprimanded in Macau. *South China Morning Post*, 3 May, EDT 1.

Hung, E. and Choi, A. 10–11 February 2012. *From Societal to State Corporatism: The Making of the 'Uncivil' Society in Macau*. Paper to the Conference 'The Dynamics of Civil Society Coalitions in Asia', Department of Public and Social Administration, City University of Hong Kong.

Jim, K.F. 2000. Analyzing the restructure of Macau Police Forces, in *The Proceedings of Public Administration in Macau During the Transition Period*, edited by G. Lü. Macau: Macau University Press (in Chinese).

Jornal, C.P. 2007. Cheong responded to the May-first gunshot but avoided talking responsibility. *Jornal Cheng Po*, 13 June 2004 (in Chinese).

Jornal, S.W.O. 2007a. The injury from strayed bullets would be properly settled: Secretary for Security Cheong says. *Jornal San Wa Ou*, 19 May 2002 (in Chinese).

Jornal, S.W.O. 2007b. The underlying reasons for the outbreak of May-first incident. *Jornal San Wa Ou*, 28 June 2003 (in Chinese).

Judiciary Police of Macau Special Administrative Region of the People's Republic of China. 2013. 'History' in Polícia Judiciária [Online: *'History' in Polícia Judiciária*]. Available at: www.pj.gov.mo/Web//Policia/history.html?lang=en[0] [accessed: 13 July 2013].

King, A. 1975. The administrative absorption of politics in Hong Kong. *Asian Survey*, 15(5): 422–439.

Macau Daily. 2006. Well-equipped police tactical unit to assume the protection of VIPs in Macau. *Macau Daily*, 20 April 2001 (in Chinese).

Macau SARG (Special Administrative Region Government). 2013. Government organization chart [Online: *Macao SARG Portal*]. Available at: http://portal.gov.mo/web/guest/org-chart [accessed: 30 July 2013].

Macau SAR Legislative Council. 2001. *Exercising the Rights to Petition (Exercicio do direito de peticao)*. Macau: Government Printer.

Macau SAR Legislative Council. 2012. *Rights to Assembly and Protests (Direito de Reuniao e de Manifestacao)*. Macau: Government Printer.

Macau SAR Administrative and Public Service Bureau. 2012. *Report on Human Resources in Public Administration of Macau, 2011*. Macau: Administrative and Public Service Bureau.

Mendes, C.A. 2013. *Portugal, China and the Macau Negotiation, 1986–1999*. Hong Kong: Hong Kong University Press.

Public Opinion Programme, The University of Hong Kong. 2007. *Archives of Macau Studies*. Available at: www.hkupop.hku.hk [accessed: 25 May 2007].

Scott, I. 2011. Social stability and economic growth, in *Gaming, Governance and Public Policy in Macao*, edited by L. Newman and I. Scott. Hong Kong: Hong Kong University Press.

Sinclair, G. 2006. *At the End of the Line: Colonial Policing and the Imperial Endgame 1945–80*. Manchester: Manchester University Press.

South China Morning Post. 2007. Macau must deal with casino boom wealth gap. *South China Morning Post*, 2 May, EDT 14.

Statistics and Census Service, Government of Macao Special Administrative Region. 2013. Latest Statistical Information [Online: *DSEC*]. Available at: www.dsec.gov.mo/e_index.html [accessed: 10 July 2013].

Wu, Z.L. and Hao, Y.F. (eds). 2013. *Blue Book of Macau: Annual Report on Economy and Society of Macau, 2012–13*. Beijing: Social Sciences Academic Press (China) (in Chinese).

Yu, E.W.Y. 2011. Executive-legislature relationships and the development of public policy, in *Gaming, Governance and Public Policy in Macao*, edited by L. Newman and I. Scott. Hong Kong: Hong Kong University Press.

9 Faint echoes of Portugal but strong accents of Indonesia

Hidden influences on police development in Timor-Leste[1]

Gordon Peake

Introduction

Since 1999, when a United Nations (UN) transitional administration was established in the wake of the East Timorese vote for independence from Indonesia, the case of Timor-Leste has been a relative mainstay in research and policy debates on post-conflict reconstruction (Hood 2007, Bowles and Chopra 2008, Call and Wyeth 2008). Timor-Leste is often characterised by scholars as a 'post-conflict' country and, as a consequence, compared to other countries that have recently emerged from political strife. This concentration is understandable but one of the consequences is that the connections, points of similarity and residual influences of the two countries that colonised and occupied the half-island state, namely Portugal and Indonesia, are obscured. This chapter concentrates on this relatively underexplored part of the story as pertains to police development, uncovering imprints of post-colonial and post-authoritarianism in the style and approach of the Timorese police, and showing that memories and history often override technical support in terms of impact. In so doing, it scopes out a potential space for further research.

The legacies of Portugal may be fainter than those of Indonesia, reflecting both the passage of time as well as the reach of respective governmental approaches, but they are still very discernible. Timorese police insignia, slogans, informational material and other pieces of paraphernalia have Portuguese titles, and laws in the former colony are written in Portuguese. Following the withdrawal of the United Nations mission in 2012 continued Portuguese presence in Timor-Leste is partially funded by the government in Dili. However, perhaps the country that has had the most potent influence and serves as a primary source of emulation for the Timorese police is the one that occupied it until 1999, Indonesia. Contemporary Indonesia is emerging as the major model of modernity and development in many

---

1 The author would like to thank Jim Della-Giacoma, Suzanne McCourt, Cillian Nolan and Edward Rees who provided useful comments on an earlier draft of this paper. The paper's three 'anonymous' reviewers all outed themselves during the re-draft of the chapter, which enables personal thanks to be extended to Jacqui Baker, Andrew McWilliam and Bu Wilson.

government spheres in Timor-Leste including policing (Nygaard-Christensen 2013). Most Timorese police officers were born after the end of Portuguese rule and so brought up and socialised in the Indonesian system; the more seasoned members of the Timorese police began their careers wearing Indonesian police uniforms, working as officers during the occupation. Some even have brothers still serving in the Indonesia police across the border. There are strong business ties between the two countries. Not only do the police *look* similar to their Indonesian counterparts, their practice has large elements of being a dated impersonation of the policing style of the rest of the archipelago. Existing cultural similarities, a long history of engagement, and language play an important role in facilitating close bonds. Many more Timorese police speak Indonesian than either Portuguese or English, creating robust informal policy networks, and facilitating the importation, re-germination and co-production of ideas, attitudes and concepts. Pragmatic international relations between the two states also play a part. The stability of independent Timor-Leste is underwritten by a consensus within the political elite to forgive and forget with Indonesia for crimes committed during the occupation and the two countries have close relations, which play out in a number of areas, including policing. Indonesia, which has pushed a policing model the least, may have been the greatest source of policy borrowing.

This chapter is composed of five parts. The first section examines how a reductionist 'conflict paradigm' has come to dominate scholarship on Timor-Leste, which has meant that relatively limited attention has been paid to the influences and echoes of either Portugal or Indonesia. The second section explores the strategies of policing employed during both colonialisation and occupation. Although different in terms of scale and reach, the paramilitary and state-security centred nature of Portugal and Indonesia echo in the attitudes and practices of the present-day Timorese police. They also indicate that UN and international efforts to create a rights-respecting, community-oriented Timorese police took place in an environment where there was little precedent for such a style of policing. The third section charts the fitful efforts of the international community to develop the Timorese police. Efforts appeared to get off to a good start – the case of Timor was frequently invoked as a poster child for capacity building – but a political crisis in 2006 that enveloped the police demonstrated such plaudits to be hasty. In the years that followed, there was a redoubling of efforts to reform, rebuild and restructure the Timorese police but these efforts appear just as ephemeral in terms of impact. A wide range of scholars, researchers and analysts have largely castigated these efforts, suggesting limited dividends are to be accrued through importing ungrounded policing ideas and concepts from afar. Along with the questions of applicability and quality is the issue of the extent to which the Timorese police were interested in the advice on offer. The fourth section examines the influences of Timor-Leste's two former metropoles, Lisbon and Jakarta. There is a most certainly a continuing Portuguese flavour to how governance and law is evolving in Timor-Leste but Indonesia dwarves this influence. At the same time as international influence (and interest) in Timor-Leste is waning, the half-island state's relationship with its former occupier has burgeoned. This is examined by

210   *Gordon Peake*

describing five facets of relations, namely historical-cultural legacy; similarities of governmentality and mimesis; shared methods of policing; pragmatic politics and business ties. A short final section offers tentative conclusions and suggests that examining how post-colonial and post-authoritarian legacies co-produce in independent Timor-Leste is an issue worthy of deeper exploration.

Before proceeding, a note on the methodology underpinning this chapter is appropriate.[2] Framed within the scholarly literature on policy transfer, post-conflict policing and the bountiful material written on Timorese policing, the arguments in this chapter emerge from my work for an Australian-funded police development program in Timor-Leste (2008–2011). During that period, I travelled extensively throughout the country in a number of capacities, including as a member of a joint assessment team that gauged the capabilities of the Timorese police. I participated in more extensive training sessions, meetings on subjects such as donor co-ordination, and grandiose policing ceremonies than I care to remember. I was an 'outside insider' (Brown 1996, Reiner 2000), having access to the inner workings of the Timorese police on a near-daily basis and privy to an unvarnished reality often shielded from outsiders. I also travelled widely throughout Indonesian West Timor.

During my period living in Dili, I became proficient in Tetun, but acquired only a passing familiarity with Portuguese, and the relationships that I developed reflected the languages that I could use. I do not speak Indonesian. The parts of the chapter that elaborate upon relations between Timor-Leste and Indonesia draw upon research material that I collected during 2011–2012 for my book of memoir and narrative history about Timor-Leste (Peake 2013).

Timor-Leste as the epitome of the conflict paradigm

This chapter is located within the growing international relations, comparative public policy and criminological literatures on 'policy transfer'. Although different labels are sometimes attached to the concept, 'policy transfer' is generally accepted to refer to 'knowledge about how policies, administrative arrangements, institutions and ideas in one setting (past or present) is used in the development of policies, administrative arrangements, institutions and ideas in another political setting' (Dolowitz and Marsh 2000: 5). The term encompasses a number of processes: policies; institutions; ideologies or justifications; attitudes and ideas; and negative lessons. Policy transfer involves primarily the state and international organisations but also a wide range of other actors including think tanks, consultancy firms, and academics (Stone 2001: 2). The agents of policy transfer are not necessarily big institutions; the literature on police transfer notes the central role of human agency and the importance of individuals and informal relationships (Ellison and O'Reilly 2008: 396–397).

---

2 This chapter is a late addition to this collection and the author did not participate in the workshop in 2011 where the initial papers were discussed.

As one scholar of Timor-Leste has noted, the small Southeast Asian nation serves frequently as 'a cautionary tale or case study for debates surrounding post-conflict fragility and the UN state-building approach' (Scambary 2015: 2). Attention has focused mainly on examining the development and state-building efforts of the United Nations and bilateral donors in Timor-Leste. By way of example, over thirty articles have been published on the topic of police development alone; this works out as a ratio of one article for every one hundred East Timorese police officers. The scholarship on police development in Timor-Leste is very much characteristic of the wider literature, with a focus on dissecting the limited return of international development efforts (Peake 2008, Lemay-Hebert 2009, Bevan and McKenzie 2012, Wilson 2012). Accounts of modest or even provisional success are few and far between within a literature that has a profoundly technical and prescriptive focus (Greener 2010, Davey and Soibada 2013). Most scholarship is in English; the bulk of accounts are based largely on written or secondary sources or interviews with educated, urban-based staff of international agencies and NGOs seemingly only too happy to get their frustrations off their chests (Sahin 2007, Simonsen 2009, Arnold 2009a, 2009b, Richmond and Franks 2008).

Asserting similarities between Timor-Leste and other countries within the 'post-conflict' space is a prominent feature of this literature. Most researchers who have published are working within the broad frame of 'post-conflict studies' and therefore tend to associate Dili more with Juba and Freetown than Lisbon or Jakarta. As scholarship on Timor-Leste accretes, this framing gets set further, with researchers building on (and referring to) each other's work, creating something of a path dependency.[3] The East Timorese government themselves embrace enthusiastically this post-conflict definition, most notably through their initiation, support and championing of the g7+, a forum for fragile and post conflict states. Large delegations of East Timorese politicians and civil society travel regularly to places like South Sudan to contribute their 'lessons learned' to other nations rebuilding after conflict.

The focus on international efforts is understandable given the size and scale of the state-building endeavour in Timor-Leste over the last decade and a half. However, it has resulted in a tendency to place the half-island state within what Bexley (2010) refers to as a 'conflict paradigm'. This paradigm has a number of features. First, it positions East Timorese as 'victims' of conflict and colours the experience of Indonesia as a 'wholly negative one' (Bexley 2010: 9). Second, the conflict paradigm examines developments in Timor-Leste through a state-centric 'security-focused' lens (Bexley 2010: 9). The conflict paradigm also views Timor-Leste within an ahistorical lens; the nation is seen as a 'tabula rasa' that began its

---

3 Ideological factors may also play a part, whether subliminally or otherwise, in emphasising differences between Timor-Leste and Indonesia. One researcher has observed how she was upbraided by fervid foreign aid-workers for speaking Indonesian, noting that the Timorese she was speaking to were less put out by her linguistic choice (Nygaard-Christensen 2013).

212   Gordon Peake

'transition' to independence following the referendum for self-determination in 1999. This paradigm is problematic because prioritising attention to internationally-led state-building and peace-building efforts means that less emphasis is placed on the extent of East Timorese agency in this endeavour. Combined with an ahistorical focus, it leaves significant gaps in our understanding about other influences on Timor-Leste, including the long relationship with Indonesia.[4] For instance, it ignores the extent to which both Portuguese colonialism and the Indonesian occupation, although oppressive, have had an enormous influence on social, political and cultural life in Timor-Leste.[5]

Colonial genealogies and historical continuities

Official or uniformed policing is a relatively recent concept in Timor-Leste, with very few references to be found to 'police' or 'policing' in pre Second World War material on Portuguese Timor. During most of Portuguese administration, local leaders, called *liurai* were joined in alliances with the Portuguese administration that maintained local order. The emphasis tended to be on military command rather than 'police' *per se*, with colonial officers utilising local auxiliaries and local leaders left largely in charge of regulating their own communities (Nixon and Hoje 2003, Nixon 2013).

The period after 1945 saw a shift towards uniformed policing which was made up of Portuguese in the lead with Timorese placed in more junior roles. Wilson (2008) notes that the police originally known as *cipaio* (or *sipao*) was established and continued until the positions were replaced with *guardas auxiliares*. There was a prying, regime-centred quality to policing, with visiting journalists remarking frequently how their movements were watched assiduously by the *Polícia Internacional e de Defesa do Estado* (International police for Defence of the State – PIDE) (Jolliffe 1978: 43, White 1967).

Even in the last few years of Portuguese occupation, when there was an uptick in scholarly interest in the colony, reference to policing is still extremely slight. Journalists and scholars visiting Dili do not recall much of a visible police presence in Timor in 1974–1975. The military were much more visible in Dili and the

---

4   The prominence that has hitherto been accorded to Timor-Leste in the 'post-conflict' space is changing to some extent, mirroring a general downscaling of international interest in this small island country. Some scholars, particularly anthropologists, have recently begun to tentatively scope out linkages between Timor-Leste and Indonesia, the country that surrounds and dominates it. For a summary of this literature see Peake, Kent, Damelado and Myat Thu 2014.

5   Locating Timor-Leste in the same bracket as countries such as South Sudan and Nepal, and apart from its neighbours, is a relatively new trend. Historians, anthropologists, botanists and geologists have long located the half-island within a broader Malay archipelago (Fox 1980) but scholars working on the country in the 2000s have tended to shy away from emphasising one regional context. Ideological predilections may also play a part, whether subliminally or otherwise, in emphasising differences between Timor-Leste and Indonesia (Nygaard-Christensen 2013).

Faint echoes of Portugal   213

hinterland. In the districts, Timorese known as *segunda linha* may have had a role in the maintenance of civil order. These were former (conscript) soldiers who wore beige uniforms and carried rifles.[6] There is little record of activities of police units during the 1975 civil war, the short-lived independent republic or the early days of the Indonesian occupation. The prime role of the police during this period would appear to be as the institutional repository from which weapons were looted.[7]

During that period, Timorese political culture had a more markedly martial ethos. Many of the country's small political elite held positions within the Portuguese military, and almost all of this group of leaders were decked out in military fatigues for the country's unilateral declaration of independence from Portugal in November 1975, ahead of the Indonesian invasion nine days later.

Indonesian approaches to policing built on, expanded and reinforced authoritarian trends developed in the late colonial period. During the Indonesian occupation, a combination of the Indonesian police (POLDA) and paramilitary mobile squad (BRIMOB) conducted policing along with local auxiliaries (HANSIP). As before, the dominant style was colonial and regime-centric with the police auxiliary to the Indonesian army and complementary to a large intelligence service. What became the Indonesian province of *Timor Timur* was classified as a *Daerah Operasi Militer* (DOM) or a Military Operations Area and therefore POLRI always the subordinate to the military commander, described by one set of authors as the 'little brother of [the] soldiers (van Klinken and Bourchier 2006: 115)

As under Portuguese rule, the leadership of the police hailed from outside the territory but a substantial number of the lower ranks were Timorese. The motivations and approach of individual officers varied. Some Timorese were supportive of the occupation, others used membership of the police as a Trojan horse to funnel information to the resistance; others were members of the clandestine movement at the same time. The colourful career of Paulo Martins, the first commander of the Timorese police, is a case in point. Martins began on the losing side during the civil war before becoming the police commander for Viqueque, one of Timor-Leste's thirteen districts. During the late 1980s, he switched political allegiances, working closely with the Timorese resistance while maintaining his official police affiliation.

The Indonesian presence was much more encompassing than the Portuguese administration. Instead of a handful of Portuguese officers based in district centres, there was a police presence in each village. These police were known as BIMPOLDA *Bimbingan Polisi Daerah (I)* – Village Guidance Police – and their role included an intelligence-gathering function. At the same time, communities

---

6 Author conversations, April 2014.

7 'They captured the police headquarters, along with its Portuguese commander, Lieutenant Colonel Rui Maggiolo Gouveia. They took control of the weapons in the armoury as well as the port, the airport and the radio and telephone facilities in Dili.' http://hass.unsw.adfa.edu. au/timor_companion/before_the_invasion/civil_war.php [accessed: 12 January 2015].

214　*Gordon Peake*

largely policed themselves with the majority of everyday disputes and crimes dealt with through a diverse amalgam of customary and village structures. Not only were these mechanisms more physically, linguistically and cultural accessible, and in accord with long-standing traditions, self-policing obviated the dual risk of unnecessary intrusion by a volatile Indonesian administration and/or earning the opprobrium of community members and the resistance.

In the run-up to the popular consultation the Indonesian police did little to act against intimation and violence directed against independence supporters. After the referendum vote, when the majority of Timorese opted for independence from Indonesia, pro-Jakarta militias embarked upon what appears to have been a pre-conceived, well-planned scorched-earth policy. According to Robinson (2009), the Indonesian police as well as the military provided extensive support to the militias, providing arms and express instructions. United Nations investigations indicted the Indonesian police commander during the 1999 violence for crimes against humanity.

The Indonesian police are long gone but the legacy of that model still very much endures in independent Timor-Leste. Despite this role, memories of BIMPOLDA are not uniformly negative and indeed there is some residual affection. During research carried out in 2012, communities spoke positively about BIMPOLDA and appeared to understand their function better than they did new post-independence incarnations of community police. The fundamental difference for communities was that BIMPOLDA were present and available for their policing needs (Wilson 2012). Speaking in 2014, Timorese police officers would regularly cite BIMPOLDA as the type of policing model they aspired to (Peake et al. 2014) Despite the application of the Indonesian model being widely discredited for its destructive influence the historical experience of the state and Indonesian model of police and military security continues to influence expectations of the role of the police (and military) in East Timor and hence the way in which those forces developed.

Lots of investment but little dividend: attempts to mould the Timorese police into an international image of best practice

Set within a wider state building discourse which one commentator has likened to 'historical amnesia' (Nygaard-Christensen 2011: 10) the literature on police development in Timor-Leste follows a similar narrative arc. It begins in 1999, when a UN transitional administration assumed temporary authority over the territory. With the departure of the Indonesian police, there was a complete vacuum of formal policing when it assumed responsibility for the territory in 1999 and created two new forces to fill it. An international police force assumed primary responsibility for actual policing, while an accelerated plan was made for founding and developing a professional, impartial and politically neutral indigenous police service to take over that responsibility. There were very few specifics about the new local police force contained in the legal instrument that created it. United

Nations Security Council Resolution 1272 did not specify the makeup of the new force, its structure or its specific tasks. The Timorese police were established on 27 March 2000, their first recruits resplendent in uniforms donated by Australia, including that country's iconic Akubra hat.

The literature describes how the UN were, essentially, making it up as they went along, working off intuition and talking points rather than any particularly detailed plan or reform doctrine (Hood 2006). Although international policing is by now an established element in post-conflict interventions and development strategies, the means by which it is organised and directed in the field remains fairly freeform. Smith's characterisation of the United Nations police in Kosovo, another transitional administration, as an endemic *ad hocracy* is also apt for its operations in Timor-Leste (Smith 2003). The approach adopted was similar to that adopted in its other peacekeeping missions, and involved the deployment of a range of different police officers drawn from around countries – everywhere from Australia to Zimbabwe – who sent for periods of time averaging six months to one year (Hansen 2002, Bayley 2007). A mismatch of experience and task was a feature throughout the decade-plus intervention with very few of the incoming officers having experience in actually building an institution. Ludovic Hood, who worked for the United Nations in the early years of police development observed that, only two members of the 1,500 strong international police had experience in this area, 'and one was politically compromised' (Hood 2007: 143).

As well as the United Nations, a range of other bilateral initiatives also provided support. Australia has had a sizable in-country program since 2004 and there have been periodic programs of assistance funded by Japan, New Zealand and the United States, among others. Additionally, there have been a myriad of trainings, study visits and symposia presented to the Timorese police from a plenitude of sources. It has been a truly global effort, ranging from courses at the FBI academy at Quantico to study visits of community policing endeavours in Bangladesh and almost everywhere in between. By way of example, the webpage itemising the work history of the current commander of the Timorese police lists over fifteen countries where he has participated in training. One scholar of Timor-Leste policing has characterised the approach as 'smoke and mirrors', 'smoke' referring to a focus more on form than substance and the 'mirrors' connoting the observed phenomena of international police builders wishing to develop a police force 'in their own image' (Wilson 2008, 2010). Continuing the analogy, it was a mirror with lots of different shards. At any one point, there would have been at least forty countries represented, with a consequent diversity in terms of skills, range of experience and approach. How to stop traffic – e.g. whether to stand in the front, or at the side or the back of the motorist – was but one of the many workaday policing tasks in which there was wholly contradictory practices (Peake 2008). Few had a shared language with Timorese counterparts; the only exception being Malaysian police contingents whose officers spoke Malay, the foundation language of Indonesian (Only a small number of Timorese police speak Portuguese to a proficient standard).

Although the rhetoric around the new institution was framed in terms of 'blank slates' and 'new beginnings', the police was certainly not composed of freshly minted police officers. The 'new' Timorese police had a strong Indonesian vein running through it. In order to expedite the development of the new institution, the United Nations decided that the backbone of the new Timorese police would be those officers who served in POLRI. The man chosen to be the first police commissioner had, prior to 1999, been the most senior ranking Timorese in the Indonesian police apparatus while other of his colleagues went on to fill senior leadership roles. The first head of the police's immigration wing and subsequently the director of the police training school was formerly a plainclothes intelligence officer (Maniaty 2009).

The connections with Indonesia did not just come through past employment. Many of the younger officers had, to a large extent, been socialised amidst the context of an authoritarian Indonesian regime. This cohort, known most frequently as *jerasaun foun* (Tetun: new generation) were born and grew up during the Indonesian occupation meaning that they were fluent in the occupying country's languages, cultures and means of doing business (Bexley 2011: 288). As Bexley writes 'while the Indonesian military remained the enemy, young Timorese became fluent in Indonesian; they were comfortable reading and writing in Indonesian, listening to Indonesian pop and rock music and socialising with Indonesians' (Bexley 2009: 10). Timor-Leste was characterised as a 'post-conflict' country but it is probably every bit as accurate to think of it as either a post-authoritarian country or one with distinctive authoritarian legacies, with all the implications that has for the introduction of a liberal-democratic model of policing.

The literature tells a narrative about the poor yield of this entire expensive endeavour. Even in the first few years of the police, when the UN was presenting the institution as the embodiment of their police-building success, observers began to question the validity of the good news story. A series of high-profile reports, including a Joint Assessment Mission of the United Nations and World Bank and an in-depth scholarly study on UN peacekeeping efforts raised a raft of issues centring on both the capabilities of the Timorese police and UNPOL (JAM 2003, King's College 2003). The tenor of these observations amplified after 2006 when widespread violence engulfed many of the country's institutions, including the police.

The 2006 crisis has complex origins. Its proximate cause was the dismissal of one-third of the Timorese defence force with a series of follow-on events awakening incipient tensions between soldiers from Timor-Leste's Eastern and Western regions. The police fractured along similar geographical lines; various factions began fighting with the defence force or fighting for the defence force. Among the brutal incidents that occurred were the killing of nine unarmed police officers who surrendered to UN officials by Timorese soldiers, and six people burnt to death in their homes. Thirty-seven people were killed in the immediate violence and many houses were destroyed. More than 150,000 Timorese – 15% of the entire population – sought refuge as internally displaced persons (IDPs) in makeshift camps for nearly two years.

The events of 2006 showed that both the Timorese police and military were as much providers of insecurity as stability. There appeared little of substance to either institution beyond uniforms and guns. The founding local police chief once again headed for the hills and abandoned his post at a time of crisis.[8] Analyses of the crisis pointed to deep and entrenched problems within the security institutions (International Crisis Group 2006, Richmond and Franks 2008, Peake 2009). Their hasty organisation, presided over by an ever-changing set of international advisers who stayed for varying periods of time resulted in anaemic, dysfunctional and deeply politicised institutions. The security sector was plagued by a legacy of antagonism and suspicion between various sectors of society divided along regional lines, insufficient senior management and an absence of sufficient civilian professionals.[9]

Police reform was a predominant feature in the mandate for a successor United Nations peacekeeping mission and enhanced bilateral efforts. UN police reassumed executive authority for policing while at the same time screening officers from the *Polícia Nacional de Timor-Leste* (PNTL) and developing a plan for this force's reform, rebuilding and reconstruction. At 1650 in number, UNPOL was by far the largest part of the mission. Officers were 'co-located' with their Timorese counterparts with the underlying concept being that, through regular interaction, 'capacity' would somehow be built by osmosis. The budget for the Australian policing program was boosted four-fold and the frequency of one-off donor-provided trips, trainings and study tours also surged.[10]

This police rebuilding process represented something of a 'do-over' opportunity for both UNPOL and bilateral donors, a chance to prove that they have addressed the deficiencies that arose in the creation of the police during the transitional administration period. The process has taken place against the backdrop of significant attention from a wide range of independent researchers, think tanks and PhD scholars. Spread out over seven years, the corpus of work reaches remarkably similar conclusions to those reached prior to 2006. The consensus is that this iteration of reformers encountered much of the same external and self-made difficulties as their predecessors.[11] The approach was practically identikit to the old style that proved so singularly ineffective: large numbers of national contingents with officers of varying styles, approaches and interests in the job who stay for insufficient times to win trust. Many of those sent to assist appeared poorly

---

8 In 2007 parliamentary elections, he became an MP for the party of Timorese Prime Minister, Xanana Gusmao, a position he retained in the 2012 polls.

9 Even the normally bland UN commentary on the crisis was pointed. 'The Ministry of the Interior . . . regularly interfered in policing activities at all levels, including in police operations and personnel decisions . . . intervened arbitrarily in disciplinary, recruitment and promotion proceedings . . . top heavy organization that lacks critical capacities at the middle and lower management levels' (United Nations 2006).

10 The program was evaluated in 2013 but the report is not publicly available.

11 The effects of all this effort are hard to measure given the paucity of published evaluations that gauges the impacts. Although post-conflict settings with large numbers of international actors such as Timor-Leste are seemingly ripe cases for charting the process of policy transfer and assessing its efficacy there have been few detailed examinations charting the effects of discrete interventions.

equipped to do the job. Incoming officers receive little guidance to assist, leaving them to default back to learning – good and bad – gleaned from their home countries. Hefty reform plans were prepared only in English, meaning it was little wonder that Timorese 'counterparts' did not meaningfully engage. To some extent, the do-over was even more flawed as the UN were working with an older (and more experienced) police. The UN and Timorese police made for a poor team. Although UNPOL and Timorese officers shared a building, they tended to work independently in separate offices and have little to do with each other (International Crisis Group 2009, Wilson and Belo 2009). I noticed a similar pattern from headquarters in Dili to the most tumbledown police post out in the rural areas: Timorese police seemed happy to have little to do with their international counterparts, save for their value as taxi drivers and couriers. Even though, officially, the two forces were working side-by-side the reality was closer to them working in parallel.

Equally skin-deep and figurative may be the influence of many other formal police development initiatives, which focused on institutional capacity building. Making judgement of impact is, again, complicated by the 'intangible' nature of much policy transfer and lack of an evaluative culture within police reform. Perhaps the only one example that can be pointed to in terms of an evident failure can be seen in terms of two sets of unoccupied and dilapidated 'police posts' dotted around the city of Dili. One set of buildings was set up circa 2005 when the Japanese International Cooperation Agency (JICA) sent PNTL officers to Singapore and Japan to learn about the *koban* system of policing while the other set of posts was built in 2010 as part of a UN Police 'quick impact' project. Following familiarisation visits intended to socialise the concept of the *koban* system, the posts were built but never staffed.

As the years went by there was increasing apathy on the part of the Timorese government and police in the advice – of whatever quality – that was on offer. Against the backdrop of greater financial resources, the Timorese government was anxious to assert sovereignty over the security sector and adamant about pursuing police reform on its own terms. This 'national ownership' includes elements askew from the liberal democratic police model advanced by the United Nations and donors. Such features included paramilitarism (with a fetish for long-barrelled weapons), complex legislation governing the security sector, a tendency towards impunity, and lack of accountability for previous actions. Frustration with the United Nations manifested often in (gleefully churlish) disregard and insouciance towards the UN and in a succession of colourful public statements disparaging the skills of the United Nations police. For example, the general commander of the Timorese police asserted, at the end of a UN training course, that the international police were the ones 'lacking capacity' while, on another occasion, the Timorese Secretary of State-Defence said 'what we do know is that if we compare the character, self-confidence and performance of some PNTL members with some UNPOL members, ours are much better' (Pinto 2009). By 2012, amidst the elaborate farewell ceremonies that marked the end of the UN peacekeeping presence, the sense was that UNPOL and Timorese police had largely outworn each other.

Post-colonial and post-authoritarian echoes

Officers of the 3000-strong PNTL have Portuguese-language designations and appellations, and frequently describe their work using mottos and dicta similar to those used by counterparts in Lisbon and Luanda. The Timorese police are *'pronto 24 oras'* ('ready 24 hours a day') and their mission, and name of their in-house magazine, is to *'servi no proteje'* (serve and protect). The former colonial power has also provided a large number of bodies to assist in police development. Portugal was a leading contributor to successive UN peacekeeping missions from 1999–2012 and provided significant inputs into police training. Many of the laws, regulations and policies governing the work of the police are written in Portuguese, drafted by expatriate advisers. Timor-Leste is a member of the CPLP (Community of Portuguese Speaking Nations)

Portugal played a significant role in all five of the United Nations missions that operated in Timor-Leste from 1999–2012. Approximately fifty Portuguese officers were deployed as civilian police and, in the last mission (2006–12), there was an additional contingent of 140 members of the GNR (*'Guarda Nacional Republicana'* – the Portuguese Gendarmarie force) who provided public order management to Dili. Although paid for out of the United Nations peacekeeping budget, the Portuguese UN contingent succeeded – whether intentionally or not – in carving some form of distance between themselves and other UNPOL counterparts. Partially, this was presentational. Portuguese police cars and trucks, for instance, were coloured moss green and not painted over with UN white.[12] To another extent their separate identity was to do with familiarity. Portugal was much more of a known country than, for example, Namibia, El Salvador or Palau, among the other countries that contributed police personnel.

Many Portuguese were also hired through other agencies, funds and programs of the UN as well as the peacekeeping mission. Portuguese police, lawyers and officials were also able to parlay their 'mother-tongue' language skills into advisory positions helping write police laws, documents and policies.[13] The Timorese police's (frequently convoluted) policy and legal frameworks are written in Portuguese but are largely inaccessible to Timorese police officers, only a small minority of whom are proficient in the language. In the latter years of the 2000s, a new source of funds emerged to hire Portuguese speakers and that was the Timorese government. Timor-Leste contributed more than half the budget to the UNDP's Justice Sector program and, separately, hired a slew of individuals to work within the government in legal and legislative drafting functions. Fifteen GNR officers remain, funded by Timor-Leste, to run recruit training at the police college.

---

12 Although failure to comply with UN 'white car' standards was a perennial complaint aired by New York based UN staff, the cars remained the same colour throughout successive UN missions.

13 Portuguese citizens were also part of the early stages of the Australian-funded Timor-Leste Police Development Program.

220 *Gordon Peake*

There are also connections between Timor-Leste and other Portuguese speaking countries. Timorese officers have participated in trainings in Angola, Brazil and Mozambique, some studying abroad in these countries for years at a time.[14] Nor is the didactic process mono-directional; currently there is a small Timorese contingent attached to the United Nations mission in Guinea-Bissau. In a formal sense, Timor-Leste is tracking along with other CPLP countries in terms of structures and laws; the country's policy to create a judicial police parallels Lusophone countries and generates intense head-shaking from police advisers hailing from common-law countries. However, on a workaday level, it is the influence of Indonesia (another civil law-based country) which tends to be much more glaring.

Even to the casual observer, there are many striking parallels between the two nations. The same sorts of minibus taxis (made in Surabaya, Indonesia's second-largest city) throng roads in urban areas in Timor-Leste as they do beyond the border. Among other points of commonality are kindred architectural styles, types of popular restaurants and the food served in them, as well as the omnipresent whiff of clove cigarettes. Police, civil servant and military uniforms are practically identikit, perhaps not surprising given that they are produced in Indonesian factories. The yellow lorries 'that speak of government funded construction contracts' (Pisani 2014: 128) are ubiquitous in both countries.

Factors such as cultural similarities, the long history of engagement between the two nations (including the 24-year Indonesian occupation of Timor-Leste) and language are all important in facilitating close economic, political and people-to-people ties. One of Indonesia's largest banks, the state-owned *Mandiri*, is based in Dili. Despite the energy reserves in the Timor Sea, all the fuel that fills the cars is Indonesian. Most of it is supplied by the Indonesian state oil company, a durable and commercial success story that operates out of the same facilities it built during the occupation and whose depot provided the fuel to burn Dili down in 1999. Substantial amounts of fuel are smuggled into Timor-Leste from Indonesian West Timor, Indonesian satellite TV beams into East Timorese homes, and the default language for web browsers and social media sites is Indonesian. There are as many East Timorese undertaking higher education in Indonesian universities as there are in Dili. Flights between the countries leave on a daily basis. According to the last census, many more East Timorese speak Indonesian than either Portuguese or English. Over 6000 Indonesian citizens live in Timor-Leste (KBRI Dili 2013).

But Timor-Leste is more than just a passive importer of Indonesian products. The links between Indonesia and Timor-Leste are strikingly apparent in the arena of policing and in the actions of the Timorese police service, the PNTL. There

---

14 Sometimes these courses are of such long duration that the Timorese officers are largely forgotten about. A number of Timorese police returned to Dili from Maputo during the course of my time in Dili; they had been sent there in 2004 during the tenure of a previous Minister of the Interior. When they returned six years later, there was a new government and no record of what the officers had been sent out to learn.

appear to be four areas of relationship and similarity beyond the historical-cultural legacies addressed already. These areas are governmentality, shared methods of policing, the ramifications of pragmatic politics and business linkages.

Although the Indonesian occupation ended, its governmental legacies endure. Like many post-colonial states, Timor-Leste has inherited more from its predecessors than nationalist rhetoric might suggest. One area in which this similarity manifests is in terms of governmentality. Similarities in terms of architecture, uniforms and police insignia are striking. By and large, the police stations and compounds that the East Timorese police occupy are former Indonesia-era buildings, which have Indonesian language slogans and insignia still very visible. Other scholars have found points of similarity in terms of political language, demonstrating how Timorese political leaders increasingly evoke, mimic and imitate Indonesian modernity discourses. Jakarta is the prime wellspring for many political visions (Kammen 2008, Nygaard-Christensen 2011, 2013).

Similarities between (enervating) public service cultures have also been explored. In an article based on a number of years living in the country, Blunt (2009) observed 'twenty-five years of Indonesian occupation have left indelible marks on bureaucratic practice and public expectation in Timor-Leste'.[15] These reverberations tend to be characterised in negative terms. Gunn and Huang, for example, (2006: 123) cite legacies of Jakarta's occupation as including 'nepotism, favouritism, corruption, and bureaucratic inertia' Other authors suggest more benign interpretations. For example, Wilson (2010) identifies similarities and resonances between Timorese and Indonesian approaches to power and governance. Looking further back, Indonesian authoritarian approaches to policing built on and reinforced Portuguese authoritarian ideas about policing, which in turn utilised and reinforced autochthonous ideas about 'policing' and authority broadly written.

Contemporary Indonesia appears to be emerging as the major model of modernity and development in many government spheres in Timor-Leste and policing is no exception (Nygaard-Christensen 2013). Beyond the existence of similar uniforms and equipment, and the fact that Indonesian words are used as police jargon, it would seem that Timor-Leste's neighbour serves as an inspiration for behaviour. Even the police uniforms of the two countries are similar, right down to practically identikit toy-town badges of individual police units.

Some of this is influenced by television. East Timorese police are avid aficionados of 'cops' style reality television shows beamed in via satellite. Professional education also plays a role, with East Timorese police regularly travelling across the border for training. According to the Timorese police's own statistics, more officers travel to Indonesia for training than anywhere else.[16]

Perhaps the most vivid similarities can be observed in the ways the East Timorese police appear to model behaviour based on the paramilitary policing

---

15 In a similar vein to this author, Blunt spent time in Dili working inside the Timorese government.
16 Copy of statistics in possession of the author.

style of the occupation (Bevan 2012, Bevan & MacKenzie 2012). The large-scale police operations appear inspired by Indonesia circa the 1990s, and the similarities between operations to protect the population from (imaginary) bogeymen are striking. From the latter part of the 1990s, the East Timorese police have engaged regularly in operations that follow a similar curvature. The operations begin with vague rumours, insinuations and tittle-tattle of threats emanating from a far-off part of the country. These rumours, spread by text message and social media and fanned by the country's febrile media, then require the country's police to mount an operation to charge off and restore calm. The operations usually involve the rounding up of a large group of people suspected of vague misdeeds, most of whom are subsequently released. The operations are large '*proyeks*' (projects), eating up hundreds of thousands of dollars in costs for staff overtime, fuel and food, and the nod to Indonesia is palpable. For example, *Operasaun 88*, purportedly an effort to round up terrorists in a mountainous part of the east of the country, was named after the Indonesian counter-terrorist unit Delta 88 (Fundasaun Mahein 2011).

Perhaps the most famous of these operations was the one to tackle an alleged 'ninja' menace in 2010, the evocative name garnering unusually high degrees of attention from the international media. The term 'ninja' in Timor-Leste doesn't evoke a real band of fighters, but a hidden, sometimes imaginary menace stalking the country. It came into the vernacular in the 1990s, when shadowy militias backed by the Indonesian army targeted East Timorese independence activists. Villages were terrorised and East Timorese were believed to be kidnapped and killed in the dark by men garbed in black (Myrttinen 2013).

Pragmatic politics have reverberated in terms of policing, with the tendency to prioritise relationships over accomplishment of policing tasks. Something of a Finland – Soviet Union complex also drives engagement between Timor-Leste and its larger neighbour. Pursuing good ties with Indonesia seems an objective of almost every leading Timorese politician. The push to forgive and forget is led by the senior political leadership, which responds to the violence of history as a matter requiring pragmatism and reconciliation, and not criminal sanctions. From Indonesia's side, the relationship is significant as evidence that a new era of political and democratic reform (*era reformasi*) has been initiated.

The consequences of good political relations were most apparent in the case of Maternus Bere, a former militia commander caught by the Timorese police and subsequently released by Timorese authorities, allegedly under intense pressure from the Indonesian Government. Bere was one of more than 400 Timorese indicted for serious crimes that took place in the run-up to and the aftermath of the vote for independence. Many of them are living in plain sight in Indonesia, and most are just over the border in West Timor. The problem of what to do with former leaders such as Maternus Bere is something that both governments prefer to keep in the background. With Bere's arrest, the matter became front-page news; the drama played out with world attention on the country, as it coincided with the tenth anniversary of the vote for independence. The decision to free Bere prompted outrage from opposition parties, civil society and human rights non-government organisations (NGOs). It even drew an unusually direct reproach from the normally anxious not-to-offend UN mission, which accused the East Timorese Government of trading victims' rights for peaceable relations. The incident also showed up the limits of the police's independence sovereignty. In arresting Bere, the East Timorese police had, in many ways, performed in a professional manner but this was trumped by political considerations.

Another facet of the relationship concerns business ties. Indonesian business dominates the marketplace across all sectors. Given the extent of Indonesia business interests in Dili, the Timorese capital city is awash with the Indonesian language in terms of private sector advertising. During 2013, Timor-Leste exported US$181 million to Indonesia (in return for goods which came in through reported customs channels), according to monthly trade reports from Timor-Leste's General Directorate for Statistics. Over the past three years, Timor-Leste's total imports of services were about 50% larger than total goods imports, and a significant part of this would have come from Indonesia as well.

This plays out in a number of obvious ways in policing. Indonesian contractors refurbish the Indonesian-era police posts, Indonesian companies produce uniforms for the Timorese police, often according to similar couture. Guns, communications equipment, trucks and assorted policing paraphernalia are sourced from Indonesian factories. Seeing senior East Timorese police officers in Dili hotels being wined and dined by Indonesian business people is a reasonably common occurrence. Some of the deals that are reported seem to result in pretty lousy products, often bought according to inexplicable and hidden off-budget payment schedules. However, when allegations of some deals have emerged, they appear to disclose close relationships between Indonesian businesses and Timorese politicians. For example, in 2012, a scandal erupted in Dili following disclosure of a commercial deal between the Timorese police chief and an Indonesian arms company for the supply of assault weapons.

Conclusion

Although much has been written about the police of Timor-Leste in the last decade and a half, scholars have rarely tied the political and governmental cultures of the new country with that of the countries that formerly ruled over it, one of which is its near neighbour. Instead, the focus has been on comparing the new country with other states and territories emerging from conflict and/or favoured with large international peacekeeping presences.

This chapter has suggested that post colonialism and post authoritarianism manifests itself in all sorts of areas in the new nation state. Some of these are obvious, such as language, but other influences appear more subtle, osmotic and permeating such as governmentality and business linkages.

The point here is not that Timor-Leste mimics or wants to be, Indonesia and, to a lesser extent, Portugal. It is, however, to suggest that, to understand Timor-Leste, one must look to its strong Indonesian and fainter Portuguese influences. Portugal and/or Indonesia is far from the only source of, inspiration for the

224 *Gordon Peake*

current attitudes, posture, trajectory and style of the Timorese police but it is perhaps one that is more significant than has previously been considered. Transposed with the existing literature, it may present a more complete picture to understand policing, and at a wider level, governance processes in Timor-Leste.

References

Arnold, M.B. 2009a. Challenges too strong for the nascent state of Timor-Leste: Petitioners and mutineers. *Asian Survey*, 49(3): 429–449.

Arnold, M.B. 2009b. Who is my friend? Who is my enemy?: Youth and statebuilding in Timor-Leste. *International Peacekeeping*, 16(4): 379–392.

Bayley, D. 2007. *Changing the Guard: Developing Democratic Police Abroad*. Oxford: Oxford University Press.

Bevan, M. 2011. *'The Hero Stuff' and the 'Softer Side of Things' Exploring Masculinities in Gendered Police Reform in Timor-Leste*. Master of Development Studies, Victoria University, New Zealand.

Bevan, M. and MacKenzie, M. 2012. Cowboy policing versus 'the softer stuff'. *International Feminist Journal of Politics*, 14(4): 508–528.

Bexley A. 2009. Getting an education: Special edition: Timor-Leste ten years after the referendum. *Inside Indonesia*, 96.

Bexley, A. 2010. *Youth at the Crossroads: The Politics of Identity and Belonging in Timor-Leste*. PhD Thesis, Australian National University.

Bexley, A. 2011. Timor's Youth: From Supermi to Sojourns. *Asian Currents*. April 2011, 7–9.

Bowles, E. and Chopra, T. 2008. East Timor: Statebuilding Revisited, in *Building States to Build Peace*, edited by C. Call and V. Wyeth. Boulder: Lynne Rienner, 271–302

Blunt, P. 2009. The political economy of accountability in Timor-Leste: Implications for public policy. *Public Administration and Development*, 29(2): 89–100.

Brown, J. 1996. Police research: Some critical issues, in *Core Issues in Policing*, edited by F Leishman, B. Loveday and S. Savage. London: Longman, 249–263.

Call, C. and Wyeth, V. 2008. *Building States to Build Peace*. Boulder, CO: Lynne Rienner.

Davey, E. and Svoboda, E. 2013. *The Search for Common Ground: Police, Protection and Coordination in Timor-Leste*. Available at: www.odi.org.uk/publications/8123-timor-leste-east-un-police-fpu-pntl-military [accessed: 28 May 2014].

Dolowitz, D. and Marsh, D. 2000. Learning from abroad: The role of policy transfer in contemporary policy-making. *Governance*, 13(1): 5–24.

Ellison, G. and O'Reilly, C. 2008. From empire to Iraq and the 'War on Terror': The transplantation and commodification of the (Northern) Irish policing experience. *Police Quarterly*, 11(4): 395–426.

Fox, J.J. 1980. *The Flow of Life: Essays From Eastern Indonesia*. Cambridge: Harvard University Press.

Fundasaun Mahein. 2011. *Saida Mak Operasaun 88*. Available at: http://fundasaunmahein. wordpress.com/2011/07/21/1216/ [accessed: 28 May 2014].

Greener, B.K. 2010. *The New International Policing*. Basingstoke: Palgrave Macmillan.

Gunn, G. and Huang, R. 2006. *New Nation: United Nations Peace-Building in East Timor*. Tokyo: United Nations University Press.

Hansen, A. 2002. *From Congo to Kosovo*. London: IISS.

Hinton, M. and Newburn, T. 2010. *Policing Developing Democracies*. London: Routledge.

Hood, L. 2006. Missed opportunities: The United Nations, Police Service and Defence Force Development in Timor-Leste, 1999–2004. *Civil Wars*, 8(2): 142–162.

Hood, L. 2007. Missed opportunities: The United Nations, Police Service and Defence Force Development in Timor-Leste, 1999–2004, in *Managing Insecurity: Field Experiences of Security Sector Reform*, edited by G. Peake, E. Scheye and A. Hills. Milton Park: Routledge, 57–76.

International Crisis Group. 2006. *Resolving Timor-Leste's Crisis*. Asia Report No. 120. Available at: https://www.crisisgroup.org/asia/south-east-asia/timor-leste/resolving-timor-leste-s-crisis [accessed 25 April 2017].

International Crisis Group. 2009. *Handing Back Responsibility to Timor-Leste's Police*. Asia Report No. 180. Available at: https://www.crisisgroup.org/asia/south-east-asia/timor-leste/handing-back-responsibility-timor-leste-s-police [accessed 25 April 2017].

Joint Assessment Mission. 2003. *Report of the Joint Assessment Mission carried out by the Government of Timor-Leste, UNMISET, UNDP and Development Partner Countries for the Timor-Leste Police Service*. United Nations.

Jolliffe, J. 1978. *East Timor: Nationalism and Colonialism*. St Lucia: University of Queensland.

Kammen, D. 2008. Fragments of Utopia: Popular Yearnings in East Timor. *Journal of Southeast Asian Studies*, 40(2): 385–408.

KBRI Dili (Indonesian Embassy). 2013. *Buku Saku Warga Negara Indonesia di Timor Leste*. [Pocket Book for Indonesian Citizens in Timor Leste]. Dili: KBRI.

Kings College. 2003. A Review of Peace Operations: A Case for Change. Available at: http://reliefweb.int/sites/reliefweb.int/files/resources/94B0FD1A8877A55FC1256D080046EF36-kings-peace-03.pdf [accessed 23 April 2017].

Lemay-Hebert, N. 2009. UNPOL and police reform in Timor-Leste: Accomplishments and setbacks. *International Peacekeeping*, 16(3): 393–406.

Maniaty, T. 2009. *Shooting Balibo: Blood and Memory in East Timor*. Melbourne: Penguin Viking.

Myrttinen, H. 2013. Phantom menaces: The politics of rumour, securitisation and masculine identities in the shadow of the ninjas. *Asia-Pacific Journal of Anthropology*, 14(5): 471–485.

Nixon, R. 2013. *Justice and Governance in East Timor*. London: Routledge.

Nixon, R. and Hoje, T. January 2003. *Reconciling Justice: 'Traditional' Law and State Judiciary in East Timor*. Report prepared for the United States Institute of Peace. Available at: www.gsdrc.org/docs/open/DS33.pdf [accessed: 28 May 14].

Nygaard-Christensen, M. 2011. Building from scratch: Aesthetics of post-disaster reconstruction. *Anthropology Today*, 27(6): 8–10.

Nygaard-Christensen, M. 2013. Negotiating Indonesia: Political genealogies of Timorese democracy. *The Asia Pacific Journal of Anthropology*, 14(5): 423–437.

Peake, G. 2008. Police Reform and Reconstruction in Timor-Leste: A Difficult Do-Over, in *Policing Developing Democracies*, edited by M. Hinton and T. Newburn. London: Routledge, 141–162.

Peake, G. 2009. A lot of talk but not a lot of action: The difficulty of implementing SSR in Timor-Leste, in *Security Sector Reform in Challenging Environments*, edited by H. Born and A. Schnabel. Münster: LIT, 213–238.

Peake, G. 2012. Disjuncture: Playing pool at the Hard Rock Café. *Local-Global*, 11: 32–35.

Peake, G. 2013. *Beloved Land: Stories, Secrets and Struggles From Timor-Leste*. Melbourne: Scribe.

226   Gordon Peake

Peake, G., Scheye, E. and Hills, A. 2007. *Managing Insecurity: Field Experiences of Security Sector Reform* London: Taylor & Francis.

Peake, G., Kent, L., Damaledo, A. and Thu, P. 2014. *Influences and Echoes of Indonesia in Timor-Leste.* SSGM Discussion Paper 2014/8, Australian National University, Canberra.

Peake, G. and Marenin, O. 2008. Their reports are not read and their recommendations are resisted. *Police Practice and Research*, 9(1): 59–69.

Peake, G., Wilson, B. and Fernandes, J. 2014. HAKOHAK (*Hametin Kooperasaun entre Kommunidade*) and TLCPP (Timor-Leste Community Policing Program Mid-term Evaluation) [copy in possession of the author].

Pinto, J. 2009. Reforming the Security Sector: Facing Challenges, Achieving Progress in Timor-Leste. *Tempo* Semanal, 18 August 2009.

Pisani, E. 2014. *Indonesia Etc.: Exploring the Improbable Nation.* London: Granta Books.

Reiner, R. 2000. Police research, in *Doing Research on Crime and Justice*, edited by R.D King and E. Wincup. Oxford: Oxford University Press.

Richmond, O. and Franks, J. 2008. Peacebuilding in Timor Leste: The emperor's new clothes? *International Peacekeeping*, 15(2): 185–200.

Robinson, G. 2009. '*If You Leave Us Here, We Will Die': How Genocide Was Stopped in East Timor.* Princeton: Princeton University Press.

Sahin, S. 2007. Building the state in Timor-Leste. *Asian Survey*, 47(2): 250–267.

Scambary, J. 2015. *When the Personal Is Political: The Dynamics of Communal Conflict in East Timor 2000–2013.* PhD Thesis, Australian National University.

Simonsen, S.G. 2009. The role of East Timor's security institutions in national integration – and disintegration. *The Pacific Review*, 22(5): 575–596.

Smith, D.C. 2003. Managing UNCIVPOL: The potential of performance management in international public services, in *Rethinking International Organizations: Pathologies and Promise*, edited by D. Dijkzeul and Y. Beigbeder. Oxford/New York: Berghahn Books.

Stone, D. 2001. *Learning Lessons, Policy Transfer and the. International Diffusion of Policy Ideas.* CSGR Working Paper No. 69/01.

United Nations. 2006. *Report of the United Nations Independent Special Commission of Inquiry for Timor-Leste.* UN. Available at: www.ohchr.org/Documents/Countries/COITimorLeste.pdf [accessed: 28 May 2014].

Van Klinken, G. and Bourchier, D. 2006. Crimes against humanity in East Timor: The key suspects, in *Masters of Terror: Indonesia's Military and Violence in East Timor*, edited by R. Tanter, D. Ball and G. van Klinken. Lanham, MD: Rowman & Littlefield, 83–156.

White, O. 1967. *Time Now, Time Before.* Melbourne: William Heinemann.

Wilson, B. 2010. *Smoke and Mirrors: The Development of the East Timorese Police 1999–2009.* PhD Thesis, Australian National University.

Wilson, B. 2012. To 2012 and beyond: International assistance to police and security sector development in Timor-Leste. *Asian Politics & Policy*, 4(1): 73–88.

Wilson, B.V.E. 2010. Smoke and Mirrors: The Development of the East Timorese Police 1999–2009. Ph.d thesis. Canberra: Australian National University.

Wilson, B. and Belo, N. 2009. *The UNPOL to PNTL 'Handover' 2009: What Exactly Is Being Handed Over.* Conflict Prevention and Peace Forum Briefing Paper, Social Science Research Council, New York.

10 Branding Rio de Janeiro's pacification model

A silver bullet for the planet of slums?[1]

Conor O'Reilly

Introduction

Brazil has emerged into the spotlight in recent years. Its newfound status as an emerging superpower being ceremonially marked by the hosting of mega-events; in this case, the 2014 FIFA World Cup and the 2016 Olympics. Such grand spectacles present unparalleled showcasing opportunities, and are held out as cultural, economic and political milestones with the potential to further accelerate development (Molnar and Snider 2011). They also represent unique opportunities to try and shift security narratives about host nations, as well as to place their security expertise on global display. Brazil provides a powerful example of such processes. Indeed, whilst the main spectacle of the 2014 World Cup played out inside shiny new stadia and was beamed to a global audience, it became apparent that security operations provided fringe 'events' that also proved significant draws. This was evident in a proliferation of documentaries and news reports about the pacification initiatives in the *favelas* of Rio de Janeiro that accompanied World Cup coverage, as well as the public protests against the costs of this event (and other societal grievances), which created a tense countdown to the curtain-raising fixture.

The elevated security profile furnished by the 2014 World Cup provides a useful entry point for this chapter. Strategic attempts to harness this event to shift negative stereotypes about both Brazil and its security institutions are integral to this analysis of branding security. However, it must be emphasised from the outset that this discussion does not provide extensive engagement with that body of research examining the links between security and mega-events (see, for example: Bennett and Haggerty 2011, Prouse 2012). Nor is it an in-depth examination of the

---

1 My thanks to Alice Hills and Erika Robb Larkins for their very helpful comments on an earlier draft of this chapter and also to Susana Durão and Marcio Darck for their input into the research process. This work was supported by funding from the *Fundação para a Ciência e a Tecnologia* through the project, '*COPP-LAB – Circulações de Polícias em Portugal, África Lusófona e Brasil* (PTDC/IVC-ANT/5314/2012). It should also be noted that this chapter was finalised in March 2015. As such it does not take into account subsequent events prior to publication of this compilation, most notably the Rio 2016 Olympic Games.

228   *Conor O'Reilly*

outworking of pacification programmes in Rio de Janeiro (on this issue, see: Denyer Willis and Mota Prado 2014, Muggah and Souza Mulli 2014, Robb Larkins 2013, 2015, Rodrigues 2014). Such topics possess undoubted contextual importance for the following discussion, however, this chapter focuses upon the transnational dynamics of promotionalism and how what I term *Rio de Janeiro's Pacification Model* (RJPM) is being constructed as a *geo-policial brand*.[2] In pursuing this line of research, I build on existing discussion of security commodification in Brazil (Robb Larkins 2015), elevating these debates through consideration of new transnational dynamics. I also extend existing theories about the reconstitution of public policing and security models as global brands (Ellison and O'Reilly 2008b) by considering a security model that has emerged from within the South, rather than those that are exports to it.

Brazil's policing institutions are prime candidates for re-branding. A wealth of critical commentary from human rights organisations and academic researchers has amassed over decades and attests to dark institutional histories that are coloured by corruption, disappearances, excessive use-of-force, extra-judicial killings and connections with drug gangs that span nefarious complicity to extra-legal suppression (see, for example: Amnesty International 2005, Chevigny 1999, Hinton 2006, Huggins 1997, Human Rights Watch 2010). The pacification programme that emerged in Rio de Janeiro must be viewed as an attempt to progress beyond such negative imagery, to break from a record of public security failure, and to achieve some tentative reforms of the police. The theoretical construct of the RJPM that is proposed in this chapter speaks to an even broader strategy of social ordering through police action than what is occurring in the *favelas* of Rio; one extending into foreign urban security contexts – for inspiration and for application – and which exerts increasing influence upon other sectors of Brazilian society. In essence, the RJPM that is presented is a control assemblage that comprises a range of policing and security agents and auspices. Whilst certainly catalysed by new public security initiatives in the *favela*, it has mutated and grown through multiple interactions: between foreign and domestic; between police and military; between public and private; and, between the militarised and the humanitarian. These dualities (examined below) are integral to its geo-policial brand appeal. It is a public security model that is attaining global recognition, that is being endorsed by peers within the transnational policing community, and that is increasingly looked upon as a solution for other complex security scenarios across the globe.

In conceptualising evolving developments regarding Brazilian pacification in terms of *branding*, a brief justification of this theoretical tool is warranted.[3] As

---

2 The compound term 'geo-policial' is constructed from the commonly used prefix 'geo' and the Portuguese term 'policial' that broadly translates as 'concerning the police'. The term 'policial' does also exist in English but is now out-dated. A geo-policial brand therefore relates to a brand that concerns both police and location.

3 Indeed, whilst this chapter makes the case for the conceptual framework of 'branding', a degree of reflexivity is warranted. In proposing the term of 'Rio de Janeiro's Pacification Model', I may actually contribute to that very branding process I set out to critique. Speaking

Branding Rio de Janeiro's pacification model 229

Anholt (2007) has observed, it would be easy to dismiss branding as merely 'a quasi-science related to shopping' (p. xii), as an inappropriate analytical lens for academic research. However, I would contest that conceptual application of branding is both worthy and instructive. Not only should this socially ubiquitous phenomenon not be discarded just because of its popular usage, but branding also captures a range of social processes that are highly relevant to the promotion of policing and security models: the manipulation of perceptions; the creation of strategic shortcuts to enhance profile; the capacity to convince others of the quality and the integrity of what is being presented. When applied to policing and security models, branding has resonance with what Young (1999) described as the 'cosmetic fallacy' of contemporary social interventions to combat crime and '. . . a general cultural predisposition to belief in the easy miracle and the instant cure' (p. 130). In a globalising neoliberal security context, branding security is a natural extension of existing patterns of commodification and promotionalism that have already taken hold domestically. Proponents of the RJPM – most notably those political actors such as former Governor, Sergio Cabral and State Security Secretary, José Mariano Beltrame – have been well aware that achieving global recognition and foreign emulation may bring domestic dividends.[4] Even if their promotionalism has perhaps been more improvisation than neatly choreographed marketing strategy and they have rarely spoken of pacification in explicit branding language, they are quite patently aware of the need to control the narrative of Brazilian public security.

It is worth nothing that the linkage between pacification and strategies of image-management is also not nearly so novel as one might expect. Pacification is a recognised feature of colonialism and can be traced back to 16th century Portuguese and Spanish imperialism in the Americas where it provided a choice euphemism to repackage exploitative ambitions delivered through military conquest and systematic control (see, for example: Neocleous 2011: 199). Indeed, Pacheco de Oliveira's (2014) historical-anthropological analysis uncovers strong parallels between contemporary '*pacificação*' and subjugation of 'others' throughout Brazilian history: the humanitarian promise of pacification interventions in the *favelas* echoes civilising missions to subjugate indigenous tribes

---

in terms of the RJPM gives form to a complex assemblage that has resulted from the, somewhat haphazard, coalescence of public security practice, contextual realities and hybrid corporate-political agendas achieved through police actions. By using this term to capture this complexity a vocabulary is provided for the geo-policial branding process, potentially lending it additional impetus, at least within those academic commentary and policy circles where it finds interest.

4 Whilst José Mariano Beltrame and Sergio Cabral are perhaps the most visible architects and advocates of pacification, the policy has also received invaluable support from powerful corporate and business interests and has been presented in a favourable light by senior policing figures as well as in the media (Robb Larkins 2015). Policy research institutes and think-tanks, indeed, even elements within academia, have also engaged in more qualified championing of this public security innovation.

230   Conor O'Reilly

centuries earlier.[5] Certainly, the multi-layered resonances of pacification that stretch from the colonial to the contemporary are highly appropriate for this volume. However, beyond historical continuities in deploying pacification to bring unreformed others 'into the fold of modernity' (Robb Larkins 2015), it should also be acknowledged that pacification strategies are also a focus of renewed scholarly interest (beyond the Brazilian context), both as regards contemporary police actions (Neocleous 2011), as well as evolving counterinsurgency strategy (González 2009).

The discussion that follows is divided into four parts. Part One establishes the theoretical connection between branding and security, presenting the RJPM as a geo-policial brand. Part Two progresses to dissect the key characteristics of the RJPM, highlighting how complex, and often contradictory, constituent elements make this model appealing to a range of security markets. Part Three progresses to examine the mechanisms through which the RJPM might be transmitted to other security contexts, assessing Brazil's ascendant role within a range of elite transnational security networks. Part Four focuses more closely on the shaping influence of international peacekeeping on domestic pacification. It examines how the security experiences that fashioned the RJPM have travelled through a feedback loop that connects the *favelas* of Rio de Janeiro with the slums of Port-au-Prince; not only are operational techniques recycled but the mantle of humanitarianism enables the consolidation of legitimacy. The conclusion reflects on the transnational potential of the RJPM, considering both the possibilities and the perils of its replication for, and its expansion into, other security contexts.

Global promotionalism and the creation of a geo-policial brand

The trend towards 'commodification' of security (Loader 1999, Goold et al. 2010) is increasingly evident at the transnational level (Sheptycki 2002). Encompassing much more than private security activity that traverses borders, public policing and security actors are demonstrating behavioural traits more typical of the commercial sphere. In essence, the transnational policing realm is rapidly being reconstituted as a hybrid transnational policing marketplace. The shift from a non-market to a market space is increasingly manifest in the promotion of various 'solutions' to

---

5 Pacheco de Oliveira (2014) identifies parallels in the treatment of indigenous population under Portuguese imperial power whereby successive tribal communities were: declared as enemies; fought and defeated; dispossessed of their lands; brought under a new normative and religious order; were governed through spatial and social control mechanisms; and, eventually provided cheap labour that facilitated the process of economic exploitation. As he previously commented:

> 'Pacification and civilization are different faces of the same process, which has/had the objective of removing the autonomy of indigenous communities and installing within them dependencies . . . making them the subjects of a tutelary administration'
> (Pacheco de Oliveira 2010: 31; my translation from original Portuguese).

Branding Rio de Janeiro's pacification model 231

complex security scenarios. Such ambitions have already been identified in the marketisation of operational templates in areas such as community oriented policing, counter-terrorism, democratic police reform and urban crime prevention (see, for example: Brogden and Ellison 2013: Ch. 4, Dixon 2005, Ellison 2007, Ellison and O'Reilly 2008a, 2008b, Newburn and Jones 2007, O'Reilly 2010). In what follows, the RJPM is spotlighted as the latest member of this cadre of globally recognised policing and security models; albeit one that is novel in that it has emerged from within the South, rather than being an export to it. As with a number of its counterparts, the promotionalism that surrounds the RJPM retains a complex duality; global ambitions are inseparable from strategies to counter negative perceptions and legitimacy deficits regarding the domestic context.

In advance of closer attention to the Brazilian case, it is important to establish the theoretical backcloth that connects branding with security. First, public policing agencies are increasingly aware that by enhancing their transnational profile they can better realise the export potential of their security wares. Elite transnational networks; knowledge-sharing expeditions; joint training initiatives; international deployments: all provide valuable platforms for such strategic endeavours. The underlying rationale is that if international recognition and foreign emulation can be achieved, then this will bestow newfound prestige and elevate the profile of those police officers, policing institutions and policy actors involved, as well as facilitating more direct, commercially beneficial, transfers. Such activities were conceptualised as attempts to create a *global brand* in Ellison and O'Reilly's (2008b) analysis of the Northern Irish policing model; concerted efforts being made to translate the seemingly incongruous experiences of counter-terrorism and democratic police reform into a best practice exemplar for other security contexts. As was the case in Northern Ireland, transnational promotionalism is often paralleled by more direct attempts to foster a brand identity at the local level, e.g. public relations and engagement strategies as well as cosmetic changes to uniforms and emblems.[6] However, when it comes to achieving global recognition, it is interaction with the 'transnational police policy community' (Marenin 2006, 2007), as well as the stimulation, and indeed the manipulation, of global media attention, that are key.[7]

---

6 In the case of Rio's Police Pacifying Units (UPPs), emphasis has been placed on a number of factors to distinguish them from traditional police officers, notably: the recruitment of a new police officer cadre, rather than retraining serving officers; provision of different training to UPP cadets; slightly better salaries for UPPs; different uniforms; and, a greater preventive emphasis within their work (Denyer Willis and Mota Prado 2014: 239).

7 There are indications that such 'brand ambition' is becoming even more commercially explicit within police organisations. For example, the constitution of the British Association of Chief of Police Officers (ACPO) – a private company composed of the most senior British police officers that was replaced by the National Police Chiefs' Council in 2015 – had somewhat optimistically listed one of its objectives as: '. . . to develop our business activities to ensure that the ACPO brand name is recognised globally as a mark of excellence in policing'. Memorandum and Articles of Association of the Association of Chief of Police Officers of England, Wales and Northern Ireland. Available from: www.acpo.police.uk/documents/ArticlesofAssociation.pdf [accessed: 25 June 2014].

232 Conor O'Reilly

Whilst the endeavours of policing and security agents to elevate their institutional knowledge and operational practice to new (transnational) levels have catalysed the application of branding concepts to policing models, it is important that a related, and equally nascent, literature on what has been termed 'security branding' (Coaffee and Van Ham 2008) is also integrated into this discussion. Embedded within strategies of what has alternatively been called 'place branding' (Coaffee and Van Ham 2008), 'geo-branding' (Van Ham 2001) and 'competitive identity' (Anholt 2007), security has emerged as an important pillar within the strategies of cities, regions and countries to manage their international reputations and 'project themselves on the world's mental map' (Van Ham 2001: 1; cited in Ellison and O'Reilly 2008b: 335). As Coaffee and Van Ham (2008) have observed,

> The marker of security has become a scarce commodity and most states and cities compete for it in the collective mind of a global audience. Moreover, being recognised as a provider of security . . . offers concomitant authority and credibility.
>
> (p. 191; see also Coaffee and Rogers 2008)

The above quotation is pertinent to this discussion in two key respects: it highlights the importance of security within place branding strategies; and, it reiterates that security actors can pursue their own promotional agendas, often in tandem with those of place branding marketeers. Indeed, whilst Coaffee and Van Ham's (2008) analysis was principally directed at the macro entities of states and international organisations, this chapter asserts that police forces are a potent institutional signifier of both security and national identity for global audiences. Such importance has already been alluded to in the context of British policing where the cultural symbolism surrounding the police 'condenses the national character' (Brogden and Ellison 2013: 90, see also, Loader 1997, Loader and Mulcahy 2003).

In something of a Weberian paradox for the transnational age (Manning 2000), police agencies are both symbolically and jurisdictionally rooted in specific contexts but are also increasingly transnationally connected and globally ambitious (Bowling and Sheptycki 2012).[8] Their international image will invariably be shaped by dominant perceptions about security levels in their domestic contexts, whilst the reputation of the police themselves can impact upon attempts to market their home location. In short, there is a complex fusion of *police* and *place* that is integral to their respective global branding ambitions. In order to capture how

---

8 Of course, any Weberian notion of the police having a monopoly over the legitimate use of force within a specific territory and its population is particularly problematic in the context of the *favela* where state presence was at best sporadic and ultraviolent prior to pacification. Even with more recent, and incomplete, programmes of pacification, the Brazilian police are still accused of coercive excess, albeit in the context of new operational strategies that have been characterised as elaborate instances of 'performative violence' (Robb Larkins 2013).

Branding Rio de Janeiro's pacification model   233

contextual origins affect the promotional strategies as regards policing models, this chapter proposes the term *geo-policial branding* to capture how perceptions about operational context are integral to marketing public security models such as the RJPM.[9] Of course, selling Brazilian policing to a global audience/market is strongly connected with ongoing attempts to sell Brazil itself internationally, both as an international player and as a global destination (Saborio 2013: 136). This is particularly evident in the hosting of mega-events – global spectacles for which the RJPM has provided the security backdrop (Prouse 2012) – as well as Brazil's increasingly interventionist role abroad (see, for example: Kenkel 2010, Sánches Nieto 2012, Viana Braga 2010).

One might think that pathological imagery of the *favela* as a site of menace combined with the atrocious human rights record of the Brazilian police would sound the death-knell for the latter's (geo-policial) brand ambitions. However, as this chapter sets out a controversial reputation need not prove an impediment. On the contrary, the experience of policing high-risk environments through, often extreme, coercive practice may actually provide what I have previously termed a 'platform of notoriety' (O'Reilly 2013); a valuable promotional resource for the global branding process. Whilst the appeal of a police force's coercive reputation to international policing deployments is later analysed in greater depth, it must be recognised that the insecurity associated with locations such as Rio's *favelas* does not necessarily present insurmountable 'country of origin' obstacles. As Anholt (2005) remarked well before recent pacification initiatives:

> The fact that there are negative associations (pollution, overpopulation, poverty, crime, corruption) within the brand of Brazil is far less of a problem in image terms than it is for the people who actually have to suffer the consequences of the problems. After all, a strong brand is rich, and richness implies a complex and intriguing mix of different elements.
>
> (p. 112)

This reality is best demonstrated by exoticised representations of the Brazilian slum that ensure that *favela* tourism is now a common feature of trips to Rio de Janeiro.[10] Located at the nexus of dark tourism and adventure tourism, the *frisson* of visiting these marginalised urban spaces was previously a niche draw (Urry and Larsen 2011: 62). However, the process of pacification and attempts to re-invent

---

9 Although not located within any explicit *geo-policial* frame, Brogden and Ellison's analysis of the "UK Police plc' brand' (2013: Ch. 4) provides another example of how a history of policing 'the other', both at home and abroad, combined with the cultural symbolism surrounding Peelian policing has culminated in concerted attempts to promote the British policing experience (for more on the British policing brand, see also: Emsley 2012, Sinclair 2012).

10 Robb Larkins (2013) observes how the contrived imagery and discourse surrounding police operations have fabricated a 'hyper-*favela*' where through 'an endless chain of empty representations . . . traffickers, police and the very *favela* itself become hyper-real: they take on constructed spectacular qualities that do not reflect reality' (p. 556)

the *favela* have also attracted more tourists and created new opportunities for *favela* entrepreneurs. Freire-Medeiros (2011) has observed how along with pacification, 'the repertoire of actions and strategies directed towards . . . "conducting conducts" of tourism in *favelas* has indeed multiplied' (p. 176; see also, Torres 2012). The prism of security refracts the 'tourist gaze' (Urry and Larsen 2011), not least during mega-events.

Consequently, the promotion of the RJPM is constructed upon attempts to govern both (in)security in the *favela* as well as external perceptions thereof. One of the challenges for those policing agents who implement pacification and for those policy entrepreneurs who advocate and promote it, is how to leverage their representations of *favela* governance into enhanced global status. Certainly, there are established techniques for managing the reputations of 'unsafe' locations that resonate with the aforementioned platform of notoriety for geo-policial branding. Avraham and Ketter (2008) speak of, 'reducing the scale of the crisis', 'tackling the reasons for the place's lack of safety', 'hosting spotlight events' and 'spinning the 'unsafe' image into assets' (p. 202; see also, Mansfield and Pizam 2006, Neill 1995). Such strategies are certainly at work in Rio de Janeiro and the focus of this chapter on the promotionalism that surrounds the RJPM speaks strongly to them. Furthermore, the storyline that is being portrayed of a war against drug trafficking twinned with the amelioration of *favela*-life is more than a little reminiscent of an earlier model for governing urban security. Whilst the following reflections from Newburn and Jones (2007) concerned zero-tolerance policing in New York, they appear remarkably apt for developments in Rio almost a decade later:

> A highly plausible policy narrative became firmly attached to a powerful dramaturgical symbol and was promoted by influential and media-literate moral entrepreneurs. There are few more potent mixtures.
>
> (p. 237; see also, Manning 2001 on the dramaturgical portrayal of the NYPD's role in the New York crime decline)

Whilst Gotham conjures up a range of fictional imagery about crime and crime fighting, the *Cidade Maravilhosa* has accumulated its own cultural folklore about the police and drug traffickers, accentuated globally in recent years through films such as *Cidade de Deus* and the *Tropa da Elite* series. As for policy entrepreneurs, New York had Rudy Giuliani and Bill Bratton (former Mayor and Chief of the New York Police Department respectively), whereas Rio de Janeiro has Sergio Cabral and José Mariano Beltrame (the former Governor and State Security Secretary respectively).[11] Of course, the contexts and the players are very different,

---

11 The status accorded to José Mariano Beltrame, for example, is reiterated by one eulogising commentary on Rio de Janeiro's pacification programmes:

> 'Secretary Beltrame has become the face of the UPP programme, as he often gives interviews and attends every important event. His presence is a constant in pictures showing the inauguration of new UPP bases, important meetings in the communities,

but the promotion of a narrative of urban security 'turnaround' (Bratton and Knobler 1998) is disconcertingly familiar.[12] Indeed, whilst also making a brief allusion to the brand-like qualities of UPPs, Muggah and Souza Mulli (2014) have remarked upon how,

> . . . the state's aggressive use of the popular media – television, radio, print – has played a pivotal role in marketing the UPP concept . . . The national media routinely advertise successes and make considerable use of metrics to back up claims of 'success.
>
> (p. 206)

The policy proponents of the RJPM have made a massive effort to ensure that this security initiative is portrayed in an overwhelmingly positive light. Whilst much of the public relations activities to bolster the RJPM have been conducted at the national level through hundreds of luncheons, interviews, press conferences and other media events, the spotlight of mega-events has witnessed global attention drawn to Rio's pacification programme. Such coverage by international media outlets is fundamental to marketing the RJPM as a geo-policial brand that might be replicated elsewhere. Not least, as this model is *ascendant* at a time when problematic urban zones have (re)emerged as a common security fault line across the globe (see, for example: Graham 2011). Whilst this model may not be the only pacification template floating on the swelling sea of urban insecurity, it is increasingly apparent that it is the RJPM that has caught the wave of global attention.

Of complex dualities and the segmented brand

The RJPM did not emerge as part of any pre-determined strategy but rather from the opportune coalescence of foreign inspiration – notably drawing from other Latin American experiments such as '*Operação Orion*' in Medellin's *Comuna 13* – with incremental developments in public security and a confluence of economic and political circumstances which made new security initiatives possible (Denyer Willis and Mota Prado 2014, Foley 2014, Muggah and Souza Mulli 2014,

---

and events such as soccer tournaments with favela youth . . . His great work is being recognized through many honors and awards that he has received, including the "Making a Difference" award for person of the year for Rio de Janeiro in 2009 and Person of the Year for Brazil in 2010'

(Gimenez Stahlberg 2011: 22).

12 Indeed, the security connection between New York and Rio is much more than a conceptual linkage. Robb Larkins (2015) notes how Bill Bratton has acted as a consultant to Rio's municipal authorities and also how the 'broken windows' policy has inspired public security initiatives such as '*Operação Choque de Ordem*' ('Shock of Order Operation') that cracks down on incivilities such as vandalism and illicit markets in legal goods.

236   *Conor O'Reilly*

Rodrigues 2014).[13] This process was further amplified by policy reverberation between domestic pacification and international peacekeeping efforts (see later discussion). Whilst the RJPM is most closely associated with Rio-based police forces and policy entrepreneurs, it comprises a much wider assemblage of actors, agencies and sponsors that transcend neat international/domestic, police/ military, military/humanitarian and public/private distinctions. Indeed, these multiple, and often contradictory, constituent elements are central to the RJPM's geo-policial brand potential. Whilst its core 'market' undoubtedly resides in policing the urban slums, its capacity to invest deployments with shifting security 'flavours' give it enduring appeal for a segmented security marketplace (Brogden and Ellison 2013: 92, 100–101, Ellison and O'Reilly 2008b: 337).

In this respect, the RJPM provides a compelling example of trends that have been termed 'armed humanitarianism' (Bjork and Jones 2005) and 'new humanitarianism' (Joachim and Schneiker 2012, see also, Amar 2013, Christie 2013). The skilful conjugation of militarisation and humanitarianism enables each of these component elements to be emphasised – rhetorically and operationally – in accordance with the audience being played to. The large-scale depiction of police operations as humanitarianism is a novel twist, albeit one that has a degree of precedent in more discrete public security interventions in Rio de Janeiro (See, Amar 2009 on Operation Princess to combat sex trafficking). It would now appear that a more comprehensive process of humanitarian 'framing' has been used to enhance the legitimacy of those implementing the RJPM. A process of image construction through official discourse that is accompanied by parallel shifts in operational tactics and overarching strategy. A degree of instruction can be taken here from a previous study regarding the framing techniques employed by private military companies to mitigate the negative imagery surrounding their industry. The RJPM similarly appears to harness the loose meaning of humanitarianism to select 'those elements of the humanitarian frame that fit [its] interests best' (Joachim and Schneiker 2012: 374). Furthermore, this humanitarian turn does not necessitate a radical disconnect from the dubious policing histories of institutions such as PMERJ (Rio de Janeiro's military police), or its elite special operations squad BOPE. As Joachim and Schneiker (2012) further observe, 'New frames . . . do not make a clean slate of the past but . . . build on already existing frames and beliefs' (p. 376). Consequently, in terms of the RJPM, militarised elements remain a fundamental part of its constructed image (Prouse 2012, Robb Larkins 2013), albeit that they are now counter-balanced by more

13 As Denyer Willis and Mota Prado (2014) set out, the UPP strategy in Rio de Janeiro – which is an integral part of the RJPM – was originally born under notions of community policing, progressing towards greater emphasis on twin strategies of occupation and proximity to now even be considered as an indirect vehicle, or 'institutional bypass' for police reform. However, this was never a coordinated plan and as they further observe: 'The strategy grew directly out of the particular circumstances of insecurity and increasing global scrutiny faced in the city. As fissures appeared, solutions were designed for that particular problem' (Denyer Willis and Mota Prado 2014: 240).

Branding Rio de Janeiro's pacification model 237

socially responsive UPPs. A multi-layered 'framing' initiative is thus taking hold and is borrowing images, language, narratives and symbols from the realms of both humanitarianism and war.[14] Indeed, in her examination of this complex framing of UPPs, Prouse (2012) notes how even the term *pacification* itself, has multiple discursive implications: 'Pacification has two common meanings: the quashing of violence by military means, and the bringing of peace to a particular place or process' (p. 10). These multi-layered implications have resonance with the military/humanitarian duality to which this chapter alludes.

The framing strategy around the RJPM is, therefore, somewhat bifocal in its effects. It is at once heavily militarised and Manichean in its operations against drug-traffickers, whilst also humanitarian, almost Salvationist, in its mission to raise *favela* residents to new levels of social inclusion and economic participation. These dual orientations may appear in marked contrast but they are reciprocally integral to the pacification process. It was previously noted how it would be premature to interpret the advent of UPPs as signalling the demise of militarised Brazilian policing.[15] Whilst the forces of neoliberalism have already further entrenched this institutional, operational and rhetorical trait (Wacquant 2008), pacification has witnessed another renewal, if not a repurposing, of militarised policing in Brazil. Whilst the operationalisation of the RJPM inevitably occurs in specific locales, this process has also been shaped by the increasing 'transnational condition' (Sheptycki 2007) of policing and security. The experiences of militarised humanitarian interventions in the *favelas* of Rio de Janeiro and the slums of Port-au-Prince – see below – have fashioned a feedback loop for urban security operations in peripheral zones. This process has not only fine-tuned the RJPM but has also managed to cultivate legitimacy for those policing and security actors involved amongst a variety of constituencies, not least the transnational policing community.

Elite transnational security networks: a scene that celebrates itself?

For much of the 20th century, the participation of Brazilian policing agencies in transnational security networks was located at the sharp end. This was most clearly manifest in receiving assistance of a distinctly American hue, training police in oppressive techniques to suppress left-wing dissent (Huggins 1998). This was

---

14 For an interesting contrast, consider the imagery that is disseminated via the twitter feeds of BOPE and UPP Social. See Robb Larkins (2013: 570–571) for an analysis of BOPE's Twitter feed.

15 Indeed, the success of the UPPs in pacified favelas has come under increased scrutiny by virtue of a recrudescence of traits of the military police. Perhaps the most striking example of this has been the widely-reported 'disappearance' of the bricklayer, Amarildo de Sousa, in Rocinha after being brought to a UPP post for questioning in July 2013 (Robb Larkins 2015, Ch. 3; Ch. 5). Notably the commander of the police station where Amarildo was taken is a former officer of BOPE, the controversial special operations unit of the military police that is often represented as the polar opposite of the UPPs.

238   *Conor O'Reilly*

followed, post-dictatorship, by support for police reforms that centred on the replication of dominant Western trends (Ellison and Pino 2012: 108–113). However, the advent of the RJPM has witnessed patterns shift and increasing attention towards this evolving urban security initiative underscores how Brazil can no longer be held out as a mere recipient but must now be recognised as inputting expertise into transnational security networks. In essence, the laboratory for security experimentation that is Brazil has sparked significant interest amongst both the transnational policing community as well as foreign political elites. In a recent commentary on security developments in Rio, it has been observed that:

> The UPP effort has already generated considerable interest across Brazil, and indeed the wider region. Official delegations from El Salvador to Kenya and the Republic of South Africa have visited Rio de Janeiro to learn more about the UPPs and potentially transfer aspects of the model to their own jurisdictions.
>
> (Muggah and Souza Mulli 2014: 212)

International recognition of Brazil as a source-nation for security expertise is at least partially attributable to the hyperactive networking activities of its policing institutions. They have proved fervent participants in 'the construction of epistemic communities around the transfer/export of policing knowledges' (Ellison and Pino 2012: 77; see also, Stone 2004), albeit that their contributions have most recently centred on two particular streams of security: policing urban slums; and, policing mega-events.

Insofar as the former is concerned, the confluence of urbanisation of poverty, economic growth and high levels of violence in slums across the Global South has witnessed security policy debates connect Rio de Janeiro with regional locations such as Port-au-Prince, Medellin and Ciudad Juarez, even extending further to cities beyond the Americas.[16] The central objective here has been comparative lesson drawing, with the principal sites from which security knowledge is currently being extracted located amongst those states that have made something of a 'transitional switch' (O'Reilly 2013); i.e. they have progressed beyond recipient status to be recognised as repositories of potentially valuable security expertise. For officials from other contexts who are also struggling with complex public security problems these locations furnish models for potential emulation. Indeed, if Latin America is the most significant global region for these trends, then pacification in Rio de Janeiro has emerged as its nucleus. Key policy actors, such as State Security Secretary Beltrame, have become frequent participants at high-profile security

---

16 A flavour of these debates is provided by the research project 'Humanitarian Action in Sites other than War' (HASOW) which although focused on Latin American and Caribbean experiences of humanitarian interventions in locations affected by enduring high levels of violence, also connects its objectives with other locations outside the orthodox conflict/post-conflict paradigm, such as: Nairobi in Kenya, Lagos in Nigeria and Saa'na in Yemen. See www.hasow. org for more information on this project.

Branding Rio de Janeiro's pacification model **239**

events across the globe. For example, in April 2014, he provided a keynote to the Stanford University convened 'Conference on Violence and Policing in Latin American and US Cities'. Whilst it would be unfair to cast such participation as unreflexive promotionalism of the RJPM, there must, at the very least, be heightened awareness that the world is watching; that there is a global appetite for more knowledge about public security policies in Rio de Janeiro. This, in itself, provides an opportunity to shift negative perceptions and to change the narrative about Brazilian policing. This is important, as peer recognition within, and acceptance into, the elite networks of transnational security can foster 'legitimacy at a distance' (Ellison and O'Reilly 2008b: 342; acceptance that might be difficult to achieve domestically can be pursued in a much more favourable international domain.

Linking to the other dominant stream of Brazilian participation in elite transnational security networks, Secretary Beltrame also spoke about the preparations for global events at a 2013 conference in London entitled: 'Policing Global Cities'.[17] By hosting the 2014 World Cup, as well as the 2016 Olympics and Paralympics, Brazil, and Rio de Janeiro in particular, are emblematic of what Molnar and Snider (2011) term, 'the mega-event security-development nexus' (p. 151). Indeed, the RJPM probably would not exist, or at least would have taken a quite different form, if it were not for the international focus that these events brought to bear on Brazilian public security. For example, it is not serendipity that most of those *favelas* prioritised for pacification are located close to key event sites (The Economist 2013). Penglase (2014) has also noted how the commander of the UPPs accompanied former Brazilian President, Lula da Silva, to Geneva when he was making his final pitch for the 2016 Olympics.

Whilst mega-events certainly helped to catalyse the RJPM, its transnational promotion may also be facilitated through the increased access to 'security knowledge networks' (Boyle 2011) that is afforded by host status. After all, as Boyle (2011) has remarked, these events are 'important pedagogical vehicles for the 'making up' and globalisation of security expertise' (p. 171). For Brazilian policing, this relates to much more than the organisational security build-up, but also post-event, when its security institutions enjoy an enhanced profile and credibility amongst their international peers. Those techniques deployed in the testing ground of Brazil will be passed on to successors.[18] Indeed, as mega-events are

---

17 Policing Global Cities, London 8–9 July 2013. Conference Report available from: http://policingglobalcities.weebly.com/uploads/4/4/0/7/44076193/policing_global_cities_report.pdf [accessed and downloaded: 6 August 6th 2014].

18 These events are also testing grounds for much more than domestic public security initiatives. The massive security spends involved – for the 2014 World Cup, the Brazilian Secretariat for the Security of Large Events (SESGE) had a budget of R$ 1.17 billion (approximately US$ 578 million) – create opportunities for a wide range of new security technologies to be purchased and deployed. One notable source for such innovations is Israel with contracts signed with defence firms that specialise in high tech surveillance, including drones, lending further strength to trends of militarisation. Brazil and Israel have also signed a security cooperation agreement (Zirin 2014).

240 *Conor O'Reilly*

increasingly used to symbolically mark developing nations emergence out of the Global South, it may well be that pacification tactics forged in Rio de Janeiro become integrated into those spatial control strategies that have already come to characterise these global gatherings (Baasch 2011). Whilst marginalised groups have often been displaced to accommodate the hosting of major events, the RJPM provides a security template for managing those situations when such relocations may be more complicated.

Of course, any participation in elite transnational security networks should be viewed through a critical lens. The sharing of policing and security knowledge often does not result in actual policy transfers. Indeed, even where patterns of transmission appear to be most explicit, participants in these fluid transnational exchanges may still primarily be driven by their own agendas (Ellison and Pino 2012: 76–80). As Boyle (2011) has commented regarding those security networks that surround mega-events:

> . . . the fact that officials often profess to voluntarily learn from others in an ostensibly free market of ideas suggests that doing so has performative value on its own that is worth considering, such as using evidence from others to justify or advance pre-formed political aims.
>
> (p. 178, original emphasis)

The stage provided by mega-events can therefore enable something of 'a scene that celebrates itself', whereby participants in elite transnational security networks obtain mutual endorsement from their peers. Of course, other valuable benefits may also be extracted, whether this is reinforcement of their own security agendas by obtaining enhanced legitimacy, credibility or prestige, or even the scope for creating lucrative new markets for their policing models and technological solutions.

In recognising that these security exchanges represent much more than conduits for policy transfer, what is to be made of the RJPM's promotion within these forums? First, there may be awareness amongst Brazilian public security actors that endorsement by the transnational policing community is an important element in 'selling' a narrative of domestic success – the aforementioned urban security turnaround. Moreover, after decades of being on the receiving end of a steady stream of Western urban security solutions and models for police reform, the Brazilian public security establishment may equally have become conscious that there is more political profit to be derived from the production of 'silver bullet' security solutions, rather than being a serial recipient of the panaceas prescribed by others. This is not to suggest that Brazil has abandoned the importation of foreign security models and technologies. On the contrary, its networking has, if anything, intensified in this regard. The significant change that has occurred, however, is that Brazil now behaves much more like a confident donor, aware of the export potential of its own institutional knowledge and holding out its reform programmes to the transnational policing community for emulation. This new reality is echoed in the field of international peacekeeping where Brazil is increasingly assuming a leadership role; a development that has also played a significant role in the evolution of the RJPM, not least insofar as the deployment of Brazilian military and police to Haiti is concerned.

International peacekeeping and the Rio-MINUSTAH feedback loop

> The UN respects Brazilian police officers . . . one of my superiors once said that as police officers we are like "war doctors", we are ready for anything. There are situations that we are prepared for, such as in operations in Cité Soleil, we were prepared to face harsh urban environments, unsanitary conditions and extreme poverty.

> Captain Fabricio Silva Bassala, Brazilian Military Police Officer who served on the MINUSTAH mission to Haiti.
>
> (Horta Moriconi 2010)

> In May, Colonel Cláudio Barroso Magno Filho, Commander of the Brazilian troops in the mission to Haiti, admitted that, 'strategic concepts used in that country [Haiti] are similar to those envisaged for Rio, particularly the integrated action of organisations at every level . . . Everything that we did here [in the favela of Morro da Providência] was planned there [Haiti].
>
> (Dantas 2007)

> In Haiti, we too have problems with violence in the ghettos, large concentrations of people in areas stricken by poverty where the geographic layout makes police action difficult.

> Marie Gauthier, participant in the Haitian National Police delegation to Rio de Janeiro in 2014 to observe the pacification programme.
>
> (Viva Rio 2014)

These quotations provide an indication of the role that Brazil's participation in MINUSTAH – the UN stabilisation mission to Haiti – has played in shaping the RJPM.[19] A complex feedback loop formed around recognition that the experience of Brazilian security institutions in Rio's *favelas* could usefully contribute to the shifting needs and mandates of international peacekeeping operations. Whilst Brazil's international ambitions were undoubtedly fundamental in the decision to join MINUSTAH, its capacity for urban-focused militarised humanitarianism was also attractive.[20] Not least given the rampant instability that engulfed Haiti in

---

19 Before examining the transfer and recycling of security experiences between Rio and Haiti, it is important to reiterate the chronology of events. Whilst policing and militarised interventions in the *favelas* of Rio de Janeiro have an extended history, the international deployment to MINUSTAH only started in 2004. However, this mission still predates the specific initiatives of pacification in Rio's favelas that would begin some four years later, in 2008.

20 Brazil's increased participation in international peacekeeping must also be set within its international ambitions and attempts to bolster its credentials as a global player, for example, to have a permanent seat on the UN Security Council. Such issues are beyond the scope of this paper but for more in-depth analyses of these issues and their interaction with Brazilian

242   Conor O'Reilly

2004, a situation further aggravated by the presence of politically affiliated gangs in the slums of Port-au-Prince. The peacekeeping experience which Brazilian military troops and police gained in Haiti was subsequently reflected back into their domestic context; new humanitarian credentials bringing further sheen to the emerging programme for *favela* pacification. Indeed, on a number of occasions some of the same marine forces that had served on MINUSTAH were deployed in *favela* pacifications, such as those of: Alemão; Morroda Providencia; and, Vila Cruserio (Chery 2011, Dantas 2007, Norheim-Martinsen 2012: 4). These pacifications represented something of a symbolic homecoming for these Brazilian security forces as they returned, with new humanitarian credentials, to this crucible of public security experimentation. As well as consolidating the RJPM and cultivating something of a local-global legitimacy cycle, to cap things off, the Haitian National Police have recently engaged in lesson drawing with the military police in Rio de Janeiro to develop pacification strategies for Port-au-Prince (Gomes 2013). Whilst ongoing efforts to achieve policing and security reforms by the integration of experiences drawn from international deployments are generally commendable (Passarelli Hamann and Costa Leite 2012: 8), the outworking of these Brazilian domestic pacification – international peacekeeping transfers have provided worrying signals that coercive institutional cultures have, if anything, become more engrained (Pina 2008). Whilst these theatres of joint police-military action could have provided useful opportunities to overcome operational disconnects and tensions between these two institutions (Savell 2014), or alternatively provided a mechanism to progress away from militarised tendencies, the Rio-MINUSTAH link has provided dubious grounds for optimism.[21] Indeed, the degree to which operational tactics have been transferred from one challenging urban security context to another, lends credence to the argument that international peacekeeping in Haiti functioned as a 'testing-ground' for techniques that were later deployed in the pacification of Rio's *favelas* (Dantas 2007, Pina 2008), as well as providing live-training and a legitimising purpose for the Brazilian military (Sánches Nieto 2012: 168).

To focus more closely upon MINUSTAH, it is noteworthy that part of pre-deployment training for Brazilian military troops was instruction in '*favela* environment operations' by BOPE, the notorious special operations unit of Rio de

---

participation in international peacekeeping, more generally, see, for example: Kenkel (2010), Sánches Nieto (2012), Viana Braga (2010).

21 Whilst both the Brazilian military and the military police have participated in the MINUS-TAH mission (military-led) as well as the pacification interventions in the favelas (military police-led), it must be emphasised that these two institutions hold very different places in terms of Brazilian public opinion. The military enjoys a high degree of respect and is viewed as something akin to guardian of the state and a highly moral organisation – even with Brazil's military dictatorship past. The military police, in contrast, is much more negatively perceived by virtue of its linkage with violent excess, illegality and corruption. As Savell (2014) discovered from her ethnographic research in Complexo do Alemão, these attitudes become even more pronounced in the *favela*, where the relationship between these two security institutions is a difficult one.

Janeiro's military police (Norheim-Martinsen 2012: 4).[22] Whilst there is undoubted logic to this training – after all the deployment was tasked with stabilising a challenging, principally urban, setting – it did foreshadow other negative parallels with Rio. As with operations in the *favelas*, there was significant criticism of the heavy-handed tactics employed by Brazilian-led UN forces to deal with gangs in Port-au-Prince. Heavily militarised incursions into urban slums to apprehend gang-members; violent weapon exchanges with scant regard for innocent residents caught in the cross-fire; a pejorative discourse regarding slum communities in mainstream media: the controversial characteristics surrounding some of the UN interventions are disconcertingly familiar (Pina 2008). In addition to extreme recrudescence of militarised excess, MINUSTAH's slum operations were also noteworthy for their use of tactics which would later (re)surface within pacification programmes in Rio: harnessing overwhelming force to subjugate gang activity (and slum residents); a shift towards intelligence-led operations more characteristic of counterinsurgency; an emphasis on territorial control, including the establishment of a permanent presence in previously gang-controlled areas (Dorn 2009, Dziedzic and Perito 2008, Norheim-Martinsen 2012). In this context, it is important that the MINUS-TAH experience is integrated into analysis of the RJPM – albeit that the dynamics of security transfers between the slums of Port-au-Prince and the *favelas* of Rio de Janeiro admittedly do require deeper empirical examination (see the forthcoming research by Stephanie Savell).

Of course, it might justifiably be asked: why even select Brazilian military police for integration within international peacekeeping given their dubious institutional history? First of all, it should be highlighted that alongside controversies regarding MINUSTAH, this primarily humanitarian mission has also had some positive impacts (Spektor 2012). Nevertheless, in considering the appeal that Brazilian police and public security institutions have for peacekeeping operations, the truth may reside in what Sheptycki (2010) has termed 'the paradox of coercion' (p. 303). Essentially, how the capacity to harness and skilfully deploy coercive force is a desirable characteristic for such deployments. Resonating with earlier discussion of how controversial institutional reputations can provide a platform of notoriety to strengthen the brand ambitions of policing models and security solutions, Sheptycki (2010) further observes that:

> Coercion is . . . a core tactic for the would be peacekeeper and peacemaker . . . in
> a variety of circumstances characterized by the potential for conflict, danger and

---

22 Those police officers deployed to Haiti – a much smaller number than those from the military – also received peacekeeping training at Brazil's dedicated peacekeeping operations centre, CCOPAB, (*Centro Conjunto de Operações de Paz do Brasil*) in Rio de Janeiro (Passarelli and Costa Leite 2012). Indeed, the merging of military, police and humanitarian dimensions of *favela*/slum interventions was demonstrated by a 2010 symposium on Civil-Military Relations in Peacekeeping Operations which alongside issues of medical treatments and humanitarian action also included a visit to *favelas* located near CCOPAB in Rio de Janeiro, in order to demonstrate UPPs in action (CCOPAB 2010).

244   *Conor O'Reilly*

disorder – what is required is "security first" and "boots on the ground"; terms that are, in fact, euphemisms for coercion (or at least its threat).

(p. 303)

This does not mean that those dispatched on peacekeeping missions must be excessively coercive in their actions; more that they should be proficient in the use of this powerful tool from the policing toolkit. They should be ready and able to use force when required, confident in their ability to do so, and most likely will already possess an established reputation for so doing. After all, 'the nastier one's reputation, the less nasty one has to be' (Sheptycki 2010: 309). Whilst not the only explanatory factor for Brazil's increased peacekeeping profile (Sánches Nieto 2012), the coercive pedigree of Brazilian policing institutions has certainly made a significant contribution to its new international role.

In bringing this section to a close, it is important to note that whilst discussion has focused on how participation in MINUSTAH has contributed to the RJPM, it should also be noted that Brazilian policing, more generally, has assumed increasing leadership roles in recent years; attracting the growing international profile that accompanies such responsibilities. Its peacekeeping actions now extend to a wider range of countries, including Timor-Leste, Guinea-Bissau and Sudan (Passarelli and Costa Leite 2012, Horta Moriconi 2010, Sánches Nieto 2012) and are further extended through training courses offered by its peacekeeping operations training centre, CCOPAB, in Rio de Janeiro. It has assumed the lead in Latin America as regards regional transnational policing action (Muggah and Diniz 2013), whilst the Brazilian Federal Police also acts as a hub for international police training at its National Police Academy in Brasilia (UNODC 2008). Brazil has also taken a prominent position within foreign police assistance to Africa (Erthal Abdenur and Marcondes de Souza Neto 2012: 5), often acting in tandem with Interpol and the United Nations Office on Drugs and Crime (UNODC). For example, it contributed to the construction of the new police academy in Guinea-Bissau (UNODC 2010) as well as engaging in other police capacity-building activities in what has been termed Africa's first Narco-state. In short, whilst this chapter has been focused upon the RJPM and its emergence as a geo-policial brand, Brazilian policing has, more generally, attained a newfound importance within and across the complex, evolving architecture of global policing.

Conclusion

In a recent work considering the phenomenon of pacification, Neocleous (2011) theorises it as security in its most expansive sense; a mechanism of social ordering for primarily economic ends. He further observes that, 'the category of "pacification". . . carries a powerful theoretical charge, linking as it does the military to the police, the foreign to the domestic, the colonial to the homeland' (2011: 204). Whilst the RJPM did not feature within his analysis, this chapter has demonstrated how it would rest quite comfortably within the theoretical framework he proposes. It has evolved from, and has been operationalised through, a series of reverberations and overlaps: between sites of intervention (domestic *favelas* and foreign slums); between security institutions (police and military); as well as between strategic approaches and agendas (militarisation and humanitarianism). Whilst the cross-contextual linkage of international peacekeeping and domestic pacification may possess superficial resonance with processes of 'internal colonialism' (Brogden 1987), the Brazilian case demonstrates much more complex patterns of security transfer. This mutation of Foucauldian 'boomerang effects' (Graham 2011: xvii–xviii) has undoubted transnational characteristics, but the reflection of security mentalities and techniques that are applied in the periphery back to the core also possesses distinctly local dimensions. Indeed, to speak of core and periphery in the Brazilian urban context is problematic. With the extremes of the class spectrum so often living cheek by jowl, it is perhaps unsurprising that tactics of subjugation initially deployed in the *favela* have seeped down on to the *asfalto*. Indeed, the RJPM is much more than a *Carioca*-version of 'weed-and-seed'. It seems to have subtly achieved a broader societal permeation that is suggestive of the sort of all-encompassing social ordering outlined by critical commentators such as Neocleous. Perhaps, the strongest indicator of this process is provided by the policing response to mass protests in the build-up to mega-events. As one commentator who participated in these popular protests – which have spanned social classes as well as diverse sources of societal discontent – observed, 'the demonstrations show another face of the urban conflict, one in which the policing tactics used in the *favela* were brought to the main thoroughfares of the city' (Santos Gutterres 2014: 904).[23] In this sense, a new form of domination seems to be emerging in the domestic context, the Brazilian security apparatus not only innovating and deploying police actions to reclaim and stabilise embedded peripheral spaces (Lindsay 2012) but also to impose order across broader social structures.

Whilst it is important to resist 'neat narratives of imperialism' (Amar 2013: 5), what is currently happening with the RJPM connects, albeit with new dynamics, with much of what has gone before in this volume. Pacification unifies the subjugating and control impulses of colonial policing with hearts and minds strategies of counterinsurgency, as well as reflecting patterns of police-military overlap; themes which have appeared across a number of the preceding chapters, in diverse Lusophone contexts (in particular, see the contributions from Rosemberg, Palacios Cerezales and Reis). Pacification also functions as something of a condensing symbol for Brazilian society and its experience of public security; shaped by its past (the legacies of colonialism, imperialism, slavery, military dictatorship and ultra-coercive policing) but harbouring global ambitions (to be a global example and a lead nation in international peacekeeping and transnational policing operations). Indeed, Brazil appears at the vanguard of a number of Southern nations that are

---

23 For more on the linkage between pacification and the public protests in Brazil, see the Special Issues of *Anthropological Quarterly* (Vol. 87, No. 3) and *Cultural Anthropology* (Dent and Pinheiro-Machado 2013).

246   Conor O'Reilly

transcending their previous status as laboratories for security experimentation to emerge as providers of security solutions for other contexts – including locations in the North. The RJPM, is certainly in an advantageous position in this regard. Not only does it possess a global profile that exceeds those of many of its Southern counterparts, as well as significantly greater political and economic clout, but in seeking to promote its expertise transnationally, it can harness a number of intersecting conduits for security transfers: policing urban slums (at home and abroad); policing mega-events; policing as peacekeeping; and, policing public protest. Even if actual transfers and emulation may often prove chimerical, the RJPM enjoys a propitious position from which to pursue such exchanges.

The RJPM certainly presents a novel case of *geo-policial branding* by virtue of its Global South origins. However, the narrative of domestic success that is fundamental to its global promotion, whilst not built on sand, remains highly suspect. This is a relatively new security initiative and representations of its 'success' are both premature and contested. There are mixed signals emerging from both the communities of pacified *favelas* as well as from those UPP police officers deployed there regarding their satisfaction with, and support for, this initiative. Also, the much-praised pacification strategy is increasingly beleaguered be accusations of violence and disappearances that are being levelled at the UPPs (most notably, the case of Amarildo de Sousa in 2013). Meanwhile in 2012, State Security Secretary Beltrame appointed Colonel Paulo Henrique Azevedo, a former head of the controversial Special Operations Unit, BOPE, as UPP commander. Indeed beyond the potential for re-militarisation of policing in the *favela* and the elusive pacification dividend, the future durability of this programme in terms of economic sustainability and political support also remains uncertain (see, for example: Muggah and Souza Mulli 2014: 207–211, Rodrigues 2014: 5).[24] This is even before we consider perennial concerns about its appropriateness for security transfers to other contexts; and the dubious assumption that what works in Rio (if indeed it does work there), is suitable for other security realities. Something that can be taken from the *geo-policial branding* of the RJPM and its presentation as triumphant security innovation, is that its champions seem well aware that selling a story of success is the next best option to achieving it. This objective may become more difficult as cracks begin to appear in the domestic pacification project and it will be very interesting to observe how promotion of the RJPM is sustained should there be a lurch back towards more militarised policing. For example, might the

---

24 The amounts required to fund Rio's pacification programme are massive and have been partially bankrolled by private interests. To give some indication of the sums that are involved, Muggah and Souza Mulli (2014) recently noted that: '. . . the state has invested more than R$650 million–$330 million in March 2013 – in the program to date. As a measure of his confidence in the agenda, the mayor committed an additional R$2 billion (1$ billion in March 2013) more in infrastructural improvements in 2012' (p. 207). Of course, it is necessary to mention that insofar as the domestic pacification programme in Rio is concerned, whilst policing and security costs are high, pacification also necessitates significant wider investment in terms of developing the *favelas* that are integral to this policy.

menace of the drug-trafficker be resurrected to legitimise more hard-line UPP activity? It will certainly be interesting to see how well a policing brand that might become tainted at home can be sustained abroad.

Nevertheless, the vested interests behind the RJPM are well aware that the momentum of positive perceptions is key to securing foreign endorsement; such recognition might furnish legitimacy in the international domain that is absent domestically. Indeed, even if the contextual specifics of Brazil do not exist elsewhere in the world, this need not discourage other policy actors from attempting to osmotically tap the international goodwill and security prestige that the RJPM has cultivated. As this chapter has highlighted, the RJPM has become integrated into a range of elite transnational security networks that are characterised by strategic endorsements and mutually beneficial exchanges. These new global connections have not occurred in a vacuum. For Brazil, they reflect a desire to shift the reputation of Brazilian policing and security actors – to re-frame, if not to reform, these institutions. Transnationally, they reflect the global appetite for 'solutions' to complex security scenarios. Indeed, as Graham (2011) has demonstrated, problematic urban zones are key sites of security experimentation and transfers across the globe. The RJPM might not be the only silver bullet for the 'planet of slums' (Davis 2007) that is currently being touted in the transnational policing marketplace. However, its potential to merge militarised occupation with humanitarianism towards wider social ordering, as well as its construction of a powerful policing dramaturgy that plays out before a global audience, does make it uniquely appealing.

References

Amar, P. 2009. Operation Princess in Rio de Janeiro: Policing 'sex trafficking', strengthening worker citizenship, and the urban geopolitics of security in Brazil. *Security Dialogue*, 40(4–5): 513–541.

Amar, P. 2013. *Global South to the Rescue: Emerging Humanitarian Superpowers and Globalizing Rescue Industries* (Rethinking Globalizations Series). Abingdon, Oxford: Routledge.

Amnesty International. 2005. Brazil: 'They come in shooting': Policing socially excluded communities [Online: *Amnesty International*]. Available at: www.amnesty.org/en/documents/amr19/025/2005/en/ [accessed: 24 November 2014].

Anholt, S. 2005. *Brand New Justice: How Branding Places and Products Can Help the Developing World*. Abingdon: Routledge.

Anholt, S. 2007. *Competitive Identity: The New Brand Management for Nations, Cities and Regions*. Houndsmills. Basingstoke: Palgrave-MacMillan.

Avraham, E. and Ketter, E. 2008. Will we be safe there? Analysing strategies for altering unsafe place images. *Place Branding and Public Diplomacy*, 4(3): 196–204.

Baasch, S. 2011. Event-driven security policies and spatial control: The 2006 World Cup, in *Security Games: Surveillance and Control at Mega-Events*, edited by C.J. Bennett, and K.D. Haggerty. Abingdon: Glasshouse, Routledge, 103–119.

Bennett, C.J. and Haggerty, K.J., 2011. *Security Games: Surveillance and Control at Mega-Events*. Abingdon: Glasshouse, Routledge.

248 *Conor O'Reilly*

Bjork, K. and Jones, R. 2005. Overcoming dilemmas created by the 21st century mercenaries: Conceptualising the use of private security companies in Iraq. *Third World Quarterly*, 26(4–5): 777–796.

Bowling, B. and Sheptycki, J.W.E. 2012. *Global Policing*. Sage: London.

Boyle, P. 2011. Knowledge networks: Mega-events and security expertise, in *Security Games: Surveillance and Control at Mega-Events*, edited by C.J. Bennett and K.D. Haggerty. Abingdon: Glasshouse, Routledge, 169–184.

Bratton, W. and Knobler, P. 1998. *Turnaround: How America's Top Cop Reversed the Crime Epidemic*. New York: Random House.

Brogden, M. and Ellison, G. 2013. *Policing in an Age of Austerity: A Postcolonial Perspective*. Abingdon, Oxford: Routledge.

CCOPAB. 2010. Symposium of civil-military cooperation in peacekeeping operations (3rd Day) [Online: *CCOPAB*]. Available at: www.ccopab.eb.mil.br/index.php/en/ccopab/noticias-do-centro/2010/120-symposium-of-civil-military-cooperation-in-peacekeeping-operations-3rd-day [accessed: 24 October 2014].

Chery, D. 2011. What happens in haiti doesn't stay in Haiti [Online: *San Francisco Bay View*, 8 December 2011]. Available at: http://sfbayview.com/2011/12/what-happens-in-haiti-doesn't-stay-in-haiti/ [accessed: 19 October 2014].

Chevigny, P. 1999. *The Edge of the Knife: Police Violence in the Americas*. New York: New Press.

Christie, R. 2013. The pacification of soldiering and the militarization of development: Contradictions inherent in provincial reconstruction in Afghanistan, in *Global South to the Rescue: Emerging Humanitarian Superpowers and Globalizing Rescue Industries (Rethinking Globalizations Series)*, edited by P. Amar. Abingdon: Oxford, 53–71.

Coaffee, J. and Ham, P. van 2008. 'Security branding': The role of security in marketing the city, region or state. *Place Branding and Public Diplomacy*, 4(3): 191–195.

Coaffee, J. and Rogers, P. 2008. Reputational risk and resiliency: The branding of security in place-making. *Place Branding and Public Diplomacy*, 4(3): 205–217.

Dantas, P. 2007. Exército Admite Uso de Tática do Haiti em Favela do Rio [Online: *Estadão de Hoje, Sao Paulo*, 15 December 2007]. Available at: http://brasil.estadao.com.br/noticias/geral,exercito-admite-uso-de-tatica-do-haiti-em-favela-do-rio,96430 [accessed: 19 October 2014].

Davis, M. 2007. *Planet of Slums*. London: Verso.

Dent, A.S. and Pinheiro-Machado, R. 20 December 2013. Protesting democracy in Brazil. [Online: *Fieldsights – Hot Spots, Cultural Anthropology Online*]. Available at: www.culanth.org/fieldsights/426-protesting-democracy-in-brazil [accessed: 6 November 2014].

Denyer Willis G. and Mota Prado, M. 2014. Process and pattern in institutional reforms: A case study of the Police Pacifying Units (UPPs) in Brazil. *World Development*, 64: 232–242.

Dixon, D. 2005. Beyond zero tolerance, in *Policing: Key Readings*, edited by T. Newburn. Cullompton: Willan, 483–507.

Dorn, A.W. 2009. Intelligence-led peacekeeping: The United Nations stabilization mission in Haiti (MINUSTAH), 2006–2007. *International Peacekeeping*, 24(6): 805–835.

Dziedzic, M. and Perito, R. 2008. *Haiti: Confronting the Gangs of Port-au-Prince*. Special Report No. 208. Washington, DC: United States Institute for Peace.

The Economist. 2013. Policing and politics in Brazil: From hero to villain in Rio. *The Economist*, 14 September 2013.

Ellison, G. 2007. Fostering a dependency culture: The commodification of community policing in a global marketplace, in *Crafting Transnational Policing: Police Capacity Building and Global Policing Reform*, edited by A. Goldsmith and J.W.E. Sheptycki (Onati International Series in Law and Society). Oxford: Hart Publishing, 203–242.

Ellison, G. and O'Reilly, C. 2008a. From empire to Iraq and the War on Terror: The transplantation and commodification of the (Northern) Irish policing experience. *Police Quarterly*, 11(4): 395–426.

Ellison, G. and O'Reilly, C. 2008b. 'Ulster's policing goes global': The police reform process in Northern Ireland and the creation of a global brand. *Crime, Law and Social Change*, 50(4–5): 331–351.

Ellison, G. and Pino, N. 2012. *Globalization, Police Reform and Development: Doing It the Western Way?* London: Palgrave-MacMillan.

Emsley, C. 2012. Marketing the brand: Exporting British police models 1829–1950. *Policing*, 6(1): 43–54.

Erthal Abdenur, A. and Marcondes de Souza Neto, D. 2012. *Brazil's Growing Relevance to Peace and Security in Africa*. NOREF Report, March 2014. The Norwegian Peacebuilding Resource Centre.

Foley, C. 2014. Pelo Telefone: *Rumors, Truths and Myths in the 'Pacification' of the Favelas of Rio de Janeiro*. Discussion Paper No. 8, March 2014. Humanitarian Action in Situations Other Than War.

Freire-Medeiros, R. 2011. *Touring Poverty*. London: Routledge.

Gimenez Stahlberg, S. 2011. The pacification of favelas in Rio de Janeiro: Why the program is working and what are the lessons for other countries [Online: *Working Paper from the Program on Poverty and Governance at the Center on Development, Democracy and the Rule of Law at Stanford University*]. Available at: http://fsimedia.stanford.edu/evnts/6716/Stahlberg,_Stephanie_-_Pacification_of_Favelas_in_Rio_de_Janeiro_(Work_in_Progress).pdf [accessed: 1 August 2014].

Gomes, M. 2013. PM do Rio Exporta Programa de Pacificaçaõ de Favelas Para O Haiti [Online: *Estadão*, 24 May 2013]. Available at: http://brasil.estadao.com.br/noticias/geral,pm-do-rio-exporta-programa-de-pacificacao-de-favelas-para-o-haiti,1035294 [accessed: 19 October 2014].

González, R.J. 2009. Going 'tribal': Notes on pacification in the 21st century. *Anthropology Today*, 25(2): 15–19.

Goold, B., Loader, I. and Thumala, A. 2010. Consuming security? Tools for a sociology of security consumption. *Theoretical Criminology*, 14(1): 3–30.

Graham, S. 2011. *Cities Under Siege: The New Military Urbanism*. London: Verso.

Ham, P. van 2001. The rise of the brand state: The postmodern politics of image and reputation. *Foreign Affairs*, 10 October 2001.

Hinton, M.S. 2006. *The State on the Streets: Police and Politics in Argentina and Brazil*. Boulder, CO: Lynne Reiner.

Horta Moriconi, L. 2010. Brazil sends record number of police officers in UN missions [Online: *CommunidadeSegura*, 5 November 2011]. Available at: https://missaodepaz.com/2010/11/11/brazil-record-number-of-police-officers-in-un-peacekeeping-missions/ [accessed: 19 October 2010].

Huggins, M. 1997. From bureaucratic consolidation to structural devolution: Police death squads in Brazil. *Policing & Society*, 7(4): 207–234.

Huggins, M. 1998. *Political Policing: The United States and Latin America*. Durham, NC: Duke University Press.

Human Rights Watch. 2010. Lethal force: Police violence and public security in Rio de Janeiro and São Paulo [Online: *Human Rights Watch*, 8 December 2009]. Available at: www.hrw.org/reports/2009/12/08/lethal-force [accessed: 24 November 2014].

Joachim, J. and Schneiker, A. 2012. New humanitarians? Frame appropriation through private military and security companies. *Millennium: Journal of International Studies*, 40(2): 365–388.

Kenkel, K.M. 2010. South America's emerging power: Brazil as peacekeeper. *International Peacekeeping*, 17(5): 644–661.

Lindsay, D. 2012. The embedded periphery: Slums, favelas, shantytowns and a new regime of spatial inequality in the modern world system, in *Routledge Handbook of World Systems Analysis*, edited by S.J. Babones and C. Chase-Dunn. London: Routledge, 345–352.

Loader, I. 1997. Policing and symbolic power: Questions of the social. *British Journal of Sociology*, 48: 1–18.

Loader, I. 1999. Consumer culture and the commodification of policing and security. *Sociology*, 33(2): 373–392.

Loader, I. and Mulcahy, A. 2003. *Policing and the Condition of England: Memory, Politics and Culture*. Oxford: Oxford University Press.

Manning, P.K. 2000. Policing new social spaces, in *Issues in Transnational Policing*, edited by J.W.E. Sheptycki. London: Routledge, 177–200.

Manning, P.K. 2001. Theorizing policing: The drama and myth of crime control in the NYPD. *Theoretical Criminology*, 5(3): 315–344.

Mansfield, Y. and Pizam, A. 2006. *Tourism, Security and Safety: From Theory to Practice*. Burlington, MA: Butterworth-Heineman.

Marenin, O. November 2006. *Global Cops: The Emergence of the Transnational Police Policy Community*. Los Angeles: American Society of Criminology.

Marenin, O. 2007. Implementing police reforms: The role of the transnational policy community', in *Crafting Transnational Policing: Police Capacity Building and Global Policing Reform*, edited by A. Goldsmith and J.W.E. Sheptycki (Onati International Series in Law and Society). Oxford: Hart Publishing, 177–202.

Molnar, A. and Snider, L. 2011. Mega-events and mega-profits: Unravelling the Vancouver 2010 security-development nexus, in *Security Games: Surveillance and Control at Mega-Events*, edited by C.J. Bennett and K.D. Haggerty. Abingdon: Glasshouse, Routledge, 150–168.

Muggah, R. and Diniz, G. 2013. *Securing the Border: Brazil's 'South America First' Approach to Transnational Organised Crime*. Strategic Paper 5, October 2013. Igarapé Institute: Rio de Janeiro.

Muggah, R. and Souza Mulli, A.W. 2014. Paving the hills and levelling the streets: Counterinsurgency in Rio de Janeiro, in *Stabilization Operations, Security and Development – States of Fragility*, edited by R. Muggah. London: Routledge, 167–181.

Neill, W.J.V. 1995. Lipstick on the gorilla? Conflict management, urban development and image making in Belfast, in *Reinventing the Pariah City – Urban Development in Belfast and Detroit*, edited by W.J.V. Neill, D.S. Fitzsimmons and B. Murtagh. Avebury: Aldershot, 50–76.

Neocleous, M. 2011. A brighter and nicer new life': Security as pacification. *Social & Legal Studies*, 20(2): 191–208.

Newburn, T. and Jones, T. 2007. Symbolizing crime control: Reflections on zero tolerance. *Theoretical Criminology*, 11(2): 221–243.

Branding Rio de Janeiro's pacification model   251

Norheim-Martinsen, P.M. 2012. Brazil as an emerging peacekeeping actor. *NOREF Report*, November 2012.

O'Reilly, C. 2010. The transnational security consultancy industry: A case of state-corporate symbiosis. *Theoretical Criminology*, 14(2): 183–210.

O'Reilly, C. October 2013. *Branding Policing in a Transnational Marketplace: A Typology*. COPP-LAB Workshop, UNICAMP, Brazil.

Pacheco de Oliveira, J. 2010. O nascimento do Brasil: A revisão de um paradigma historiográfico. *Anuário Antropológico*, 1: 11–40.

Pacheco de Oliveira, J. 2014. Pacificação e tutela militar na gestão de populações e territórios. *Mana*, 20(1): 125–161.

Passarelli Hamann, E. and Costa Leite, I. 2012. A experiência do brasil em contextos instáveis. Strategic Paper 3, September 2012. Igarapé Institute: Rio de Janeiro.

Penglase, B. 2014. Pacifying Rio's favelas: Innovation, adaptation or continuity? [Online: *Anthropolitea*, 16 May 2014]. Available at: http://anthropoliteia.net/2014/05/16/pacifying-rios-favelas-innovation-adaptation-or-continuity/ [accessed: 6 August 2014].

Pina, K. 2008. Brazilian military's experience comes full circle in Haiti. *HaitiAction*, February 20th, 2008.

Prouse, C. 2012. Framing the world cUPP: Competing discourses of favela pacification as a mega-event legacy in Brazil. *Recreation and Society in Africa, Asia and Latin America*, 3(2): 1–17.

Robb Larkins, E. 2013. Performances of police legitimacy in Rio's hyper favela. *Journal of Law and Social Inquiry*, 38(3): 553–575.

Robb Larkins, E. 2015. *The Spectacular Favela: Violence in Modern Brazil*. Berkeley, CA: University of California Press.

Rodrigues, R. 2014. The dilemmas of pacification: News of war and peace in the 'Marvelous City'. *Journal of Security and Development*, 3(1): 1–16.

Saborio, S. 2013. The pacification of the favelas: Mega-events, global competitiveness, and the neutralization of marginality. *Socialist Studies*, 9(2): 130–145.

Sánches Nieto, W.A. 2012. Brazil's grand design for combining global south solidarity and national interests: A discussion of peacekeeping operations in Haiti and Timor. *Globalizations*, 9(1): 161–178.

Santos Gutterres, A. 2014. 'It's not easy, I ask for public mobility and the government sends skulls against me': An intimate account of the public protests in Rio de Janeiro (June and July 2013). *Anthropological Quarterly*, 87(3): 901–918.

Savell, S. 2014. The Brazilian military, public security and Rio de Janeiro's 'Pacification', [Online: *Anthropoliteia*, 7 July 2014]. Available at: http://anthropoliteia.net/2014/07/07/the-brazilian-military-public-security-and-rio-de-janeiros-pacification/ [accessed: 19 October 2014].

Sheptycki, J.W.E. 2002. *In Search of Transnational Policing: Towards a Sociology of Global Policing*. Aldershot: Ashgate.

Sheptycki, J.W.E. 2007. Criminology and the transnational condition: A contribution to international political sociology. *International Political Sociology*, 1(4): 391–406.

Sheptycki, J.W.E. 2010. The Constabulary Ethic reconsidered, in *International Police Co-operation: Emerging Issues, Theory and Practice* edited by F. Lemieux. Cullompton: Willan, 298–319.

Sinclair, G. 2012. Exporting the UK police brand: The RUC-PSNI and the international policing agenda. *Police Quarterly*, 6(1): 55–66.

Spektor, M. 2012. Humanitarian intervention Brazilian style? [Online: *Americas Quarterly*, Summer 2012]. Available at: www.americasquarterly.org/humanitarian-interventionism-brazilian-style [accessed: 29 October 2014].

Stone, D. 2004. Transfer agents and global networks in the 'transnationalization' of policy. *Journal of European Public Policy*, 11(3): 545–566.

Torres, I. 2012. Branding slums: A community-driven strategy for urban inclusion in Rio de Janeiro. *Journal of Place Management and Development*, 5(3): 198–201.

UNODC. 2008. South-South cooperation fights organised crime [Online: *United Nations Office on Drugs and Crime*]. Available at: www.unodc.org/unodc/en/frontpage/south-south-cooperation-fights-organized-crime.html [accessed: 19 October 2014].

UNODC. 2010. UN anti-crime agency to help set up police academy in Guinea-Bissau [Online: *United Nations News Centre*]. Available at: www.un.org/apps/news/story.asp?NewsID=33569 [accessed: 19 October 2014].

Urry, J. and Larsen, J. 2011. *The Tourist Gaze 3.0*. London: Sage.

Viana Braga, C.C. 2010. MINUSTAH and the security environment in Haiti: Brazil and South American cooperation in the field. *International Peacekeeping*, 17(5): 711–722.

VIVA RIO. 2014. UPP project is presented to Haitian police officers [Online: *VIVA RIO*, 5 February 2014]. Available at: http://vivario.org.br/en/upp-project-is-presented-to-haitian-police-officers/ [accessed: 19 October 2014].

Wacquant, L. 2008. The militarization of urban marginality: Lessons from the Brazilian metropolis. *International Political Sociology*, 2(1): 56–74.

Young, J. 1999. *The Exclusive Society*. London: Sage.

Zirin, D. 2014. Exporting gaza: The arming of Brazil's world cup security. [Online: *The Nation*, 30 June 2014]. Available at: www.thenation.com/blog/180465/exporting-gaza-arming-brazils-world-cup-security# [accessed: 6 August 2014].

Comment

'Never mind the similarities, focus on the differences': imposition, imitation and intransigence in post-colonial global policing reform

Andrew Goldsmith

Introduction

In this Comment, I seek to draw key lessons from the chapters making up this section in terms of what can be learned today from recent efforts in post-colonial policing, especially in relation to the wider phenomena of transnational and transitional policing. I shall argue that while we will inevitably be struck by the commonalities of approach that straddle different national, cultural and linguistic groups in an era of globalisation, there is merit still in attending to the differences that remain, in terms not just about what these differences reveal about the enduring weight and influence of past associations upon present practices, but also about how such differences can be, and are being, exploited both by donors and by recipients for their own agendas. As with the case of its predecessor, colonial policing, I shall suggest that the imperial contribution of transnational policing to post-colonial policing is often more partial, less effective, and dependent on local power and authority than some 'grand narrative' views of the significance of globalised policing convey or imply.

A decade or so ago, the notion that Lusophone police delegations would or could play a significant role in peacekeeping or nation-building efforts over the next ten years would have struck many Anglo-American, or indeed Australian, observers of transnational policing developments as improbable and indeed strange. After all, the conflicts and calamities that had afflicted parts of the globe between the early 1990s and the early 21st century had, for one reason or another, become the 'responsibility' of international entities such as the United Nations (UN) and the European Union (EU) and a few countries such as the United States, the United Kingdom and Australia. This meant that ideas about promotion of the rule of law, security sector reform, and police development in conflict-affected or post-conflict states typically emerged from these (mostly English-speaking) quarters.

The footprint of the Anglophone world in this field has been very clear. The discourse of transnational policing in this period among academics and policy developers was heavily influenced by ideas, philosophies, and practices drawn from

254   *Andrew Goldsmith*

these countries (Goldsmith and Sheptycki 2007, Ellison and Pino 2012, Bowling and Sheptycki 2012). It explains, for example, the high level of interest among many Western reformers in community policing as a potential template for re-establishing or initiating public police forces in hitherto conflict- afflicted places. It was hoped by many Western policing donors that implementing such a model would lead to local policing approaches that were more respectful of civil liberties and local concerns about crime than had been the case previously.

In the past decade or so, perhaps unsurprisingly given the prominent role of multilateral peacekeeping forces under the UN and African Union (AU) umbrellas, the role of non-Anglophone countries has become more apparent, as Francophone and Lusophone contributions have become more visible in the field. As demonstrated by O'Reilly's contribution regarding Brazil's leadership role in the UN mission to Haiti, in some cases, it is the former colonies such as Brazil that have come to play a prominent role in the export of policing reforms (see, Amar 2013). As one might predict, though not irrelevant, the more recent trends exhibit less fealty to historical colonial and linguistic associations as particular 'brands' of policing reform become global in nature.

Imperial impositions

In any consideration of the Lusophone contribution, it is inevitable that comparisons will be drawn with contributions from non-Lusophone sources in this area, begging questions of similarity and difference in the models proposed and implemented.[1] Beyond variations of policing approach, comparisons need to address the implications of transnational policing trends for contributions of whatever provenance. Talk of 'neo-liberalism' and 'globalisation' in relation to global policing reform (see, for example: Bowling and Sheptycki 2012) implies or invokes processes of harmonisation, homogenisation, and convergence among once relatively distinct philosophies and practices of policing. As hallmarks of an emerging 'common agenda' for policing at the global level, one would expect to witness a decline in the influence of particular nation-based or linguistic-based contributions to the nature of policing being offered by donors.

Nonetheless given current as well as past associations between European powers and their erstwhile colonies, it is only natural and sensible to ask – what are the legacy effects of these past associations in the light of recent and current transnational and global reform developments in policing? Also, what contemporary expressions, even renewals, of differentiated policing approaches along the lines of past colonial associations are visible, defying assumptions of convergence? In looking to the past as a reference point for comparison, commonalities of approach arising from the *colonial* aspect of such ventures, included shared

---

1 Of course, the reliance of UN police missions upon personnel contributions from different countries reflecting often quite different approaches to policing ensures that such comparisons often emerge within the context of a single mission.

experiences of counter-colonialism, should be anticipated and given weight where appropriate. The recent establishment of links between Cape Verdean and Angolan police forces is an example of a counter-colonial commonality contributing to the development of contemporary relationships.[2]

Another factor making comparisons complicated is that the export model of policing cannot be assumed to resemble or imitate the domestic model of policing. In fact, it is widely accepted that the 'policing by consent' model associated with Peelian policing in England was predominantly not the English export model, but rather a 'policing by coercion' model involving armed mounted police was more commonplace in colonies as close to home as Ireland and as far away as Australia (Brogden 1987, Ellison and O'Reilly 2008a, Sinclair and Williams 2007). Not only did countries such as the United Kingdom develop a different model in its Irish colony that was replicated elsewhere in its empire, rather than slavishly promoting the domestic model; in addition, as various policing scholars have noted, there can often be a 'reverse learning' or reverse capacity-building (Harris and Goldsmith 2009) outcome, in which the home country's experience with the export model in its colonies subsequently influences its revision of its domestic approach to policing (see, in particular, the contribution from Diego Palacio Cerezales to this collection).

If there are happy histories of colonial policing, they are difficult to find. Historical assessments of many former British colonies, including Canada and Australia, point to significant negative experiences with colonial and post-colonial models of policing (see, for example: Finnane and Paisley 2010, Nettlebeck and Smandych 2010). In many outposts of the different European empires, policing was experienced by native populations and to some extent, settler populations, as external and imposed by colonial authorities, rather than as incorporating indigenous perspectives or being suitably adapted to local conditions. The calibre and orientation of policing services clearly varied from place to place and over time, but typically exported colonial models privileged the interests of the colonial authorities over those of locals (see, for example: Killingray 1986). Tendencies towards subjection and control of local populations by force during moments of crisis, and relative neglect during more peaceful times, rather than to service to the community, have been documented in many places, not least in the earlier contributions to this volume.

The reasons why imposed policing models were so often widely resented can be differentiated in a number of ways. In some cases, local resentment was due to overt violence by police agents towards the local people and what some scholars have called processes of 'pacification', suggesting the imposition of a model of order and governance upon a reluctant population. Pacification was often the secular counterpart to Christian missionary expeditions, component parts of a wider (typically European or American) 'civilising mission' (for more on 'pacification' see O'Reilly, this volume) Not all colonial experiences of policing were

---

2 This linkage was drawn to my attention by Dr Conor O'Reilly.

256   *Andrew Goldsmith*

however equally intense, ambitious or indeed violent. In addition to plenty of examples of brutal suppression or extensive influence, there are cases of 'light footprint' colonisation and post-colonial governance approaches. These are more resonant of neglect and indifference towards the local population, rather than of active domination or even exploitation. As the chapters from Ho and Lam on Macau and Peake on Timor Leste indicate, the approaching end of Portuguese administration coincided with a withdrawal of interest as well as investment in processes of policing reform.

Amidst the talk of empires and colonialism, therefore, the deliberate or accidental outcome of limited colonial *infrastructural power* (to use Michael Mann's (1984) useful term) during colonial times can reasonably be expected to limit the extent or durability of any enduring colonial influence in the post-colonial period. Imperial indifference or neglect at the local level inevitably allowed room for indigenous ordering processes to continue or to re-emerge. Empires, in terms of control of geographical space, have always been partial as well as expensive and difficult to establish and maintain,[3] making indirect rule an inevitability. In the case of Timor-Leste, for example, a '*laissez-faire*' approach by Portuguese authorities during their tenure enabled certain indigenous administrative structures to persist as systems of governance and indeed policing at the local level. These structures persist today, even after the successive Indonesian colonial period (1975–1999). In the case of Macau, the Chinese population effectively self-regulated their affairs while living alongside or in close proximity to the colonial administration, whose policing 'contribution' to local people was frequently limited to bribe-taking and suppression of political dissent. Such an exploitative, partial, even parasitic arrangement between police and colonial subject is not adequately captured by the almost clinical sounding phrase 'limited infrastructural power.' There is a level of intentionality implied in such arrangements that is suggestive of a more cynical, rent-seeking agenda.[4]

Despite such histories, it is impossible to dismiss the contemporary relevance of enduring cultural affinities and delusions of ongoing imperial relevance on the part of some leaders in European states. There is, it would appear at least to a degree, a kind of learned forgetfulness at work in which past shortcomings are put to one side and not allowed to prejudice expressions of continuity between former colonial powers and their erstwhile colonies in areas such as trade, development and security. Thus, with little apparent sense of irony or historical memory, former European colonial powers once again can be seen in the 21st century to be engaged in efforts to project power into former colonies (among other places) in the form of police peacekeeping and development. A real question for exploration and analysis here is the extent to which past experiences (of at best a mixed kind)

---

3 As Killingray (1986) observed, 'vast areas of colonial Africa were unpoliced by central government' (p. 426).

4 Many scholarly critiques of imperialism reach this conclusion across a range of colonial administrative and military practices promoted by European imperial powers.

in recipient former colonies might be expected to inject a degree of sensitivity and even humility, rather than echoes of imperial hubris, in proposals for police reform being touted on behalf of donors from these erstwhile colonial powers?

Another related question, aside from matters of sensitivity or appropriateness of what is being offered by donors by way of policing reform, is how past associations influence the types of police models being chosen (familiar versus unfamiliar), and the relative ability of donors from different countries to influence local politicians in making their selections of the models to be implemented. While clearly an empirical question, one subject to the changing array of participants and the incentives on offer by donors, the maintenance of linguistic and cultural attachments, albeit ones based on past colonial relationships, might be expected at times to at least to favour the positions and offerings of those European or metropolitan sources with those shared attachments over others. As we can see at least in the case of Timor-Leste (Peake, this collection; Goldsmith 2009), the common Lusophone background of the first generation of post-colonial Timorese leaders and the Portuguese government played a not insignificant part in shaping the policing reform debates and outcomes in that country.

Intransigence and resistance

As has been the case with many other imperial impositions, disregard of local circumstances often led to limits upon the influence and effectiveness of police reform efforts. In the chapters in this section, we see that the Lusophone police influence in recent times has been underestimated by many and that it continues to play a significant role in the increasingly transnational circulations of policing knowledge and practice. We shall also see that while it is often associated with a different model of police reform from many others offered by international agencies and other Western countries, there have also been mistakes of a similar kind in the way reforms have been introduced. Equally, and counter-intuitively, there have been similar forms of 'push-back' at the local level, often in subtle ways, that not simply frustrates the goals of foreign reformers but paradoxically that enable modes of adaptation of imported practices and ideas to survive and become, at least to some extent, sustainable. Such forms of resistance and expressions of intransigence at the local level are important and often neglected elements of the progressive narratives underpinning many foreign-led police reform ventures (but see Blaustein 2015).

These chapters can be seen in the context of recent attempts to capture in an overtly systematic manner the significance of various forms of transnational policing. The narratives of colonialism, re-colonisation and Western hegemony are readily found in the relevant literature seeking to make sense of this phenomenon. They are used to try to capture and summarise certain features of recent trends in practice, namely the dominance of agencies such as the United Nations, its various off-shoots, and the security and development establishments of major Western powers in setting the tone of, and engaging in, significant efforts at police reform in a variety of places around the globe. The banners of humanitarian intervention, the 'wars' on drugs and terrorism, and nation-building have in their own ways legitimated versions of police reform, whether in the form of training, resources, sharing of knowledge, or exchanges of personnel. The very notion that these programs and resources come from dominant Western countries and that they are in some sense imposed on receiving countries conforms neatly with critical understandings of interventionism and past colonial practices.

While there is a strong element of truth to such critiques, what is arguably as interesting, and which remains still relatively unexplored and hence underappreciated in the literature on transnational policing and international policing reform, is the extent and forms of resistance and co-optation at the local level to many externally-led initiatives. As noted, where, as there often is, significant push-back from different local elements, a more nuanced understanding of how transnational policing occurs and what it means at the local level is required. There are arguably a number of factors enabling locally-driven resistance, indifference or creative adaptation to these initiatives. So far as Lusophone influence is concerned, one of the interesting phenomena at work in many places, including in the places covered in this section (particularly Mozambique and Timor-Leste), is the marketplace for police-related reform ideas, reflected in various externally-driven proposals and embodied by the presence of police delegations from different countries, each simultaneously attempting to shape in some respect the final contours of the receiving policing agency. As a consequence, the policing models offered by Portugal and Brazil sit on the same shelf as offerings from Australia, the US or the UK.

A semblance of choice now has emerged from this competitive police reform environment. The actual or attributed differences between the models on offer means that they serve as counterpoints to each other, empowering local police chiefs, politicians and others to compare, contrast, and at times reject elements of these models or approaches. The unforeseen consequences of global police reform – the perverse empowerment of local people and authorities arising from donors competing to influence the direction and format of local police reform – remain a largely unexamined phenomenon (but see Blaustein 2015). As noted earlier, while the different competitors superficially seem to be offering similar or identical products (e.g. 'community policing'), the philosophies, priorities set, and modes of implementation mean that what is delivered in the form of training and resources ensures some substantial differences between policing approaches on the ground.

As we have seen from the contributions to Part Three, another aspect of the Lusophone impact has been the various ways in which superficially identical or similar notions, such as 'community policing' and 'professional policing' are prioritised as reform models, and then interpreted and implemented in particular settings. Given the enormous geographical, cultural and experiential gaps that separate foreign and local police in most reform settings, it should hardly be surprising that different understandings of reform objectives might emerge, not just as between foreign and local parties, but also within the constellation of foreign actors engaged in police reform activities. These differences may be quite material

Comment   259

in terms of the ways in which these ideas are implemented on the ground. Local preferences for particular interpretations over others can often be significant, resulting in 'in' and 'out' groups among contributing foreign police.

'Cherry pie or knuckle sandwich?'[5]

One theme to emerge across several chapters is the apparent resilient demand, at a local level among key players at least, for strong forms of policing in areas such as public order policing as well as crime control. Here, it can be observed, a potential tension emerges between prioritising public order policing (as supporting in the first instance, the post-colonial regime) and crime-fighting as a local general community requirement. In settings where new governments have only recently emerged from long periods of internal conflict, often following the withdrawal of colonial governments, one could predict that new leaders would place considerable importance on ensuring that political opposition did not undermine their recently obtained governance roles. This was evident in each of Timor-Leste and Mozambique, though interestingly how this was delivered locally varied in each case, as will be discussed further shortly.

Variation in response to local perceptions of serious crime threats also provides a marker in terms of what policing areas are prioritised and how policing reform is approached. Local crime gangs may exert political as well as criminal influence in local settings, leading to conflict over how and whether policing reform should focus on ways of targeting these groups. Perhaps it is hardly surprising that many people living in zones of current or recent conflict would seek effective responses to rising levels of crime and violence in those zones. Effective responses to gang activity often implies a robust policing approach, one that may simultaneously of course suit regime protection as well as gang suppression objectives. The presence of powerful, armed criminal gangs, as evident in Haiti in the 1990s and early 2000s, called forth a demand, and arguably a need, for strong militarised policing in order to subdue and contain the previously unchecked activities of some gangs in Port au Prince, the national capital. As O'Reilly observes in his chapter, the contribution of Brazilian police in this role was not only substantial but also subsequently significant at home in Brazil in terms of shaping approaches to the policing of the urban *favelas* in Rio de Janeiro.

The preference for robust policing units as key components of policing reform can also be seen in Peake's account of Timor-Leste policing and Kyed's account of the Mozambique case. What both chapters point to is the strong influence of local politics upon both the agenda-setting and ultimate implementation phases of police reform. While a 'foreign' model of policing (or a version of it) is in some sense adopted, it is one locally chosen from a menu of offerings. The degree of local influence over choice of models adopted or adapted points to the inadequacy

---

5 With this title, I am obviously drawing upon Mike Brogden's piece (1999), referring to the export of community policing by the US as something distinctly American like cherry pie.

260   Andrew Goldsmith

of seeing recent developments in terms of imposition rather than negotiation, resistance, and on occasion rejection or refusal. It could be argued, legitimately, that many systemic critiques of transnational policing (e.g. Bowling and Sheptycki 2012) have glossed over this critical point, tending to over-predict the strength of foreign reform efforts in shaping the agenda and influencing how policing takes place on the ground. In the case of Timor-Leste, as Peake points out, analysts too often fail to observe the recalcitrance and resistance among locals towards foreign reform templates that ignore or ride roughshod over the power sharing arrangements and political agendas at the local level. While the UN and countries such as Australia have over time provided training in public order policing and attempted to influence the overall approach by local police towards the population through community policing programs and other capacity building endeavours, these attempts have arguably had little effect, and sometimes even have drawn criticism among the Timorese political leadership, in large measure because local police and politicians have often shown a clear preference for more robust or muscular forms of general patrols as well as public order policing.

The presence in Timor-Leste of Portuguese paramilitary police, the *Guarda Nacional Republicana*, alongside contingents of police from Australia, New Zealand and elsewhere under bilateral and UN arrangements, meant that locals could look and compare the 'brands' on offer. As Peake confirms in his chapter, on several fronts there was strong preference among many locals, community members as well as some political leaders, for what appeared to be offered as the Portuguese version of public policing. This model was viewed by locals in terms of its provision of rapid response units composed of well-equipped fit young males, capable of chasing and catching young gang members involved in causing trouble, as well as of dealing quickly and effectively with disorderly crowds. This, in the eyes of at least some locals, could be contrasted with perceived shortcomings of other policing units. These shortcomings were that the other units were too slow, under-equipped, too old, or work-shy, or a combination of the above. In Timor-Leste, the Portuguese policing model on offer in the second half of the first decade of this century was seen by locals, at least, as being a far cry from the more 'softly softly' approaches associated with New Zealand and Australian police, that attempted to operate on more conciliatory community policing lines. For many local Timorese in 2006 or 2007, these were not priorities for policing reform when gangs were fighting each other and attacking other residents on a daily basis (see also Goldsmith 2009).

Glocality, co-optation and hybridity

Much of what has already been discussed in this Reflection can be understood in relation to the term 'glocal policing.' Following its usage by Blaustein (2015), it reflects the idea raised in the previous section of this Reflection, that while 'the global increasingly influences the local . . . the local inevitably exerts a mediating influence upon the convergent pressures generated by the global' (p. 3). This notion implies a less harshly defined relation of the centre to the periphery, in which the 'local' 'pushes back' in some way. The pushback can come from any one or a combination of players at the local level. However clearly the attitude of key political actors normally matters enormously in terms of how these negotiations proceed and which outcomes are achieved. As we saw in the case of Brazil, it is now the case that the 'local' can be seen to lead in international and transnational dealings rather than simply follow or temper the foreign/export model, thereby influencing not only practice in the home countries but also elsewhere in places not characterised by a pre-existing metropole/empire relationship (Sinclair and Williams 2007).

The potentially destructive and regressive impact of local politics in transitional police reform has been visible in the case of Timor-Leste. The politics of the last decade in critical areas such as policing reform has shown the frequent links between those in political office, certain elements of the police, and criminal gangs, as well as the military. In the run-up to the 2006 crisis, it has become evident since, the Minister of the Interior at the time, Rogerio Lobato, was equipping certain police units and militias with military-grade weapons in anticipation of struggles with the military and other elements in political office (Peake, this collection). The deliberate formation, in effect, of a praetorian guard within the Timorese system is one expression of how local agendas can seek to divert or hijack the agendas of outside reformers with, at times, as in this case, disastrous effects in terms of political stability and social order. One might see such developments in part as a local political response to the functional and administrative separation of police from military forces. Such separation exercises, as in the case of Timor-Leste's massive neighbour (and former occupier), Indonesia, while consistent with the modernist narrative of reform of civil-military relations, also can set the scene for rivalries between armed security units of the state. These administrative restructuring exercises often fail to address, at least successfully, the cultural conditions and political divisions that enable those divisions to persist, and thereby contribute to the subversion of the objectives of the restructuring.

From missionaries to marketeers

While there are clear signs today of market competition for 'brand' policing reform models (O'Reilly, this compilation), the transnational condition of recent decades has meant inevitably that differentiation of offerings between policing donors has at times been exaggerated in order to seek influence, while simultaneously an homogenisation of approach has been often taking place in the background, often quietly and unstoppably. Platforms such as multilateral police missions (e.g. involving UN Police), and modern communications and transportation, have made processes of awareness across traditional national boundaries and distinctions around legal systems (Continental versus Common Law) commonplace. Practice harmonisation is also implicitly or explicitly required in relation to the demands for international cooperation in areas such as counter-terrorism and organised crime (Andreas and Nadelmann 2006).

What we are witnessing, it can be suggested, is the incremental assimilation of different policing approaches towards a common approach defined by shared

262 *Andrew Goldsmith*

normative commitments of a formal legal and professional kind. In this sense, there is a clear retreat from, if not indeed active rejection of, the past policing model in many respects. It is interesting that sometimes these processes can move in a common direction in different countries at or around the same time despite some clear distinctions of an economic and political kind retaining their pertinence. In other words, contexts can vary while changes remain similar at least superficially. This point is made, for example, in Ho and Lam's chapter dealing with Macau. As the former Portuguese colony was transitioning to joining the People's Republic of China in 1999 and immediately after this time, it became clear that the new leadership in Macau saw the need for a modernised, distinctly post-colonial model of policing, one that rejected the past Portuguese model that had a separate judicial police force in addition to a public police, and that ensured new levels of transparency and accountability.

The case of Brazil is an interesting one, compared to many transnational policing stories, because of the way it seems to have turned a disadvantage into an advantage. Out of the adversities faced at home dealing with the *favelas* of Rio de Janeiro and Sao Paolo, the Brazilian police have been able to build a brand for dealing effectively with hardened urban crime groups. O'Reilly's chapter focuses on the re-framing exercise involved, noting how, strangely, it operates on two fronts simultaneously. One is a presentation of the effective, muscular urban patrols of violent areas, while the other, developed largely it might be argued in relation to its overseas missions, particularly in Haiti, as the defender of the marginalised urban dwellers. While Brazilian police have undoubtedly inherited much in respect of police training and orientation from their own, and indeed other, colonial masters (Rosemberg, this volume), like many other New World countries, they are now operating in the international arena very effectively, in fact more so, it might be argued, than their former colonial masters. One can see certain parallels and ironies in common with the Northern Ireland example, in which the Royal Ulster Constabulary, later the Police Service of Northern Ireland, turned its experience policing highly divided communities, despite its highly contested record, into an export marketing bonus (see, Ellison and O'Reilly 2008b, Ellison and Pino 2012).

Conclusion

Summing up in relation to the contemporary Lusophone contribution to transnational and transitional policing, it is possible to point to three identifiable phenomena of current theoretical and practical significance. One is the conversion of previous colonies of empires into new free-standing exporting countries of policing reform ideas and practices. Here, in addition to Brazil's growing role elsewhere in the Americas and through the United Nations even further afield, we can point, albeit on a much lesser scale, to the contributions of Timor-Leste policing personnel to UN policing missions across the globe. No-one should ultimately be surprised that the recipients of development assistance and institutional reform might one day seek to play the role of donor, trainer, or developer to others in these areas. That the 'child' might grow to be bigger and stronger than the 'parent,' at times reversing the directionality of influence, is hardly surprising either.

The second point is the inevitable convergence trends in this area. There is undoubtedly a 'transnational police policy community', as Marenin (2007) has noted, that exists among police professionals as well as among scholars, some of whom have contributed to this volume. The leading role of UN police deployments in this field, drawing together into single missions contingents from dozens if not scores of different contributing nations, makes contact and communication across cultural and linguistic, as well as national lines, inevitable. Through doctrinal as well as rhetorical commitments at the mission level to notions of the rule of law, human rights and community policing, serving police officers are drawn into a common language relating to police practice. Such trends are only likely to continue and become more pronounced, in the process effacing some at least of the differences of practice as well as of philosophy in policing across the globe.

Lastly, as one might predict in the context of any transnational policy transfer, there is inevitably some degree of discernible local reaction to impositions from outside in an area as sensitive as policing. The reactions obviously vary from case to case as well as between different groups in each setting. As well as acceptance and compliance, there are plenty of examples of keen negotiation and adaptation as well as rejection and indifference. As I have suggested, there are various signs of local agency in many transitional and post-colonial police reform stories, whether they be politically, professionally or societally driven. Local reactions may exploit and benefit, almost perversely, from such impositions or attempts at imposition, as they can manipulate donors in ways often not easily seen by them. The duping of donors and the ascendancy of the once-colonial subjects over their one-time masters are stories increasingly evident to many of those working in or studying this field. In making sense of terms such as 'glocal policing' (Blaustein 2015), there are instances, as in Timor-Leste, in which the mediating influence of local interests has arguably been quite powerful. Like their colonial predecessors, many contemporary donors in the policing reform space, are coming to terms with their limited infrastructural power in these dynamic and often contested settings, as much if not more out of necessity as of respect for local sovereignty.

References

Amar, P. 2013. *Global South to the Rescue: Emerging Humanitarian Superpowers and Globalizing Rescue Industries* (Rethinking Globalizations Series). Abingdon, Oxford: Routledge.

Andreas, P and Nadelmann, E. 2006. *Policing the Globe: Criminalization and Crime Control in International Relations*. New York: Oxford University Press.

Blaustein, J. 2015. *Speaking Truths to Power: Policy Ethnography and Police Reform in Bosnia and Herzegovina*. Oxford: Oxford University Press.

Bowling, B. and Sheptycki, J.W.E. 2012. *Global Policing*. London: Sage.

Brogden, M. 1987. The emergence of the police: The colonial dimension. *British Journal of Criminology*, 27(1): 4–14.

264   *Andrew Goldsmith*

Brogden, M. 1999. Community policing as cherry pie, in *Policing Across the World: Issues for the Twenty-first Century*, edited by R.I. Mawby. London: Routledge, 167–186.

Ellison, G. and O'Reilly, C. 2008a. 'From Empire to Iraq and the War on Terror': The transplantation and commodification of the (Northern) Irish policing experience. *Police Quarterly*, 11(4): 395–426.

Ellison, G. and O'Reilly, C. 2008b. 'Ulster's policing goes global': The police reform process in Northern Ireland and the creation of a global brand. *Crime, Law and Social Change*, 50(4–5): 331–351.

Ellison, G. and Pino, N. 2012. *Globalization, Police Reform and Development: Doing it the Western Way?* Basingstoke: Palgrave Macmillan.

Finnane, M. and Paisley, F. 2010. Police violence and the limits of law on a late colonial frontier: The 'Borroloola Case' in 1930s Australia. *Law and History Review*, 28(1): 141–171.

Goldsmith, A. 2009. 'It wasn't like normal policing': Australian police peace-keepers in Operation Serene, Timor-Leste 2006. *Policing & Society*, 19(2): 119–133.

Goldsmith, A. and Sheptycki, J.W.E. 2007. *Crafting Transnational Policing: Police Capacity-Building and Global Policing Reform*. Oxford: Hart.

Harris, V. and Goldsmith, A. 2009. International police missions as reverse capacity-building: Experiences of Australian police personnel. *Policing: A Journal of Policy and Practice*, 3(1): 50–58.

Killingray, D. 1986. The maintenance of law and order in British colonial Africa. *African Affairs*, 85: 411–437.

Mann, M. 1984. The autonomous power of the state: Its origins, mechanisms, and results. *European Journal of Sociology*, 25: 185–213.

Marenin, O. 2007. Implementing police reform: The role of the transnational policy community, in *Crafting Transnational Policing: Police Capacity-Building and Global Policing Reform*, edited by A. Goldsmith and J.W.E. Sheptycki. Oxford: Hart.

Nettlebeck, A. and Smandych, R. 2010. Policing indigenous peoples on two colonial frontiers: Australia's Mounted Police and Canada's North-West Mounted Police. *Australia and New Zealand Journal of Criminology*, 43(2): 356–375.

Sinclair, G. and Williams, C. 2007. 'Home and away': The cross-fertilization between 'Colonial' and 'British' policing, 1921–85. *Journal of Imperial and Commonwealth History*, 35(2): 221–238.

Index

Africanism and militarism 48–50;
integration of metropolitan and
colonial armies 50
Angola 6, 8, 17, 21, 24, 25, 29, 32,
69, 71, 76, 77, 79, 82, 83, 91–104,
110, 129, 136, 142–4, 153–6, 158,
220, 255 *see also* Luanda: PIDE; anti-
colonial politics 94; counterinsurgency
144; MLNA 96–7; mobile police
columns 25; multinational nationalist
movement 96; nationalist groups
95–6; PIDE's racial strategy 91–104;
racial segmentation 91–4; Salazar
dictatorship, and 91–2; shantytown
massacres 98–9; UN Sub–committee
on Angola 93
army as police 39–43; capture of criminals
47; contrast between Portuguese
and Spanish case 40; criticisms of 42;
elections 47; GNR 50; military budget,
and 41; military weaponry 47; network
of barracks 41–2; principles 46–7; role
40; statistics 48; training 46–8

Beresford, William Carr: reconstruction
of Portuguese army 40
Brazil 2, 3, 6, 7, 9, 10, 20, 40, 56–7,
58–9, 62, 64, 68, 70–3, 74, 76, 77,
81, 83, 100, 220, 227–52 *see also*
militarism in the São Paulo police
force; Rio de Janeiro; São Paulo;
image–management 27–52;
pacification 227–52; policing
institutions 228
British ultimatum 48

Cape Verde 4, 6, 30, 95, 98, 255; Praia
police force 23
circulation of police personnel 25–31;
Project COPP-LAB – *Circulation of*

*Police Officers in Portugal, Lusophone
Africa and Brazil* 5–6
coercive modes 79; non-racial 81;
physical punishment 79–80
colonial policing and Portuguese
Empire c.1870–1961 17–34;
circulation of police from Lisbon to
colonies 25; Ministry of Interior,
and 24; policing perceived as army
function 21; research studies 17;
scramble for Africa 17; sources 18–19
commodification 3, 228–30 *see also*
geo–policial branding
community policing 163–82, 254
Companhias Móveis ('CPs') 132
Confidential Questionnaire on Islam
106; delays in data–collection
118–19; field surveys, and
121; governance strategy, and
122–3; implementation 117–21;
interrogation 116, 118; manifestation
of colonial governance, as 124;
negative images 119; objectives 115;
Orientalist approach 115; success
of outcome 121; suspicion towards
Muslims 120–1; threat–centric
perceptions 119
Costa, Eduardo 21–5; appearance of
colonial police, and 21–5; chaotic
nature of policing structure, on 22;
civil police forces in urban colonial
settlements 23; legislative reforms,
and 23; Mozambique, on 22; science
of colonial administration 21–2; types
of police, on 22
counterinsurgency 4, 5, 8, 9, 108,
112, 124, 129–51, 155–6, 230,
243, 245; Algeria 134; Angola 144;
Britain 134; British doctrine 139,
143; cohesive imperial intelligence

266 *Index*

community 146; denying insurgents status of lawful combatants 137; diffusion as high policing 138–44; *Dispositifs Opérationnels de Protection* (DOPs) 140; framing as policing 133–8; France 134, 137–8, 140–1; intelligence, and 140, 143; intelligence-centric 129–51; intelligence-centric policing 142; interrogation 139; late colonial policing, and 129–51; Malaya 135–6; minimum force issue 145–6; paramilitary units 136–7; PIDE, and 142–3, 144; police state, and 147; Portuguese colonial intelligence 141–2; resistance to political pressure for 136; SCCI 143; transnational networks, and 141; treatment of prisoners, and 137

de S. Januario, Vizconde 42–3

elections: policing by army 47

forced labour 82
FRELIMO 112, 116, 123, 155, 165–7, 168, 171–3, 175–6, 179–81; Mozambican Islam, and 109
FUA: failure of 101; nature of 99–100; PIDE, and 99–101

gendarmerie 35–6; resistance to 42
geo–policial branding 10, 228, 230–5, 236, 244, 246
globalisation of policing 1, 239, 253–4
glocal dynamics of policing 10, 260–1
GNR 50
Goa 20, 24, 36, 49, 51, 83, 153
Guinea–Bissau 6, 8, 71, 220, 244

high policing 8, 73, 111, 113, 130, 132, 137, 138–44, 146–8

imperial policing 50–1
institutional landscape of Portuguese early colonial policing 25–31
internal colonialism 43–6; intervention in rural disturbances 45; propaganda missions 46

learning to police 46–8
Luanda: Police Corps 24
Lusophone community 1–2
Lusophone policing: research projects 5

Macau 183–207; adjournment of salary scale and amount 200; assessing reform 202–3; attempts to reform police agencies and policies 199–203; China's SAR 183–207; civic groups 184–5; CPSP 188–9; de-monopolisation of gaming industry 195–7; dual police forces 187–92; emergence of new civil groups 197–8; emergence of outspoken media 198–9; events triggering changes in policing 184; future developments 203–4; government-society relations 183–4; informant profiles 205; JP 189–90; key organisational features of colonial policing 186–7; Labour Day Rally 2007 198–9; limited capacity and professional ability 193–5; non–local police forces distant from community 192–3; operational conflicts between PSP and JP 190–2; police corps 23; policing 20; PSP 188–9; public relations 202; transformation of policing 183–207; triggers for police reform after 1999 195–9; Unitary Police Services 199–200; upgrading police professionalism 200–2
militant decolonisation movements 8
militarism in the São Paulo police force 55–66; ambivalence of military ethos 63; heraldic use 63–4; hierarchy-disciplinary scheme 57; identity crisis 55; impediments to training 59; local police 60; material contingencies 64; militarism of uniformed police machine 61; military police organisational model 59–60; policy of social control 61; power and presence of state, and 58–9; public police patrols 59; urban base, and 61–2
military: *raison d'être* 56
military and policing 35–6, 69, 71, 72–4, 129, 131–49, 241–3 *see also* counterinsurgency; militarism in the São Paulo police force
military model: criticism of 56
Ministry of the Realm 43
Ministry of War 43
MINUSTAH 241–4
MLNA 96–7
Mozambican Islam 105–28; colonial governance during liberation war 105–28; *Confidential Questionnaire*

on Islam 106; Council of the Notables 122–3; data collection and surveillance 105–6; FRELIMO, and 109; institutional apparatus of colonial powers 106; negative view of 108–9; PIDE, and 109; repression 109–10; SCCIM, and 106, 107, 110–14; statistics 107–8; threat to colonial rule, as 108; wider racial discrimination, and 109

Mozambique: autonomous actions 173–5; community policing 163–82; community policing model 169–72; contested police reform process 165–9; CPCs 170; development of police services 26; everyday policing 173–5, 176–9; FRELIMO 166–7; international involvement 167–9; legal defiance 176–9; MINT 170–2; national expansion 170–2; new civilian agents of state police 172–5; new neighbourhood court 175–9; pilot projects outside official reform 170–2; Police Company 23–4; political instrumentalism 176–9; post–conflict, police reforms in 9; post–war police reform 163–82; professional policing model 164; Rapid Reaction Force 167; Renamo 166–7; state outsourcing 173–5; UNDP-led process 167–9; *see also* Mozambican Islam

New State ('*O Estdao Novo*') 6, 19, 26, 27, 29, 30, 31, 32, 91, 108, 109, 111, 129, 131, 144; colonial policing during 26–31; reform movement during 29–30
Nova Goa City: Civil Police 24

Okuma, Thomas: Angolan European 92–3

pacification 25, 227–52; Brazil 227–52; neat narratives of imperialism, and 245–6; origins and meaning 229–30, 237; Rio de Janeiro 227–52; security, and 244–5
parish constables 38–9
PIDE 91–104 *see also* Angola; Angola, in 95–6; arrests of Angolan nationalities 97; divide to rule 97–8; FUA, and 99–101; key features 94–5; Mozambican Islam, and 109; origins 94–5; racial strategy 8, 91–104;

racialised incarceration 97–8; reform of 12; role of 142–3; success of racial strategy 101
police–military blur 4–5, 7–8, 133 *see also* militarism in the São Paulo police force; military and policing
Police Pacification Units 55 *see also* pacification
police reform: 1860s metropolitan Portugal, in 20–1
police state: counterinsurgency, and 147
police under the Republic 60–4; federal states' rights 62; material limitations 62–3; nascent workers' movement 61; political composition of regime 61; shift in axis of power 60; social controls 62
policing alternatives in early years of liberalism 37–8
policing Brazil in the 19th century 57–60; civil police 58; civilising pressure of social groups 58; uniformed military police 58
policing transfers 4, 6, 7, 9, 10, 36, 68, 72, 231, 240, 242–3, 246–7
policing without a gendarmerie 35–6
Portugal 1–2, 4–5, 8–10, 17–21, 23–4, 26–9, 31, 35, 36–7, 39, 40–2, 44, 45, 48–50, 62, 68, 70, 72–3, 75, 77–8, 79–83, 92–5, 98, 129–33, 135, 141–2, 145, 147–8, 152–9, 166, 183, 187–90, 192, 202, 204, 208–26, 258
Portuguese army: archives 41
Portuguese colonial administration: weakness of 20
Portuguese colonial policing mission 67–87; agents 78; assimilation project 81; British officers, and 72; carrot and stick measures 80; centrality of military 72–3; civilising mission 79–83; coercive modes 79 *see* coercive modes; coercive levels 69; comparative perspective 67–87; concessionary regimes 75–6; crime control 74; defence of state 73; differences between fighting and policing 73; endemic extra-legal violence 69–70; exploitative purpose 68; forced labour 82; French policing influences 72; high policing *see* high policing; imposed state of order 74; indigenous authorities 78; influence of colonial periphery 85; inter–imperial comparisons 71; knowledge

268 *Index*

circulation 71–2; knowledge transfer between empires 72; magistrates, and 67; more democratic forms of policing by consent, and 133; multilayered control 75–9; non–concessionary colonial areas 76–7; non–military layers of policing in Portugal 77–8; official violence 70–1; operational flexibility 68; policing 68–71; preventive policing 74; private policing regimes 75–6; professionalization 83–4; rank and file police and soldiers 78; slavery 77; social tranquillity, and 74; sources of coercion 68; state expectations 69; success of pacification 83; surveillance of population 70; systematic infliction of pain 81–2; terror, use of 69; third phase of global Empire 7; toleration for indigeneity 80; transnational standard of policing professionalism 131–2; winning hearts and minds 82–3

Portuguese colonial rule 129–30

Portuguese later colonial policing 91–103, 105–28, 129–50, 152–9; anti–colonial wars 153–4; army protest movement 157; civil–military friction 152; civil war, and 155; decolonisation process 157; intelligence gathering 156; Lisbon dictatorship 152, 153; overthrow of dictatorship 153; SCCIM 155; settler colonialism 154

post–colonial global policing reform 253–64; cherry pie or knuckle sandwich 259–60; co–optation 260–1; from millionaires to marketeers 261–2; glocality 260–1; hybridity 260–1; imitation 253–64; imperial impositions 254–7; imposition 253–64; intransigence 253–64; intransigence and resistance 257–9

povo 44–5

private policing 19, 22, 60, 75–7, 175

Project Alcora 5

PSP organisational structure 31

Rego, Salgueiro 26–31; career of 27; colonial policing system, on 28; diversity of policing, and 29; organisational diversity, on 30

Rio de Janeiro 227–52; complex dualities of pacification 235–7; creation of geo–policial brand 230–5; elite transnational security networks 237–41; *favelas* 10; global promotionalism 230–5; international peacekeeping, and 241–4; pacification model 227–52; Rio-MINUSTAH feedback loop 241–4; segmented brand 235–7

rural policing: revamping of 45

Salazar dictatorship: Angola, and 91–2

São Paulo 4, 7, 68, 72, 75, 82, 84; militarism in police force 55–66 *see also* militarism in the São Paulo police force

São Tome and Principe 26, 27, 28, 30, 51, 76, 83

SCCI 143

SCCIM 8, 110–14; governance aims 113; influence of 114; Mozambican Islam, and 110–14; surveys 113

self-policing 38

slavery 77

territorial occupation: emergence of colonial policing, and 19–21

the Other 3

Timor–Leste 10, 208–26; attempts to mould police into international image of best practice 214–18; colonial genealogies 212–14; epitome of conflict paradigm, as 210–12; hidden influences on police development 208–26; historical continuities 212–14; little dividend 214–18; loss of investment 214–18; port-authoritarian echoes 219–23; post-colonial echoes 219–23

Wardrop, J.C.: Angolan European, on 93